William Edward Birkhimer

Historical Sketch of the Organization, Administration, Matériel and

Tactics

of the Artillery, United States Army

William Edward Birkhimer

Historical Sketch of the Organization, Administration, Matériel and Tactics
of the Artillery, United States Army

ISBN/EAN: 9783337018986

Printed in Europe, USA, Canada, Australia, Japan

Cover: Foto ©ninafisch / pixelio.de

More available books at **www.hansebooks.com**

Historical Sketch

OF THE

ORGANIZATION, ADMINISTRATION, MATÉRIEL AND TACTICS

OF

THE ARTILLERY, UNITED STATES ARMY,

BY

WILLIAM E. BIRKHIMER,
FIRST LIEUTENANT, THIRD REGIMENT, U. S. ARTILLERY.

WASHINGTON, D. C.:
JAMES J. CHAPMAN,
AGENT.
1884.

TO

BREVET MAJOR-GENERAL

HENRY J. HUNT,

COLONEL (RETIRED) UNITED STATES ARMY,

WHOSE DISTINGUISHED SERVICE IN PEACE AND CONDUCT IN WAR, DURING

FORTY-FOUR YEARS OF ACTIVE MILITARY LIFE,

EVER CONTRIBUTED TO THE HONOR OF THE ARTILLERY ARM,

THIS WORK IS RESPECTFULLY INSCRIBED.

ERRATA.

Page 7, thirtieth line, for 1776 read 1777.
Page 135, seventeenth line, for (U) read (M).
Page 180, twenty-sixth line, omit 'a.'
Page 231, seventh line, insert 'had' after 'also.'
Page 269, eighth line, for 'representative' read 'representatives.'
Page 273, the *note* belongs to paragraph above.
Page 322, second line from bottom, insert the words "'battery' to the" before 'front.'
Page 328, in both fifteenth and nineteenth lines, insert (3) before 'guide.'

PREFACE.

When the writer of this work joined the army as a commissioned officer, in 1870, he cast about with a view to learning something of the career in this country of the arm to which he had been assigned—the artillery. The result was unsatisfactory. Of record there was almost nothing, and that little was sometimes glaringly erroneous. Experienced officers who were consulted could give little information regarding matters of a date anterior to their entry into service, and when they wished to speak positively concerning those things of which they were personally cognizant their memories were frequently so defective as to surprise even themselves.

All this was a subject for wonder to the writer. It seemed strange that with our admiration for and knowledge of foreign services our own had not received more attention; but, on the contrary, the study of its organization and administration had been neglected. Since the Civil war much has been said and written concerning our military establishment. The matter has received no little attention in the deliberations of the National Legislature; but it has always seemed that such legislation would be none the less certain of being wise and permanent if more were known of the history of our army, especially of its combatant branches.

Of late years there has been a seemingly increasing disposition with us to inculcate the precepts, if we could not attain to the practice, of European services. There are undoubtedly many admirable features in the organization of some foreign armies; but instead of blindly following them, it would be wiser to first thoroughly familiarize ourselves with our own service and its relations to our civil institutions, to see whether principles which lead to such happy results elsewhere would be equally applicable here; indeed, whether they would not be positively injurious. As to the artillery, however, there is left no room for doubt. The technical and the combatant branches are everywhere else united under a single superior direction, and so they must be with us before either can attain to highest efficiency.

It would have been interesting to have touched upon the subject of projectiles and powder, in the manufacture of which there has been vast improvement. Indeed, powder has largely revolutionized methods of gun construction. But these advances in the refinements of modern warfare are of so recent date as to remove them from the domain of history according to the plan of this work. On the other hand, questions involving the construction of carriages, the metals of which cannon should be made, and the character of the 'artillery system' which would best meet the necessities of Government have been of constant recurrence since the beginning of the Revolutionary war. For this reason the latter alone have been considered in treating of MATÉRIEL.

With us the employment of guns in masses was not practiced, and was almost unknown even in theory, before the Civil war. In earlier days, nothing beyond the manœuvres of a single battery was attempted. Hence, but a passing notice has been taken of the use of artillery, in conjunction with the other arms, as an important factor on the battle-field. Yet, broadly speaking, this is the true province of ARTILLERY TACTICS. To have entered it would, however, have transcended the limits within which it was determined to restrict the consideration of tactical questions, and which did not extend beyond a brief review of the main points of difference between successive systems of instruction which have been adopted. Until quite recently there is discernible, running through the latter, evidence of an effort being made to maintain the tactics abreast with improvements affecting artillery organization and matériel. When pieces were hauled around by drag-ropes, field exercises were very limited. The prolonge greatly added to the mobility of the system. This was again enhanced many fold by the introduction of the stock-trail carriage. Requisite mobility being secured, the next feature appearing in our works of instruction related to administration, and embraced a comprehensive article on the interior œconomy of the battery, in so far as related to strictly artillery affairs. Lastly, there was formulated the 'assimilation' idea, in which the dominating principle seems to be to convert as nearly as possible both artillery and cavalry into infantry: to consider the questionable advantage of mere similarity in commands as of more consequence than the preservation of the natural elements into which experience has divided the different arms of service: and to leave the light artilleryman and the cavalryman in doubt whether, after all, the most important part of their service is not performed on foot, where they are at every disadvantage when compared with their more fortunate coadjutor—the infantryman.

Researches, the results of which are given in the following pages, were begun in 1872-'73, when the writer was at the artillery school of practice. It was not with the intention of publishing a book that they were commenced, but simply to increase knowledge of a subject of great personal interest. The scope of his labors has been enlarged since that time, due in great degree to the suggestions of friends and others interested, and to a hope he was led to entertain that in this way the army, particularly the artillery, would acquire information which would be acceptable to it. The work has been prosecuted with as much assiduity as circumstances would permit. Facilities afforded at the ordinary military post for the collection of facts which could be utilized are not worth considering. But the writer was fortunate in being stationed for some time in the vicinity of New York, and afterwards in Washington city, where he availed himself of opportunities to gather together data other than is found in ordinary histories. He was also generously assisted by friends, who placed their collections of papers at his disposal. Press of official duties for several years precluded attempts to arrange in a connected manner any portion of what he had accumulated; but, so far as affects the artillery, the first available moments have been made use of for this purpose.

Others may possess knowledge which would have enabled them to perform the task here essayed in a more thorough or acceptable manner. If so, it is to be regretted that they have not published and made it available to those who are interested.

The writer is under obligations to the Honorable Robert T. Lincoln, Secretary of War, to Adjutant-General Drum, and to General Benét, chief of ordnance, for facilities extended to him in the prosecution of his work, in the course of which the wisdom of the existing relation between the ordnance department and the artillery regiments is brought in question. To be known, however, it needs not to be pointed out here, that the chief of ordnance is not responsible for a state of affairs which he did not create. It is only regretted that the gentleman at the head of that department is not now, what it is hoped he may yet be—chief of a reorganized and reunited artillery.

To General Henry J. Hunt and Lieutenant-Colonel Robert N. Scott the writer is under particular obligations for suggestions, the use of documents and books of reference. To Mr. David Fitzgerald, the efficient librarian of the War Department, he desires to make acknowledgments for courtesies so willingly extended on every occasion; while to General E. P. Alexander, late C. S. army, to Major J. P. Sanger and Lieutenant E. S. Dudley, of the artillery, and to Captain James Rockwell, Jr., of the ordnance, who kindly read over and corrected different portions of the manuscript, he now returns sincere thanks for their valuable assistance.

LITTLE ROCK BARRACKS,
    ARKANSAS, *November 1st*, 1884.

CONTENTS.

CHAPTER I.
ORGANIZATION—GENERALLY.

CHAPTER II.
ORGANIZATION—FIELD ARTILLERY SINCE 1821.

CHAPTER III.
ORGANIZATION—FIELD SERVICE.

CHAPTER IV.
ORGANIZATION—ARTILLERY RESERVES.

CHAPTER V.
ADMINISTRATION—INSTRUCTION.

CHAPTER VI.
ADMINISTRATION—DUTIES: TECHNICAL.

CHAPTER VII.
ADMINISTRATION—DUTIES: AS AN ARM OF SERVICE.

CHAPTER VIII.
ADMINISTRATION—DUTIES: CHIEF OF ARTILLERY IN THE FIELD.

CHAPTER IX.
MATÉRIEL—CARRIAGES.

CHAPTER X.
MATÉRIEL—METAL.

CHAPTER XI.
MATÉRIEL—SYSTEMS OF ARTILLERY.

CHAPTER XII.
TACTICS—GENERALLY.

CHAPTER XIII.
TACTICS—FIELD ARTILLERY.

APPENDICES.
[A], ORGANIZATION; [B], ADMINISTRATION; [C], MATÉRIEL.

HISTORICAL SKETCH

— OF —

THE ARTILLERY, UNITED STATES ARMY.

ORGANIZATION—GENERALLY.

THE ARTILLERY OF THE UNITED STATES ARMY dates from the beginning of the American Revolution, when, as part of the continental forces, it became a recognized arm of the military establishment. Prior to that time, however, some of the colonies had limited experience in the organization and management of this branch of service. Companies had been formed and trained at Boston, Philadelphia, Charleston, S. C., and other cities, some of which saw active service in the wars with the French North American possessions, wherein were associated with them companies of the English Royal Artillery Regiment. When Louisburg was captured in 1745, three companies of the latter, with some Massachusetts militia, manned the artillery of the besiegers. Braddock, ten years later, was accompanied by a company of the Royal artillery in his disastrous expedition.

At the epoch of the American Revolution the British artillery, after a protracted but triumphant struggle with prejudice, had vindicated its right to be, and was, considered an important combatant arm. Its laws, customs, and traditions were ingrafted into the new-formed artillery of the Colonial army. This naturally resulted from that association of Colonial with the Royal artillery to which allusion has been made. The organization of the first artillery regiment arrayed against the forces of the Crown, at Boston, in June, 1775, gave proof of this. Raised by the Colony of Massachusetts and adopted by the continental Congress, the regiment was commanded by Colonel Richard Gridley, a half-pay British officer, who had rendered distinguished service as an engineer and artillerist. The number and designations of the officers, and of the rank and file, were very similar to those of a battalion (at the time four in number) of the Royal Artillery Regiment, the most marked difference being that a greater number of field officers was given the American regiment than belonged to a battalion of the English artillery. The difference was not accidental, but well considered, and was to the advantage of the colonists. It showed that Gridley, under whose advice the regiment was raised, had profited by his experience with the Royal Regiment, in which, because of the few field officers, it had been found necessary to organize a new battalion every few years, in order that those who remained in service should have a reasonable chance of promotion. (Organization of Gridley's regiment, Appendix A [1]; Organization of Fourth Battalion, Royal artillery, 1771, Appendix A [2].)

There was associated with Gridley at the siege of Boston a company of Rhode Island artillery, commanded by Major John Crane. The personnel consisted of one major and commandant, one captain, three lieutenants, (no distinction as to grade,) two sergeants, four corporals, two bombardiers, four gunners, four musicians, (drums and fifes,) seventy-four matrosses, and one conductor—who was the company ordnance officer. This was a large number of men to manage the four field guns which constituted their armament; but in those days, and for many years afterwards, field artillery in this country was manœuvred by drag-ropes, manned by matrosses, who occupied the grade now corresponding to that of private soldier.

The field officers of Gridley's regiment, under the colonel, were: William Burbeck, lieutenant-colonel; David Mason, first, and Scarborough Gridley, second major. The latter was dismissed the service in September, 1775, for misconduct at the battle of Bunker Hill, where the artillery did not cover itself with glory, as five of its six pieces present remained in possession of the enemy. The influence of the colonel on the discipline of the regiment does not seem to have been good, as in the report of a committee sent by the continental Congress to visit the army at Boston in the fall of 1775, it is stated that he had become very obnoxious to that corps (the artillery regiment), and would prove its destruction if continued in command. It was recommended that he be superseded in some honorable way, Congress making good the half-pay he had renounced on entering the service of the colonies. Mr. Henry Knox, a young man of twenty-five, and who had been serving as a volunteer in the army under General Washington, was recommended as his successor—an appointment duly conferred by Congress on the 17th of November following.* He was announced as colonel of the artillery in general orders dated December 12th, 1775. At that time Knox had been sent on special duty to New York, Albany, and Ticonderoga to procure siege material for the army before Boston. Gridley continued to command the regiment until January 1st, 1776, on which date the term of service for which the latter had enlisted expired.

Meanwhile Congress, at the instance of the commander-in-chief, had resolved to reorganize the regiment, with one colonel, two lieutenant-colonels, two majors, and twelve companies. It was recruited immediately upon the old regiment being mustered out, and to a great extent by re-enlisting for one year the discharged artillerymen of Gridley's regiment, together with Crane's company of Rhode Island artillery. (Organization of Knox's regiment, Appendix A [3].) The field officers were: Henry Knox, colonel; William Burbeck, first, and David Mason, second lieutenant-colonel; John Crane, first, and later in the year John Lamb, of the New York artillery, second major. These officers had rendered service before the enemy, all except Lamb at the siege of Boston, and he, with Montgomery, at the assault on Quebec, where he fell, severely wounded, into the hands of the enemy. The appointment to Knox's regiment was given him by General Washington as a reward for his conduct on that occasion.

It was fortunate for the artillery that there was placed thus early at its head an officer of acknowledged ability, experience in business affairs, and an aptitude for the duties of that arm. Under Knox's command it took and maintained a position second to none during seven years of an eventful war. When compared with the best appointed of the present day, it is true that the artillery of our Revolutionary army seems a crude affair; but when tested

---

*General Henry Burbeck, in a letter of April 30th, 1847, stated that the colonelcy of this regiment was offered his father, at that time lieutenant-colonel, but he declined, and recommended Knox, whom he knew, and who was a soldier in every way; that his father, though well informed as an artillerist and in laboratory duties, was by habit nothing of a soldier, and was about sixty years of age.

by the true standard—the character of its officers and its efficiency in the field—it appears favorably when placed side by side with other artilleries of that time.

The straightened condition of the force invading Canada, after Montgomery's death and the failure of the attack on Quebec, determined General Washington, after the enemy had left Boston, to detach two companies of the artillery regiment to the assistance of the commander (Arnold) in that quarter. With them were dragged through the wilderness two thirteen-inch mortars. Nine companies moved with Knox to New York city in April, 1776, while one remained in the defenses of Boston. To replace the three absent companies, there joined and did duty with the regiment two New York artillery companies, one under Captain Sebastian Beauman, afterwards major in the Second Regular Artillery, and the other under a youth destined to act a distinguished part in the history of his adopted country—Alexander Hamilton. Of the field officers before mentioned, Lieutenant-Colonel Mason and Major Crane were present; Lieutenant-Colonel Burbeck, having refused to leave Boston when the army marched, was in May summarily dismissed the service; Major Lamb was still a prisoner.

After the defeat of the Americans on Long Island, August 27th, 1776, and their retreat from New York city, Congress resolved upon an entire reorganization of the army. The number of infantry battalions was, September 16th, fixed at eighty-eight. As to the artillery, nothing was immediately determined on; but the congressional committee appointed to investigate the subject of army reform called upon Knox for suggestions concerning that arm. These he communicated as follows:

"1. I recommend that there be one or more capital laboratories erected at a distance from the seat of war, in which shall be prepared large quantities of ordnance stores of every species and denomination.

"2. That there be at the same place a number of able artificers employed to make carriages for the cannon of all sorts and sizes, ammunition wagons, tumbrels, harness, &c.

"3. That, as contiguous as possible to this place, a foundry for casting brass cannon, mortars, and howitzers be established upon a large scale.

"4. And, *as officers can never act with confidence until they are masters of their profession*, an academy established upon a liberal plan would be of the utmost service to the continent, where the whole theory and practice of fortification and gunnery should be taught, to be nearly on the same plan as that at Woolwich—making allowances for differences of circumstances—a place to which our enemies are indebted for the superiority of their artillery to all who have opposed them.

"5. That these and all other matters respecting the artillery and artillery stores be under the direction of a board of ordnance, whose business shall be the regulation and management of the affairs of this department, and to whom returns shall be made.

"6. The corps of artillery now in the service of the United States is exceedingly insufficient for the operations of an extensive service. It consists of a little more than 600, officers included; of these, 100 are in the northern army, where their numbers are very unequal to the service. His excellency General Washington has, to supply the deficiency of this corps, drafted from the different regiments 600 men, and General Gates a proportionate number. This is a temporary remedy, attended with a variety of inconveniences.

"7. There ought to be a respectable body of artillery established which shall be equal to all the services of the war. In proportion to every 1000 men of the marching regiments, there ought to be one company of 60 men, including officers. This number will be found to be small when the various contingencies of the artillery shall be considered. Supposing, then, the army to consist of 80 battalions of 726 men each, making nearly 60,000 men, the number of artillery requisite will be 3360. These may be thrown into two or three battalions, as may be thought best.

"8. If any circumstances shall happen to render the movement of this army necessary, one hundred covered wagons will be wanting to transport the stores; three hundred strong horses to draw the travelling artillery; (the heavy artillery on garrison carriages and the heaviest stores are not included in the above estimate;) wagons and drivers for the above; a wagonmaster to be established for the artillery; also a quartermaster for the horses and wagons, whose business it shall be to purchase hay, horses, &c., as may be needed.

"9. Exclusively of the artificers at the fixed laboratories, there must be 100 of different branches attached to the artillery, to repair carriages when broken, make platforms, and a thousand other matters belonging to the artillery.

"10. Besides the commissary of stores, it will be necessary to have a deputy commissary, who shall be a capable, active man; the number of conductors and clerks to be twelve; if the service should require more, they to be added during the pleasure of the commander-in-chief; the commanding officer of artillery to have a clerk attached to him, for the purpose of arranging and disposing the various returns of cannon and stores.

"11. The following brass field pieces are wanting, (and as there is a considerable quantity of copper collected, it is to be wished that the founder might be employed to cast some immediately,) viz., eighteen six-pounders and eighteen three-pounder cannon."

These recommendations evince that the commander of artillery was cognizant of the requirements of that arm, and of the proper means to secure them; and, though not always in the manner contemplated, most of the measures here proposed were favorably acted upon by Congress. The prominence given to the supposed excellence of the English artillery system is worthy of notice. It was upon this as a model that Knox sought to build up the United States service, and not upon the French, as has been erroneously supposed. It is true that several officers of the latter service sought and obtained positions in the continental army; that in their own country the new and improved system of Gribeauval was at last, spite of every opposition, firmly established; but in the American army English ideas of organization and matériel had taken too deep root to be shaken; as to organization, this has already been illustrated. And though much artillery matériel was purchased in France, it was almost entirely confined to the one item of cannon without carriages. It was the not unnatural expectation of French officers to give shape to, and command, the American artillery; but they found already on the ground those capable of conducting its management, in every detail, with distinguished success.

The elaboration of a plan for establishing the artillery upon a scale commensurate with the requirements of the contemplated regular army, of possibly more than one hundred regiments, embracing troops of all arms, was a task devolved upon Colonel Knox. He recommended to the commander-in-chief that the number of artillery *battalions* be fixed at five, each to consist of one colonel, one lieutenant-colonel, one major, and twelve companies; each company one captain, one captain-lieutenant, four lieutenants, six sergeants, six corporals, six gunners, six bombardiers, and twenty-eight matrosses. From this it appears that each company was to manœuvre two pieces, with their ammunition wagons. The "*battalion*" was in fact a regiment; the former designation was given in conformity with the English system that Knox so much admired, and which, he remarked, "we will have no reason to blush for imitating."

Alarmed at the retreat of the army through New Jersey and the proximity of the enemy to the seat of government, Congress adjourned from Philadelphia to Baltimore, first delegating to General Washington, December 12th, 1776, power to "order and direct all things relative to the department and operations of war." By virtue of this authority steps were at once taken for raising three of the five battalions proposed by Colonel Knox.

(Appendix A [6].) This action was confirmed by Congress, December 27th, when Knox was chosen brigadier-general of artillery —a grade which, in the *regular* army, has been held to this day by that officer alone.

The five battalions proposed by Colonel Knox were intended to supply artillery to all the armies of the United States. That number was organized in a few months, but one of them was converted into an artificer-regiment, and ingrafted into the "Department of the Commissary-General of Military Stores." (Appendix A [11].)

Of the four remaining, one was recruited in Virginia, pursuant to resolution of Congress, November 26th, 1776, and embraced two companies raised in that State by General Charles Lee. The field officers of the regiment were: Charles Harrison, colonel; Edward Carrington, lieutenant-colonel; Christian Holman, major. Two regiments were raised pursuant to the orders of the commander-in-chief, issued under the extraordinary powers conferred by Congress, December 12th, 1776. The other artillery regiment raised pursuant to this authority was that converted into artificers. The commanders of the latter regiments were Colonels Crane and Lamb for the artillery and Flower for the artificers. The other artillery regiment necessary to complete the number came from Pennsylvania. This was raised, pursuant to resolution of the State authorities, in February, 1777, and on the 20th of June following was taken by Congress into the continental establishment. Its field officers were: Thomas Proctor, colonel; John Martin Strobagh, lieutenant-colonel; Thomas Forrest, major.

The regiments of Colonels Harrison, Crane, Lamb, Proctor, and Flower constituted, therefore, the artillery of the regular army after June, 1776. Of these, Flower's was never arranged properly as a regiment; it was never anything but an assemblage of mechanics, with some degree of military organization. It will, therefore, not hereafter be considered as belonging to the artillery, which, omitting this, was made up of the four other regiments mentioned. It may remove misapprehension to mention that the terms "regiment" and "battalion" were synonymous as they appear in the resolutions of Congress and in the army orders of the time.

No sooner were the four regiments, or, for that matter, any two of them, brought together than disputes arose as to their order of precedence and the relative rank of their officers. The difficulty was enhanced by the fact that some officers of service under previous engagements had now commissions of a more recent date than others who had originally entered the service long after them. To put an end to daily bitter controversies, a board of officers was assembled at general headquarters in August, 1779. The board decided that the colonels ranked in the following order: Crane, Lamb, Harrison, and Proctor; but that their regiments should be designated and take precedence as follows: First, Harrison's; Second, Lamb's; Third, Crane's; Fourth, Proctor's. This decision was never afterwards modified. Those are the designations which will hereafter be given the four regular regiments.

By reference to Appendices A [5], [6], [7], [8], [9], and [10] it will be seen that the organizations of these regiments or battalions were dissimilar. This was to be expected from the various sources whence they came. When originally organized, both Harrison's and Proctor's were State troops; but Lamb's and Crane's were recruited from the States at large. It was not until May of 1778 that all were given, on paper at least, the same organization.

There was difficulty in obtaining the complement of field officers for Crane's and Lamb's regiments. John Popkins was lieutenant-colonel of the former and Eleazer Oswald of the latter; but in neither was the office of major filled until September, 1778, when William Perkins was appointed major of Crane's and Sebastian Beauman major of Lamb's regiment. At the same time that the latter appointments were made, Oswald's resignation caused the assignment to the Second Artillery of Lieutenant-Colonel Ebenezer Stevens, commander of artillery in the northern department. The position of the latter officer was anomalous. In the fall of 1776, when the terms of service of the two companies of Knox's regiment, in command of which Captain Stevens had marched to join the northern army, had expired, General Schuyler, commanding that department, had authorized him to recruit a corps of one artificer and three artillery companies. This he did, principally in Massachusetts, where, at the same time, Colonel Crane was enlisting for his (3d) regiment. The latter officer claimed Stevens' corps as part of his regiment, in which he had the support of the authorities of Massachusetts, as well as the favorable indorsement of General Knox. Stevens, however, maintained that he was independent; and as he served altogether in the northern department until the fall of 1778, removed from all other artillery, he succeeded in practically sustaining his claim. His companies formed what was known as "Stevens' Corps of Artillery," which never acknowledged any connection with Crane's regiment, although the latter, without these, had but nine of the twelve companies authorized by Congress. (Organization of Stevens' Corps, Appendix A [7].) In the movements of the army towards Canada at various times under Generals Schuyler, Gates, and St. Clair, the services of Stevens' corps and the ability of its commander were conspicuous, particularly in the campaign terminating in the surrender of Burgoyne. Congress conferred upon its commander the brevet of major, May 22d, 1777; the brevet of lieutenant-colonel, April 3d, 1778; November 24th, 1778, passed a resolution conferring the full rank of lieutenant-colonel of artillery, to date from the preceding 3d of April, he to be assigned to the first vacancy in that grade happening in the four regular artillery regiments. When, therefore, in the fall of 1778 Oswald resigned, on a point of rank, Stevens was assigned to the Second Artillery. The companies of his corps were incorporated into Crane's regiment; his artificers were at the same time attached for general service to the artillery of the main army.

While the four regiments before mentioned formed what was considered the regular artillery, there were other companies and battalions of that arm organized by the colonies, some of which were in continental pay, and in a limited sense might be considered as belonging to the continental establishment. New Jersey raised two companies—one for the eastern, the other for the western division of the colony; each of one captain, one captain-lieutenant, one first and one second lieutenant, one fire-worker, four sergeants, four corporals, one bombardier, and fifty matrosses. Rhode Island raised more than three hundred artillerymen to guard her coast. In Massachusetts there was an artillery regiment, intended for local defense alone, with a personnel of one colonel, one lieutenant-colonel, one major, one adjutant, one quartermaster, and ten companies. The provincial Congress of South Carolina, in November, 1775, put on foot an artillery battalion of three companies, one hundred men each. (Appendix A [12].)

This organization, in which the men were enlisted for two years, was taken by Congress into continental pay. Owen Roberts was lieutenant-colonel commandant and Barnard Elliott major. The former was mortally wounded in the affair of June 20th, 1779, at Stono River, and the regiment, with the volunteer companies of Charleston artillery, was captured at the surrender of that city to the British, May 12th, 1780. Georgia contributed her artillery quota, concerning which the continental Congress, February 6th, 1777, resolved: "That as soon as the artillery companies already ordered to be raised in Georgia are completed, one other be raised, to consist of one captain, two lieutenants, and fifty privates." What the organization of these was, except the last, is not known; but Captain Defatt was appointed inspector of the whole, and a French officer—Major Roman de Lisle—commander.

Although the expenses, including the pay of the foregoing State organizations, were borne by the United States, their status was different from that of the four regular artillery regiments. The companies of South Carolina and Georgia were not expected to, nor did they, move beyond the immediate boundaries of those States; the continental Congress bore their expenses with this understanding, and for the reason that the States themselves were not able to do it. Knox, as head of the artillery, never exercised any control over these organizations.

While the army lay at Valley Forge in the winter of 1777-'78 many measures, some of which affected the artillery, were adopted by Congress. It was then that a junto in that body, aided by the Conway cabal in the army, was endeavoring to undermine the influence and prestige of the commander-in-chief. To understand the course of legislation at this time it is necessary to appreciate the character of this short-lived intrigue.

With the exception of the surprise at Trenton, the forces under the immediate orders of General Washington had been defeated wherever they met the enemy in the open field. Gates, on the contrary, had compelled a splendidly-equipped British army to lay down their arms. The opponents of the former were not slow to institute comparisons which were to the disadvantage of the commander-in-chief. This movement was strengthened by the caustic pen of General Charles Lee, who hinted at General Washington's indecision of character. The first act in the programme to supersede the latter was the remodeling of the Board of War and Ordnance. This board, organized in June, 1776, was at first composed of Members of Congress. Its duties, in brief, were to see that military affairs were conducted properly, that supplies were furnished, and proper care taken of those not in use. It was the direct military organ of Congress. The duties of the Secretary of War to-day, in his relations to the President, are analogous to those of the Board of War at that time. It was proposed, after eighteen months' trial, to relieve Congress of this duty, so extensive, important, and demanding, for proper performance, both technical knowledge and unremitting attention. To do this, gentlemen were to be selected who were in no way connected with that body, yet who would, as a board, be subject to its orders and direct supervision. Quartermaster-General Mifflin, Adjutant-General Pickering, and Colonel Harrison—General Washington's secretary—were the first members appointed, the latter declining. A few days later Gates was chosen by Congress president of the board, with Joseph Trumbull and Richard Peters as additional members. There can be little doubt but that General Mifflin was mainly instrumental in bringing about this readjustment of the board. He was clever enough to discern that if he could control the Board of War, with Gates as its nominal head, he would virtually command the army. Arrangements were now complete for General Washington's opponents to assume direction of military affairs. The first act was to bring to the front an officer—General Conway—more obnoxious to the commander-in-chief than perhaps any other in the army, and make him inspector, with the increased rank of major-general. It is to be understood that Congress alone had the authority to originate this or any other measure affecting the organization of the army; but at this time it was very willing to adopt any suggestions emanating from the Board of War; so that, in effect, the latter controlled military measures. The Quartermaster's Department was remodeled under the auspices of the new board, which rightly judged that the building up of the administrative bureaus was a long step in the direction of that consolidation of powers in their own hands for which they planned, and for the consummation of which nothing was left undone. A blow was struck at the efficiency of the artillery by the organization of the "Department of the Commissary-General of Military Stores." (See Technical Artillery.) This temporarily rendered the commander of that arm—one of General Washington's trusted lieutenants—powerless to effect reforms or improve his service. But this attempt to concentrate authority in the hands of those who knew not how to use it failed of any useful purpose, and was but ephemeral in its effects. Concerning the board itself, little more need be said. Its efforts to render the commander-in-chief impotent at the head of his army failed signally. Its influence faded away in that majestic presence as dew before the sun. No effort was made to enforce the new inspectorship, to put in operation the machinery of the new Quartermaster's Department, or to carry into execution many other resolutions of Congress based on the recommendations of this new Board of War. Those members who had been moved more by ambition than by patriotism naturally became disgusted. Gates sought, and was given, a command. Mifflin requested a similar favor, but, finding himself unpopular, resigned from the army. The prestige of the commander-in-chief, and the confidence reposed in him by his countrymen, had but gathered strength under factious opposition.

Congress resolved, January 6th, 1778, to send a committee to the camp at Valley Forge to concert measures for the reduction of the number of regiments, and placing those retained upon a more efficient footing. One of the results was the reorganization of the army the 27th of May following, by which, in each branch or arm of service, the regiments (called battalions) were arranged uniformly. For the first time the artillery was now placed on the same basis in all the regiments; the same personnel given each. (Appendix A [8].) This was simply bringing Harrison's and Proctor's regiments to the same standard fixed for both Crane's and Lamb's when (January 1st, 1777) they were first authorized.

Harrison's was brought up to twelve companies by attaching to it two companies from Maryland, commanded, respectively, by Captains Brown and Dorsey. Lamb had twelve companies; but Crane, due to the fact that Stevens would not join him, had but nine companies, until, as before narrated, Stevens' corps was absorbed in the Third Regiment in the fall of 1778. The First, Second, and Third regiments had, therefore, their complement of companies, and were organized, as contemplated by Congress, before the end of the year; but Proctor's retained the eight companies with which it was organized the year before, and gained none. The Fourth Artillery never had the organization provided by the resolution of May 27th, 1778, nor was it given ten companies even, until 1780, when the other regiments were razeed from twelve to ten companies each, and two of the surplus companies attached to the Fourth. The resolution of May 27th provided further that in all the regiments the adjutants and quartermasters should be chosen by the field officers, subject to the approval of the commander-in-chief or the commander of a separate department; and that the regimental paymasters, who also had charge of the clothing, should be selected by the officers of their own regiment from among the captains and subalterns.

The new regiments had but three field officers. Gridley's regiment in 1775 had four, and Knox's five in 1776. The change had not been for the better. The lessons which in the British service were at that time being taken to heart, causing the organization of new battalions in the Royal Artillery Regiment, in order that more field officers might be appointed, thus giving promotion to the lower grades, were unheeded. The battalion organization of the enemy—the weakness of which the enemy himself acknowledged—was blindly followed. The result was a foregone conclusion: promotion in the artillery was so slow as to deter many from entering that arm, and caused others of its best officers to leave it in despair. After the four regular regiments were established in 1777, and until the end of the war, not more than a half-dozen or so captains were promoted, or at a rate but little greater than one captain a year for the Artillery Brigade. This state of affairs, which should not exist, was partially due to the mistake, made after the year 1776, of reducing the number of field officers, as before indicated. Gridley, who knew from a long experience the inconvenience of this arrangement, understood the proper organization for this arm, and the regiment he commanded gave proof of it. It had been better had his precepts and example in this particular been followed by his successors in service.*

---

*Incidents trivial in themselves often, from their associations, indicate a great deal. As illustrating the manner in which the British idea had taken possession of their rebellious subjects, it will not be uninteresting to note that in some of the official returns Knox's command is designated the "American Regiment of Artillery," of which the four regular regiments were styled "battalions." To those acquainted with the organization of the Royal Artillery Regiment at that time it need not be pointed out that a more complete case of military and official plagiarism, with slight foundation to base it upon, can scarcely be conceived of.

In common with the rest of the army, the artillery was next reorganized, pursuant to resolves of Congress of October 3d and 21st, 1780. On the former date a proposition was carried through that body to retain as the artillery of the "regular army of the United States" the four existing regiments, but with the number of companies cut down to nine, each of sixty-five enlisted men, the commissioned officers remaining as before. Upon consultation with General Washington this was modified, on the second date mentioned, so as to fix the number of companies at ten per regiment. (Appendix A [13].) The change here contemplated was effected by transferring two Pennsylvania companies from the Second to the Fourth Artillery. In the First, natural causes so reduced the number of companies that neither consolidation nor muster-out was necessary. It went south with Gates, and suffered severely at Camden; never rejoined the main army, but the fragments remained in the Carolinas and in Georgia until the end of the war. In the Third, two companies were absorbed, the men transferred, and the surplus officers, as provided by Congress, placed on the list of supernumeraries. The organizations here given were retained unchanged until the end of the war.

When the regular army was being prepared for the field in 1776–'77 it was given out that the artillery was to be recruited at large, and without regard to State limits, as is customary now for all branches of service; but those regiments soon found, to their cost, that it was far better to be assigned to the quota of some particular State, each of which, to some extent, furnished its own troops with food and clothes. .Accordingly, under the resolves of October 3d and 21st, 1780, the First Artillery was assigned to Virginia, the Second to New York, the Third to Massachusetts, the Fourth to Pennsylvania. To the latter State was also accredited a regiment of artificers; but as it afterwards became a matter of doubt whether Congress intended to retain Flower's artillery artificers or Colonel Baldwin's quartermaster artificer-regiment, both were mustered out of service, and the artificers, as a distinct organization, entirely disappeared.

The Fourth Artillery served a short time in the southern department with the First Regiment. The former moved to join Greene after the siege of Yorktown, with the commands of St. Clair and Wayne. The Second, with the Fourth, composed the artillery in the trenches at that memorable siege. Except this service of the Second, and the detachment with Lafayette into Virginia of part of the same regiment, under Lïeutenant-Colonel Stevens, early in 1781, the Second and Third regiments served wholly in the northern section of the United States, and mostly with the main army.

The rule of promotion in the artillery during the Revolution underwent several changes. In the first period of that war, and before the regiments were organized into a brigade, promotions were regimental. This is stated in a letter from General Washington to Major Forrest, of the Pennsylvania artillery (Proctor's), in 1777. Replying to a complaint that Major Popkins had been, July 15th, 1777, promoted to lieutenant-colonel of Crane's regiment, when Forrest antedated him in the former grade, the commander-in-chief remarked: "Each regiment of artillery is as distinct as are the regiments of foot belonging to the various States, and promotion in Crane's regiment does not affect you." When, however, the brigade had been formed, there was established a closer bond of union than was here indicated. This will appear in the following letter of Knox to General Washington, dated New Windsor, March 27th, 1781:

"There is now no established rule for filling vacancies that occur in the artillery. Some doubts have arisen since the last regulation of the army (October, 1780) whether the right of appointment is in Congress, as usual, or in the States to which the artillery regiments were then assigned. New appointments, made since the regiments were originally organized and placed on the continental establishment, have been made by Congress on requests and certificates of regimental commanders, countersigned by the general commanding the corps. All line officers have been promoted regimentally, field officers in line of the corps at large; this principle connects the artillery regiments; without it they would be four separate and distinct organizations. If States interfere with the appointments, this connection between the regiments will be destroyed. The principles of appointments and promotions should be fixed in the most explicit terms. * * * I propose that appointments originate with the colonels, as before indicated, with certificate of qualifications. Unless something of this kind be done, the best officers, seeing how uncertain promotion is, will leave the service. The present state of the artillery, the work of years, may be ruined in an hour unless this matter be settled."

It will not escape notice that the principle of promotion here announced as that which cemented together the various parts of the artillery is precisely that which governs in the premises at this time —one hundred years later. The only instance during the Revolution in which it was practically illustrated was the case of Captain

Benjamin Eustis, of the Third Artillery, who, December 2d, 1778, was promoted to major of the Fourth Artillery. On that date Lieutenant-Colonel J. M. Strobagh, of the latter, died, and Major Forrest, of the same regiment, succeeded him. Eustis was the ranking captain of artillery, and for this reason was promoted major, *vice* Forrest. (Appendix A [10].) The principle on which this was done, however well it might have been understood in the army, was little understood outside of that institution. The officers of the Fourth Regiment remonstrated against Eustis' transfer, nor was President Reed, of Pennsylvania, inclined to look with favor on this injection of a Massachusetts officer into what was looked on as the artillery of the State of Pennsylvania. Mr. Reed was satisfied when the commander-in-chief explained the rule to him, but the officers of the Fourth Regiment were slower to acquiesce in what they considered an infringement on their rights; and it required all the authority of the commander-in-chief to sustain Major Eustis in his position, which he filled until his death, October 6th, 1781.*

The assignment in the reorganization, October, 1780, of the artillery to certain States for recruitment was followed by a resolution of Congress, May 25th, 1781, making promotion regimental. But the power to appoint officers of the line up to and including colonels was, by the adoption of the Articles of Confederation, March 1st, 1781, given the States, each for its quota. This, whether intended or not, wrought new and diverse rules of promotion. The power to appoint was found to carry with it that of prescribing how the officers should advance from one grade to another. Hence each State both appointed and promoted officers as it saw fit. These frequent changes where there should be, and in every

---

*Writing to President Reed concerning the remonstrance of the Fourth Artillery officers, General Washington remarked: "From 1777, when it was taken on the continental establishment, until October, 1780, Proctor's regiment was not credited to the quota of, nor did it belong to, any State. In consequence, the various resolutions of Congress regulating promotions in State quotas did not apply to this regiment. When Forrest was promoted, *vice* Strobagh, Eustis was the ranking captain of artillery. Up to that time there had arisen no occasion for promoting field officers of artillery, or it would have been done on the principles here used." In the latter statement, however, the commander-in-chief was not strictly correct, as the case of Forrest, who sought the lieutenant-colonelcy of Crane's regiment, evinces. (See p. 15.)

well-regulated system is, stability, caused misunderstandings, bitter controversies, and consequent disappointment. This was particularly the case when Proctor resigned, April 9th, 1781. Carrington, as ranking lieutenant-colonel of artillery, claimed the vacancy. He at the time was deputy quartermaster-general of the southern department, but Greene permitted him to leave that station and assume command of his (supposed) regiment. His claims were supported by General Washington; but the matter being referred to Congress, that body decided that, under the Articles of Confederation, it was not legal to appoint a Virginia lieutenant-colonel to the command of a Pennsylvania regiment. Carrington's pretensions were therefore disallowed. He resumed his duties of deputy quartermaster-general, which he performed with distinguished ability until the end of the war. The vacant colonelcy was never filled. Forrest remained lieutenant-colonel of the regiment until October 7th, 1781. The ranking major—Andrew Porter—commanded until January 1st, 1782, when he was promoted to lieutenant-colonel commandant. The vacancy in the rank of major thus created was filled December 24th, 1782, by the promotion of Captain Francis Proctor, Jr., to date back to January 1st, 1782, when Porter was promoted. The vacancy caused by Eustis' death, was filled by the promotion of Captain Isaac Craig. All these officers belonged to the Fourth Artillery. Under the provisions of resolution of Congress of August 7th, 1782, consolidating and reducing the number of regiments and retiring supernumerary officers, Major Proctor retired from active service January 1st, 1783.

As the time for disbanding the Revolutionary army approached, the serious consideration of Congress was directed to providing a proper peace establishment. A committee composed of Messrs. Hamilton, Madison, Ellsworth, Wilson, and Holten was appointed to examine into and submit a report on the subject. They solicited the views of numerous officers of rank in the army; and as some of the views elicited, as well as those contained in the committee's report, are interesting and pertinent, they will be inserted here. Du Portail, the chief of engineers, in a letter to General Washington, September 30th, 1783, gave as his opinion that, for the following among other reasons, it would be best to unite the artillery and engineers:

"The preliminary knowledge of each is the same. There is a

very great relation between the professions themselves. The most important use of cannon is in attack and defense of fortified places. In some European countries they are united, and where they are not, it is in contemplation. In France they were united at a time of active hostilities, and the scheme for uniting was bad; besides, the private interests of some of the first officers were injured by the union; add to this the injury to their corps pride, one of long standing, and the opposition to the union, upon the wisest basis, can be accounted for. However, almost all officers of engineers are persuaded of the advantage of it.

"In making my calculations of force, I suppose, agreeably to his excellency's letter, that it is to be used solely to protect ourselves against the British; for if the United States are to have fortified harbors, what I am proposing will be insufficient. I propose two regiments, each five companies of gunners, one of bombardiers, one of sappers and miners, one of artificers; each company in peace to have three sergeants, six corporals, twenty-four privates, commanded by one first and one second captain, one first and one second lieutenant; in time of war the number of privates to be doubled; each regiment to have one colonel, one lieutenant-colonel, one major, one adjutant, one paymaster, one quartermaster, two surgeons, one sergeant-major, one drum-major, six drums and fifes; total to each regiment, 327.

"The four officers to each company provides for detached service on fortifications, &c.

"The British frontier should be divided into three parts; at the head of each a brigadier-general or colonel will control what concerns artillery and fortifications in that part. Above and commanding all these must be a director-general of the United States artillery and fortification. All officials of the department are accountable to the director; he is the head of the administration of the corps. Through him the orders of Congress and of their Board of War will be transmitted to the corps. Such an officer as director seems absolutely necessary to have that important branch of the administration governed upon the same plan and constant principles. If there be at the head of the department of artillery and fortification many officers, independent one of another, great inconvenience will result.

"The necessity of an academy to be a nursery for the corps is too obvious to be insisted upon. It must be commanded, under the director, by a field officer, assisted by a captain. The students should spend three years at least at the academy. Ten or twelve students would be sufficient to keep the corps complete. To secure places in the corps as soon as possible for men of theory and knowledge, keep vacant the second lieutenancies for the first graduates. At the academy there should be one master of mathematics, one of natural philosophy and of chemistry, and one of drawing. As for military matters, it belongs to the officers of the head of the academy to give that kind of instruction."

Colonel Hamilton penned the committee report submitted to Congress, when all suggestions had been received and considered. In this it was recommended "that the military peace establishment of the United States shall consist of four regiments of infantry, one of artillery, into which regiment the engineers will be incorporated, the consolidated body to be called the Corps of Engineers."

Each regiment of infantry "to contain two battalions of four companies each ; the companies to have each sixty-four rank and file, to be recruited to one hundred and twenty-five rank and file in time of war, preserving proportion of corporals to privates. The entire personnel of the infantry regiment to be : one colonel, two majors, eight captains, eight first lieutenants, thirteen second lieutenants, (to furnish paymaster, quartermaster, and adjutant, and also two ensigns, one to each battalion,) one chaplain, one surgeon, one mate, two sergeant-majors, two quartermaster-sergeants, two drum and fife majors, thirty-two sergeants, sixty-four corporals, (included in rank and file,) four hundred and forty-eight privates, sixteen drums and fifes. The corps of engineers to consist of one regiment, or two battalions of artillery; each battalion four companies; each company, sixty-four rank and file; and a corps of artificers. The personnel of the corps of engineers to consist of one major-general commandant, one colonel, two lieutenant-colonels, four majors, eight captains, sixteen first lieutenants, nineteen second lieutenants, (to provide corps paymaster, quartermaster, and adjutant,) one professor of mathematics, one professor of chemistry, one professor of natural philosophy, one professor of civil architecture, one drawing master, one chaplain, one surgeon, one mate, one sergeant-major, two quartermaster-sergeants, one drum and fife major, thirty-two sergeants, (four to a company,) thirty-two bombardiers, (included in rank and file,) three hundred and eighty-four cannoneers, ninety-six sappers and miners, sixteen drums and fifes." The artificers forming part of the engineer corps were to be workers in brass and iron, armorers, engravers, cutters, blacksmiths, carpenters, wheelwrights, masons, saddlers, cartridge-box makers of the first, second, and third classes. The committee thought, also, that "there would be necessary one commissary of military stores, five deputy commissaries, and a certain number of conductors, all of whom should be taken from among the non-commissioned officers."

Of the general staff in time of peace there would be necessary, in the opinion of the committee, one general commanding the troops, one general commanding the artillery and engineers, and one inspector-general.

As to a military academy, that would not be advisable; active service, in the opinion of the committee, was the school of the soldier. To disseminate throughout the military establishment the necessary scientific knowledge, the professors in the corps of engineers were provided, and would be sufficient.

Touching the subject of appointment to office in the peace army, as well as promotion therein, the report proceeds: "The idea of the Confederation being adhered to, the number of troops to be raised must be distributed to the several States according to the proportion of their respective populations, and each must appoint regimental officers in proportion to the number of men furnished; but as no State will have to furnish a complete regiment, this apportionment of the officers will become extremely difficult, if not impracticable, on any satisfactory footing, and the filling up vacancies as they arise will create endless perplexity. It would be much to be preferred that the States could be induced to transfer this right to Congress; and indeed without it there can never be regularity in the military system. It would also be much for the best that the men should be enlisted under continental direction, which will be a more certain and frugal mode."

The rule of promotion suggested by the committee was that of seniority in each regiment, to include the advancement of captain to major, and after that in the arm at large; and if dragoons should be introduced into the army by subsequent resolution of Congress, then the officers of infantry and dragoons to be placed on one roster for promotion to lieutenant-colonel and colonel. In the engineer corps, advancement to follow strictly the rule of seniority. It was provided, however, that in no part of the army could an officer claim exemption from being overslaughed by another for brilliant services or peculiar talents; but this exception to the ordinary rule was never to be made but on recommendation of the general commanding the army, accompanied by facts and reasons, and with the approval of the Secretary of War.

General Washington, to whom this report was referred, strongly indorsed the views therein set forth respecting the appointment and promotion of officers; but with reference to those relating to the necessity for a military academy, he stated that he would pass them by without remark. He favored the establishment of that institution, as did also Colonel Hamilton when he had more maturely considered the importance of the measure.

But not even Colonel Hamilton's array of facts, nor his forcible method of presenting them, could remove the insurmountable obstacles that arose to the formation of a peace establishment. The opinion very generally prevailed that it was a violation of the fundamental principles of the Confederation to maintain a standing army in time of peace; that each State should maintain order within her own borders, and without others helping to bear the expense. Militia only, according to this theory, could be lawfully brought into service, except when a national danger called the whole country to arms; when that time arrived, the Confederation involved in war, a regular army was admissible. It need not be mentioned that these views were not those entertained by Colonel Hamilton, who struck at the root of these dangerous heresies when he urged that the States should surrender to Congress the power of appointing and promoting officers in the proposed national army. The States would surrender nothing; and when afterwards General Knox, as Secretary of War, attempted to lay down rules governing the relative rank of officers in the army, he found they could not be enforced; the States accepted them, or not, as they chose. As a consequence, diversity prevailed in these matters; and when, in 1789, President Washington nominated the officers of the Confederation army for appointment in the army of the United States, he remarked: "It is to be observed that the order in which the captains and subalterns are named is not to affect their relative rank, which has hitherto been imperfectly settled, owing to the perplexity of promotions in the State quotas conformably to the late Confederation."

Various causes operated to prevent the Revolutionary army being entirely disbanded November 3d, 1783, as directed in the proclamation of Congress the preceding 18th of October, and the remnant designated which was to remain in service. The portion of the army thus retained formed in no sense a peace establishment. When the time came to disband the troops there were large quantities of public stores scattered at numerous places all over the country; these had to be guarded; it was expected the British would vacate the posts they occupied within the northwest boundaries of the United States, and it was necessary that troops should occupy them. For these and other necessary purposes one infantry regiment five hundred strong, and one battalion of artillery composed of one hundred and thirty-eight officers and men, with a few from the invalid regiment, were kept in service. They were all selected from the army on the Hudson River, which was under the immediate orders of General Washington. (For statement of force retained, see Appendix A [14].) Except the small battalion here mentioned, the four regular artillery regiments had disappeared, the First and Fourth under Greene to the southward, the Second and Third in the north. Of the battalion, four officers and fifty-five men were from the Third Artillery; the rest from the Second. Those were retained who, by the terms of their enlistments, had longest to serve.

The maintenance of any military establishment was beset by so many difficulties—the principal of which seemed to be the expense attending the measure—that many expedients were proposed in Congress whereby the absolutely necessary military service of the Government could be performed. Colonel Hamilton's plan for an army dropped apparently out of sight. Another committee, to which had been intrusted the duty of devising measures for taking possession of the forts held by the British, submitted May 12th, 1784, a scheme for this purpose which embraced the formation of three battalions of infantry, one battalion of artillery, and a few engineer officers. (Appendix A [15].) It was understood that these troops were for the purpose specified, and not to form a permanent force; the term of enlistment three years, each State furnishing a contingent. This report, like its predecessor, was rejected; and as the terms of service of the few men of the old army were about expiring, it was resolved, as a preliminary step to the raising a proper peace establishment, to discharge all those who had been retained. This was accordingly done by resolution of Congress June 2d, 1784, but eighty men—fifty-five at West Point and twenty-five at Fort Pitt—being kept to guard stores, with a proportionate number of officers, none above the rank of captain. (Appendix A [16].) The next day it was resolved that, "as it appeared absolutely necessary to have seven hundred non-commissioned officers and men properly officered, it was recommended to the following States, as most convenient to the posts shortly to be vacated by the British, to furnish from their militia: Connecticut, 165; New York, 165; New Jersey, 110; Pennsylvania, 260—to serve twelve months, unless sooner discharged."

The Secretary at War was directed to form these troops into one regiment of ten companies—eight of infantry, two of artillery; the officers to be one lieutenant-colonel commandant, from Pennsylvania; two majors, one from Connecticut, the other from New York, each major to command a company; eight captains, to be taken from the States in proportion to their quotas; ten lieutenants, one to act as adjutant; ten ensigns, one chaplain, one surgeon, and four mates. As there was no Secretary at War until March, 1785, the duty of arranging the organization, further than here given, devolved on the States furnishing the troops and upon the regimental commander.

Among those kept to guard stores, under resolution of June 2d, 1784, was the artillery company of Brevet Major John Doughty, Alexander Hamilton's successor* in the New York artillery. Doughty's, with one from Pennsylvania under Captain Thomas Douglass, late of the Fourth Continental Artillery, were assigned as the two artillery companies of Lieutenant-Colonel Harmar's regiment.

Thus, in the fall of 1784, the only force in the service of the United States—aside from a few of the old Maryland line at Fort Pitt—was a regiment of detached militia enlisted to serve one year, and styled by the War Department the "First American Regiment." Upon this as a basis was gradually built up the regular army, into which passed by absorption several companies of the First American; among others, the artillery company of Captain and Brevet Major Doughty.

By resolution of March 31st, 1785, it was determined to discharge that part of the regiment not actually in service on the frontier. It was soon evident that the term of engagement was too short for any useful purpose; and in April, (1st, 7th, 12th,) 1785, it was resolved to replace the one-year militia by others to serve three years. The quotas of States remained unchanged, and in fact the personnel of the new regiment was little else than the old re-enlisted. The former officers were generally retained, among others Captain Doughty; but Pennsylvania replaced Captain Douglass by Captain William Ferguson, also late of the Fourth Continental Artillery. At this time a change was made in the designations of enlisted men of artillery. In Douglass' company they had been divided into sergeants, corporals, bombardiers, gunners, drummers, fifers, and matrosses; whereas in Ferguson's the terms bombardier and gunner did not appear, and matross was supplanted by the term private. The personnel of Douglass'. company, on December 1st, 1784, as shown by his return, was: one captain, one lieutenant, four sergeants, three corporals, three bombardiers, three gunners, two drums and fifes, and thirty-five matrosses. That of Ferguson's, August 7th, 1787, was: one captain, one lieutenant, three sergeants, three corporals, two drums and fifes, and forty-two privates.

Resemblance to Colonel Hamilton's plan, or that reported by the committee May 12th, 1784, will be looked for in vain in the organization of the army actually adopted. A regiment composed partly of infantry and partly of artillery companies was not apparently thought of by those to whom had been intrusted the devising a plan for a military establishment. The regiment served on the northwest frontier, where its duties were principally to keep the Indians in good order; but small as was the force, insignificant as were its operations, the uniting artillery and infantry in the same regiment was found to be as inconvenient as it was incongruous. When, therefore, the military establishment was, October 20th, 1786, increased to 2040 enlisted men, including those in service, and Secretary Knox given authority to organize the whole, he formed them into a legion, the artillery, under a major, making a separate battalion. (Appendix A [17].) From that day —January 30th, 1787—to this the artillery has been organized as an arm distinct from the infantry, though generally in peace, and sometimes in war, performing the duties of the latter. The major and commandant of the new artillery battalion was John Doughty. The captains were William Ferguson, of the Pennsylvania company ; James Bradford, late first lieutenant Second Artillery, and who, remaining in service with him, was now promoted, *vice* Doughty ; Henry Burbeck, (son of Lieutenant-Colonel Burbeck, of Gridley's regiment,) late captain of the Third Artillery ; and Joseph Savage, late captain in the Second Artillery.

Excepting the companies of Burbeck and Savage, the troops enlisted pursuant to resolution of October 20th, 1786, were, by resolution of April 9th, 1787, ordered to be discharged. This vacillation was due to the deranged state of the public finances. It was felt that the protection of the frontier and the vindication of the national honor required these troops, but economy was more important. This left in service Harmar's eight companies of infantry and Doughty's four companies of artillery.

The re-enlistment of the seven hundred men engaged under resolution of April 12th, 1785, and their rearrangement with Burbeck's and Savage's companies into an infantry regiment of eight and an artillery battalion of four companies, was authorized by Congress October 3d, 1787. All companies were given the same organization. (Appendix A [18].) The staff remained unchanged. This regiment and this battalion, commanded, respectively, by Lieutenant-Colonel and Brevet Brigadier-General Harmar and Major Doughty, were adopted, September 29th, 1789, as the regular army of the United States under the constitutional Government. The former had received the brevet of brigadier-general, with the emoluments of the office but without the pay proper. He remained lieutenant-colonel of the regiment of infantry, and performed the duties of the latter office as well as those of commander of the forces in the northwest. (Appendix A [19].)

Affairs on the frontier had, under the Confederation, gradually grown worse, the Indians more haughty ; and there was reason to believe they were urged on by the British, who still, seven years after the Revolutionary war had ended, held to the posts they were expected to deliver up on the ratification of peace. Under these circumstances the infantry regiment, by act of April 30th, 1790, received an addition of four companies, and the twelve of which it was now composed, were arranged to three battalions. Except a slight increase in the rank and file, this act left the artillery unchanged. (Appendix A [20].) It was with these troops that Harmar marched against the Miami Indians, by whom he was defeated October 20th, 1790. This disaster caused a further increase of the army by one regiment of infantry similar to that in service, the appointment of St. Clair to the position of major-general and Samuel Hodgdon to the office of quartermaster-general.

Major Commandant John Doughty, of the artillery, was nominated and confirmed lieutenant-colonel commandant of the new regiment of infantry. The ranking artillery captain—Ferguson—was confirmed, *vice* Doughty, as commandant of the artillery. Doughty, however, declined the appointment thus tendered; but as Ferguson had been confirmed major of artillery in his stead, he was considered as ousted from the service. The battalion, under its new commander, accompanied St. Clair on his expedition against the Miami Indians, when, on the 4th of November, 1791, Ferguson, with other officers and many men, fell by the side of the guns they could not take off the field. Bradford, the ranking captain, having been killed, Ferguson was succeeded as major commandant by Captain Henry Burbeck.

The defeats in succession of Harmar and St. Clair caused the army, by act of March 5th, 1792, to be still further increased to 5120 men; and, under the authority given him in the act, President Washington arranged this force to one legion and four sub-legions. This plan had been advocated by Baron Steuben, who often during the Revolution pressed the principles and advantages of the legionary formation upon the attention of the commander-in-chief. A few months after Steuben's arrival in this country and his appointment as inspector-general, an attempt was made in Congress (May, 1778) to have the army organized in this manner, but it failed of adoption. Replying in 1783 to General Washington's request for suggestions upon the subject of a peace establishment, Steuben had again urged the legionary as the best organization. It was doubtless under his influence that Knox became imbued with the same views, as is evinced in his arrangement of the army in January, 1787, and his celebrated, but utopian and impracticable, plan of 1790 for the organization of the militia of the United States.

As the army was arranged in 1792, the major commandant was of the legionary staff, and one company of artillery was assigned to each sub-legion. (Appendix A [21].) Under St. Clair's successor, Major-General Anthony Wayne, the Americans at last defeated and dispersed the Indians at the Miami Rapids, August 20th, 1794.

Meanwhile, on the 9th of the preceding May, (1794,) the artillery had been (for those times) largely increased in numbers, and had received an important change of organization. Since the disbanding of the artillery of the Revolution, that arm had been maintained in but insignificant numbers, with an eye single to economy, at whatever sacrifice of efficiency. The infantry and artillery had been organized and used together on the frontier, and the only difference between them was that the artillery, in addition to duty as infantry, managed their guns, repaired and kept in order every species of armament, small-arm or otherwise, with which the troops were equipped. For this extra service they received neither pecuniary nor other reward. The pay of the same grade of officers in different branches of service was the same. In one word, the artillery, except in name, had been only infantry, with the additional duties imposed of acting as artificers for the army, and managing the pieces of ordnance with which the western forts and the Indian expeditions were supplied.

The act of May 9th, 1794, by combining the artillery with the engineers, contemplated a very different status for the arm from that to which it had been relegated since the Revolution. For furnishing merely a combined infantryman, gunner, and artificer, without regard to efficiency, former practices had been sufficient. When, however, the scene of operations was transferred from the wilderness to the sea-coast,—the objects to be defended, instead of log forts became populous cities, the repositories of the nation's wealth; the enemy, instead of the wild Indian became a military nation supported by the most powerful navy in the world,—the necessity for reorganizing and increasing the artillery to meet the new order of things became apparent. That this was the matured judgment of the country, proof was given in the prompt passage by Congress of the act of May 9th, 1794. The Executive evinced his appreciation of the situation by appointing to the first positions in the new corps gentlemen of approved scientific attainments. The field officers were: Stephen Rochefontaine, lieutenant-colonel commandant; to the original vacancies, Lewis de Tousard, John Jacob Ulrich Rivardi, Constant Freeman, majors; and, as the artillerists and engineers absorbed the old artillery battalion, Burbeck, by virtue of his former rank, entered as major.

Rochefontaine and Rivardi were at the time civil engineers in the employ of the Government, constructing fortifications; Tousard was an accomplished artillerist; Constant Freeman, late captain-lieutenant Crane's regiment, was an officer of great experience, and had a thorough knowledge of his duties as an artillery officer.

The plan of organization for the artillerists and engineers (Appendix A [22]) had some of the features proposed by both General Du Portail and Colonel Hamilton's committee, before mentioned. But, like many other attempts at army legislation, there was more form than substance in it. Both Du Portail and the committee, while proposing to unite the artillery and engineers in one corps, contemplated the organization of that corps into one compact and well proportioned body, with a regular chain of surbordination extending from top to bottom, so that unity of purpose and action might characterize every movement. Both recognized the necessity that existed in such a corps for the subalterns receiving special instruction to teach them the fundamental principles of their profession. The act of May 9th, 1794, was drafted apparently with the same general principles for a groundwork. But, while the form was there, the practical facilities to secure efficiency were lacking. The section of the law authorizing cadets to be instructed, and the procurement of the necessary apparatus for the purpose, while well meaning, was never, except to demonstrate the inadequacy of educating officers in this manner, of any utility whatever. Then the absorption of the old battalion of artillery was a mistake; it had never, in fact, been anything but infantry, except in name, and the personnel was not possessed of the theoretical knowledge and scientific attainments which it was intended should distinguish the officers of artillerists and engineers. The scattered condition of the corps on the western frontier, in the east and on the sea-board, was prejudicial to its interests; the parts did not serve together; were unknown to each other, and the colonel, serving constantly as an engineer, was given no opportunity to attend to the interior arrangements of his command. Moreover, though Rochefontaine and his associates were capable officers, there was an element of weakness in having a corps French at the head and American at the foot. Opportunity was not given for the cultivation of that sympathy between these parts which grows out of a community of interests;

thus the naturally delicate and difficult task of uniting heterogeneous elements into one harmonious whole, with the cultivation of a proper *esprit de corps*, was practically impossible. The disadvantage of this situation was something for which no one was responsible; the attempt had been made to build up the corps with the best material obtainable, and it was but an incident of the imperfectly developed resources of the country that features which it was expected would, and which actually did, give strength to the system, were at the same time sources of weakness. Under all the circumstances, however, it was not a matter to excite wonder that the artillerists and engineers failed to accomplish what was expected, or that in eight years the corps passed away leaving scarcely a trace to show that it had existed.

This was but facilitated by the organization of a regiment of artillerists and engineers, in addition to the corps, by act of April 27, 1798. (Appendix A [23].) The two organizations were separate and distinct, and the sequel verified the prediction of Du Portail years before that: "If there be at the head of the department of the artillery and fortifications many officers, independent one of another, great inconvenience will result."

The field officers of the regiment were: John Doughty, lieutenant-colonel commandant; Benjamin Brooks, Adam Hoops, and Daniel Jackson, majors. Of these, Doughty was the old major commandant of artillery, and Jackson had been a first lieutenant in Crane's Revolutionary artillery.

It will be noticed that, whereas a preponderance of rank and influence had been given foreign officers when the *corps* was organized in 1794, in the *regiment* of artillerists and engineers all the field officers were native Americans. The presence of the former at this juncture was a source of solicitude to the President, which, from the friends of government in his confidence, he did not attempt to conceal. He summarily dismissed Rochefontaine in May, 1798, although for what reason is not known. When Inspector-General Hamilton urged the appointment of Major Tousard to the position of inspector of artillery—an office created by act of July 16th, 1798—the President replied that there was so much uneasiness felt because of the French officers of artillery, he expected much trouble; and although Tousard, in April, 1801, received this appointment to date back to May, 1800, there was no denying the fact that President Adams was right; at that early day, when the machinery of government was not yet in working order, it was dangerous to intrust the inspection and proof of artillery to any officer with whose native country the United States was preparing to go to war.

By the same act which created the office of inspector of artillery, the President was authorized to appoint not exceeding four teachers of the arts and sciences, for the instruction of the cadets of artillerists and engineers. They were to do the duties contemplated for the professors in Colonel Hamilton's plan for an army before given, and it is reasonable to suppose their employment now was suggested by that gentleman, whose influence with Secretary McHenry was unbounded. Concerning these teachers the Secretary remarked: "Their employment would give the intended effect to the provision of the law of May 9th, 1794, authorizing the appointment of two cadets to each company of artillerists and engineers, who would, it was supposed, form a nursery from which qualified officers might be drawn to fill vacancies." It is not known that these teachers were appointed. It is probable that they were not, as, when the cadets were drawn together in 1801 at West Point, they gave little evidence of having been the subjects of scientific instruction. "The school as started at this time was under the direction of a private citizen, and was nothing more than a mathematical school for the few cadets then in service. It was found that the government of young men was incompatible with the ordinary system of schools, and consequently the institution ran into disorder and the teacher into contempt."

The act of March 3d, 1799, reorganized the army upon a plan drafted by Lieutenant-General Washington. It provided for placing the corps and the regiment of artillerists and engineers upon the same footing, giving the latter, like the former, four battalions. (Appendix A [24].) Thereafter the two organizations were called, respectively, the first and second regiments of artillerists and engineers.

The United States had but few more scientific officers in 1798 than the colonies had in 1775. In both instances the Government turned abroad—to Europe—for the desired knowledge and experience not found at home. To the corps of artillerists and engineers the country had looked for the requisite talents and knowledge, and the personnel in 1795 gave promise that this confidence was not misplaced; but events had unexpectedly changed. Those for-

ORGANIZATION—GENERALLY. 31

merly relied upon were now mistrusted; and, through neglect to cultivate native talent, the attainments essential to an army scientific corps had now, in face of the enemy, to be picked up wherever found. These facts made a profound impression on thoughtful men of the day. The revival soon after of the attempt to re-establish the military school, which for years had languished from inattention, gave proof that the lesson had been taken to heart. Adverting to this subject in a letter of December 24th, 1798, Mr. McHenry said:

"It is deeply to be regretted that a precious period of leisure was not improved toward forming among ourselves engineers and artillerists, and that, owing to this neglect, we are in danger of being overtaken by war without a competent number of characters of these descriptions. To form them suddenly is impracticable; much previous study and experiment are essential. If possible to avoid it, war ought not to find us unprovided. * * * In the meanwhile it is considered to be advisable to endeavor to introduce from abroad at least one distinguished engineer and one distinguished officer of artillery. They may be sought for preferably in the Austrian, and next in the Prussian armies. It is also suggested that an inspector of fortifications is much wanted. * * * The officer may be drawn from the corps of artillerists and engineers, or it may be left discretionary with the President to choose him where he pleases."

These suggestions had been made to Mr. McHenry by Lieutenant-General Washington in his letter submitting the plan for the reorganization of the army. In conformity therewith, the President was authorized, by act of March 3d, 1799, to engage and appoint two engineers with rank of lieutenant-colonel, distinct from the corps, and also an inspector of fortifications, who, if not taken from the corps, should have the rank of major.

There at this time entered the artillerists and engineers as major of the Fourth Battalion, Second Regiment, Jonathan Williams, a gentleman of ability and attainments, the result of combined talent, travel, study and reflection. He at once took a prominent position among those who were to re-establish confidence in the native American officers of the army. He was, December 14th, 1801, made inspector of fortifications, and at the same time superintendent of the military school for cadets at West Point, into which it was proposed to instill new life. His appointment in 1802 to the corps of engineers separated Major Williams from the artillery; but, as superintendent of the military academy, he laid the foundation of an institution which, for its special purposes, is second to none.

President Adams contemplated the appointment of a civilian to be commander of the corps of artillerists and engineers in place of the dismissed Rochefontaine; but the nomination of the Hon. Jonathan Dayton of New Jersey to the office was not confirmed, as it should not have been, being a most dangerous innovation upon the well-understood rule for making appointments and promotions in the army. No successor to Rochefontaine was appointed until February 20th, 1799, when Henry Burbeck, ranking major, was promoted to the vacancy, to date from May 7th, 1798, the day of Rochefontaine's dismissal. The office of lieutenant-colonel commandant of the Second Regiment of artillerists and engineers, vacated by the resignation of Doughty, May 26th, 1800, was filled by the promotion of Tousard, the ranking major in that arm of service. But fate had decreed that neither Tousard's nor his compatriot Rivardi's connection with the American artillery was to be prolonged. They were not in favor with Secretary Dearborn, a rough, practical soldier, who had imbibed military ideas in the field during the Revolution, and who then conceived what he never overcame—a prejudice against foreigners and their ways of doing things. The correspondence between the Secretary and these officers was often of such nature that no one familiar with it was surprised when, in Mr. Jefferson's political reorganization of the army in 1802, both were mustered out of service.

In this reorganization the artillerists and engineers as a combined arm disappeared. Out of a part of the old material a regiment of artillerists was formed, while a corps of engineers was created as a distinct part of the military system. The colonel of the former was Burbeck, ranking lieutenant-colonel commandant of artillerists and engineers; the lieutenant-colonel, Constant Freeman; the majors, Daniel Jackson, Decius Wadsworth, Moses Porter, and William MacRea. This absorbed all the field officers of the late artillerists and engineers save four. Of these, Williams was appointed major of the engineer corps; Tousard and Rivardi, with Mahlon Ford, were discharged. The arm was here deprived of some of its best educated and most capable officers.

Before the reduction the artillerists and engineers embraced one hundred and eighty-two officers, surgeons, mates and cadets. In the regiment of artillerists there were one hundred and seven of these grades. The enlisted force was at the same time cut down from 2152 to 1520. But though forty per cent. of the first mentioned left service, it will be noticed that both Burbeck and Freeman were promoted by the change, thus going up in the scale, while many others went not only down but out of service. As illustrating the mutability of military fortune in those days of frequent changes, it may be mentioned that both these officers—Burbeck in 1815 and Freeman in 1821—were placed to one side to make room in their turn for others.

If we compare the organization of the artillery under the act of March 16th, 1802, (Appendix A [25],) with that of the artillerists and engineers before that time, it will be found in some respects to have gained by the change. True, the staff of the regiment and the battalions were either wanting or entirely inadequate; but this disadvantage was far more than offset by the fact that the arm was again given a single head. The complete failure of the artillerists to rise to a plane of scientific excellence commensurate with the needs of service—a fact which led directly to the separation in 1812 of the technical from the combatant artillery and the formation of the technical branch into an ordnance department—was due not to faults of organization but to incompetent personnel.

The large number of musicians given each company, (four out of seventy-six enlisted,) was for the purpose, as the Secretary of War explained, of providing the colonel with a fine regimental band,—a luxury in which Crane, Proctor, and perhaps other artillery commanders were indulged during the Revolution.

There was little in the history of the artillery between 1802 and 1812 to call for remark except that important event, the organization of the light artillery regiment. On the 26th of February, 1808, Mr. Jefferson recommended to Congress that, in view of complications growing out of the Napoleonic wars, an addition should be made to the regular army. Accompanying the communication of the President was one from Secretary Dearborn, suggesting that this increase should be fixed at six thousand men, arranged to five regiments of infantry, one of riflemen, one of light artillery, and one of light cavalry. This was authorized by act of April 12th, 1808. (Organization of Light Artillery, Appendix A [26].) Profiting by experience, the introduction of unnaturalized foreigners as officers was prevented by a clause restricting such appointments to citizens of the United States.

Examination of all correspondence bearing on the subject leads to the belief that, when the light artillery was recommended by the Secretary and authorized by Congress, the question as to its equipment had not been decided. No provision, based on the hypothesis that it would be mounted, was made for any part of the establishment; in fact, as provided for in the law, the light differed from the other artillery only in name. The expense that necessarily attended fitting out a regiment of this character was more than the administration was willing to authorize, and no sooner were the light companies recruited than they were, with a single exception, marched off with muskets. To such lengths was this spirit of economy carried, that the lieutenant-colonel was not appointed until December, 1811, and the colonel for some months later. Captain John Saunders of the artillerists was, January, 1809, appointed major of the new regiment, but this was after the companies were nearly, if not quite all, fully recruited. The captains and subalterns were active young men, who eagerly sought opportunity to distinguish themselves in an arm of service rendered famous in the contemporaneous wars of Europe. George Peter, who had the honor of commanding the first properly equipped light artillery company in the American army, headed the list of captains; Winfield Scott, afterwards general-in-chief, stood second on the list; Abraham Eustis, who rose, 17th November, 1834, to be colonel of the present First Artillery, was third. These and many others who started with them rendered distinguished service. The regiment was full of life, the officers young enough to be ambitious, and had opportunity offered under anything like favorable conditions, the light artillery would have made a record honorable alike to itself and to the service of which it formed a part.

Secretary Dearborn lost no time in organizing the first company as field artillery proper. The following is his letter of instructions to Captain Peter, then stationed at Fort McHenry, Baltimore, Maryland:

"WAR DEPARTMENT, 6th May, 1808.

GEO. PETER—*Sir:* As soon as you can have two six-pounders properly mounted, with one ammunition wagon and one light horse wagon, for conveying four men besides the wagoner, prepared for service, I will order the purchase of a sufficient number of horses for making an experiment with one field piece, with its ammunition wagon containing, say, fifty cartridges, ten of which ought to have round shot, and ten of grape or canister. The officers, with one sergeant and three men on horseback, and four men in the light wagon, are to proceed, at the rate of five or six miles an hour, from Baltimore to this city, and to make some experiments at this place by manœuvring the cannon in different directions. * * * For one six-pounder, one ammunition and one light wagon, and for the officers and others on horseback, it will, I presume, require from thirteen to sixteen horses. I wish you to endeavor to have a sufficient number of suitable men well trained to the business before the general experiment is made."

On the 16th of the same month, ten days after the Secretary's letter was written, Peter replied that he had the requisite number of horses in training, and that the carriages, harness, saddles, bridles, &c., would be ready in a few days. Upon this letter the Secretary indorsed an order to the surveyor of supplies directing that he send twenty-six suits of light artillery uniform to Captain Peter as soon as possible. Everything having been put in order for the purpose of making a display with the new arm, the novel feature of the succeeding 4th of July parade in Washington city was Captain Peter's field artillery company.

This was properly looked upon as an important event, and one of great interest both to the Secretary and the President. Artillery moving at the rate of five or six miles an hour was a great advance on anything that had been seen before in this country. The equipment was unique, and must have originated with Secretary Dearborn. Different from anything then practiced elsewhere, it was, both in simplicity and mobility, certainly not second to the system at the time in vogue in some parts of Europe, and of which the Wurst caisson formed a prominent feature. The gun carriages and limbers, of nearly the Gribeauval pattern, were made by the artillery artificers stationed at Fort McHenry.

Orders having been issued directing that the light artillery companies raised south of New Jersey should be concentrated at New Orleans, Peter, augmented in men and guns, left Baltimore December 24th, 1808, and marched to Pittsburg *en route* to that city. Writing to Secretary Dearborn from Pittsburg, January 9th, 1809, Captain Peter said: "The performance of the light artillery in the late march has exceeded my most sanguine expectations. The gun carriages, ammunition wagons, fixed ammunition, &c., have arrived without the smallest injury, and I really believe that the march could have been performed in ten days could the baggage 'wagons have kept pace with us." In conjunction with other forces destined for New Orleans, the company, with men, guns, and horses, were embarked on the Ohio in the latter part of January. After many delays, due to inclement weather and other causes, the command reached its destination in the latter part of March, 1809. Soon after, the army moved to Terre au Bœuf, below the city, and Peter resigned his commission. The company, left in command of Lieutenant James Gibson, was in 1812 absorbed in the companies of the artillerist regiment in that vicinity; while Gibson, returning north, raised and marched to the field one of the first horse artillery companies, which joined the army on the Niagara frontier.

Ere this, Secretary Dearborn had been succeeded, under the new administration of Mr. Madison, by Doctor William Eustis. This gentleman had been surgeon of Gridley's regiment in 1775. He had seen something of military affairs, but wholly from the standpoint of a non-combatant. In this he was a marked contrast to his predecessor, and, unlike him, failed to appreciate the importance of maintaining some portion of the field artillery, equipped as such, in a state of efficiency. On the 2d of June, 1809, he wrote to General Wilkinson: "I am informed by the accountant that the amount of expenditures at New Orleans is great; the charges for house rent, forage, and other articles are such as, if admitted and continued, will soon devour our appropriations. The inclosed memorandum will give you an idea of them. I beg of you to interpose your authority to put an end to them. Horses for the artillery cannot be maintained at such an expense; they must either be sent to some part of the country where they can be maintained at one-fourth of the present expense, or they may be sold. On those waters I should suppose they might be dispensed with. The drivers should be taken from the line; there is no lawful authority for the employment of other persons. Imagine for a moment the whole regiment of light artillery on this scale of expense. Consider the prejudices against the army in general which an inspection of such charges by members of the Government is calculated to impress on their minds." Replying to this, August 27th, 1809, Wilkinson said: "Finding that it is impossible to maintain the light artillery horses on anything like the terms you stipulate, I have ordered them to be sold at vendue." Thus, after a service of little more than one year, the first light artillery company of the United States army, serving as such, was dismounted.

From the date of this event until war with Great Britain became inevitable, nothing was done to further the interests of the light artillery arm beyond preparing the matériel necessary for its equipment, which was to be on the Gribeauval system.* In this Secretary Dearborn had resolved on uniformity, and his successor followed in his footsteps. Meanwhile a bold front was put on when the subject of adding to the efficiency of the practically-discarded arm was suggested as a measure worthy the attention of Government. To a French gentleman who had presented a memoir on the advantages of horse artillery organized as in Europe, pointing out the deficiencies of the United States in this particular, Secretary Eustis, January 10th, 1810, replied: "The use of horse artillery has been suspended in practice for reasons which cannot at this time be entered upon. The importance of this limb of an army has never been uncontemplated or undervalued. The measures of availing ourselves of it are not so remote as may be imagined." But in fact there was little upon which to base this air of confidence. The means at hand to form an efficient horse artillery were too meagre to be relied upon for this purpose. They consisted of a so-called light artillery—but really an infantry—regiment, possessing neither a horse nor a gun, and

---

* In the spring of 1810, the death of Major John Saunders gave rise to a controversy regarding the right to promotion of an officer under suspension which, because of the important precedent established by the decision, as well the subsequent prominence of the person at the time principally affected, is of interest. Captain Winfield Scott, the ranking officer of light artillery after Saunders, claimed the majority, under the regular rules for promotion. But he was at the time under suspension by sentence of a court-martial, and the Secretary of War, not being acquainted with the precedents in the case in our army, referred the matter to a board, of which Colonel Burbeck was president, for advice; the report was adverse to Captain Scott's pretension, and was to the effect that officers forfeited their right to promotion while under suspension, and the next on the list eligible in other respects acquired them. Under this ruling Eustis overslaughed Scott, and was made major of the light artillery. Although this was not in accordance with precedents, had the Secretary but known what they were, it is an eminently just decision, and has governed similar cases in the army since.

of some matériel for its equipment, when mounted, scattered at the arsenals and artillery posts.

It was not until February, 1812, that the officers, even when mounted, were authorized by law to draw forage for their horses, having previously been required to feed them at their own expense. At the same time the President was empowered to mount the entire regiment, while to each company thus mounted there was allowed one saddler and one farrier. This was four years after the organization was put on foot, and shows what erroneous ideas prevailed as to the requisites for a proper light artillery. In the following May, when preparing to take the field, each company was, by law, allowed twelve drivers, who, when the companies were not mounted, were at all times liable to do duty in the ranks. This was a wise measure. Enlisting drivers in the company with which they served was far more conducive to efficiency and discipline than the practice then in vogue in some European armies of having them drawn from corps attached to the artillery, yet independent of it.

The condition of the light artillery at the commencement of the year 1812 demonstrated the impossibility of combining the duties of that arm with those of the infantry. The attempt failed; it was seeking to obtain something for nothing—to have the moral effect and prestige of this powerful auxiliary arm without paying for it. That there was not an efficient horse artillery during the war of 1812, resulted from the fact that the Government was not willing to complete the work it had begun. The personnel was of the best; the matériel was practically equal to that of the enemy, (owing to the relatively slight use made of field artillery;) but from first to last the policy was pursued of dismounting the companies almost as fast as equipped, to the discouragement of the men and the disgust of the officers, who could not reasonably be expected to take pride in a light artillery regiment which existed as such in name only.

Under the pressure of impending war, larger additions were made to the army by act of January 11th, 1812. The combatant force thereby authorized embraced two regiments of artillery, one of dragoons, and ten of infantry. (Organization of Artillery, Appendix A [27].) The two artillery regiments were designated the Second and Third, the old artillerists being, for convenience, known as the First Regiment of regular artillery. But, as regards promotion of officers, these regiments were always distinct. The First belonged to what was officially known as the "peace establishment;" the Second and Third to the "additional military force;" and if during the lifetime of the latter two regiments—January 11th, 1812, to March 30th, 1814—there had happened, in either, a vacancy in the grade of major, for instance, the ranking captain of the artillery line could not claim it. After the original vacancies in the Second and Third regiments were filled, advancement in each was distinct; it was not until the reorganization of March 30th, 1814, when the regiments were broken up and formed into a corps, that promotion, under existing rules, became general throughout the foot artillery arm.

Captain George Izard, formerly of the artillerists, was appointed colonel; Captain Winfield Scott, of the light artillery, lieutenant-colonel; William Lindsay and Daniel M. Forney, majors of the Second Regiment; the other lieutenant-colonel, Francis K. Huger, was not appointed until 1813. Concerning the colonel of the Second, it is proper to remark that there was not in the United States his superior in military knowledge. Educated in the military schools of France, he had, by several years' experience in the army, supplemented by study and reflection, methodically digested in his mind the whole subject of army organization and supply. This fact made his counsel particularly valuable at the beginning of the war, upon which, with little preparation, the Government had now embarked. Both the colonel and lieutenant-colonel of this regiment rose to the grade of general officer.

The Third was not completed in organization so rapidly as the Second Artillery. Of the field officers, only the colonel, Alexander Macomb, late of the engineer corps, and Major George E. Mitchell from civil life, were appointed in 1812. Early in 1813 the complement of field officers was completed by raising Mitchell to the grade of lieutenant-colonel, transferring into the like grade Captain James House, of the First Artillery, and appointing a civilian, Mr. Samuel Nye, with Captain George Armistead, of the First Artillery, majors.

When Izard was promoted, March 12th, 1813, he was succeeded by Lieutenant-Colonel Scott; the latter by Major Lindsay, and he by Captain Hindman—all agreeably to the regimental plan of promotion.

Macomb was appointed brigadier-general January 24th, 1814,

and Scott on March 9th following. The vacancies thus created were not filled; in the corps of artillery organized from the three regiments March 30th, same year, the grade of lieutenant-colonel was the highest for which provision was made by law.

The artillery was generally well officered during the war of 1812, but it suffered then, as it has since, from not having a single head to direct its affairs. Prior to the year mentioned, Burbeck was theoretically serving as such; but by July, 1812, three other officers of equal rank were appointed in that arm, viz., Porter of the light artillery, Izard and Macomb. These officers were independent the one of the other, and neither was appointed to the command of the artillery of the whole army, as might easily have been done. While Secretary Eustis expressed himself as deeply impressed with the importance of training *all* troops at the service of artillery, and sought to render the arm itself efficient, he failed to appreciate the fact that, to do this, unity in purpose and action, which alone can exist under the supervision of one directing mind, was the first thing to be secured. The Secretary was a man of peace, not of war, and seems to have lost his head amidst the multiplicity of affairs that pressed upon him, and which soon drove him from his office in despair. Not only was no one appointed to command the whole, but the principal officers were scattered everywhere except with their own arm. Izard did not serve a day with the artillery, although from taste, education, and experience he was well qualified for it. Burbeck was not acting as an artillery officer proper, although, first in New York Harbor and afterwards at New London, he had troops under him of that arm, but always in conjunction with infantry, in a general command. Porter was commander of artillery on the Niagara frontier from the fall of 1812 until he retired through sickness, one year later. Macomb was commander of the artillery brigade at Sackett's Harbor in the summer of 1813, and at other times was chief of artillery in Wilkinson's army, but it was, except for a very short time, merely as an adjunct to his duties as an infantry commander. His own regiment, the Third, served almost wholly as infantry. Lieutenant-Colonel Fenwick commanded the light artillery under various generals whose armies operated on the Canadian frontier, but he was transferred to a staff department.

Thus it was with the most prominent and efficient officers; that they were efficient was considered a reason for assigning them to duty elsewhere. As a result, commanders were embarrassed in the management of their artillery, and, to secure its even tolerable service, it was often necessary to assign to duty therewith officers from other branches of the army. Writing, August 29th, 1812, from his grand camp at Greenbush, near Albany, N. Y., General Dearborn said: "I am in want of experienced artillerists. We have none here of any kind, excepting light artillery unprepared for actual service. Whatever relates to our artillery and ammunition remains in a chaotic state for want of suitable officers." In the summer of 1813 General Hampton complained that he was left with only raw captains just entering the artillery service, and asked authority to appoint Lieutenant Lomax an assistant adjutant-general, that he might be assigned to the command of that arm over the heads of those officers. Soon after Major McRee, of the engineer corps, was appointed chief of artillery in Hampton's army. The instances cited sufficiently illustrate the difficulties experienced in securing the services of competent artillery officers, who, instead of being with their commands, were performing what was considered indispensable duty elsewhere; but it was at a sacrifice of the efficiency and credit of their own arm. It all resulted from one cause, viz., the want of a chief of artillery for the whole army, as Knox was in the Revolution, who could assign duties to his own officers, each in the sphere for which he was best fitted. Colonel Izard well understood this fact. He urged on the Secretary of War, early in 1812, a reorganization of the artillery to secure its efficiency, stating at the same time that he was willing to serve in a subordinate capacity; but his suggestions came too late to work a practical reformation. War was at hand; all were preparing for the field; the time for wisely carrying out the proposed work, which must always be the result of deliberate reflection, had passed, and, though Mr. Eustis was favorably disposed, he resigned before congressional action could be taken; the artillery was left to drift without a directing hand; and finally, March 30th, 1814, a distorted plan, miscalled a reorganization, entirely devoid of the substance, while having in some degree the form of a scheme proposed by Colonel Izard, was enacted into law; but by this, the regiments, instead of being drawn more closely together, were broken into still smaller fragments, each independent of the other. (Izard's Plan of Organization, Appendix A [29].)

In common with each regiment of dragoons, infantry, and rifles, the light artillery was, by act of January 20th, 1813, given another major. This was more particularly to facilitate recruiting, as it was intended that the extra major should supervise that service for his regiment. In addition there were, as to every other in the army, added to each company of light artillery a third lieutenant and a fifth sergeant.

Thomas Pitts, senior captain of the light artillery, was appointed to the original majority thus created in his regiment. He resigned August 31st, 1814. The President appointed Captain McPherson to be Pitts' successor, overslaughing Captain William Campbell. This was during the recess of the Senate, which body did not consent to the appointment. Captain Campbell's name was then sent in, and he was confirmed major in the light artillery, to date back to the day of Pitts' resignation. The circumstance receives significance from the fact that it was an attempt, on the part of the Executive, to ignore, in the interests of favorites, the rules of promotion *established by law*. It is one of the many instances in which *the Senate stood firm in defense of right. To that body, and to it alone, the army owes it that promotions are made otherwise than at the will, perhaps the caprice, of the President.*

By the law of March 30th, 1814, the First, Second, and Third regiments of artillery, as has been mentioned, were arranged to a Corps of twelve battalions. (Appendix A [28].) The light artillery remained unchanged. The pay of all was, for the first time, fixed at that of dragoons. The President was authorized to assign one of the second lieutenants, of which each company of the Corps was given two, to duty as conductor of artillery, *i. e.* company ordnance officer, for which he received ten dollars per month extra compensation. The artificers introduced into the artillery in 1802 were not provided for in the corps organization; they were generally superior workmen, and since their introduction in 1802 had made much of the matériel, such as carriages, caissons, &c. Their loss now deprived the artillery of some of its most useful members, whose duties under the law of 1812 were devolved on the ordnance department.

It is to be regretted that no authentic information has been obtained concerning the reasons which led to the formation of the Corps of Artillery. Before this law was enacted promotion was regimental, and afterwards it followed the general rule, only the Corps was considered a single body. This undeniably tended to unity throughout the system, and thus far the change was for the better ; but this advantage was dearly purchased at the price of a still further dispersion of the arm into twelve instead of, as formerly, four independent units. Though the law contemplated the consolidation of many organizations and the mustering out of supernumerary officers, more of the latter were provided for in the Corps than in the three old artillery regiments. This increase was, however, in the lower and at the expense of the upper grades. Macomb and Scott had recently been promoted. Burbeck was a brevet brigadier, assigned to duty as such. At the date of the passage of the act of March 30th, 1814, there was not a colonel serving with these three regiments. The fact might have been used as an argument for abolishing the grade ; but, if so, it was illusory, illogical, and struck a fatal blow at soldierly ambition. Because, forsooth, colonels of artillery proved themselves worthy of promotion, the vacancies thus created were not to be filled! The men upon whose conduct they had to a great extent built up their fame were not worthy to succeed them ! If this is to be their reward, what incentive to honorable action can subordinates have?

But whatever may have been the motives which actuated the legislature, the practical effect of the reorganization upon the artillery was prejudicial to its interests. Denominated a Corps, it was such in no sense indicating unity either in mind or body. It had no head. It was only small, separate fragments thrown together. The many distinguished subordinate officers of artillery who had won brevets on brevets *in battle* were now given to understand they need expect no more substantial rewards. The battalions of the so-called "Corps" were composed of four companies each, half commanded by lieutenant-colonels and half by majors—an incongruity at variance with the simplest rules ot correct military organization. The radical defect, however, lay in the fact that no officer commanded the different parts of the Corps.

By Colonel Izard's scheme for the reorganization of the artillery, it was proposed to replace the regiment by a battalion, to unite the engineers with the artillery, and to impose on the new corps all the duties devolving by law upon the artillery, the engineer corps, and the ordnance department. This was in substance what Du Portail and Hamilton had advocated in

1783. Izard favored an artillery corps composed of battalions; the act of March 30th, 1814, provided such a Corps. So far as names—words—were concerned, the act supplied what Izard had advocated; but here similarity ceased. Words are not things. The organization actually given was but a soulless form, devoid of life, or that which could impart animation to the system.

Brevet Brigadier-General Burbeck ceased now to be colonel of artillery, but he continued in service until the reduction and disbanding of the army the following year, when, after having served almost continuously for forty years, he was relegated to civil life.

The act of reorganization, March 30th, 1814, increased by one the number of lieutenant-colonels in the artillery, to which original vacancy Major MacRea, of the First Regiment, was appointed; and as there existed a vacancy in the grade of major in one of the regiments, but one other field officer besides Burbeck was retired from the service. This was Major A. Y. Nicoll, late adjutant and inspector-general of the army, who resigned June 1st, 1814.

The act fixing the military establishment, approved March 3d, 1815, authorized the President to determine what proportion of the ten thousand men forming the peace army should be artillery, infantry, and riflemen. Regarding the former, the law provided that the Corps should retain its existing organization, and that the light artillery should be maintained as organized in 1808, thus mustering out of the latter the second major, the third lieutenant and fifth sergeant for each company, the drivers, saddlers, and farriers. (Appendix A [30].)

There were mustered to form the Corps of Artillery the old corps, the regiment of dragoons, the 41st, 42d, and 43d regiments of infantry. Seven of the eight field officers retained were from the old corps; the eighth and junior was Major W. H. Overton, of the 3d rifles, who resigned a few months later, and was succeeded by Major James Bankhead, late of the 7th infantry.

To form the new light artillery there were mustered the existing regiment, the 15th, 26th, 30th, 31st, 33d, 34th, and 45th regiments of infantry. All the field officers of the old light artillery regiment and four of the ten captains were retained. Among those transferred to the light artillery at this time was Captain Nathan Towson, of the Corps of Artillery, afterwards paymaster-general, whose good fortune it had been to be present with his company in almost every affair of importance on the northern frontier during the years 1812–'14.

By the War Department order which reduced and reorganized the army, (17th May, 1815,) the territory of the United States was divided into nine military departments, five of which made up the northern and four the southern division. The dividing line between the divisions may be roughly stated to have been the parallel of Washington city. In assigning the artillery, the light regiment, with four battalions of the Corps, were apportioned to the northern; the other four battalions to the southern division. The battalions were officially known as the first, second, third, and fourth of the divisions to which they belonged. In each division the companies of the battalions were designated by the letters of the alphabet from A to Q, both inclusive, excluding the letter J. (Appendix A [32].) To point out a particular company it was necessary to specify, for instance, "Company (Q) Fourth Battalion, southern division," and they are so designated in the official records. If Company (Q) of the southern were ordered into the northern division, a company must leave the latter to take its place; whereupon these two changed their official designations, which were, consequently, never permanent. This attempt to maintain an artillery equipoise in the two great military divisions was as inconvenient as the organization of the Corps itself was impotent. The awkwardness of the arrangement was clearly demonstrated before the reorganization of March 2d, 1821, when the army was reduced from ten thousand to six thousand men, and the Corps of Artillery put an end to.

By act of April 20th, 1818, slight changes were made in the personnel by giving each company of the Corps one captain, two first lieutenants, two second lieutenants, and to each company of light artillery one captain, one first and two second lieutenants; while to each battalion of the Corps and to the light regiment there was allowed one armorer. It was further provided that in each artillery company one of the second lieutenants should be conductor, for which $10 per month extra pay was allowed. The act affected the commissioned officers to the extent that in the Corps of Artillery each company was given another first lieutenant and its third promoted to second lieutenant; while in the light artillery an additional second lieutenant was given each company.

The 1st, 2d, 3d, and 4th regiments of artillery of the present regular army date from the act of March 2d, 1821. Although the number of companies in each regiment has been increased, and other modifications have been introduced as circumstances have made them proper, the organization then given these regiments has remained essentially unchanged. (Organization, Appendix A [31].) In Appendix A [32] will be found a statement showing which companies of the Corps and of the regiment of light artillery were retained, and their designations, in the new regiments. Under the terms of the reorganizing act the light artillery regiment ceased to exist; but provision was made for this species of troops by a mandatory clause in the law directing that one of the nine companies in each regiment *should be designated and equipped as light artillery.* (See Field Artillery.)

The field officers of the artillery regiments retained were: Moses Porter, Nathan Towson, Walker K. Armistead, John R. Fenwick, colonels; George Bomford, James House, G. E. Mitchell, William MacRea, lieutenant-colonels; John B. Walbach, J. Hindman, James Bankhead, Abraham Eustis, majors. Of these, Armistead was transferred from the head of the engineer corps; Bomford from the ordnance department; while Towson was taken from the head of a civil department, the pay corps. When the name of the latter officer came before the Senate, that body refused to give its consent to the appointment. Then commenced a struggle between the Executive and the Senate which it is believed is without a parallel in the history of the Government. Three successive administrations became involved in the controversy, and finally, after eleven years, during which time the Second Artillery remained without a colonel, *the matter was settled by a compromise.**

---

* The President maintained in the 1821 reduction that he had a perfect right to make the new corps of the army out of the old, in any manner he saw fit. That no officers could claim legal exemption from being deranged, nor could any have legal claim to being retained. The selection of officers for the new army, from those belonging to the former, was a matter entirely at the discretion of the President.

From these broad propositions, all and singular, the Senate dissented. Many interesting points were raised in the ensuing discussions that must be considered as corollaries to the main proposition stated above.

The President maintained that the pay department was one of the "corps" of the army; the Senate denied it and rejected the nomination of the paymaster-gen-

ORGANIZATION—GENERALLY.   47

The law of April 5th, 1832, introduced into the army a class of under officers (ordnance sergeants) who, while belonging neither to the ordnance department nor to the artillery, are intimately connected with both. During the Revolutionary war the office of conductor of artillery was one of the subordinate positions assigned to artillery officers. It disappeared with that war, and was revived again by section 17 of the act of March 28th, 1812, which directed the President to appoint four conductors, to be entitled to the pay and emoluments of a lieutenant of artillery. As has been noticed, the acts of March 30th, 1814, and April 20th, 1818, had imposed the duties of conductor on one of the two second lieutenants given each artillery company, and for the performance of which $10 per month extra pay was allowed. These duties had been to receive, account for, issue, and keep in repair the artillery and other material of the company, garrison, brigade, or other organization to which the conductor was attached. It was a position in war of great property responsibility, and, though sometimes intrusted to warrant officers and at others to those holding commissions, it had been the practice to allow additional compensation to the incumbent. The reorganizing and reducing act of March 2d, 1821, neither made mention of nor provision for

---

eral for the colonelcy of one of the regiments. The President held that no particular officers were entitled to the colonelcies of the eleven new regiments. The Senate held that, by directing the Executive to *arrange* the officers of the old army to the new, he was bound to put the eleven old colonels in these new places. Therefore, according to the Senate's views, the colonels dropped out were still legally in service.

The President mentioned that he was prepared to take the ground that Congress could not, constitutionally, limit by law his choice of individuals to fill original vacancies from the whole body of his fellow citizens. The Senate remarked, incidentally, that they were prepared to combat that proposition ; basing their argument on the clause of the constitution giving Congress power to prescribe rules for the government and regulation of the land and naval forces.

The Senate held that the offices that Towson and Gadsden were nominated for were created during a session of the Senate, and therefore the President had no right to fill them during a recess of that body. Here again the President was at issue with them.

The House also became involved in the controversy. So far as the views of that body can be gathered, they at that time sustained the Senate in all points upon which they (the House) expressed an opinion.

The Senate and House maintained that, in the new army, officers should be

conductors of artillery, and their duties devolved upon commanding officers, who thus, instead of being able, if so disposed, to devote their time and attention to other and relatively more important matters, were compelled to give a large part of it to petty details connected with the keeping in order of ordnance and other property. It was with the double object of relieving commanding officers of the duties of receiving and preserving "the ordnance, arms, ammunition, and other military stores," and transferring them to meritorious non-commissioned officers of long sérvice, with an increase of pay and a permanency of station, that the grade of ordnance sergeant was created.

The Seminole war having drawn all the troops into the field and strained to the utmost the resources at his command, the Secretary of War, in his report of 1837, recommended, among other measures looking to the perfection of the military system, the increase of the number of companies in each regiment of artillery. This was done by act of July 5th, 1838. One company was added to each regiment, and the number of privates in each

---

kept, when possible, in same corps as before the reduction ; and rejected Gadsden for adjutant-general on that ground, he having formerly been an inspector.

The House became interested in this controversy from the fact that, through a transfer of Lieutenant-Colonel Lindsay back to the artillery from the infantry, Major Eustis was kept out of his lieutenant-colonelcy. Major Eustis had an uncle, the Hon. William Eustis, formerly Secretary of War, who was chairman of the House Military Committee, and who was looking after the major's interests.

The Senate having rejected the paymaster-general's nomination for colonel of the 2d artillery, the regiment was without a colonel. Of the four colonels discharged, viz., Wadsworth, Smith, King, and Bissell, the first and third died soon afterwards. Smith was appointed a U. S. judge, leaving Bissell alone to be provided for. The President maintained he was out of service ; the Senate that he was in service ; he took the latter view, and reported regularly to the War Department, but was not assigned to duty. When Mr. J. Q. Adams became President, Bissell reported for duty as usual. He was not assigned, but Mr. Adams nominated him as from citizen life for the colonelcy that the Senate had contended all along of right belonged to him. The Senate did not act directly on the nomination, but expressed the opinion that Bissell was entitled to the place, and, as he had never been out of service, the President might *arrange* him to the 2d artillery. To this proposition Mr. Adams would not agree. He renominated Bissell, but nothing came of it. In his annual message, December, 1826, he recommended such legislation as the case might require, as there was no hope of the President and Senate agreeing. A bill was reported by the Senate Military Committee looking to the legislating of Bissell into office,

company was increased from forty-two to fifty-eight. At the same time the number of second lieutenants allowed each artillery company was reduced from two to one, but the filling original vacancies created by the new companies, together with the enlargement of several staff corps, obviated the necessity for mustering any officer out of service. (Appendix A [31].)

The vacancies in the grade of captain created in the four regiments were filled by appointing in each, except the First, the ranking first lieutenant. For particular reasons, that officer in the First Artillery stood still and was overslaughed. This was the first instance in the history of the artillery that offices newly created (original vacancies) in that arm had been filled, preferably, by selections made from those already in service. The practice in the early years of the Government was the reverse. When the corps of artillerists and engineers was raised in 1794, the regiment of the same arm in 1798, the 2d and 3d regiments of 1812, officers of the army received very few of the appointments thus made available to them; they were, with rare exceptions,

---

but it failed to become law. The House Military Committee also reported a bill looking to the same end, but its fate was like the other. In presenting this bill the House Military Committee was called on to express an opinion on the construction of the reducing act of 1821. They sustained the Senate so far as Towson was concerned, but maintained, with the late President, that the old colonels had no legal right to the new colonelcies; in which view they were opposed by the Senate. The House Military Committee, therefore, in 1827, concurred in President Monroe's view expressed in 1822, that the only limitation placed on him was that he should take the officers of the new army from those of the existing army; but they disagreed from his views as to who were officers of the army before the reduction. The House Committee intimated very strongly, but did not say, that in their opinion Bissell was entitled to the colonelcy.

President Jackson suggested that an explanatory act be passed, designating the class of officers from which the colonelcy of the 2d regiment of artillery should be filled. This called forth a report from the House Military Committee, January 18th, 1830. In this it was held that Bissell was *not* entitled to it, but the vacancy belonged to the ranking lieutenant-colonel of artillery, Lindsay. The Senate Military Committee was now under the leadership of Mr. Benton. It can readily be surmised that it would not assent to these views of the House Committee. The bill did not become a law. But the same end was attained, as the ranking lieutenant-colonel was promoted in accordance with this idea, April 26th, 1832; and thus, after being eleven years without one, the 2d regiment of artillery was given a colonel. (See Niles' Register, vol. 22, p. 406, *et seq.* Mil. Affairs, vol. 2, p. 395; Vol. 3, Ibid., pp. 259, 290; Vol. 4, Ibid., p. 248.)

conferred upon civilians. The experience of the war of 1812 had demonstrated the superiority, as a rule, of officers versed in their profession over those newly selected from civil life. One of the results has been, and the general augmentation of 1838 initiated the system, that since then, in the matter of new appointments, those already in the army have received consideration in some degree commensurate with their professional services and attainments.*

There was begun a movement this year which, in its effects on the artillery, has been, to a degree, unsurpassed by any measure of reform, permanent and salutary. Reference is made to the mounting, as horse artillery, in the fall of 1838, of Captain Ringgold's company C, of the 3d regiment. Followed the succeeding year by the equipping one company in each of the other regiments as field artillery, it resulted, as did many other improvements of that arm, from the intelligent, earnest efforts of the gentleman at the head of the War Department. Of the many measures set on foot for building up the department over which he presided with singular, conspicuous, and universally acknowledged ability, none contributed more to that end, or to the glory of his country's arms in the field, than did the re-establishment, as contemplated in the act of March 2d, 1821, of this arm of service. The subject will be treated of elsewhere; for the present it suffices to remark that the field batteries of the regular army, with their honorable records, owe their existence to the military sagacity of Secretary Joel R. Poinsett.

The Mexican war brought an augmentation and a slight change of organization to the artillery. In his annual report, December 5th, 1846, Secretary Marcy pointed out that the efficiency of the regular troops in the field was greatly impaired by the absence of the field officers. This, he stated, was in great degree due to their

---

* "To the House of Representatives of the United States, whose vote † of the 10th of April, 1846, in the Twenty-ninth Congress, gives hope of a recognition of military service as a necessary qualification for command, this work, of four years' labor, is humbly inscribed, by C. K. Gardner." (Dictionary of the Army of the United States.)

† The vote was for this:

"*Provided*, That all the officers of the aforesaid regiment of riflemen shall be selected from the regular line of the United States army." (Intending to embrace, for the selection, the whole army then in service. Being defective, the proviso was stricken out by the Senate.)

physical incapacity. As there was no retired list on which they could be placed, the Secretary urged, as a means of infusing younger blood into the system, the appointment in the artillery of an additional major for each regiment. An increase also in the number of artillery troops seemed to be a proper measure from the fact that the old organizations were absent at the seat of war, leaving public property inadequately guarded and the forts on the maritime frontiers almost without garrisons. Ships of the most insignificant nation can insult with impunity the strongest coast devoid of defenders. These considerations moved Congress to augment the artillery and to add slightly to the staff, to make the whole more complete, by acts of February 11th and March 3d, 1847. Two additional companies, a major, quartermaster, two principal musicians, and a principal teamster, were given each regiment; two teamsters to each company; while the President was authorized to designate four additional companies to be equipped as light artillery. For the first time since 1821 the officers and men of the light artillery, when serving as such, were given dragoon pay and allowances. This resulted from the brilliant actions of the field companies on the battle-fields of the Rio Grande valley, where they astonished the army and the country by their manœuvres, efficiency, and power. (Appendix A [33].)

The artillery was given the benefit of the original vacancies created by the acts cited, in filling which, as well as in the resulting promotions flowing therefrom, due regard was paid to the actual rank of officers concerned, who were advanced to newly-created offices upon the principle of regular promotion established by law for all branches of the army.

From the Mexican war until the breaking out of the Civil war in 1861, the artillery retained its organization unchanged, although attempts to modify it in various ways were made during that time. Mr. Shields, chairman of the Senate Military Committee, made a report, March 23d, 1852, advocating the appointment of a head to the artillery, and accompanied by a bill to secure this desired amelioration. (Appendix B [2].) During the session of 1854–'55 a bill favored by Secretary Davis was introduced, which provided for reducing the arm to two regiments, to be thereafter equipped and trained strictly as artillery proper. At the same time it was proposed to cut off all below the grade of field officer in the ordnance, and detail the captains and subalterns of that department from the line of the army. In the latter particular the measure was similar to that proposed in 1878 by the congressional committee on army organization. These measures received the approval of many of the first officers, in point of intelligence, in the army.

It was expected that officers for service in the ordnance would be drawn from the artillery; they would ultimately become the field officers of that department; these two branches of service would thereby be drawn more closely together, and, while one would not interfere with the other, the interests of both and of the service in general would be enhanced. As to the effect on the artillery, one of the advocates of the measure—an ordnance officer* second to none for faithful, intelligent, and successful labors for the improvement of artillery matériel—remarked that, "Being thus reduced to the part of the military force of the nation that can be spared from the Indian frontiers, it will be restricted to duty appropriate to artillery, either with field, garrison, siege or sea-coast guns—*a service requiring much greater and much more difficult instruction than that of foot troops.*"

None of these attempts had the effect to change the status of the arm. The general-in-chief strenuously opposed the reduction contemplated in the last-named measure, and carried the point with Congress. What could not be effected by legislation, viz., placing the artillery in a more advantageous position professionally, was next sought through the re-establishment of the artillery School of Practice at Fort Monroe, the organization of field artillery schools, and providing a systematic course of instruction for artillery troops at permanent fortifications. (See Instruction.)

The scattered condition of the regular army in 1861 rendered it impracticable for the Government at the beginning of the Civil war to avail itself of the services of the troops in that prompt manner which the emergency demanded. This, so far as the artillery was concerned, resulted, at least ostensibly, from the attempt to carry out an elaborate scheme of instruction for that arm. To meet the necessities of the case the President, by proclamation of May 3d, that year, increased the regular establishment by one regiment of artillery, one of cavalry, and eight three-battalion regiments of infantry. The Constitution provides that "Congress

---

* Major Mordecai.

shall have power to raise and support armies;" but this was an instance where delay was not to be tolerated, and the Executive, conceiving that it was always constitutional to save the Government from overthrow, raised these troops on his own responsibility. The day following the President's proclamation a general order was issued, fixing the organization and pay of the additional regiments. On June 18th (G. O. 33, A. G. O., 1861) a roster of the commissioned officers was promulgated. In the artillery, the higher positions in the original vacancies thus created were filled by selections from the old artillery regiments. The colonel was taken from the line of majors; the lieutenant-colonel and majors from the captains. In every instance they overslaughed several in their own arm of service. The commissions of all were dated May 14th, 1861. Nearly three months after this addition to the regular army had been organized, the act of July 29th, 1861, was passed, giving legislative sanction to the increase. As was the case with the two companies added to each regiment of artillery by the act of March 3d, 1847, it was stipulated that the additional troops should serve only during the existing war; but when the rebellion was put down circumstances had changed, and the Fifth Artillery became a part, as it has remained, of the permanent military establishment. (Appendix A [34].) It followed that during the Civil war the artillery regiments had different organizations. This was changed by act of July 28th, 1866, which, except as to the commissioned staff, (made uniform for all,) placed the four old regiments on the same footing with the Fifth. This, with some slight changes in the non-commissioned staff, affecting all regiments alike, is the status of the artillery at the present day. (Appendix A [35].)

CHAPTER II.

ORGANIZATION—FIELD ARTILLERY SINCE 1821.

The part of section 2 of the act of March 2d, 1821, which directed that one company of each artillery regiment should be designated and equipped as light artillery,* remained for seventeen years practically inoperative. Aside from announcing the companies, a matter of form merely, and giving their uniform some slightly distinctive feature, nothing was done during that time to carry the law into effect.

Mention has been made incidentally of the equipping by Mr. Poinsett of the light companies in 1838–'39. When finally the time came to execute the law in earnest, no attention was paid to the previously existing light artillery designations, which had been made on the authority of regimental commanders; companies were selected regardless of either service or associations, and more particularly with a view to obtaining efficient captains.

The first to be mounted, (C) of the Third Artillery, retained its light battery organization until 1849, and, except during one interval of eighteen months, has been equipped as a field battery since then. The captain of (C) company at that time was Brevet

---

* *Light* artillery is *horse* artillery, but the *practice* in our service has been so opposed to the correct military usage of the former term that with us it signifies both horse artillery, *i. e.*, wherein each man serves on horseback, and mounted artillery, in which the cannoneers mount on the carriages for rapid movements only. The person to initiate this was Mr. Poinsett, who, as mentioned in the text, in 1838 and 1839 fitted out one company as horse and three as mounted artillery, when he essayed to execute the law of 1821, directing that, in each regiment, one company should be "designated and equipped as light artillery."

Economical considerations caused *indirectly* that to be called light artillery which was not such in fact, and the confusion has continued since. The term "light" is now made to do duty for "field" artillery. At the present time there are, under the authority of the law allowing ten light batteries, that number of mounted (field) batteries in service. Correctly speaking, there is not in our army to-day a single battery equipped as light artillery.

The difficulty has not been in the law, where proper terms have always been used; it has arisen from the erroneous practice under the law.

The Artillery Tactics have until quite recently made correct use of military

Major Samuel Ringgold. It was engaged in the Florida (Seminole) war, whence its commander had returned north on sick leave. The intention of the Secretary of War to give vitality to the almost obsolete law was conveyed officially to Major Ringgold in the following communication :

"ADJUTANT-GENERAL'S OFFICE,
"WASHINGTON, *September* 18*th*, 1838.

"SIR: Having been selected by the Secretary of War to organize, equip, and command the first company of light artillery authorized by act of 1821, you will repair to Carlisle barracks and lose no time in proceeding to execute the views of the department. The number of horses necessary for the purpose being now in depot, will require your immediate attention. As the convenience of the general service will not, at this time, justify the ordering of your company to Carlisle, you will see by my requisitions on the colonels of the First and Second regiments of artillery of this date the measures which are, for the present, to be adopted for the formation of the proposed company. The ordnance, equipments, and all other supplies will be furnished in due time by the proper departments. You will forward to this office your requisitions for the approval of the Secretary of War."

The horses referred to in this letter were those used by the Government in removing Indians from their lands east of the Mississippi River to the Cherokee country. Upon these horses, now no longer needed, the Secretary relied for a proper mount, and they alone were used for this purpose. Mr. Poinsett was not one to be deterred by lack of means; having the will, he found the way to the building up of this important but neglected branch of the artillery service.

The following is the letter to the colonels of the First and Second artillery regiments, referred to in Major Ringgold's instructions :

"The Secretary of War being desirous to equip one company to act as light artillery with as little delay as practicable, deems it most expedient, for the present, to organize the proposed company as a detachment to be formed by

---

terms. In the assimilated edition, now in use, the term "light artillery" has, however, been introduced with the erroneous signification above indicated.

During the Civil war many regular batteries were equipped as horse artillery, as was Ringgold's, (C) of the Third, from 1838 to 1849. So far as the author is aware, no other regular batteries have in time of peace been so equipped since 1821.

In the text, the term "light artillery" is used with its customary signification ; the work of reform in the use of technical language in our army is too onerous to be undertaken here.

detail or selection from the First and Second regiments of artillery. Accordingly he desires that you select three good men, such as you may suppose best calculated for the object in view, from each of the companies of your regiment, which, on being mustered and inspected as a detachment, you will order to Carlisle barracks with as little delay as practicable. You will also please to assign two sergeants and two corporals to the detachment, who will be reported on the same service."

A first lieutenant was ordered from the First and a second lieutenant from the Second Artillery to act as subalterns in the new company for the time being. Lieutenants Aisquith and Barry were selected for this duty. The latter here laid the foundation for that knowledge of light artillery service which, twenty-three years afterwards, he turned to good account as chief of artillery when the Army of the Potomac was being organized in 1861.

November 5th, 1838, by orders from the War Department, the men thus detached were formed into a new (C) company, Third Artillery; Ringgold's old company in Florida was broken up, the subalterns ordered to join the light company, and the detached lieutenants just mentioned of the First and Second ordered to join their regiments. Lieutenant Barry was, however, at his own request, allowed temporarily to remain; and at Major Ringgold's request, the books of his old company, with one sergeant and one private soldier of his own selection therefrom, were sent to his new command.

How the light artillery should be mounted—whether the cannoneers should ride on the limbers and caissons, or each man on horseback as light artillery proper—was a question yet to be settled. There was at the time sitting in Washington city a board composed of Fenwick and Ewing of the artillery, Talcott, Baker, and Mordecai of the ordnance, and which had been assembled to fix upon a system of artillery for field service, as well as to determine other questions of a proper artillery matériel. (See Matériel.) The question of light artillery equipment was a peculiarly appropriate one to be decided by the board, to which it was referred by the following letter:

"ADJUTANT-GENERAL'S OFFICE,
"WASHINGTON, *October 24th*, 1838.
"*Brevet Brigadier-General* JOHN R. FENWICK, *Fourth Artillery,*
"*President of Board of Ordnance, Washington.*

"GENERAL: I am desired by the Secretary of War to inform you that he wishes the board to communicate its views as to the preferable mode of mounting the company of light artillery now being organized at Carlisle; that is, whether it be preferable that every man be mounted, as is usual in what is generally known as horse artillery, or that as great a number be accommodated on the guns and caissons, as is generally practiced in the equipment of field artillery. The Secretary himself would prefer the latter mode, inasmuch as the expenses of the outfit would be less, and he being desirous in making his estimates for this branch of service, in fulfillment of the provisions of the act of 1821, not to swell the amount beyond what may be absolutely indispensable. The opinion of the Secretary as to this point is not communicated with any view to control that of the board, but only to show the expediency of the lesser expenditure, in order to insure the chances of better success in obtaining the necessary appropriation by Congress."

The gentlemen addressed seem to have had little difficulty in determining the point, and adversely to the predilection of the Secretary, as the next day an answer, signed by the president of the board, was transmitted to the adjutant-general, as follows:

"SIR: In reply to your letter relative to the preferable mode to mount the light artillery company at Carlisle, I have to state that the views of the ordnance board relative to light artillery are that *it should be organized as horse artillery*, and consequently that the men should *not* be carried on the guns and caissons, but that each man should be mounted separately, as is usual in the service of that arm; otherwise the exercise and manœuvres of the company must be conducted as for foot artillery, instead of light horse artillery."

Notwithstanding the prompt action of the board, the question was not finally decided for a month afterwards. The matter of relative expense was one of grave moment, as the Secretary well understood, and as subsequent experience has fully demonstrated. October 25th, 1838, the adjutant-general wrote Major Ringgold:

"SIR: I am instructed to inform you that your company will be mounted as horse artillery, and consequently the men should *not* be carried on the guns and carriages, but that each man be mounted separately, as is usual in the field service of that arm."

The company was equipped as directed, and continued to serve as horse artillery until dismounted at Santa Fé, New Mexico, whither it had been marched after the Mexican war.

Particular attention is here given to the mounting of Ringgold's company for the reason that doubts are sometimes expressed as to its having been horse artillery. The letters quoted will dispel those doubts, which have arisen perhaps from the fact that the light artillery companies of the other three regiments, equipped the following year, were organized into what was technically known as mounted artillery, *i. e.*, the cannoneers habitually walked, and mounted the limbers and caissons for rapid movements only.

It seemed a peculiarly appropriate circumstance that General Fenwick should be the officer to announce the decision as to what should be the equipment of the rehabilitated arm; for, although he was not the first to organize a company of that description in the United States army, he was the first to lead one into the presence of the enemy. This was in September and October, 1812, when, as lieutenant-colonel of the light artillery regiment, he marched a section of Captain Gibson's company, fully equipped as horse artillery, together with a train of heavier ordnance, to the relief of General Van Rensselaer, just before the battle of Queenstown Heights.

Having embarked in the scheme of restoring the light artillery to the service, Mr. Poinsett followed it up with his usual vigor. In his report of December, 1838, he pointedly called the attention of Congress to the importance of the measure, remarking: "We are without light artillery entirely, and have yet to learn its management. There is not at present a complete train of artillery for a single one of the four regiments in service. I beg leave to suggest the necessity of an appropriation for the purpose of furnishing the number of pieces required to arm the existing regiments properly, as well as to furnish batteries for two battalions of light artillery."

The opportunity to still further put into execution his views on this subject was given the succeeding year, when, following up his efforts to improve the condition of the troops, not of one but of all branches of service, sadly impaired during a protracted war in the pestilential swamps of Florida, Mr. Poinsett, by General Orders No. 28, Adjutant-General's Office, May 20th, 1839, established a camp of instruction for the practice and discipline of detachments from all the fighting arms. The order was as follows:

"With a view to the better instruction of the troops and improvement of the discipline of the army, such portions of the regiments of dragoons, artillery, and infantry as may be withdrawn from their stations without detriment to other interests of the service, will be concentrated during the summer months at some convenient point best calculated for a camp of instruction.

"The arduous and desultory service in which the troops have been so long engaged, the unavoidable dismemberment of the regiments, and separation of so many officers from duty in the line while employed on other service, could hardly fail greatly to impair the *esprit de corps* of the army, as well as its discipline and efficiency. These must be restored, and every proper effort speedily made to place the service on a foundation which will insure its steady and uniform advancement.

"The occasional concentration of companies of the same regiment, and the bringing together troops of different arms where all the duties of the officer and soldier of the several corps of the army may be strictly and systematically performed, from the school of the company to the evolutions of the line, are necessary steps to be taken to effect this desirable amelioration.

"Major-General Scott is charged with the formation and direction of the proposed camp of instruction, the immediate command of which will be assigned to such officer as he may designate. In choosing a position for the camp, regard will be had to health, cheapness, and facility of transportation, both of troops and supplies.

"The rules and regulations and established systems for each arm of service will be punctually observed and strictly practiced, and no other than the prescribed military dress will be worn.

"All necessary supplies and transportation will be promptly furnished by the respective departments of the staff, and two officers of each branch of that service will be ordered without delay to report to Major-General Scott for duty at the camp of instruction."

The camp, named "Camp Washington," was established near Trenton, New Jersey, and Brevet Brigadier-General Abraham Eustis, major of the light artillery regiment of 1808, and at this time colonel of the First Artillery, was appointed commandant. To this camp Ringgold marched his company of horse artillery, fitted out with an entirely new armament, prepared by the ordnance department. Here were found also (K) of the First Artillery, a new company, added to the regiment by act of July 5th, 1838; (A) of the Second, and (B) of the Fourth Artillery, all destined to become the field companies of their respective regiments. (A) received its battery at the camp of instruction; (K) at Plattsburg, New York, immediately after the camp was discontinued; while the order dated September 27th, 1839, Headquarters Eastern Division, breaking up the camp, directed the dragoon-horses to be turned over to (B), Fourth Artillery, which was then equipped as a field company.

Simultaneously with the equipping of the last three companies, there appeared a tactics adapted to the service of this species of troops. This was the "Instruction for Field Artillery, Horse and Foot," translated from the French and arranged for the service of the United States, by First Lieutenant Robert Anderson, Third Artillery. This work, the appearance of which was most opportune, was, by orders from the War Department, April 20th, 1840, adopted as the authorized field artillery tactics, except that portion relating to horse artillery, which it was directed was not to be put in practice until further orders—a suspension which was terminated by General Order No. 46, Adjutant-General's Office, August 19th, 1841. From this date until 1845 Anderson's translation was the prescribed field artillery tactics for the army.

The opposition to that part of the tactics relating to horse artillery has been stated by good authority to have been due to the influence of Major Ringgold. Previous to his company being mounted he had studied the exercises of the British light artillery, upon which he had modeled his own, and his wish was to adhere to their system. The adoption in 1845 of a course of field artillery instruction supplanting Anderson's work, in a measure accomplished his wishes in this respect. (See Tactics.)

It has been mentioned that, by act of July 5th, 1838, the number of enlisted men in the companies of artillery had been increased to seventy-one. This sufficed to enable the captains of the light companies to man (in a most imperfect way to be sure) six pieces; but the return of a general peace, after the Seminole war, having caused a reduction to be made in each company of one artificer and sixteen privates, the number of pieces in each was restricted by Special Orders No. 96, Adjutant-General's Office, 1842, to four; the other two in each company being stored for use when required.

To still further reduce expenses, and in total disregard of those considerations for public interests which had but recently led to their proper equipment, the question began to be agitated whether or not it would be expedient to dismount the field companies, either wholly or in part. As had been the case in 1809, the successor to the Secretary of War, who had attempted to place this branch of the artillery upon an eligible footing, did not appreciate as did that officer the value to the combatant arms of this species of troops. Change of policy followed change of administration in the War Department. Fortunately for the artillery, at this juncture there was a staunch old soldier in the office of adjutant-general who knew something of war and its necessities from *experience*, and who had the courage to avow and defend his convictions.

In a communication addressed to the Secretary of War, Mr. J. M. Porter, and commenting upon the proposition mentioned, he remarked:

> "The arming and equipping of the light companies of artillery with their appropriate arms has been attended with the best results. Considering the character of our maritime frontier, rendering field and horse artillery peculiarly efficient as a means of national defense, and the little knowledge of their management possessed in the country even among the educated classes, this powerful arm is, in my opinion, vitally important and ought to be encouraged; and therefore it would be inexpedient to dismount any of the companies now mounted as light artillery."

On this letter General Scott indorsed the brief but expressive sentence, "I fully concur in the above."

The companies in question were in the meantime being brought in an unobtrusive manner to a high state of excellence as regards discipline, drill, and generally whatever would enhance their efficiency. The selection of their commanders—Captains Ringgold of the Third, Taylor of the First, Washington of the Fourth, and Lieutenant Duncan of the Second Regiment—had been well calculated to bring about that result. They were men well fitted by nature, taste, and training for the work here given them in hand. The duty was attended by positive pecuniary disadvantages. Although subjected to all expenses attending mounted service, they did not receive mounted pay. This circumstance, which was in effect a discrimination against the field artillery, made the duty undesirable to many officers, captains as well as subalterns. Few men have the virtue, *esprit de corps*, or whatever it may be called, to sacrifice themselves and their material interests for sentiment's sake and without compensation; few can afford to do it even if so disposed; nor does sound policy require it at the hands of public servants. Yet this was demanded of the commanders in question. Undeterred, these officers pursued the even tenor of their ways, faithfully attending to whatever would enhance the professional standing of their companies. The battle-fields of the Mexican war, on which the latter soon after acted so conspicuous a part, bore testimony before the army and the country to the thorough manner in which they had been prepared for their as yet untried and arduous duties in the field.

It is not intended here to do more than mention the field artillery companies that did service in Mexico. What that service was is a matter of history, written more eloquently than elsewhere in the brief but spirited and business-like official reports of the various commanders under whom they won their way to the first rank in the fighting arms of service. Company (E), Third Regiment, Lieutenant Bragg commanding, was, under War Department instructions, furnished with a battery consisting of two guns and two howitzers in the summer of 1845. It joined General Taylor's army, and immediately after the first battles, in May, 1846, was fully equipped as field artillery. Captain T. W. Sherman, subsequently one of the most distinguished officers of that arm, succeeded to the command of this company, by regular promotion, May 28th, 1846. The companies organized by Mr. Poinsett were also with General Taylor in his advance into the enemy's territory; Ringgold's equipped as horse artillery; the others continuing, as they had started in 1839, to be what is now technically known as mounted artillery. Major Ringgold was mortally wounded at Palo Alto, May 8th, 1846, and died three days later. His successor, Morris S. Miller, assistant quartermaster, relinquished the captaincy June 18th, to be followed by Braxton Bragg, who proved himself to be a worthy successor to the first commander of the horse artillery company.

By the act of May 13th, 1846, the number of privates in companies of the regular army was authorized, at the discretion of the President, to be increased to one hundred. This enabled the field artillery companies, if filled, to man six guns each. Of Ringgold's old company, an officer who joined it at Monterey says:

"It was then commanded by Bragg, and was in the highest state of efficiency, discipline, and drill of any organization, of any arm, that I have ever seen. It had six guns, six caissons, two battery wagons, and two forges, each having six horses as teams, and each gun served by a detachment of twelve men mounted, not on the boxes, but on high-mettled and well-trained horses, which followed the guns as they moved at a gallop, and swept over the plain of exercise like a whirlwind."

That its action on the field of battle was as conspicuous as were its manœuvres on the drill-ground, it gave ample proof, particularly at Buena Vista, where its service is best described in the language of the commanding general:

"Captain Bragg, who had just arrived from the left, was ordered at once into battery. Without any infantry to support him, and at the imminent risk of losing his guns, this officer came rapidly into action, the Mexican lines being but a few yards from the muzzles of his pieces. The first discharge of cannister caused the enemy to hesitate; the second and third drove him back in disorder, and saved the day."

The services of the field artillery companies proving so valuable, Congress, by act of March 3d, 1847, provided that, "in addition to the four companies authorized by the act of March 2d, 1821, to be equipped as light artillery, the President is hereby empowered, when he shall deem it necessary, to designate four other companies, one in each regiment, to be organized and equipped as light artillery. * * * That the officers and men of the light artillery, when serving as such and mounted, shall receive the same pay and allowances as provided by law for the dragoons." By War Department General Orders No. 16, April 15th, 1847, the duty of designating the four additional field companies was imposed on the general-in-chief, then in the field. Accordingly, in General Orders No. 218, Headquarters of the Army, Pueblo, Mexico, July 16th, 1847, the following companies were so announced: Captain J. B. Magruder's, (I) of the First; J. F. Roland's, (M) of the Second; T. W. Sherman's, (E) of the Third, and Captain S. H. Drum's, (G) of the Fourth Artillery. So far as (E) of the Third Regiment was concerned, the order simply legalized a state of affairs that had existed for a year. All the companies, except (M) of the Second, had participated in the battles either in the Rio Grande valley, or in General Scott's campaign on the southern line of operations. (M) was one of the companies added to the Second Regiment by the same act which increased the number of light artillery companies, but it was not organized in time to render services in the field during that war.

After the close of hostilities with Mexico all the field companies of artillery, with the exception of (C) and (E) Third, and (B) Fourth, turned their horses over to the quartermaster's department at New Orleans, in compliance with orders from Headquarters First Military Department. They were legally, however, field companies, and all hoped to be remounted; but a circular from the Adjutant-General's Office, September 30th, 1848, directed that but one in each regiment should be equipped as a company of field artillery. In compliance therewith the original four field companies were retained as such, and (E) of the Third turned in its horses accordingly. (K) of the First and (A) of the Second were provided with horses in November, 1848, and, with (C) of the Third and (B) of the Fourth, formed the mounted field companies of the regular army. This was but a temporary arrangement. It was soon resolved to equip four other companies, as contemplated by the law of March 3d, 1847; and as the assignment of these companies by the general-in-chief while in the field was considered to be but provisional in its nature, it was deemed proper to announce them anew. This was accordingly done in General Orders No. 22, War Department, Adjutant-General's Office, April 21st, 1849, as follows:

"1. Under the provisions of the act of March 3d, 1847, authorizing four additional companies 'to be organized and equipped as light artillery,' the President directs the following designated companies to be so organized and equipped:

"First Regiment of Artillery, Company (I), Captain Magruder.
"Second do do do (M), Captain Roland.
" Third do do do (B), Captain Shover.
"Fourth do do do (G), Captain Freeman.

" Four pieces and forty-four horses will be allowed each company, and all the necessary supplies will be furnished, on requisitions duly forwarded to the proper departments of the staff, agreeably to regulations.

"Company (B), Third Artillery, will proceed, without unnecessary delay, to take post at West Point, for the purpose of aiding in the practical instruction of the cadets in this important branch of the military service, under its captain, Brevet Major Shover, the present instructor of artillery at the academy. The lieutenants on extra duty will join the company."

The only change made by this order was that affecting (E) of the Third, for which (B) of the same regiment was substituted. This was a discrimination against the former company which its commander, Captain T. W. Sherman, energetically and successfully combated. The company had earned in the field honorable distinction as field artillery even before the law authorizing its equipment was passed. The proposed substitution for it of (B) Company was not carried into execution, as in General Orders No. 29, Adjutant-General's Office, May 12th, 1849, it was announced that "the execution of paragraph 2 of General Orders No. 22, dated April 21st, 1849, having been suspended, and Company (B), Third Artillery, ordered to rejoin its station at Fort Adams, considerations of the public service no longer require a deviation from the rule observed in designating the companies

ORGANIZATION—FIELD ARTILLERY SINCE 1821.

of the other regiments of artillery to be remounted. Accordingly Company (E), Third Artillery, Captain T. W. Sherman, will be organized and equipped as light artillery, instead of Company (B)."

The selection of field artillery commanders was about the same time regulated by General Orders No. 12, War Department, 1849, which were dictated by Secretary Marcy, and to the following effect:

"If a vacancy happen in the grade of captain of a company designated as a light artillery company, it will be filled by the order of the Secretary of War on the recommendation of the colonel, who will name the captain best qualified for the service."

This has been the rule by which the assignment of captains to this duty has been *supposed* to be regulated down to the year 1882, when captains, equally with lieutenants, were made detailable according to seniority, and the former for a tour of three years.*

Under the provisions of the orders of April 21st and May 12th, quoted, (I) of the First, (E) of the Third, and (G) of the Fourth Artillery were equipped as directed. Company (M), Second Regiment, was not so equipped up to 1851.

The supposition, based in error, that, the war being over, the field companies had fulfilled their appointed purpose, and were no longer useful, led (March 31st, 1851, by General Orders No. 18, War Department) to the dismounting of six companies of the field artillery, leaving only (K) of the First and (C) of the Third equipped with the proper arm. Referring to this in his annual report of that year, Secretary Conrad remarked:

"Prior to the late war there were only four light artillery companies. After the war broke out four more of the artillery companies were converted into light artillery, making in all eight companies. This description of troops, although extremely effective in regular war, are utterly useless in the kind of service in which the army is now employed. The department did not hesitate, therefore, to direct that six of those companies should be dismounted. Of this number four will continue dismounted, unless Congress should otherwise direct. But as it is deemed important to preserve a portion of this description of force, two others will be mounted as soon as the department is provided with the means of doing so. This will make in all four companies, or one to each regiment of artillery, which seems to have been contemplated by the act of 1821."

---

*Changed by G. O. 86, H. Q. A., series of 1884, to *four* years for captains.

The "means of doing so" were forthcoming the next fiscal year; and accordingly Sedgwick's (A) of the Second and Hunt's (G) of the Fourth Artillery were remounted by General Orders No. 36, Adjutant-General's Office, September 25th, 1852.

The statement of the Secretary of War that four of the field companies would "continue dismounted unless Congress should otherwise direct," was a direct appeal to the sense of the legislature upon the propriety of dismounting the artillery, a measure the wisdom of which was doubtful even to himself, and which had been entered upon in opposition to the advice of the most experienced and distinguished officers in service, including the general-in-chief. The response was of such a character as, to some minds at least, would have carried conviction as to the wishes of Congress in the premises; it was announced by that body appropriating, during the session of 1852–'53, the sum of eighteen thousand five hundred dollars, to be expended under the direction of the President of the United States, *for the specific purpose of mounting the four remaining field artillery companies.* This expression of congressional will was sufficiently emphatic to impress even Secretary Davis, no friend to the artillery, who, in War Department General Orders No. 15, May 26th, 1853, directed that (M) of the Second, (E) of the Third, and (B) of the Fourth Artillery should be remounted. Of the field companies, (I) of the First alone remained now without horses and proper artillery equipments.

Commenting upon the fact that Congress had in the most explicit manner expressed a desire to have all the field companies mounted; that Secretary Davis, while partially carrying it into effect, had acted with apparent desire to defeat the spirit of the law, General Scott, in a communication of May 22d, 1857, to Secretary Floyd, said:

"The Congress, during the winter of 1852–'53, made an ample, specific appropriation for the purpose of mounting the four dismounted light companies. The next Secretary (Mr. Davis) gave horses, &c., to only three of these, and sent them to the Indian frontier, where, according to Mr. Secretary Conrad and all military men, they were utterly useless, and in fact soon fell into decay, after an enormous cost in forage. To correct this blunder (by another), Mr. Secretary Davis (General Orders No. 9, Headquarters of the Army, October 30th, 1856) dismounted three companies and ordered them to Fort Monroe, with Magruder's company, (I) of the First Artillery, (which had not been mounted in many years,) to constitute a school of practice, as sea-coast, garrison, and siege artillery. Of that school of practice I think well, but consider it a blunder to have dismounted those companies. In conclusion, I hope that they, together with Magruder's, may soon be remounted."

It was at this time that General Scott expressed the urgent desire to assemble the field companies in pairs, at the posts best adapted to that end, for purposes of instruction; forming, in fact, field artillery schools.

The companies dismounted, as mentioned, by General Orders No. 9, of 1856, were (M) of the Second, (C) of the Third, and (G) of the Fourth Artillery; (C) had not before been dismounted, except temporarily and for change of station, since it was organized as a horse artillery company, in 1838. Having marched to Santa Fé, New Mexico, after the Mexican war, it was there for a time converted into a company of cavalry, the matériel, guns, caissons, &c., being stored. In 1850 the remaining personnel, without the guns, &c., returned to Jefferson Barracks, Missouri, where Captain Bragg joined it, and rehabilitated the company as field artillery; but this time as mounted, not as horse artillery.

Acting on General Scott's suggestion, Secretary Davis' successor had scarcely assumed the duties of his office before he began seriously to consider the advisability of remounting the companies of field artillery dismounted but six months previously. One week after General Scott's communication was written, Magruder's company, (I) of the First, was, by General Orders No. 6, Adjutant-General's Office, May 29th, 1857, ordered to be equipped as field artillery. This was followed by the equipment of (M) of the Second, pursuant to "Special Orders No. 70, Headquarters Troops Serving in Kansas," dated September 18th, 1857, issued under instructions from the War Department of the 7th of that month. It was fitted out completely as a four-gun battery.

By Special Orders No. 52, Headquarters of the Army, April 10th, 1858, Captain and Brevet Major J. F. Reynolds' company, (C) of the Third, was directed to proceed to Leavenworth, Kansas, for horses, and thence to Utah to receive the guns, caissons, and other matériel from a detachment of the ordnance, in whose charge they had been placed by the commanding general of the army in Utah.

Touching the subject of this transfer, the remarks of Colonel H. K. Craig, head of the ordnance department, are worthy of record as illustrating the spirit of fairness regarding the proper service of artillery which had succeeded to the intriguing of the disgraced late head of that bureau. In a letter to the Secretary of War, Colonel Craig observed :

"The efficient performance of his ordnance duties will occupy Brevet Captain Reno's time and that of his ordnance detachment. It was not supposed that he would be diverted from these legitimate and proper duties to be assigned to those which pertain properly and exclusively to the artillery. Every consideration of justice and propriety demands that all batteries of artillery, and especially those in active service, should be manned and served by artillery troops, under the direction of officers of that arm; and the assignment of such duties to ordnance officers and soldiers, or to any other, is wrong. It is also adverse to the interests of public service, inasmuch as it tends to lessen the artillery *esprit de corps*, and assigns very important military service to troops who cannot be supposed to take much interest in it, or to be as efficient for its performance as those to whom it legitimately pertains."

It is all the more pleasurable to note the views here expressed upon the relative proper functions of the artillery and the ordnance, under the existing organization, from the fact that it has been found necessary elsewhere in this work to expose and animadvert upon the manner in which the latter usurped, in large degree, the functions of the former during the Mexican war.

The resuscitation of (C) of the Third restored to their proper status seven of the eight field artillery companies, leaving (G) of the Fourth Regiment alone dismounted. The pieces of this company were inspected and condemned at Fort Leavenworth, Kansas, May 18th, 1855. The following month it was mounted as cavalry, and acted as such during the Sioux expedition, returning to Fort Leavenworth in November, 1856. It was not again equipped as field artillery until June, 1861.

Six of the seven mounted field artillery companies were either in Utah, or marching to join the army there, when the adjustment, in a measure, of the difficulties that had caused the Government to concentrate its troops in that quarter left the "batteries," as they were now often officially designated, free for duty elsewhere.

It was at this time that War Department Order No. 10, of 1859, was issued, elaborating a plan for "the better instruction of the artillery in its appropriate duties, and at the same time to secure an efficient disposition of it for actual service." (See Instruction.) Notwithstanding the expressed views, already quoted, of the general-in-chief, that "according to Secretary Conrad and all military men" they would thereby be rendered "utterly useless," the batteries were distributed at various points on the Indian frontier, where, as it proved, they were not available, but utterly useless when most needed, in 1861, and those in Texas only escaped the enemy by sacrificing their horses and matériel.

It was this dispersed condition of the companies, resulting not from Secretary Floyd's treachery, as is sometimes asserted, but from a desire in certain quarters (not, so far as known, on the part of the Secretary) to experiment with an impracticable system of instruction, which brought the Government face to face, in 1861, with the necessity for providing itself with more field artillery, and was the immediate cause of the Fifth Regiment being organized; for although, when the Civil war broke out, the companies were called in as quickly as possible, in many cases it could not be done soon, and in some instances it was not known that it could be done at all.

The law designated as "batteries" the tactical units of this regiment. This was the first time this designation was legalized, although for several years the terms "light company" and "battery" had been treated as synonymous in orders from army headquarters. The Fifth was equipped throughout as field artillery; but the law did not, as was the case with the eight old companies, direct that this *should* be done; it followed from the necessity that existed for fitting out many more batteries, commanded by regular officers, for service with the armies then being organized.

The importance of placing on a field artillery footing every company of the old regiments that could by any means be made available was quickly appreciated; and, for the reason that the enemy was not a maritime power, it became the easier and more reasonable thing to do, to take for this work the companies from the sea-coast as well as those from the interior. August 23d, 1861, General Barry, chief of artillery, Army of the Potomac, addressed General McClellan on the subject as follows :

"To insure success, it is of vital importance that the army should have an overwhelming force of field artillery. To render this the more effective, the field batteries should, as far as possible, consist of regular troops."

A few days after, the commanding general urgently appealed to the Secretary of War to send in the Third Artillery from the Pacific coast, to give him half the companies forming the late artillery school at Fortress Monroe, and followed it up later with the recommendation "that the whole of the regular artillery, old and new, be ordered to report here [Washington], excepting the mounted batteries actually serving in other departments, and the minimum number of companies actually necessary to form the nucleus of the garrisons of our most important permanent works." These earnest representations had the effect to bring into the Army of the Potomac, as field batteries, half the regular artillery of the United States.

As usual with that arm, the service was by detachment, the regular batteries forming the nuclei around which gathered the volunteers. This important principle of organization, conformable to the sound and settled policy on which the regular army has been maintained in time of peace, was observed in every phase of organization that the artillery experienced, and whether assigned to brigades, divisions, corps, or armies, and with or without reserves. That portion of the regular artillery which was not with the Army of the Potomac served elsewhere in the field, save four companies which remained in permanent works, but from necessity it was scattered very sparsely over the various theatres of operations; nevertheless, all except those mentioned were, at one time or another during the Civil war, organized and equipped as either mounted or horse artillery.* In view of the fact here stated, it is a rather curious circumstance that the official army registers issued during the years of the Civil war set forth that "*two* companies in each of the 1st, 2d, 3d, and 4th regiments of artillery being equipped as light artillery, are allowed sixty-four instead of forty-two privates per company."

Horse artillery was early recognized as the associate of properly organized cavalry. Accordingly, some time in the fall of 1861, Tidball's company, (A) of the Second, was equipped for that service at Washington, D. C., forming the first company of horse artillery in the army since Bragg's company was dismounted at Santa Fé after the Mexican war. This was soon followed by the similar equipment of (M), Second, and, March, 1862, by (B–L), Second, (consolidated for want of men,) and (C), Third Artillery. These companies were formed into a horse artillery brigade ; and so efficient did they prove that by the date of the battle of Chan-

---

* Companies (H) and (K) of the Second, and (B) and (D) of the Third, were not at any time equipped as field artillery.

cellorsville (May 2d–4th, 1863) their number had been doubled. After this battle the horse batteries of that army were organized into two brigades, that they might alternate campaigning and recuperating, in their arduous service with the cavalry. The strength of these brigades gradually increased in personnel and fighting power as their utility became manifest and their management understood, until, under Meade, May 4th, 1864, on the eve of the Wilderness, the First Brigade embraced the Sixth Battery of New York light artillery, (B–L), (D), and (M) of the Second, (A) and (C–E) of the Fourth Artillery; the Second Brigade, (E–G), (H–I), and (K) of the First, (A) and (G) of the Second, and (C), (F), and (K) of the Third Artillery. Of the twelve batteries composing the two brigades, seven were six-gun and five were four-gun batteries.

Associated with the cavalry of other armies than that of the Potomac were horse batteries, the armaments being generally 3-inch rifle guns, which were served with an enterprise, élan, and effectiveness unsurpassed up to that time by the first artilleries of the world. (See Organization of Artillery for an Active Army.) Of the companies equipped for longer or shorter periods as field batteries from the regular army during the Civil war, about one-third served as horse artillery.

A general dismounting of both regular and volunteer batteries commenced within a few days of the surrender, May 26th, of the last Confederate army in the trans-Mississippi. By General Orders No. 105, Adjutant-General's Office, June 2d, 1865, commanders of military geographical departments were directed to reduce at once their batteries of volunteers to the lowest number absolutely required. General Orders No. 126, same office, July 20th, following, directed that two companies of each of the regular regiments, to be selected by the colonels, should be, as previous to the war, retained as mounted batteries, while the remaining companies, except those serving west of the Mississippi, were dismounted. Pursuant to the provisions of this order, the following were designated by General Orders No. 139, Adjutant-General's Office, September 28th, 1865, as the field batteries of the regular regiments, viz.: (I) and (K) of the First; (A) and (M) of the Second; (C) and (E) of the Third; (B) and (G) of the Fourth; (F) and (G) of the Fifth. It will be noticed that the original field artillery companies were retained in the four old regiments. Of the two batteries retained in each regiment, one had for armament 3-inch rifles, the other 12-pounder Napoleons. The personal armament of the men were revolvers and sabres for chiefs of pieces and of caissons, sabres for cannoneers, while the drivers were unarmed.

Though the term "field artillery" does not appear in the act of July 29th, 1861, legalizing the organization of the Fifth Artillery, the personnel of the battery therein prescribed was, with slight modification, that which had been fixed upon for field artillery in the authorized tactics of that arm. This, together with the other fact of the mounting, equipping, and sending out as field artillery all the batteries of the regiment, does not leave in doubt that Congress intended the Fifth to be a field artillery regiment.

Prior to the organization of the Fifth there were authorized by law but eight field artillery companies. The equipment of that regiment added twelve batteries to the number; and as the act of July 28th, 1866, directed that thereafter the organizations of the four old regiments should be similar to that of the Fifth, the designations of their tactical units—"companies"—were thereby changed to "batteries," each of which, like the batteries of the Fifth, was eligible for equipment as light artillery.

Such was the state of affairs when, in 1874, the enactment of section 1101 of the Revised Statutes re-established to a degree the laws of 1821 and 1847 relative to the selection of batteries for light artillery service by providing that "one battery in each regiment of artillery, to be designated by the President, shall be equipped as light artillery, and one other battery may be so designated and equipped when the President may deem it necessary." Under the law as it exists to-day, therefore, but five of the batteries are *required* to be equipped as light artillery, while five others may or may not be, at the option of the President, who, by General Orders No. 96, of 1882, Adjutant-General's Office, in the exercise of the discretion here given, increased the field batteries to the full number authorized. As previously mentioned, however, they are equipped not as light artillery proper, but as mounted batteries.

It is not known that the President, acting under the requirements of the law, formally announced the five batteries which "shall be equipped as light artillery." It was probably thought to be unnecessary. The organizations designated under the act of 1821, with (F) of the Fifth, were, at the date of the enactment of the statutes, so equipped, and have so continued. But had the President, *pro forma*, selected certain batteries for this duty, instead of recognizing the continuation of the existing state of affairs as a full compliance with the statute, there was every reason which sound military policy and public spirit could dictate why he should have chosen the four original companies. They were the pioneers in the field of light artillery under the present regimental organizations. The blaze of their guns had shed unfading lustre over every battle-field, from Palo Alto to the crushing of the last army of the Rebellion. Nothing could be more conducive to a proper *esprit de corps* than a recognition of this fact, for both officers and men must see with peculiar satisfaction these honored organizations allowed permanently to retain the armaments with which they had become veterans, and which they had ever served to the credit of the artillery arm and to their country's glory. This pleasure seems vouchsafed to them, for there is no reasonable doubt but that the continuation as field artillery of the batteries indicated, subsequent to the enactment of the Revised Statutes, fixed on them the character of permanent field artillery organizations, as contemplated by the law.

Of the ten batteries equipped pursuant to General Orders No. 139, of 1865, (I) of the First, (M) of the Second, (E) of the Third, (G) of the Fourth, and (G) of the Fifth were, in accordance with provisions of General Orders No. 6, of 1869, Adjutant-General's Office, dismounted; and at the same time four of the five batteries remaining were ordered to Fort Riley, Kansas, to form a school for field artillery practice and instruction. (See Instruction.)

The five batteries retained by the order of 1869, quoted, remained the field artillery organizations of the regular army until the number was increased by five additional batteries, agreeably to the requirements of General Orders No. 96, of August 15th, 1882, Adjutant-General's Office. In the meantime, however, (L) of the Second, in Texas, was, by Special Orders No. 25, of February 4th, 1878, Adjutant-General's Office, directed by the President to be temporarily equipped as field artillery, and so remained until it was transferred from that military department pursuant to instructions from army headquarters and Special Orders No. 208, of October 13th, 1880, Department of Texas. The captain of (F) of the Second, which remained in Texas, having applied to have his battery equipped as field artillery, the request was favorably considered, and in Special Orders No. 246, of November 17th, 1880, Adjutant-General's Office, the President, in conformity with section 1101 of the Revised Statutes, directed that battery to be temporarily so equipped. As (F) of the Second was one of those designated by General Orders No. 96, of 1882, before mentioned, to be mounted and equipped as an additional field battery, its temporary service has been exchanged for one more permanent in character. (For G. O. 96, A. G. O., 1882, see Appendix.)

It will not escape notice that, of the batteries designated in General Orders No. 96, of 1882, not one was of the additional companies equipped as field artillery in 1846–'47. While the competency of the President to select for this service from all dismounted batteries is not here denied,* it must be conceded that it would have been a particularly appropriate thing had the four old batteries been allowed to once more buckle on the harness in which, on the hotly-contested fields of two wars, at least three of them—(I) of the First, (E) of the Third, and (G) of the Fourth—had been greatly distinguished. The regiments had learned to regard their field artillery companies with affectionate pride; and it will be remembered that, in 1865, when the selection of companies to remain mounted was left to colonels of the artillery regiments, and their expressed wishes respected, the original light companies of 1821 and 1847 were, without exception, retained. The traditions of an honorable arm of service are worthy of respect—a fact recognized by every nation in which the profession of arms has been cherished, and forgetfulness of which has in every instance been the surest evidence of military and political decadence; those who disregard them stifle the noblest sentiment that can actuate the soldier's breast, while evincing an ignorance of human nature well calculated in its effects to freeze up the fountains of

---

* Whether or not recent laws and the enactment of the Revised Statutes have abrogated the legal rights of the eight batteries designated as light artillery under the acts of March 2d, 1821, and March 3d, 1847, is an open question. It is not intended here to enter upon its legal aspects. Suffice it to say, there are the strongest reasons upon which to base an argument in support of the negative view, though the logic of orders since the Civil war tends to the affirmative of the proposition.

true military spirit by the chilling blasts of official indifference or neglect.

To be known, it need not be repeated here; but it will not be amiss to recall that (I) under Magruder, (E) under Sherman, and (G) under Drum all won in Mexico the plaudits of the army and the country, and, with (M) of the Second, did faithful service during that interval of vacillation and perpetual change intervening between the Mexican war and the Civil war; all this when not a single battery designated in General Orders No. 96, of 1882, had as yet been equipped as field artillery. As a result, the old field batteries were looked upon with affectionate regard by their respective regiments, each of which doubtless would have been glad to see ancient and honorable associations perpetuated by having these, preferably to any others, equipped for a service with which their careers had been so intimately connected. It would have tended, therefore, to the development and maintenance of proper professional spirit had the field batteries of 1847 been selected as those to be rehabilitated in 1882; and it is to be hoped, should changes be hereafter made, that their claims—based on services, merit, their own pride and that of the artillery arm—may not be denied the recognition to which they are justly entitled.

CHAPTER III.

ORGANIZATION—FIELD SERVICE.

At the epoch of the Revolution (1775-'83) it was customary to attach two field guns to each infantry battalion, the rest being kept in a general reserve. General Washington early and urgently recommended to Congress the procurement of sufficient field guns from Europe to supply two to each regiment of infantry of the continental army. This, however, was not a matter easily accomplished in the crippled state of the finances and trade of the colonies, and the plan was adopted of attaching a company of artillery with two or three guns to each infantry brigade. The remainder of the pieces with the army were held in reserve. Battalion guns, *i. e.*, those attached to battalions alone, have never had any place in the armament of our regular army.

The first assignment thus made was by General Orders No. 9, Headquarters· of the Army, New York city, August· 9th, 1776, which directed that two pieces should be attached to, and manœuvre with, each brigade, the horses and ammunition carts being kept at some convenient place and for this special service.

The following are the instructions given the officers commanding the brigade artillery companies, or detachments, by General Knox :

"Much is required from an officer of artillery when on detachment, as he hath then the whole weight of duty on·his mind. He must be careful in disciplining and exercising his men at least three times a day. He must see that they keep themselves clean, and will himself set the example. He will particularly attend to the manner of the men cooking their provisions, which ought always to be boiled or roasted, never fried, baked, or broiled, which modes are very unhealthy; they must be taught to use vinegar freely. The officer must frequently examine his ammunition and air it, view his pieces, apparatus, the horses and harness, and be sure that everything is in the most perfect order to move at the shortest notice after he shall receive orders. The reputation and promotion of the officers, and that of the corps, will depend on the most punctual performance of their duty in every point; no excuse will be admitted for any omission. The orders of the day must be constantly taken by every officer commanding a detachment, and when the brigade manœuvres the artillery must be out and exercise with them. The limbers belonging to the guns must not, on any pretense whatever, be taken for any other use, but always kept with them."

These instructions give sufficient proof of the intimate relations existing between the commander of the artillery and the various portions of that arm, even when the latter were detached from the main park and serving with other troops.

Afterwards, and doubtless for the reason that divisions became reduced until they were no larger than brigades had formerly been, artillery, as we learn from the orders of the day, was sometimes attached to divisions; but these were exceptional cases, the rule remaining as before.

There was at that time no uniform system of artillery tactics for the whole army, nor any system of evolutions for the guns with their brigade. This is told us by Captain Stevens, who, in 1797, wrote the first artillery tactics published in this country, and who was an officer of Lamb's regiment during the Revolutionary war. To supply the deficiency indicated, this author informs us that General Knox appointed boards to determine the simpler manœuvres of the pieces with the troops. Tousard, also, reproduces in the Artillerist's Companion some of the evolutions performed by the artillery when paraded and drilled with the infantry. We are led to believe, therefore, that, though uniformity of practice was wanting, the manœuvres of the artillery were characterized by sufficient mobility to meet every demand of service.

The principle of organization for the artillery was this: The general of artillery commanded the whole; that with the main army, in person; that with other armies, through their respective artillery commanders. During the inactive season all the guns and matériel of each army were drawn together into one park. When the campaign opened the various detachments were attached to the brigades, and, for *fighting purposes*, were exclusively under the orders of the brigade commander. In *disciplinary* matters the authority of the commander of the artillery extended over these detachments, he alone having power to grant furloughs to either officers or men.

During the war of 1812 the only attempt known to have been made to systematically apportion the artillery was that of General Izard, made at the beginning of the campaign of 1814, and was after the Revolutionary method. This solitary effort was short-lived, and passed away without having been of any practical benefit. During that war the artillery was, as a rule, scattered without semblance of system.

For administrative purposes, Izard adopted a plan similar to McClellan's in 1862. In this respect he placed the artillery and cavalry on the same footing. McClellan's orders will be found further on; Izard's were promulgated in General Orders of July 25th, 1814, which, after designating the several regiments of infantry to be assigned to the brigades of the army, directed:

> "The detachments of artillery and of light dragoons will join the several brigades as occasion may render the measure advisable. When not so detached these corps will be under the immediate orders of their respective commanding officers, and report directly to the headquarters of the army."

We thus see that in 1814, as during the Revolution, artillery attached to brigades was on the footing of troops *attached for service merely*, returning to the main body at general headquarters, and passing again under the orders of the officer commanding that arm, when their services with the troops were no longer necessary.

With the rise of the Military Academy, and the increased interest in military affairs manifesting itself when officers commenced to look to the army as a permanent profession, the proper adjustment of its parts became a subject for study and reflection. From this followed the elaborate and in some instances very able discussions which grew out of the reductions of 1815 and 1821, in the latter of which Mr. Secretary Calhoun, with that earnestness and energy of style, plainness of proposition, and closeness of logic for which his public papers stand unrivalled, reviewed the field of controversy, and for the first time formulated those principles on which should rest the organization and maintenance of our regular army.

The Mexican war enabled, in a limited degree, application to be made of theoretical knowledge acquired by officers. But although the services of the arm in Mexico were brilliant, and brought the field artillery especially to the front rank in the combatant arms of service, the operations of that war were conducted on too small a scale to enable practical knowledge to be acquired as to the best organization to be given artillery to accompany a large army. Not only this, but what was there learned, being acquired by experience with small forces, contracted the field of vision, and to many officers was a detriment, by leading them to suppose the same principles should govern in the distribution of the artillery in large armies like those of the Civil war. On the northern line of operations—General Taylor's—the field batteries were attached one to each brigade of infantry ; on the southern line—General Scott's—the artillery was attached to divisions. The strength of the brigades was about 1200 men present; of the divisions, 2400 men present. The brigades which took the field in 1861, North and South, were much stronger than these divisions of the preceding war; and this circumstance led to the faulty system of attaching artillery to brigades in the first months of the contest; but, with the large armies which then took the field, the system was found wretchedly inadequate for either administrative or fighting purposes, and was speedily abandoned.

Many of the regiments taking the field at the commencement of the Civil war had batteries attached to them, but they were found to be practically useless, and the first regiments bringing them out were also the last.

When the Union army marched to the first Bull Run the batteries not belonging to regiments, and most of which were regulars, were attached to brigades. The average strength of the latter was 3000 men present. No attempt was made to provide an artillery reserve. No organization looking to the efficient tactical use of the arm had yet been effected. One of the batteries, borrowed from the navy, was hauled by drag-ropes, as were the guns at Bunker Hill in 1775.

Elsewhere than on the Potomac the Federal forces distributed their artillery in a similar manner. In August, 1861, General Lyon's army in Missouri was organized into brigades, each of which had its battery ; so likewise with General Grant's troops in the vicinity of Cairo, Illinois, in October of that year ; and, without particularizing farther, it can be stated that the same remarks are true with reference to the numerous other armies which took or prepared to take the field in the first campaign of that war. To those who were capable of learning, a brief experience was sufficient to demonstrate the disadvantages of the system. In an army exceeding 10,000 men it sacrificed that concentration which alone renders artillery-fire formidable. It was soon found that brigade commanders either could not or would not give both their regiments and their battery proper supervision; neither did they better understand the question of artillery supplies, through what channels they came, or who was responsible that they came at all; in one word, the brigade system, in both the Army of the Potomac and that of Northern Virginia, broke down; nor was it more efficient in other armies of any magnitude.

General McClellan assumed command of the army at Washington July 27th, 1861. It embraced about 50,000 infantry, less than 1000 cavalry, and 650 artillerymen, manning nine incomplete batteries aggregating but thirty guns. In the reorganization at once set on foot the following principles formed the basis for the organization of the artillery:

"1st. The proportion of artillery should be in the ratio of at least two and one-half pieces to 1000 men, to be expanded, if possible, to three pieces.

"2d. The field guns should be restricted to the systems of the U. S. ordnance department and of Parrott, the smooth-bores (with the exception of a few howitzers for special service) to be exclusively the 12-pounder guns, model of 1857, variously called the gun howitzer, light 12-pounder, or the Napoleon.

"3d. Each field battery to be composed, if practicable, of six, and none to have less than four guns, those of each battery to be of uniform calibre.

"4th. The field batteries to be assigned to divisions and not to brigades, in the proportion of four to each division, one of which should be a regular battery, the rest volunteers; the captain of the regulars to command the artillery of the division. In the event of several divisions being united into an army corps, at least one-half of the divisional artillery to be withdrawn from the divisions and formed into a corps reserve. [*Note.*—The contingency provided for having arisen, the corps reserves were formed as contemplated, when the army was on the Peninsula.] (See Appendix.)

"5th. The reserve artillery of the whole army to consist of one hundred guns, comprising, besides a sufficient number of light mounted batteries, all the guns of position, and, until the cavalry be massed, all the horse artillery.

"6th. The amount of ammunition to accompany the field batteries to be not less than four hundred rounds per gun.

"7th. A siege train of fifty pieces to be provided [subsequently expanded to one hundred pieces at Yorktown, including 13-inch sea-coast mortars and 100-pounder and 200-pounder Parrotts].

"8th. Instruction in theory and practice of gunnery, as well as in the tactics of that arm, to be given to the officers and non-commissioned officers of the volunteer batteries, by the study of suitable text-books and by actual recitations in each division, under the direction of the regular officer commanding the divisional artillery.

"9th. Personal inspections, as frequent as circumstances will permit, to be made by the chief of artillery of the army, to see to a strict observance of the established organization and drill, of the special regulations and orders issued from time to time under authority of the commanding general, to note the improvement of officers and men of the volunteer batteries, and the actual fitness for field service of the whole, both regulars and volunteers."

These principles for the organization of artillery were proposed by the chief of that arm, and are worthy of special notice. At other and various times in this country commanders and writers had essayed in the same direction. Still, from force of circumstances, the artillery before this had been either small in amount or imperfect in appointments, often both. And although books on the subject were not wanting, it is believed that the plan here proposed by General Barry was the first comprehensive scheme for organizing artillery to accompany a large force into the field ever promulgated to the United States army, with the expectation that it would be brought to the test of practical experience. It may be remarked, however, that the assignment as here contemplated, of batteries to divisions and of artillery reserves to corps and armies, was then practiced in the principal States of Europe, though the army reserves have been since abandoned. Although in some respects the preceding principles were departed from in actual practice, they formed the groundwork on which was built the artillery service of the Army of the Potomac.

McClellan says in his report: "The creation of an adequate artillery establishment was a formidable undertaking, and had it not been that the country possessed in the regular service a body of accomplished and energetic artillery officers, the task would almost have been hopeless." He drew together all the regular batteries he could lay his hands on; and when the three corps—eight divisions—embarked for the Peninsula campaign they were accompanied by forty-nine batteries aggregating two hundred and ninety-nine guns, of which one hundred were in the artillery reserve. Of the forty-nine batteries, twenty were regulars; the latter represented twenty-six batteries, some being consolidated for service. Of the eighteen batteries of the reserve, fourteen were regulars, of which five were formed by two batteries being consolidated into one. The First Corps (McDowell's), which did not accompany McClellan, is not included in the preceding.

It will not be uninteresting to note the changes which the organization of the artillery of the Army of the Potomac underwent at different periods subsequent to its establishment upon a proper, scientific basis—changes which resulted partly from experience acquired in campaign and battle, and partly from the caprices of the numerous generals who at various times commanded that army.

First of all, an increase in the number of army corps caused a draught from the reserve artillery which almost annihilated it.

On the Peninsula, McClellan had three corps; and two divisions joining subsequently, made ten divisions altogether. Four months later, at Antietam, the army embraced six corps and one cavalry division; total, nineteen divisions. There accompanied the army at Antietam sixty-two batteries; seven were in reserve; fifty-five were distributed to divisions and to the Twelfth Corps, the latter having its seven batteries organized as corps artillery, and not distributed to divisions. There were attached to the cavalry division four batteries of horse artillery. Except in three divisions, one regular was associated with the volunteer batteries, in accordance with the original plan. Of the sixty-two batteries, twenty-two were regulars, five of the latter being formed by uniting two distinct batteries, thus making twenty-seven the number of regular organizations represented at Antietam. It will thus be seen that the creation of new divisions had in a few months well-nigh absorbed the whole of that superb artillery reserve which took the field under McClellan at the beginning of 1862.

At the close of the Peninsula campaign General Barry, under whose immediate supervision the artillery of the Army of the Potomac had been organized, was appointed inspector of artillery, and commander of that arm in the defenses of Washington, being succeeded, September 5th, 1862, as chief of artillery, by Colonel Henry J. Hunt, late commander of the artillery reserve. McClellan remarks, in his report dated August 4th, 1863, concerning this officer, that he "had commanded the artillery reserve with marked skill, and brought to his duties as chief of artillery the highest qualifications. The services of this distinguished officer in reorganizing and refitting the batteries prior to and after the battle of Antietam, and his gallant and skillful conduct on that field, merit the highest encomiums in my power to bestow." General Hunt continued in this position during the rest of the war, stamping on the service of which he was the head the impress of a cultivated mind stored with knowledge of the uses and capabilities of the artillery arm, the result of extensive experience, profound study, and reflection.

At the battle of Fredericksburg General Burnside's army consisted of six corps, each of three divisions, and of two cavalry divisions. He had sixty-seven batteries, nine of which were in reserve. Of the sixty-seven, twenty-six were regulars, four of them being composed of two batteries each, thus representing thirty regular organizations. All the horse artillery belonged to that branch of service. The fifty-eight batteries attached to troops were with the divisions, a number varying from one to four being with each, depending on the arm of service and the strength of the division. In the cavalry service each division had one horse battery; drawing on the reserves for a greater number when needed. Of the infantry divisions, seven had two, three had three, and eight had four batteries. The strength of the divisions (effective) was about 5000 men; of the corps, 15,000 men. The batteries were two-thirds six-gun, the rest having four guns each.

At Chancellorsville General Hooker had eight corps, including one of cavalry, a total of twenty-three divisions. Of the seventy-one batteries with the army, twelve were in the reserve; the rest, except two attached to the provost guard, were arranged to the divisions. Of the seventy-one batteries, twenty-one were regulars, representing twenty-three distinct organizations; in the Eleventh and the Cavalry Corps, half the artillery was formed into a corps reserve. Of the twenty-three divisions, fourteen had two, five had three, and four had four batteries attached. The effective strength of the divisions averaged about 5000 men; of the corps, about 15,000 men; the average number of guns, including the general reserve, was three per 1000 men.

Down to this time the principles originally adopted as those upon which the artillery should be organized had been adhered to, and even the Twelfth Corps, which at Antietam had its guns massed under one commander as corps artillery, at Chancellorsville had its batteries distributed to divisions, in accordance with the original plan.

As, however, regiments had been compelled to surrender up their artillery to brigades, these in their turn to divisions, so, as experience in manœuvring and fighting large armies was gained, did it become manifest that, to most effectively organize the arm for administrative and fighting purposes, divisions must give up their artillery to army corps. Accordingly, after Chancellorsville this change was effected, the batteries of each corps being organized into what was designated an "artillery brigade," the commander of which had, or was supposed to have, his own staff, adjutant, quartermaster, commissary, medical officer, &c.

As illustrating the disadvantages under which artillery officers often labor in the matter of rank, it may be noted that while these artillery brigades were considered equal in importance and fighting power to divisions of infantry, the latter were commanded by generals, the former, as a rule, were commanded by captains or lieutenants.

The number of batteries in a brigade varied according to the strength of the corps to which it was attached. Of the eight corps at Gettysburg, the first battle after this reorganization was effected, four had five and two had four batteries to a brigade; the Sixth Corps brigade had eight batteries; the Cavalry Corps had nine of horse artillery, the latter in two brigades of four and five batteries respectively. Four-fifths of all the batteries of the army had six guns, the rest four guns each. Each brigade included at least one regular battery.

The advantages to be derived from assigning the artillery to larger commands were that the batteries were better cared for and capable of more efficient employment on the field of battle. As a result, fewer guns were required to perform the same amount of work. Consequently, in 1864 the number of pieces was reduced to two and one-half per 1000 men of other arms, having previously been in the ratio of three guns per 1000 men.

The Confederates had anticipated us in this style of organization for artillery. Immediately after the Peninsula campaign, in 1862, they commenced to draw their batteries together into battalions, which embraced from three to five batteries, and had a complete battalion organization, perfect in all its parts, *i. e.*, each battalion had a proper number of field officers, with a regular staff, the quartermasters and commissaries being officers of those departments.

There is an error made by those who sometimes affect to understand the use and management of artillery, *i. e.*, to consider the battery as necessarily the unit of the artillery arm. This must mean that it is either the fighting or the administrative unit for the artillery, as the battalion is for the infantry. So far from this being the fact, the reverse is true in every well-organized army. As for fighting purposes, it is well known that allowing batteries to go into battle alone is avoided when it can be done, and every effort made to bring all the batteries of the brigade into action at the same time, that concentration of fire and weight of metal thrown may produce decisive results. The battery is not, therefore, the only fighting unit. No more is it the sole administrative. In Germany batteries are assembled together in divisions, each commanded by a field officer, with a proper staff; and, though the designations are different in some, the same is true in every other army in Europe. These divisions are made up of three or four batteries, and are similar in purpose, essentially so in organization, with the brigades of the Union and the battalions of the Confederate artillery. In each and every case the battery ceased to be the only administrative unit, and those functions were conjointly assumed by the brigade, the battalion, or the division. (Appendix A, No. 52.)

The erroneous ideas to which attention has been drawn led to others, and to an invidious discrimination against the artillery in our own army. Accepting as an established fact that the battery was the artillery unit, the conclusion was drawn that there was nothing about the service of that arm higher than a battery which could be legitimately the subject of command. This doctrine, at variance alike with our experience and the facts as they exist in every active army of respectable proportions in recent times, was announced in General Orders No. 126, of 1862, from the War Department, which provided that, "as a general rule, artillery will be called for and received by batteries, thus rendering the field and staff unnecessary." As a result, when these batteries were assembled into brigades, the field and staff, here pronounced unnecessary, had to be drawn from captains and subalterns, thus increasing the duties of these officers, and turning over the artillery brigades to those whose rank was in nowise commensurate with their commands. The arrangement was most unjust, and drove many of the first officers of the artillery, in point of merit, into the staff or into other branches of service, where they received the promotion they deserved.

The laws of the Confederacy allowed general and field officers at the rate of a brigadier-general to every eighty guns, a colonel to every forty, a lieutenant-colonel to every twenty-five, a major to every twelve; and although the complement under this rule may never have been appointed, still it appears from the records that their battalions, made up of independent batteries, were always commanded by a field officer, while many of them had more than one officer of that rank.

Neither the brigades of the Union nor the battalions of the Confederate artillery were creations authorized by the legislature; they sprang out of the necessities of war, supplanting the battery as the artillery fighting and, to a great extent, as the administrative unit, the progress of the war only demonstrating more clearly their efficiency.

When the Army of the Potomac took the field in 1864, the number of corps had been reduced from eight, with 277 regiments, to four, with 226 regiments; the artillery from sixty-seven to fifty batteries of field artillery, with which were serving two regiments and three battalions of foot artillery, the latter armed as infantry for guards and escort duty. The regular batteries which were with the army the year before remained with it, though from the reduced number of men it was in several instances found necessary to unite two or three organizations in a single battery, which, even then, in no instance had the maximum strength authorized by law. To each corps' artillery brigade there was attached a battalion of foot artillery for the various duties, artillery and other, required of foot troops. The two heavy artillery regiments formed part of the Artillery Reserve, which, May 4th, 1864, embraced twenty-four of the fifty field battery organizations of the army.

Soon after the first movements of troops in the Wilderness campaign (1864), General Grant resolved to dispense with this artillery reserve. It was accordingly ordered back to Washington. The reason for this step was that the theatre of operations, as well as the plan of campaign determined on, did not permit the use of artillery to advantage, or with decisive effect. The attack was generally against breastworks of greater or less strength, in a swampy or wooded country, where artillery could only manœuvre with difficulty. Instead, however, of ordering the guns to Washington, the reduction of impedimenta was, upon the representations of the chief of artillery of the army, effected in the following manner:

"HEADQUARTERS ARMY OF THE POTOMAC, *May* 16th, 1864.
"[Special Orders No. 136.]

* * * * * * * * *

"2d. Each six-gun battery in this army, except the horse artillery and Taft's New York independent battery, will at once be reduced to four guns, retaining all its caissons. The surplus ordnance stores and horses will be sent to Belle Plain to-morrow, and turned in to the proper departments at that place. The batteries of the Artillery Reserve will be distributed as follows, after sending back the surplus guns: To the Second Corps, Major Hazard, with Clarke's (B) First New Jersey, McKnight's Twelfth New York independent, and Burton's Eleventh New York independent. To the Fifth Corps, Major Fitzhugh, with Bigelow's Ninth Massachusetts, Hart's Fifteenth New York, Sheldon's (B) First New York, Barnes' (C) First New York. To the Sixth Corps, Lieutenant-Colonel Monroe, Brinkle's (E) Fifth United States, Stevens' Fifth Maine, Hexamer's (A) First New Jersey, Ewing's (H) First Ohio. Taft's Fifth New York battery will report to-morrow to Major-General Warren, commanding Fifth Corps. The batteries transferred from the Reserve will join their corps to-morrow. Lieutenant-Colonel McGilvray will remain in charge of the general ammunition column, with staff officers attached to it.

* * * * * * * * *

"By command of General Meade.
, "S. WILLIAMS,
"*Assistant Adjutant-General.*"

By this arrangement the organizations of all the batteries were retained, together with the field officers belonging to the reserve; a matter of importance in an army where, as we have seen, that class of officers was proscribed; only the surplus guns were sent away. The retention of all the caissons with the reduced batteries enabled the ammunition wagon-trains to be correspondingly reduced, besides furnishing a better means of transport, as caissons are acknowledged to be superior for this purpose to wagons.

Prior to the issuing of the special order just quoted, the artillery brigade of the Second Corps had nine, of the Fifth Corps had eight, and of the Sixth Corps had eight six-gun batteries. The Artillery Reserve had six six-gun batteries, besides Taft's six-gun 20-pounder battery. Under the terms of the order, therefore, thirty-one field batteries were changed from six to four guns, and each of the three corps mentioned was given a brigade of twelve batteries—forty-eight guns.

At the date of breaking up the Artillery Reserve the Horse Artillery was composed of twelve batteries, with sixty-four guns, organized into two brigades. On the 31st of May, 1864, these were reduced to eight batteries, four guns each, the whole arranged to one brigade for the Cavalry Corps. This reduced the number of guns in the Horse Artillery by thirty-two, or to one-half the original number, thus making a total reduction in the field artillery of ninety-four guns in that army before the campaign had gotten well under way. In each horse battery one section—two guns—was 12-pounder Napoleons, one 3-inch rifles.

Most of the pieces ordered away when the Reserve was broken up were returned when the army arrived before Petersburg, to be used as guns of position in the siege operations. Besides these, there was a siege train, which embraced twelve 8-inch siege howitzers, sixty-seven siege mortars, seven sea-coast mortars, thirty-six Coehorn mortars, ten 100-pounders, thirty-eight 30-pounder Parrotts, fourteen 4½-inch rifles, and one 30-pounder Brooke rifle. The artillery operations before Petersburg, from the arrival of the army, June, 1864, until March, 1865, when the final campaign was vigorously opened, were almost wholly in the nature of the siege, and, by Special Orders 42, of 1864, Headquarters Armies of the United States, were carried on under the supervision of the chief of artillery of the Army of the Potomac.

On taking the field in 1865 the artillery was distributed as follows: The Second Corps artillery brigade had twelve batteries; that of the Sixth Corps nine, and of the Ninth Corps six batteries. Four batteries were in the Artillery Reserve. The horse batteries were attached to the cavalry. The Second, Sixth, and the Reserve had each six Coehorn mortars, this species of cannon proving so efficient in the previous campaign as to recommend them to more general service.

On the 29th of March the batteries for field service were ordered to be reduced to six for the Second and Sixth Corps, and five for the Fifth and Ninth Corps. The surplus batteries were either left temporarily in position on the lines, or sent to the Artillery Reserve, which had, by sheer force of circumstances and in absence of specific instructions, re-established itself with nineteen batteries, the supply (artillery) and ammunition trains of the army.

This reduction in the number of guns with the troops resulted

ORGANIZATION—FIELD SERVICE.

from a desire to strip the army of all impedimenta not necessary for the campaign then opening, and of which the pursuit of the enemy was rightly expected to be one of the main features. Besides, it had been shown that the large artillery brigades of twelve batteries organized when the Reserve was broken up were unwieldy; moreover, the Corps, accustomed as they had been from the beginning to send broken-down or surplus batteries to the general artillery reserve, were now at a loss for means to take care of or recuperate them. Then followed a reaction in favor of returning to the former practices; the brigades were reduced to a less number of batteries than they had before the order of May 16th, 1864, was issued, while the Artillery Reserve was re-established with a larger number of batteries than it had before that time.

Thus the organization of the artillery of this army changed frequently during the four years of the war. An understanding of the causes for these changes and their results will prove neither uninstructive nor uninteresting.

We have seen that when the war began it was not unusual for regiments to bring their guns into the field, after the practice of the last century in Europe; while the generally accepted plan was to attach a battery to each brigade of infantry, then four batteries to each division, and finally from five to twelve batteries, organized as a brigade and with a distinct administrative staff, were attached to each army corps.

Experience has everywhere demonstrated that in a large army the smallest tactical unit which should be made complete in all fighting arms of service is one numbering 10,000 men at the minimum. When large forces are involved a less number than this cannot be expected, if detached for any purpose, to effect important results. When the Army of the Potomac was organized, and prior to its embarkation for the Peninsula, the divisions numbered about 10,000 men each, as will be seen from the following official list selected at random from the returns: Present for duty—Sedgwick's, 9296; Hooker's, 10,751; Porter's, 11,335; Couch's, 11,013; Casey's, 10,998. The batteries were accordingly assigned to divisions; but the necessity for a distinct administrative staff for the divisional artillery was not understood, and during the three campaigns of the ensuing twelve months those duties were imposed upon the corps chiefs of artillery.

Casualties of service soon reduced the strength of the divisions, which at Antietam averaged but 6190 men. This is too small a force to be made an independent unit in a large army, but the divisional plan having once been adopted, it was not easy to effect a change, even though the necessity for it became clearly manifest. This difficulty was enhanced by the frequent changes of army commanders.

At Chancellorsville the average strength of army corps was 15,000 men; of the divisions, 5000 men. It was resolved after this battle to withdraw the batteries from the latter and assign them to the former, giving to the corps artillery what the divisional never had, viz., a distinct organization with an administrative staff. These organizations were designated "artillery brigades." Experience served only to multiply proofs of the efficiency of the new system. Each corps of 15,000 men was now a complete, compact fighting body, capable of making its power felt with effect, whether acting in concert with other corps or detached and acting independently. In Europe to-day the same principles govern in this matter. There the divisions, which as a rule number 15,000 men, are the smallest commands to which distinct artillery organizations are assigned. In artillery, as in other arms, concentration is favorable to instruction, to discipline, and to efficiency, and in active service is absolutely necessary to secure that weight of metal which renders its fire formidable. From the time that artillery was attached to battalions of infantry to this day the tendency has been in that direction, and it is always accompanied by marked improvement and economy. In all active armies it has resulted in substituting the artillery brigade attached to a fighting unit of 15,000 men for a single piece attached to a battalion 500 strong, with very great advantages both of command and administration, as well as increased efficiency on the field, which has enhanced the importance, relatively to others, of the artillery arm of service.

In the consolidation of corps effected by General Orders No. 115, of March 23d, 1864, Adjutant-General's Office, no change was made in the principles of artillery organization. Thereafter the corps, numbering about 23,000 effectives* each, were com-

---

*The Second, Fifth, and Sixth Corps aggregated 69,884; Cavalry Corps, 11,839; Ninth Corps, 18,995 effectives.

posed of three or four divisions of the same strength as formerly—five to six thousand men. The same reasons which rendered artillery brigades advisable existed still, and continued until the end of the war. The only changes were in the number of batteries assigned to these brigades, these varying from five at Gettysburg to nine and twelve in the campaign of 1864, and returning as the war progressed to their original numbers.

The artillery of this army was never in better condition than at the beginning of the Wilderness campaign. The batteries were well equipped both in personnel and matériel. The brigades were commanded by experienced officers, and associated with each was a battalion of foot artillery for guard, escort, and other infantry duty, besides furnishing drafts, if needed, to keep the batteries full. The Reserve embraced about one-third of the batteries with the army, organized into brigades of a size convenient for manœuvre or detached service with other troops, and it was accompanied by two regiments of foot artillery armed as infantry. These regiments furnished parties for the construction of works on the field or elsewhere, the fabrication of gabions and fascines, the building of magazines, the preparation and laying of platforms, and other duties of similar nature requiring special instruction and practice to insure rapidity and perfection, and generally all those duties connected with artillery service that men of the batteries cannot well be taken to do, and which uninstructed infantry had previously been detailed to perform, at great sacrifice of time, labor, and economy. Its principal defects were, first, a want of general and field officers, a subject to which attention had been called by the chief of artillery in all his reports of battles; and, second, of a code of regulations for its government which should be binding on all branches of the service. These defects injured its efficiency and usefulness to the prejudice of its reputation, caused a misapplication of its powers, and added to its cost; but they were defects for which the artillery itself was in no way responsible.

It was at this time that the Artillery Reserve was broken up, the artillery brigades given a larger number of batteries; and although circumstances rendered a return to former practices necessary before the campaign closed, thus demonstrating the necessity that existed for that Reserve, the excellence in both a military and economic point of view of the artillery brigades was never brought in question, but, on the contrary, made more clearly manifest as the war progressed. With us, evolved out of the necessities of actual service, this organization was that adopted by our enemies under precisely similar circumstances; it is that put in practice by the armies of Europe during both peace and war. It may therefore be considered as that which, at this stage of the military art and science, is best for the artillery accompanying a large army into the field.

It does not follow from this that the distribution of single batteries to brigades may not, under certain circumstances, be proper, and indeed necessary. With a small force like that which fought under General Taylor in the Mexican war, for instance, it may be the only thing to do; and what in an army like that of the Potomac would cause the power of the artillery to be frittered away in inefficient driblets, the cost of its maintenance to be greatly increased, might, under the circumstances supposed, have been highly advantageous. It was by overlooking the fact here brought to view, viz., that the proper organization of artillery will vary with, among other things, the numerical strength of the army, which caused much of the delay in putting it on a proper footing when the Civil war broke out; *and fortunate will it be for us if the results of practical knowledge then acquired do not pass beyond recall forever with the lives of those who then learned the proper use and management of the artillery arm in campaign and in battle.*

Particular attention has been paid to the principles on which the artillery of the Army of the Potomac was organized, and the changes made in that organization, for the reason that it was the most important army of the Nation. Its opponent was the grand army of the Confederacy, in which was concentrated the bone and sinew of the rebellious States, their warlike resources, organized and guided by the highest order of military talent at their command.

In other armies than that of the Potomac, in their diverse fields of action, the artillery was variously organized, depending greatly upon the character of the country, the magnitude of the operations, including that of the forces engaged, and the views of commanding generals; but, except in some of the western armies, it will be found, as a rule, that as the war continued, as the resources of the combatants became compressed essentially into two or three well-organized masses, the tendency was to withdraw the artillery from control of subordinate commanders, and place that arm under orders only of generals commanding the larger tactical unit—divisions and army corps.

Although reference has been made to changes of artillery organization in the Army of Northern Virginia, a more particular yet general review of these may not prove uninteresting.

August 23d, 1861, the chief of artillery of McClellan's army wrote to that general:

"To insure success it is of vital importance that the Army of the Potomac should have an overwhelming force of field artillery. To render this the most effective, the batteries should, as far as practicable, consist of regular troops. With every disposition to do their best, the volunteer artillery do not possess the knowledge or experience requisite for thoroughly efficient service. I would therefore recommend that companies of regular artillery may be withdrawn from many of the forts on the Atlantic and Pacific sea-boards and ordered to this point [Washington] at as early a date as practicable, to be mounted as field artillery."

This, seconded by the influence of the commanding general, had the effect, before the army took the field in the spring of 1862, of increasing the number of regular batteries in McClellan's army from thirteen when this written, to twenty-nine when the campaign commenced. The expectation, however, of creating a field artillery overwhelmingly stronger than that of the enemy was not realized. The enemy were equally alive to the importance of the measure, meeting gun for gun the artillery of the Union army. Shortly before that battle the Confederate army which met McClellan at Antietam had seventy-three batteries, to oppose which that general had but sixty-seven; and, although the data is not at hand by which an accurate comparison can be made of the metal-throwing powers of the two artilleries, there is reason to believe that the total number of pieces with each army was about the same. At Gettysburg, General Meade's sixty-seven batteries were met by sixty-eight of the Confederates. Afterwards the number went on increasing until, when preparing for the final struggle in the campaign of 1865, the Army of Northern Virginia embraced eighty-one batteries in its various army corps.

In the arrangement of this artillery the same principles controlled as in the Army of the Potomac, in so far as to lead to forming battalions analogous to our brigades; but in other respects the practice of the two armies was very different. Just prior to the second Bull Run, August 29th–30th, 1862, forty-seven batteries of General Lee's army were attached to brigades and divisions, while twenty-six were held in reserve. This was long after brigade artillery had become a thing of the past in the Army of the Potomac; but, as to the reserve, the same organization was given it in each of the opposing forces at this time, that is, it embraced about one-third of all the field artillery.

One year after, when the Army of the Potomac met that of Northern Virginia at Gettysburg, the artillery reserve, having in the interval nearly vanished, (at Antietam it embraced but seven, at Fredericksburg but nine batteries,) was as large in the former as when first organized, while in the latter it had entirely disappeared. At this time, and afterwards, the Confederate artillery in this army was attached to divisions, each army corps having its own reserve. Here again there was a marked contrast, as divisional artillery was unknown in the Army of the Potomac after Chancellorsville.

It is proper to place on record the fact that the Confederates were the pioneers in the plan of artillery organization and administration at this time universal in Europe. They were the first to break up and do away with grand army reserves, distributing the artillery to divisions and retaining corps reserves only. Prussia and Austria followed after 1866 and France after 1870; and although the details of both organization and supply are more perfect in those armies than was possible in that of the Confederacy, still the prominent and more important features are those put into practical execution in the Army of Northern Virginia, under General Lee, early in 1863.

In the west we find that General Albert S. Johnson organized his army October 28th, 1861, in the same manner as McClellan on the Potomac; but afterwards the Confederates in that section had their artillery almost wholly distributed to brigades—a faulty system in a large army, delivering as it does piecemeal what should be a powerfully concentrated fire—and one which had been abandoned by the most important and best equipped armies on both sides. After General Johnson had given a proper direction to this matter, it is to be wondered at that this objectionable plan should have been resorted to, thus carrying the army backward instead of forward in organization. Whether or not General Beauregard's influence effected this change is not known; yet certain it is that his recommendations of March 4th, 1862, after he joined the western army, would, if acted upon favorably, have brought about that result. His proposition, in brief, was to assign to "each brigade of 2500 men one battery of six guns, either four smooth-bores and two howitzers, four rifles and two howitzers, or six rifle guns; to give to each grand division [corresponding to corps of Union army] as large an artillery reserve as practicable, and to attach to the staff of the general-in-chief a chief of artillery."

In Lieutenant-General J. C. Pemberton's command—Department of Mississippi and East Louisiana—as organized in April, 1863, there is not discernible any systematic distribution of the artillery, although most, but not all, of the brigades had one battery attached; some of the so-called divisions had artillery reserves, while others had not. The dispersed condition of this army may account for the want of system here manifest.

When General J. E. Johnston assumed command, after Pemberton's surrender, he distributed the batteries to brigades in all the infantry divisions, retaining one battalion of three batteries in reserve. The cavalry, numbering three small divisions, had but one battery, as shown by the returns; but it is inferred the reserve was to supply that or any other deficiency.

At Chickamauga, Bragg's artillery was distributed one battery to each brigade, except in Longstreet's corps from the Army of Northern Virginia, organized as already indicated. Of the forty-three batteries with the army, excluding the battalion of six batteries with Longstreet's corps not yet arrived, six were in reserve.

After Chickamauga, and previous to the battle of Chattanooga, November 23d to 25th, 1863, Bragg's army was organized into corps, and the artillery then distributed, in battalions of three batteries each, to divisions; seven batteries of the thirty-two with the army constituting a general reserve.

It will be seen that South as well as North, when necessity for and the great advantage of thorough organization became more apparent, the artillery was assigned in the principal armies to the larger commands, the batteries being arranged in battalions. This was an outgrowth of experience acquired in war, which sifts from crude and ill-digested notions the germs of good they contain. If proof were wanting that the true military idea had been seized upon, it will be found in the armies of Europe to-day, where briefer experience has rendered the adoption of the same principles of artillery organization for an active army universal.

CHAPTER IV.

ORGANIZATION—ARTILLERY RESERVES.

General Artillery Reserves have formed a feature of our active army organization at various times, commencing with the Revolution; but the opinions of military men have differed regarding their formation, management, and utility. The reason seems to be that this, as the light artillery brigade, being a creature of active campaign, is not, with us, thought of or provided for in peace, and its existence depends upon the particular views of each army commander, the magnitude of the operations, and the topographical features of the theatre of war.

We find the artillery of the Revolution was provided, in a limited degree, with this as with most other essentials to a respectable field service. As early as August 9th, 1776, General Washington apportioned, in orders, the artillery of the army to infantry brigades, giving each two pieces, while the remainder were directed to be kept parked near headquarters, under the eye of the colonel commanding that arm. In an estimate dated January 3d, 1777, this latter officer, now promoted to brigadier, submitted the following list of the ordnance necessary for the main army to take into the field the ensuing campaign: For seventeen infantry brigades, four pieces to each, total 68; to be 3-pounders, 4-pounders, and 6-pounders, brass; and for a reserve, two 24-pounders, four 12-pounders, four 8-inch and eight $5\frac{1}{2}$-inch howitzers, and twenty 3-pounders, 4-pounders, and 6-pounders, all of brass;—or, more than one-third of all the guns were kept directly under the control of the general. That these pieces could be brought up and put into action with effect, the battle at Monmouth gave proof, as did other contests in which the arm acted an honorable part. In general orders congratulating the army on the affair at Monmouth, the commander-in-chief remarked that he could "with pleasure inform General Knox and his officers that the enemy has done them the justice to acknowledge that no artillery could have been better served." Without doubt, however, it was not so much to act a part by throwing its weight at vital moments into the scale of battle that the reserve was expected to prove its utility in those days, as by becoming a base of supply for brigade artillery, or a depot where could be sent broken-down guns and matériel to be either repaired, or their places supplied with new. The master mind destined to teach men the true use of an artillery reserve, launched on the foe at the right point with the force of the thunderbolt, had not, at that time, received the impress of a first lesson in the military art.

Neither the second war with Great Britain nor the operations in Mexico furnish any examples of the use of artillery in the manner indicated. During the former, throughout two of its three campaigns the vital powers of the army seem to have been paralyzed by the want of military knowledge at the War Department, the incompetency of most of the officers who one after another were assigned to command, and the factious, unpatriotic opposition to the war on the part of one of the great political parties. In the Mexican war the forces engaged were too small to render necessary any artillery reserve for fighting purposes; and, besides, the efficiency of the horse and modern field batteries was first taught our commanders, the army and the country, in the Rio Grande valley. It is true that under General Taylor were several heavy pieces, 18-pounder guns and 24-pounder howitzers, which had not the mobility demanded of field artillery; pieces of position they might be called, but they in no sense formed, either in fact or design, an artillery reserve. Under General Scott, on the southern line, the siege train, equipped by the Ordnance Department and manned by its artificers, would, under ordinary circumstances, have formed part of the reserve; but in this instance, as in the other mentioned, there was nothing with the army which could properly be designated by that name.

Accompanying the Army of the Potomac when it took the field in 1862, there appeared, for the first time in this country, an artillery reserve placed upon a proper footing, to be used both for purposes of fighting and of supply, commanded by officers conversant with its functions, and capable of developing, organizing, and directing its powers.

Of the two hundred and ninety-nine guns which accompanied McClellan's army, one hundred were in this reserve, with calibres ranging from the 3-inch to the 20-pounder rifle. The first brigade of horse artillery (four batteries) formed part of the reserve, which embraced eighteen of the fifty-two batteries with the army. Its commander was a colonel, and aid-de-camp to the commanding general, appointed under the act of August 5th, 1861. To assist him there was a regular staff, though it was incomplete.

The operations attending the withdrawal of the troops from the Peninsula, reforming them for the Virginia and Maryland campaigns, well-nigh swept the reserve from existence. The first troops landed from the Peninsula were hurried forward to the Army of Virginia, and no attention paid to whether they had or had not their regularly assigned artillery; in this way many of its batteries were attached to and remained with divisions. New divisions absorbed many more. When preparing for the Antietam campaign it was found that some batteries had lost more or less guns, others were greatly deficient in men and horses, and a number were unserviceable from these causes combined. Batteries were supplied from the reserve to the corps and divisions deficient in guns, horses were taken from the baggage trains, and men transferred from the infantry; and by the time the army reached Antietam its artillery was in very fair condition, having been reorganized on the march and in the intervals of conflict. On this field the reserve embraced but seven of the sixty-two batteries with the army, the rest having disappeared as just indicated. The number of divisions had increased from the eight which accompanied McClellan to the Peninsula, to eighteen at Antietam, including the cavalry. These had all to be supplied, and it could only be done by reducing the number of batteries attached to the old divisions and to the artillery reserve.

Thus matters stood at the battle of Fredericksburg, where but nine of the sixty-nine batteries (two with siege guns being unattached) with the army constituted the reserve. The enemy was on the opposite side of the river; and, in order to control his movements, command the town of Fredericksburg, cover the throwing of the bridges and the crossing of the troops, a powerful and well-sustained artillery fire was necessary. To this end it was determined to temporarily attach to the artillery reserve some of the batteries of the divisions. This being done, they were grouped into four artillery divisions for the work before them, two being made up of seven, one of eight, and one of nine batteries. It may be remarked that many of these were 20-pounders and $4\frac{1}{2}$-inch rifles, thus demonstrating, as was done on many other occasions, the advisability of carrying heavy guns of position with every army in the field.

Prior to this battle General Burnside contemplated breaking up the artillery reserve, distributing its batteries to divisions of infantry and cavalry, half of which had but two batteries each; but the experience there acquired not only put an end to this, but brought out in stronger light than ever before the necessity of the commanding general retaining a respectable mass of artillery in his own hand to meet the possible exigencies of the conflict.

One of the specious arguments in favor of breaking up the reserve was, that if artillery *en masse* were needed, it could be obtained when the occasion arose by *withdrawing batteries from troops*. This theory was put to a practical test when, as mentioned, it became necessary to temporarily increase the reserve, while covering the army during its passage of the river in face of the enemy. The theory signally failed; many division commanders, although the guns were to be restored as the troops crossed, protested against their being taken for this short time, and declared they would not be responsible for the consequences. The batteries were, however, restored to the divisions, as had been stipulated they should be, and, as a result, eleven of the nineteen which debouched into the town were jammed together in the streets, idle spectators of the fight, obstructing the movements of other troops, and in many instances returning to the north bank without having fired a shot. The logic of this circumstance was to negative propositions for placing more artillery at the disposal of subordinate commanders when they could not use what they already had, yet were willing to make its temporary withdrawal a cause of embarrassment to the commanding general.

At Chancellorsville twelve of the seventy-one batteries were in the reserve, and among them were several siege batteries, which proved very efficient. The mismanagement here of the artillery, a fact for which the arm itself was not responsible, led to a return to first principles, and an augmentation of the reserve, which at Gettysburg, two months later, embraced twenty-two of the sixty-seven batteries present on the field—the proportion to the whole artillery that it bore when McClellan started for the Peninsula. But things did not stop here; the consolidation of March 23d, 1864, threw still other batteries into the reserve, and when the army moved—May 4th, 1864—on the Wilderness campaign, that organization embraced twenty-four of the fifty light batteries with the army, together with two regiments of foot artillery armed as infantry. This was by far the most complete organization the general artillery reserve ever had, and it was that to immediately precede its dissolution. The twenty-four batteries were arranged to brigades of six batteries each, fully appointed and well commanded, while the foot artillery served as escorts, guards, skilled workmen for the various duties devolving on that species of troops, and supplied on requisition details to keep the batteries full. But the campaign just opening was in a country with few and bad roads; it was therefore desirable to reduce to the utmost practicable limit the impedimenta; the fighting was in places where artillery could only with difficulty be manœuvred, or, rather, could not be manœuvred at all, and it was resolved to send all surplus guns back to Washington. The details of this reduction are given elsewhere. It suffices here to remark that its disappearance was short-lived, as, during the summer, it was partially resuscitated with as many as eleven batteries at one time; that the morning report of the Army of the Potomac, March 31st, 1865, shows the artillery reserve contained 35 officers, 1127 enlisted men, 47 guns, and some mortars; that on the 6th of April a brigadier-general was assigned to its command, and that before the brief campaign ended it embraced nineteen of the forty-two batteries actually with that army. .

As with other parts of the combatant arms, the most important service of the reserve was by hard blows to help beat the enemy, and this, early in its history, it did at Malvern Hill, where every gun was employed, and with such effect that it confessedly saved the army from serious disaster. At Antietam, Fredericksburg, and Gettysburg every battery present with the army was sent into action, and always at critical moments. The belief which, with many other erroneous ideas, prevailed at the beginning of the war, that a reserve was to be kept out of the battle, was, not figuratively speaking but in fact, effectually exploded by its shells at Malvern Hill, and its subsequent services in action sustained the reputation it there earned. If a particular point was to be defended as the key to the position, its guns were placed there; when, as we have seen was the case at Fredericksburg, bridges were to be thrown and the army crossed in presence of the enemy, it was the reserve artillery, augmented by batteries withdrawn if necessary from the troops, which covered the perilous undertaking. These facts set at rest the suspicion that this mass of artillery was, merely because of its designation, to play a secondary part on the field of battle—a suspicion founded on ignorance of the functions of the various parts of every army organized upon sound military principles, and of which the first in our service was the Army of the Potomac under McClellan.

Batteries attached to divisions and corps losing their efficiency, either from the want of men or matériel, the incompetency of their officers, or other casualties of service, were at once replaced from the reserve, thus keeping the army corps fully effective, and giving the broken-down batteries the necessary opportunity and supervision to restore them. In this way was maintained the efficiency of the artillery of the whole army; but its utility as a centre of supply for this purpose was apparently never appreciated by the army itself until after May 16th, 1864, when its batteries, with a diminished number of guns, were distributed to army corps. When, from the natural accidents of service, after this, batteries became run down in men or matériel, there was no satisfactory way for the corps to take care of them; they were accordingly sent to the army ammunition train, which was all that was left of the old reserve, to recuperate and be refitted. Thus this train became the nucleus around which a new reserve grew up, without special orders, and merely from the force of circumstances; it lacked, however, the well established administrative machinery of its predecessor, which led to delays in the performance of duties assigned it; but for this it was not responsible.

From its earliest organization the reserve was accompanied by an ammunition train, which was conspicuously useful on numerous occasions. At Malvern Hill its one hundred wagons supplied the guns engaged after (as was the case in many instances) their ammunition chests were emptied. The division trains had been mixed up with the baggage wagons, and sent away with them. Had it not been for this ammunition column many of the batteries would have been idle during a great part of the battle.

Though not to such a degree, the same trouble existed at Antietam, there being a great deficiency in the divisions of certain kinds of ammunition, which this column supplied. At Gettysburg the Third Corps left all its artillery ammunition behind, the Second Corps half its trains, and many others were, from similar or other causes, deficient in this essential item.

There had been formed while preparing for this campaign, and attached to the reserve, a special ammunition column containing twenty rounds per gun for every gun in the army over and above the number (two hundred and fifty rounds per gun) fixed by orders as the campaign supply. From this source was mainly drawn ammunition to meet the deficiencies mentioned, the disastrous consequences of which were in this manner luckily provided against.*

There were expended in the three days of this battle 32,781 rounds, averaging over 100 rounds per gun. Of this number many were lost by explosions or other accidents to limbers and caissons. The supply, as just seen, was 270 rounds per gun; hence there was sufficient left to fill the chests and enable the army to fight another battle. There was for a short time, during the progress of the fight, a fear that the ammunition would give out, caused by the large demands made by commanders who had left their trains, or part of them, behind. It was in this emergency that the special ammunition column supplied every requisition made upon it.

When the general reserve was broken up, in May, 1864, it was this column which was ordered to be retained, with a battalion of foot artillery, armed as infantry, for escort. Several Coehorn mortars—a species of cannon proving so useful during the progress of the campaign as to cause the number to be afterwards increased—were also retained with it. These formed the groundwork on which, as has been mentioned, a new artillery reserve grew up to vindicate the principle of this organization in a large army.

The establishment, fitting out, and maintenance of ammunition columns was a part of the duties of the reserve to which no glory attached. In time of peace, particularly, very little attention is

---

* This special ammunition train was organized by Brigadier-General Henry J. Hunt, chief of artillery of the army, upon his own motion, and without special orders to that effect. Upon his requesting it, the quartermaster of the Army of the Potomac furnished the wagons. General Meade knew nothing about it until some time afterwards. The intelligent foresight evinced in the formation of this train becomes apparent when we contemplate the situation at Gettysburg, where, owing to the fact that much ammunition with some of the commands was left behind in the hurry to arrive on the field, its absence might have led to serious embarrassment, not to say disastrous results.

given to these matters in our army; in war the machinery for their adjustment is complicated; yet they are of the first importance. In Europe this is not only well understood, but the practice is in accordance therewith, the arrangements for supplying ammunition to a battery being as clearly defined as is the organization of the battery itself. Under control of the artillery arm, through the ammunition columns and depots, there extends an unbroken chain of supply connecting the batteries in line of battle with the arsenals in their rear. With us, requisitions for ammunition have first to be submitted to one department, and, when obtained, turned over to another for transportation to the front. All ammunition should be transported in caissons, in charge of properly organized companies, and not, as with us, in ordinary army wagons. It was to attain this desirable end, at least partially, that all caissons were retained in May, 1864, when many of the reserve guns were sent to the rear. The chief of artillery with the army should have charge of these columns, the immediate commanders of which should be officers selected from that arm. In this way only can supplies under all circumstances, on the field of battle as elsewhere, be certainly provided when wanted.

In the Union armies other than that of the Potomac there was not the completeness of organization inaugurated by McClellan; hence in few of them is there found any trace of an artillery reserve. In the Army of the Ohio such an organization was not deemed necessary by either Buell or Rosecrans; but General Thomas, who relieved the latter October 19th, 1863, distributed eighteen of his batteries to divisions, while a general reserve embraced twelve more, including the six regular batteries with that army.

In the Confederate Army of Northern Virginia there was, as early as the Peninsula campaign, a large artillery reserve. It does not seem, however, to have well answered its purpose, as we are informed by one of the first artillery authorities of their service that this body, "not being in intimate relation with the infantry, which always develops the situation, and being invariably put on the march either behind the infantry commands or on some road to itself, was never promptly available on an emergency. Indeed, if the history of the general reserve artillery during its entire existence be investigated, it will be found that, although excellent in material and comparatively so in equip-

ment, the service that it rendered was greatly disproportionate to its strength." It is not to be wondered at, therefore, that in February, 1863, all the reserve, except two battalions aggregating six batteries, were assigned to corps, and that when a new corps was formed in June of that year these two battalions were taken away and the general reserve broken up, never to reappear. Each army corps had its own train to which disabled guns were sent, from which spare parts were supplied, and which thus acted for the corps the part that· the general reserve train is supposed to perform for all the corps of the army.

The similarity of artillery organization adopted by the Confederates at this time to that now practiced in Europe may be judged of by the following: At Gettysburg, each division of General Lee's army had attached to it an artillery battalion of three or four batteries, while two battalions formed the corps reserve; in the German army, each division of infantry has a division of artillery of three or four batteries, and the corps artillery (called corps reserve with us) embraces two divisions of three batteries each; in the English army, each infantry division has attached three batteries, and the corps artillery embraces five batteries; the same principles govern in Austria and Italy; and in all these armies, as in that of Northern Virginia, there is no general artillery reserve.

It must not be accepted from what precedes that the artillery organization of the Army of Northern Virginia was more in consonance with advanced military ideas than was that of the Army of the Potomac. Judged only by the present organization of European armies, this might be conceded; but, on the other hand, there are reasons disassociated from any army, and based on general principles, for maintaining a general artillery reserve.

The extended fronts of modern lines of battle render rapid concentration at a decisive point, when the enemy has shown his hand, the natural method of attack. "After a defensive army has developed its strength, and the weak parts of its line have been ascertained, a powerful reserve artillery will have little difficulty in bringing about a preponderating cross or enfilade fire·upon an exposed flank already engaged in front, or upon one or more points of a defensive line, that will inevitably cause disaster." The only certain way to have artillery ready when wanted, as here described, is to have it massed under the direct control of the commanding general. Division and corps commanders view with

ORGANIZATION—ARTILLERY RESERVES.

alarm any attempts to take from them their batteries in time of action—witness Fredericksburg!—while to the practical impossibility of withdrawing artillery from the corps, and bringing it to bear upon the decisive point of attack, was attributed by some of the ablest generals of the Confederacy the failure of Pickett's charge at Gettysburg.

From the success attending the employment of the German artillery in the war of 1870–'71, it seems to be a widely accepted principle that the entire artillery of the main body ought to be kept at the head of the columns and brought up at the very commencement of an attack, when all the guns should go at once into action—the objects to be attained being to prevent the enemy destroying the artillery in detail as it forms, and also by numbers and concentration of fire to obtain ascendency of the latter as quickly as possible.

It is very desirable that these objects be attained; but it is not admitted that this is the only proper method, nor must we lose sight of other important duties of the artillery arm. Nothing is more fallacious than to suppose that, a certain tactical principle having been practiced successfully, it must needs prove equally so under all other circumstances; and the brilliant movements of the artillery in that war are not likely to prove an exception when attempted against a formidable and enterprising foe.*

Bringing from column into line to the front the large mass of artillery takes time, and the mass extends over considerable ground, where it is but very inadequately protected until the infantry in rear arrives; thus a fearless and energetic enemy is given an opportunity of which he would not be slow to avail himself. When the other troops arrive the very length of line occupied by the artillery may seriously impede their deployment, and cause them to mask the guns while doing so. It offers from the first a conspicuous object for the concentrated fire of the enemy; essays what must always be considered the hazardous experiment of leaving the general empty-handed to meet the critical phases of battle; and even though it be possible, when an emergency

---

* What might not the French have accomplished had they, at 10 o'clock A. M., September 1st, 1870, energetically attacked the poorly supported mass of guns, with the defile of St. Albert at its back, on the fatal field of Sedan! The desperate valor of Ducrot's last effort with the cavalry came four hours too late!

arises, to take from corps and divisions to supply new demands elsewhere in action, it would at best be using troops partially exhausted, while those from a general reserve would be fresher for their work. It is one of the first tactical principles in the use of the arm that artillery should avail itself of accidents of the ground, adding by the position taken up to the effectiveness of its fire. If it be massed regardless of this principle, much of its power will be sacrificed.

In every carefully selected line of battle there will be positions of importance—key points—the successful defense of, or attack on, which will decide the conflict. These should be both attacked and defended by heavier guns, which in every well-appointed reserve forms part of its armament. When bridges have to be thrown or rivers otherwise crossed in face of the enemy, these guns, even if they cannot properly be attached to troops, will be found, if not indispensable, at least greatly to facilitate the difficult operation.

Let, then, corps and division artillery come into action with their respective commands, and a reserve, under the direct control of the commanding general, be kept free to act at his bidding at the supreme moment of the battle.*

Napoleon first taught the tactical use and power of this organization. Having developed the strength and position of his adversary, he brought up at the right time and place the artillery reserve to sweep everything before it, preparatory to advancing a strong column to penetrate and roll up the enemy's line. These tactics were little practiced during the Civil war, the nearest approach to it being the Confederate attack of July 3d at Gettysburg; but this was lacking in the elements which made Napoleon's tactics formidable, viz., a sweeping of the ground at which the assault was to be made by a powerful and sustained fire from fresh masses of artillery held in reserve for this very purpose.

Rapidity and precision of modern fire render future successful attacks in column improbable; but the extended line in which the column is now deployed will offer opportunities for decisive results if promptly taken advantage of, and artillery must be at

---

* At the battle of Gravelotte, Prince Frederic Charles, commanding the Second Army, held the *corps* artillery of the Third Army Corps directly under his orders as an artillery reserve.

hand to do the work. This can certainly be depended upon only when held at the commander's disposal.

In the United States there is another than the purely tactical reason here given for the organization of an artillery reserve in a large army like that of the Potomac. It arises from considerations affecting the composition of such armies. From necessity they are composed of volunteers, with a little leaven from the regular army to set an example in discipline and in methods of administration. A reserve in such an army, under an efficient officer, will be an absolutely necessary source whence supplies may be drawn, including replenished and properly-equipped batteries, to take the places of those that have been run down and knocked to pieces. It is also necessary in such an army that the commanding general should have at his bidding and immediately under his control a powerful weapon, such as this is, to throw upon the vital point when the latter is developed, either to pave the way for piercing the enemy's line, or to repel his onslaught.

If we are to abandon well-established principles and adopt the practices, at present in high repute, of certain military nations, without considering the different circumstances under which our armies are raised and take the field, it is difficult to indicate at what point in the model system we should commence to copy. If it be not at the fountain-head—the plan for recruitment, by which each man is compelled to take his turn with the colors—the result may not be the same with us as with those who lay the foundation for success in that true principle of democracy—universal service in the ranks of the army.

CHAPTER V.

ADMINISTRATION.

From the organization of the colonial forces, in 1775, the artillery took and maintained an advanced position. Numerous artillery companies, formed in the principal cities, and invariably composed of the first young men of the community, gave respectability to the arm, prestige to its service, and a personnel far above the average in character, intelligence, and professional attainments. The question of the relative rank of its officers with those of the infantry and cavalry had been fought over in England, and decided, in 1751, in favor of the artillery. Since then the superior scientific knowledge of its commissioned personnel in the mother country had raised that arm still higher in its own and in the estimation of others; while in the colonies, due to causes just mentioned, it was regarded as a more elevated branch of service than any except the engineers. There was no aristocracy. The high-born commissioned gentlemen of the English infantry and cavalry, whose deeds of bravery lent honor to the troops they led, and gave eclat to those services, were not to be found among the forces assembled to oppose them, where, as regards birth, all, in theory at least, stood on the same plane, and where, therefore, other things being equal, the better education of the artillery officers not unnaturally raised that branch of service in public esteem. Colonel Gridley, commander of the first artillery regiment, was the most accomplished and experienced artillerist and engineer in the colonies, and, though too old for the duty, his selection in the first instance evinces the belief which prevailed—that to be a competent artillery officer required both attainments and acknowledged ability.

The provisions of Articles XLVIII and XLIX of War, adopted by the continental Congress June 30th, 1775, strengthens this general view of the subject. It was declared by the former that "all officers, conductors, gunners, matrosses, drivers, or any other persons whatsoever receiving pay or hire in the service of the continental artillery, shall be governed by the aforesaid rules and articles, and shall be subject to be tried by courts-martial, in like manner with the officers and soldiers of the continental troops;" and by the latter, that "for differences arising amongst themselves, or in matters relating solely to their own corps, the courts-martial may be composed of their own officers; but where a sufficient number of such officers cannot be assembled, or in matters wherein other corps are interested, the officers of artillery shall sit in courts-martial with the officers of the other corps." This language might leave in doubt whether officers of artillery were considered too good, or not quite good enough, to sit on courts-martial with those of other corps. When made part of the English code, whence they were transcribed bodily into our own, they were intended to establish that officers of artillery were as good as those of other arms—a fact which the infantry and cavalry had strenuously denied. The origin and significance of the law was, however, when adopted by the continental Congress, either misunderstood or lost sight of, and an interpretation given it the reverse of what was originally intended—the artillery was placed a little above the others. The air of superiority thereby engendered was no doubt disagreeable. To curb their pride and let them know their true position, Congress, in the revised Articles of War adopted September 30th, 1776, provided that, when sitting on courts-martial with those of other corps, officers of the artillery should take "rank according to the dates of their respective commissions, and *no otherwise.*"

That the artillery was not unconscious of its position there is abundant evidence. The fact crops out in the correspondence of the times, particularly of its own members, and was encouraged in various ways by the Revolutionary Government. When the provincial Congress of New York authorized Captain (afterwards Colonel) Lamb to raise a company of artillery, and then resolved to attach the company to McDougall's regiment, the sturdy captain objected "that it placed the artillery on a level with the infantry—a practice unprecedented in any service," and thereupon tendered his resignation. This was not accepted, but, instead, the obnoxious resolution was repealed. In his estimates Colonel Pickering, when quartermaster-general, inserted the items forage and horses for captains of artillery, who, at least until 1782, were mounted at Government expense—a consideration shown these officers, the quartermaster-general remarked, based not on law, but on unbroken custom, which he was not at liberty to disregard.

The pay of the artillery, established by Congress, was better than that of either the infantry or cavalry. The first adjustment of the pay of the army provided, among other things: Per month, captain of infantry, $20; of artillery, $26⅔;—lieutenant of infantry, $13⅓; of artillery, $18⅓;—sergeant of infantry, $8; of artillery, $8½;—private of infantry, $6⅔; of artillery (matross), $6⅛. When, May 27th, 1778, the different arms of service were first uniformly organized, the pay of certain officers was established as follows: Per month, colonel of artillery, $100; of cavalry, $93¾; of infantry, $75;—major of artillery, $62½; of cavalry, $60; of infantry, $50;—a surgeon of artillery, $75; of cavalry and infantry, each $60.

A superiority claimed by the members of a particular branch of service, and recognized by Congress, could not have been maintained without something of solid merit to rest upon. The foundation consisted in (1) a department controlled by a single directing mind, intelligent, fertile in resources, imbued with a love of the special duties of the arm; (2) excellent subordinate officers, any one of whom was known to be equal to the performance of any duty the exigencies of service might require. There was, besides, even among the best informed people, a very general ignorance of the art and science of artillery, which no doubt added to the seeming importance of those versed in what was generally considered occult. Referring to the arrival of a captain of artillery with his company *en route* to join in Montgomery's invasion of Canada, Schuyler wrote to the commander-in-chief: "I am glad he has arrived, as there was not in this whole department a single person who understood the business."

Regarding the qualifications of the personnel, Knox wrote: "No officer should be appointed to the artillery who does not possess a proper knowledge of the mathematics and other necessary abilities for the nature of the service." Not only were they able to point and fire guns, but—down at least to captains, inclusive—they were conversant with the laboratory arts, knew enough of engineering to build a work adapted to the site, and place the guns therein advantageously for defense.

Early in the war the necessity of procuring, for the service of the colonies, scientific engineers was made manifest, and many there were who, ignorant of the capacity of our own artillery officers, imagined it would be necessary to secure, as well, officers of experience in that department. To this end, Mr. Silas Deane, the agent of the colonies at Paris, entered into negotiations with several artillerists of the French army. Benjamin Franklin, before leaving this country as one of the commissioners at that capital, had also entered into correspondence on the subject. On June 10th, 1776, Barbue Dubourg wrote the distinguished patriot:

"Many military men agree in thinking that the colonies have more need of artillerymen than of engineers. This is particularly so with the most capable judge in Europe, the Count De St. Germain. Mr. De Gribeauval, lieutenant-general of the King's armies and director-general of artillery, thinks you ought to have three officers of that arm: one to be chief, and set the whole going, one to direct in the northern and one in the southern colonies. For chief he has fixed his eye, with St. Germain, upon Mr. Du Coudray, whose talents in Corsica raised him over one hundred and eighty seniors."

Upon these flattering recommendations Du Coudray was accordingly employed to collect the cannon, ammunition, arms, and clothing purchased by the colonies pending the settlement of the terms on which he could enter their service. (See Appendix B [1].) The arrival of this gentleman with a retinue of officers on the 20th of April, 1777, produced an explosion in the army which threatened serious consequences, several of the first officers, including Knox, Sullivan, and Greene, protesting to the President against the confirmation of the Deane-Coudray compact in such vigorous language that Congress voted their letters to be an infringement on the liberties of the people, as tending to influence the decisions of that body, and called upon the offenders to apologize for so "singular an impropriety." This was not done, however; the pressure brought to bear was too strong for Congress to resist, and the compact was disapproved, on the ground that Mr. Deane had exceeded his authority. It was at this time that General Washington, writing to the President of Congress, spoke of Knox as "one of the most valuable officers in the service, a man of great military reading, sound judgment, and clear conceptions, and who, combating almost innumerable difficulties in the department he fills, has placed the artillery upon a footing that does him the greatest honor." From this time on there was no attempt made to supplant the commander of the artillery in the position which, according to the highest authority in the land, he was so eminently qualified to fill, or to disturb by foreign influences the workings of a department which, at that time and afterwards, met every demand of service promptly and efficiently.

The administration of artillery affairs will, for convenience of arrangement and clearness of thought, be considered under the following heads: (1) Instruction. (2) Duties: (A) technical; (B) as an arm of service. (3) Duties of the chief of artillery in the field.

INSTRUCTION.

Aside from the experience acquired in war, this may be considered under three heads: First, Instruction at Posts; second, Instruction at Schools; and third, Practice-Firing. The first is both (A) practical, and (B) theoretical. The second embraces (C) schools for foot artillery, and (D) the field batteries.

INSTRUCTION AT POSTS: (A) PRACTICAL.

During the Revolutionary war the experience of the field supplied that practical instruction which enabled the artillery to come to the front rank in the army. Aside, however, from the mere duties of the gunner—pointing and firing the piece—the commander of that arm and many of his officers improved every opportunity to elevate their branch of service by both experiment and research, all conducted with a view to rendering themselves and those under their command more efficient in the field. Until February, 1778, the commander of the artillery had charge of the procuring all arms and stores, *i. e.*, warlike matériel. In this service he employed many civilians, some companies of artificers, and such artillery officers as were available and whose services could be thus utilized to advantage. Although nothing elaborate was attempted in those primitive times, the experience of all kinds gained by artillery officers was such as to make them thoroughly efficient in their specialty.

Although the establishment (1778) of the department of commissary-general of military stores took from the artillery the manufacture of matériel and the charge of the arsenals, the necessity for schooling of this kind for officers of that arm was fully appreciated; and accordingly, the next year, February 13th, 1779, it was resolved by Congress "that, when it shall be thought necessary, the commanding officer of artillery shall send officers of artillery to visit the laboratories, foundries, and manufactories, to the intent that they may thereby gain an insight into the mechanical branches of their profession. And such number of artillery officers as, in the opinion of the commanding officer of artillery, with the concurrence of the commander-in-chief, can be spared from their duties in the field, shall, at every convenient season, be stationed at all or any of the principal laboratories, to be instructed in the laboratory art, that a knowledge thereof may be disseminated through the corps." The same resolution of Congress provided for a surveyor of ordnance, to be taken from the colonels of artillery. This officer was really an inspector of artillery manufactories and matériel, and the creation of this office again brought these matters under the surveillance of the commander of that arm, who was thus in fact, though not in name, made chief of artillery technical affairs.

From this time on, the manufacture, inspection, and acceptance of artillery matériel were duties performed by artillery and ordnance officers acting jointly; the manufacture, however, being almost exclusively intrusted to the latter, under instructions prescribed by General Knox. It is deserving of notice and remembrance that, in the midst of campaigns, many artillery officers of the Revolution not only practiced their profession in the field, but in the inclement seasons supplemented the knowledge there acquired by researches in the laboratory and workshop. In this way practice and theory went hand in hand. The result was that no branch of the army stood so high, professionally, at the end of that war as did the artillery.

From the close of the Revolution until the end of the eighteenth century the artillery did little else than infantry duty. It was armed as infantry even when manning the small field pieces which were taken into the Indian country. What technical duties it was called upon to perform in this interval, the writer has not been able to determine. It is presumed, however, that they were limited to making or repairing carriages. Certainly the requirements of the service were very meagre, and all artillery supplies were obtained, by contract, under the direct orders either of the Secretary of War, or of the Treasury Department. If artillery officers had anything to do with the matter, it was doubtless to act as inspectors, the necessity for which, in order that uniformity might be introduced, was so generally recognized, that, when the army was augmented in anticipation of war with France, in 1798, an inspector of artillery for the army was authorized—to be taken from the artillery arm. He was the legitimate successor to the surveyor of ordnance of 1779, although Congress had defined the duties of the latter but not those of the inspector, which were left to be regulated by the War Department. Colonel Louis Tousard, commanding the Second Regiment of artillerists and engineers, was, April 14th, 1801, appointed inspector of artillery, his commission dating back to May 26th, 1800, when, it is presumed, he formally assumed the function of the office, although prior even to this date he had acted as inspector, as appears from his work, The Artillerist's Companion. His duties were: (1) to take an inventory of all ordnance and ordnance stores, note where kept, and see that they were properly cared for; (2) inspect all artillery matériel after manufacture; (3) devise models for all such matériel, and allow no deviation therefrom in construction. Scarcely had Colonel Tousard assumed the direction of affairs when the reduction of the army, March 16th, 1802, retired him from active service. Although it was questioned by some of the best authorities whether that act abolished the office of inspector of artillery, it was held by the War Department that it did.

The law reducing and reorganizing the army provided eight artificers to each artillery company, whereas there were only four each of sergeants and corporals; moreover, the pay of each artificer was $10 per month, the same as that of a cadet and more than a sergeant-major. The object of this apparently singular provision was to convert each artillery post into a small arsenal, where would be manufactured all the gun carriages and other artillery matériel required in service, except the guns and projectiles; hence the proportionately great number of mechanics and their comparatively very high pay. These mechanics continued in service until the reorganization of March 30th, 1814, although in the meantime the ordnance department had assumed their functions as constructors of artillery matériel.

It must not be presumed for a moment that the services performed by these artificers were merely nominal. This was far from being the case. The records of the War Department covering this period are, to a great extent, preserved; and they evince that at all the posts garrisoned by artillery, either in the interior or on the sea-board, the manufacture of matériel of all kinds, except that of the foundry, was very generally carried on, particularly under the business-like administration of Secretary Dearborn. Although this enabled officers to acquire valuable practical experience, it of necessity led to great diversity in constructing the same articles, as Colonel Burbeck had never, like Tousard, been authorized and directed to prepare working models and then to see that they were adhered to.

With the organization of the ordnance department the labor devolving on the artillerists, and for performing which the artificers had been provided, was transferred to that department, one of the duties of the commissary-general of ordnance being "to direct the construction of all carriages, and every apparatus for ordnance, for garrison and field service, and all ammunition wagons, pontons, and travelling forges." The artificers were indeed retained until the reducing act of March 30th, 1814, but their occupation was gone, and the officers were deprived of the practical experience secured them by the law of 1802.

From 1802 until May 14th, 1812, when the ordnance department was organized, artillery officers had in charge, as part of their practical duties, the manufacture of whatsoever matériel the service required at their various stations. The colonel of the regiment of artillerists was the principal, though by no means the only, inspector of artillery, having in that capacity succeeded to the duties formerly devolving on Colonel Tousard.

From the date of the establishment of this department until 1821, when it was merged in the artillery, the practical duties of the latter were confined, as at present, to taking care of and manœuvring their guns on the field or elsewhere, and to drills at their posts. It was made the business of the inspectors-general of the army, among other things, to report half-yearly the progress made by each regiment or corps in military discipline in general, and particularly in knowledge of the evolutions prescribed for the practice of the troops—whether the officers knew their duties, and were able and willing to perform them. There was during this time no uniform system of artillery matériel. The text-books authorized were meagre in detail; so it is fair to infer that the course of practical instruction for the artillery, from the end of the war of 1812 until the reorganization of 1821, was very limited.

It was the wish of Secretary Calhoun to place the artillery in this country on something like the same plane it occupied in

Europe. To this end, under his supervision, the ordnance department was merged in the artillery at the reorganization mentioned. This was maintained until the partial re-establishment of that department in 1832, and its final resuscitation as a staff corps of the army in 1838; for, although under the provisions of the act of 1832 lieutenants of artillery alone were eligible for detached service with the ordnance, it was not the practice after 1838 to detail them on that service. In the meantime other influences had been brought to bear in the matter of artillery instruction. The school of practice at Fortress Monroe, to which reference will hereafter be made, was one. Lieutenant Daniel Tyler of the artillery had, in 1829, secured complete drawings of the French stock-trail system of gun carriage, limber, caisson, &c. In 1830 several were constructed, and that series of experiments begun which resulted in the adoption of the system of artillery substantially as it exists to-day.

From the date of breaking up the artillery school of practice, in 1836, at the beginning of the Seminole war, down to the Mexican war, practical instruction was confined, of necessity, to drills with various kinds of old-fashioned artillery with which, in limited quantities, the army was supplied. But there was inaugurated during this period a system of instruction which, for practical benefits, were it properly carried out, could not be surpassed. Reference is here made to artillery target practice, first in our service enjoined and regulated by General Orders No. 21, series of 1842, Adjutant-General's Office. The provisions of this order will be found embraced in paragraphs 72 to 85, inclusive, Regulations of 1847, and, with slight modifications, paragraphs 57 to 70, Regulations of 1863. Article XXXVII, of Regulations of 1881, contains the rules of artillery practice originally adopted in 1842, with all subsequent modifications. However slight may have been the facilities for this practice, it cannot be doubted that the institution of the system of firing at targets was most important. The practical value of the experience thus acquired, if the firing be conducted properly, can scarcely be overestimated; and it may be looked upon as second to no other means of acquiring valuable knowledge now open to the artillery arm.

At the date of the Mexican war the new system of field artillery, based upon the researches of Lieutenant Tyler, before mentioned, supplemented by those of numerous artillery and ordnance boards, had become familiar to the army. The labors of that officer, of these boards, and of the distinguished head of the ordnance department, Colonel Bomford, resulted in supplying, also, about the same time, new siege and sea-coast armaments. In 1851 tactics for mountain and heavy artillery were also supplied the service, so that the ten years from 1850 to 1860 were more favorable for practical instruction of artillery at posts than any previous equal interval had been. More attention was directed to the subject by the authorities than before, and the re-establishment of the artillery school of practice in 1857 was an encouraging step. This was followed May 9th, 1859, by the promulgation of General Orders No. 10, Adjutant-General's Office, directing the establishment of a more complete and systematic course of practical and theoretical instruction. It failed of any useful purpose, for the reason that thereby the artillery was scattered over the interior of the continent, and, as a result, experience obtained under the newly-inaugurated system was of little value. The scattering of the arm, the field batteries especially, was particularly unfortunate; nor did more practical good result to those companies serving as infantry at posts which, by the order, were organized as artillery schools of instruction. One provision of this order, however, deserves particular notice; and if ever any system of instruction is to be made of value, it will be by enforcing its requirements. The feature here referred to was the appointment of *inspectors of artillery*, whose duties were, under the direction of the general-in-chief, to inspect periodically (at least once a year,) the artillery within the geographical limits assigned them. The inspection embraced a thorough examination into the proficiency of every company officer in the practice as well as theory of the arm, and the result was reported through regular channels to the adjutant-general of the army. Another feature of the system of instruction provided for an annual change between the companies on the sea-coast and those stationed at the field artillery schools, one-third of the whole changing yearly. Whether or not this could have been carried into practical execution is not known, but it is doubtful; the Civil war, however, put an end to the scheme.

After the war, in 1866, one of the first duties performed by the permanent artillery board convened by General Orders No. 16, Adjutant-General's Office, March 12th of that year, was to submit one project for the re-establishment for the second time of the artillery school of practice at Fortress Monroe, and another for instruction at the various posts occupied by the artillery. The result will be considered when treating of theoretical instruction. For the present it suffices to state that General Orders No. 10, of 1859, was, so far as field artillery was concerned, partially revived, not, however, upon the recommendation of the permanent artillery board. It is, for all practical purposes, that which governs in the artillery to-day. It has been shown to be wanting in nearly every feature which would render it efficient as a course of practical instruction for that arm of service.

INSTRUCTION AT POSTS: (B) THEORETICAL.

If we except the study of tactics required of all arms, there does not appear to have been any course of theoretical instruction prescribed for the artillery previous to that promulgated in General Orders No. 10, of 1859. Efforts, though feeble in their nature, had before been made to keep up an appearance of instruction; but in this order, for the first time, was there a course of studies prescribed. A consideration of those paragraphs affecting the field artillery will for the present be deferred, and only those referring to the foot artillery will now be noticed.

For this branch the order provided: "At each artillery station there will be established a thorough system of instruction, theoretical and practical, in the more essential elements of the artillery service. At the fortifications it will necessarily be confined, for most part, to heavy artillery; but in every case it will be carried to all the duties of the arm which the means at hand will permit, including those of the laboratory."

The following named text-books were designated: (1) Instruction for Field Artillery; (2) Instruction for Heavy Artillery; (3) Ordnance Manual; (4) Aide Mémoire d'Artillerie.

Recitations were to be had twice a week, work in laboratory one day per week, the whole under supervision of the commanding officer, either directly or through some officer designated by him. No account was rendered by commanding officers of the nature and extent of recitations. The only reports called for were those of the artillery inspectors.

It is not to be expected that any project for instruction in any part of the army will be perfect at first; the aim of those having these matters in charge is to have them grow in excellence. It is presumed that the present system would have been no exception to this rule, but, as previously mentioned, the breaking out of the Civil war suspended its operation during several years. When it reappeared, in 1866, there were some modifications in the original plan. Instead of the commanding officer of each post being the instructor, this duty was transferred to the commanders of batteries, supervised in each regiment by the colonel, who was directed to require quarterly reports to be made by battery commanders of (1) means of instruction at posts; (2) progress and kind of instruction given; (3) numbers and dates of drills, exercises, and recitations—the colonels to forward abstracts of these reports direct to the headquarters of the army. The text-books prescribed were: (1) Parts I and II, Instruction Field Artillery; (2) Heavy Artillery Tactics; (3) Gibbon's Artillerist's Manual; (4) Roberts' Hand-book of Artillery; (5) The Ordnance Manual. The handbook was intended for the use of non-commissioned officers and enlisted men; and it is worthy of remark that the order in question (General Orders No. 67, of 1866) was the first to provide a theoretical course for the rank and file of the regular artillery, their instruction, in all preceding orders covering the subject-matter, having only in general terms been enjoined upon their officers. It was intended by the board which submitted projects for the artillery school at Fortress Monroe, and for instruction at posts, that the former should be supplementary to the latter, and that the two should be so arranged as to insure the progress of officers at posts equally as at the artillery school. It was not contemplated that the prescribed course of instruction at the former would remain in force longer than two years, when it was expected that a revised course would be adopted, thus maintaining the studies of artillery officers at posts abreast with the progress of the age. No attempt has been made to carry this plan into execution. The course of study has been changed very little since 1866.

In 1876 the new field artillery tactics were substituted for Parts I and II of the old, and in 1880 Tidball's Manual of Heavy Artillery was prescribed as a text-book for artillery troops garrisoning the sea-coast forts. It may be objected to these books—our field artillery tactics—Tidball's, Gibbon's, the Ordnance Manuals, and Roberts' Hand-book—that they treat in great measure of antiquated matériel; and while this is true as regards some of them, it is also true that a thorough study of these books would give the best artillerist many practical hints; but, with any text-books that could be devised, it is doubtful if the present system of instruction is capable of accomplishing anything of great value. The method contemplated in 1859, to insure an execution of the orders of the War Department, was to have inspectors, officers of rank in the artillery, visit the posts and personally examine into the proficiency of every company officer. The plan adopted in 1866 to secure the same object, and which still governs, was a system of *paper inspections, i. e.*, quarterly reports of instruction and progress. The former of these two plans, *if intrusted to competent inspectors*, sustained as they should be, was capable of accomplishing something creditable. The latter has not been, nor will it ever be, of great practical utility. What is needed to give vitality to the subject of instruction at posts is, first, a course of study which keeps the officers up with the improvements of the times; second, that artillery inspectors visit and examine, find out and report upon the practical and theoretical knowledge of every officer. *One active and capable inspector would have done the artillery more good, and have given the authorities a juster insight into the condition of the matériel and the acquirements of the personnel, than all the quarterly reports that have ever been written.*

INSTRUCTION: (C) SCHOOLS FOR FOOT ARTILLERY.

The establishment of artillery schools was first suggested, in our service, in a letter written by Colonel Henry Knox, September 27th, 1776, to a congressional committee at the time visiting army headquarters. Among other recommendations having in view the efficiency of the arm of which he was the head, was the following: "As officers can never act with confidence until they are masters of their profession, an academy established upon a liberal plan would be of the utmost service to the continent, where the whole theory and practice of fortification and gunnery should be taught; to be nearly the same as that at Woolwich, making allowance for the difference of circumstances—a place to which our enemies are indebted for the superiority of their artillery to all who have opposed them." Although the academy was not established during that war, proof is here given that early in the lifetime of the artillery in this country the necessity for study by an officer of that arm was recognized, and, in providing that officers should visit laboratories, workshops, and arsenals, when they could be spared from other duties, an important movement was made in the interests of efficiency. In the midst of campaigns, when experience was every year impressing deeply on the mind those invaluable lessons which unaided theory in vain essays to teach, officers of artillery were never allowed to forget that the profoundest knowledge is acquired by learning first the theory and then practicing the details of their profession.

Attaching cadets to the regiment of artillerists and engineers in 1794 was doubtless the first attempt to establish anything like a course of instruction for that arm; but it is generally admitted to have been a very imperfect scheme, and productive of no practical benefit, except to demonstrate the inherent weakness of a travelling military academy, or one without a thoroughly complete organization. Referring to this subject, the Secretary of War, in letter dated June 28th, 1798, said: "It was supposed that these cadets would form a nursery from which qualified officers might be drawn to fill vacancies; but it must occur that, without proper masters to teach them the sciences necessary to the engineers and artillerists, this nursery can produce no valuable plants." It is not intended here to trace the origin of our military academy. That has been done by others. It suffices to say that the provisions of law authorizing the appointment of cadets continued to be practically as unsatisfactory in results as at the time mentioned by Secretary McHenry, until the corps of engineers, constituting a military academy, was organized in 1802, and had placed at its head that accomplished scholar and soldier, Colonel Jonathan Williams. Not even the talents and address of Colonel Williams could, however, speedily put the school on a respectable and satisfactory footing, and it was not until after the war of 1812, when cadets were appointed, not in the artillery and engineers alone, but in all branches of service, and attached to the academy for instruction, that the latter was started on its distinguished career as a *preliminary* military and scientific institution.

It was soon discovered that it did not suffice that cadets pass through the course at West Point; it was found that they were then only prepared to begin in earnest the practical duties of their profession. The advantages of concentration, to insure uniformity of instruction and a higher degree of discipline among the troops, were also speedily recognized. These two considerations were mainly instrumental in causing to be established at Fortress Monroe a practical school for artillery. This was effected by Orders No. 18, dated Adjutant-General's Office, Washington, April 5th, 1824, which directed that eleven companies of artillery should be stationed at that fortress, the whole to constitute a "corps for instruction," the companies to be detached from the several regiments. A colonel was placed in command. He was assisted by a lieutenant-colonel and a major, one director and one assistant director of artillery, one instructor and one assistant instructor of mathematics. These officers formed the staff of the school. Concerning this institution, the general-in-chief remarked, in 1825, one year after its establishment:

"As a remedy for the evil resulting from its dispersed condition, the artillery arm has, in the school of practice at Fortress Monroe, a most favorable earnest of the advantages that may be expected from concentration. Among the numerous benefits to be derived from the institution, there appears to me none more important than those to be reaped by the graduates of the military academy, in the incipient formation of their ideas and character with reference to the practical duties of their profession. Our commissioned ranks are periodically recruited from this source—young men of high moral worth and scientific attainment; and sanguine hopes have been entertained that on this fundamental source of excellence a military establishment would be formed for the Nation to which it might look with confidence and pride for those attributes on which, in a future exigency, its glory and perhaps its safety might depend. It seems to be, however, almost in vain that military education should be fostered, if it terminate with the course of studies at West Point; and a school of practice has been anxiously looked for as a supplemental institution, in which the theoretic instruction of the academic graduate might be applied with good effect to the practical duties and relations of the military service."

In accordance with these views, the cadets assigned to the artillery were, after the organization of the school, sent to that institution for a practical course before joining their regiments. In this view of the subject the West Point education was considered in its true light, viz., *as a preparatory course of training, fitting those who had enjoyed its benefits for beginning, under favorable auspices, the practical life they would be called upon to pursue in the army.* To educate a man in four years is an impossibility. To give him in that time the *foundation* for an education is entirely feasible. That is what West Point then did and continues to do. Hence the necessity that existed and always will exist for supplemental courses of instruction, both practical and theoretical; for the science and art of war are progressive, essentially practical, and he who is content to stand still will fall rapidly to the rear out of sight. Special schools are as necessary for our officers, élèves of West Point, as is sea service to the graduate of the naval academy, or law and medical practice to the graduates of our colleges who adopt those professions. None of these schools give young men, however great their aptitude or talents, a practical knowledge of professions evolved from centuries of experience and study of details. There is no royal road to learning for the practical artillerist. He must have instruction in his specialty; and, for foot artillery, this can, perhaps, best be given in our service at a single school, where the necessary matériel can be collected, expenditures economized, and the course made complete and thorough. If, when thus established and made efficient, the studies and practice at this school be brought into harmony with the instruction which officers receive at posts, the whole being supervised by an adequate inspectorship, the hope can be rationally indulged that the artillery arm may, in so far as its disjointed organization will permit, enter upon a career of professional efficiency honorable to itself and reflecting credit upon the country.

These seem to have been the views of Mr. Calhoun and his successors in the War Department, under whose fostering care the school of practice, amidst many difficulties, continued in some, although not full, degree to meet the expectations of its friends. In his report of December 1st, 1825, Secretary Barbour said: "The good effects resulting from the establishment of the school of practice at Fortress Monroe are daily developed in the increasing improvement of the artillery corps, that important arm of the public force."

It was the custom to change the companies annually—a practice to-day happily abandoned, as the attendant expense very greatly prejudiced the interests of the school, which, as soon as established, in 1824, became the favorite experimental ground upon which were tested the guns, carriages, and other artillery matériel before they were either discarded or issued to troops. Boards for the purpose of advising the Secretary of War on artillery matters were assembled at the school, which was intended to be a headquarters whence would emanate well-digested opinions, based on actual experience, concerning artillery matters.

It would seem, however, that eleven companies were more than could be accommodated at the fortress. Mr. Calhoun's desire to form a "perfect regiment" thereat was never realized. Although there were plenty of troops, the amount of matériel available for practice was small, and, contrary to the hopes of its founders, no horse artillery was organized there, though the grounds for manœuvring that arm were provided.

The death of General Brown, commanding the army, an event which took place February 24th, 1828, deprived the school of its steadfast friend and advocate. His successor, Major-General Alexander Macomb, though an old artillery officer, was of opinion that the institution could best accomplish its purpose by giving up some of its companies for duty at ordinary artillery posts. Accordingly, by Order No. 58, Adjutant-General's Office, 1828, the number of companies was reduced to six, all from one regiment (the First), and a stop was put to the plan of rotating the various companies as set on foot by Mr. Calhoun. The new arrangement was not intended to interfere with the school of practice, and graduates of the military academy, when assigned to the artillery arm, were directed to repair there as usual. It was also provided that either companies or officers found deficient, when inspected, should be sent to the school of practice, with a view to their instruction and improvement. Referring to this change, the general-in-chief remarked: "It may be proper to state, in regard to this institution, that the want of means has prevented its establishment to a full extent upon the plan originally contemplated. It is believed, however, that, as at present arranged, it may be made instrumental in diffusing throughout the artillery the practical knowledge necessary to the efficiency of that arm." We were at this time on the eve of an important revolution in artillery matériel; knowledge of the stock-trail system of carriages was being put in possession of the Government, but many years passed before its adoption, and, in the meantime, circumstances had operated to break up the school of practice. In 1831 eleven companies were stationed at the school; in 1832, six companies, Indian and other troubles having removed the rest; in 1833, nine; in 1834, nine; in 1835, four companies, at which time the Seminole disturbances in Florida caused all the troops to be transferred to that theatre of hostilities. Fortress Monroe then became an experimental ground for the ordnance department, and so remained until the reorganization of the school of practice, which was brought about in the following manner:

In 1855 Mr. Jefferson Davis, Secretary of War, writing to the chairman of the Senate Military Committee, said: "Much may be effected for the improvement of the artillery by the establishment of schools of instruction, causing all the companies to pass periodically through the course, remaining for a term of, say, two years." This was followed by General Orders No. 9, Headquarters of the Army, October 30th, 1856, directing that (M) of the Second, (C) of the Third, (G) of the Fourth, and (I) of the First Regiment should be thereafter designated as garrison, sea-coast, and siege artillery; that they should be concentrated at Fortress Monroe, Virginia, and form a school of practice for service with heavy guns. These companies, which had previously been equipped as field artillery, and were legally light artillery companies, were accordingly brought together, and by General Orders No. 15, Headquarters of the Army, December 29th, 1857, Brevet Lieutenant-Colonel Harvey Brown, Second Artillery, was instructed to proceed to organize the school, submitting to the general-in-chief a code of regulations and plan of instruction.

The code of regulations and the plan of instruction ordered to be submitted, as just indicated, were published in General Orders No. 5, Adjutant-General's Office, May 18th, 1858. The school was very much on the plan adopted in 1824, except the number of companies was fixed at eight—two from each regiment. The course extended over two years, one company from each regiment being relieved annually. The companies were given their complement of officers. Graduates of the military academy assigned to the artillery were, as in 1824, to serve one year at this school before joining their companies. The instruction was quite complete, embracing, so far as practicable, the whole range of studies and practice which go to make up the education of an artillery officer. Provision was also made for the examination in their duties of the non-commissioned officers. The official designation was "*The Artillery School.*" There is every reason to suppose that the institution, started under circumstances so much more favorable than those surrounding it in 1824, would have been productive of much good to the artillery arm, had not the breaking out of the Civil war put an end to its existence before the first companies selected had completed the prescribed two years' course of instruction.

That feature of the code of regulations which required graduates of the military academy to serve at Fortress Monroe before joining their companies is considered to have been a mistake, though sanctioned by previous practices.

Young graduates of West Point need practice more than anything else. They possess already the groundwork of a thorough professional education, but it is nearly all theoretical. Let them, after completing their academic course, first join their respective commands, where they will mingle with the army such as it is in every-day life, and not such as is found at schools of any kind. Here the *observant young officer* will have leisure to think over what he has learned, to compare the theory of the school-room with the practice he sees around him, and draw therefrom many useful conclusions. He will soon find that there are many things of first importance in the management of military affairs which he learned nothing of in his four years' course, yet a knowledge of them is indispensable to the officer who is to command troops. Instead, therefore, of crowding the heads of young graduates with more theories, when they have not been able to digest those already learned, let them go first to their stations, and mingle with the arm with which they are to be thenceforth identified, and acquire some practical knowledge of army life as it really is. Having done this they will be much better prepared to appreciate the true value and importance of what is taught at any well-organized school of practice.

One of the first things to be attended to after the Civil war was to reorganize the school upon the old site. There then arose a practical difficulty in devising any course of study to be pursued by all artillery lieutenants, resulting from the diverse attainments of these officers, some of whom were from civil life, some from the military academy, and others promoted during the war from the ranks of the army.

In order that all lieutenants should have opportunity to prepare themselves, it was proposed that there should be established at the various posts *instruction batteries* for the foot artillery, similar to those already existing in each regiment for field artillery; the captains and the non-commissioned officers of the foot *instruction batteries* to be permanent, the lieutenants and privates to be assigned temporarily.

At the school of practice it was proposed to adopt different courses of study to meet the acquirements of the various classes of officers. For those requiring it, there was to be a course in the common branches of an English education, embracing so much mathematics and natural philosophy as would enable those pursuing it to comprehend in a very general way the principles on which their ordinary practical duties depended. It was not thought just to require more than this of officers promoted for *field service* in inferior grades. For all graduates of the military academy a higher standard was prescribed. The distinction here made was based on the principle that in peace the only claims to commissions should be knowledge and education; in war, courage and conduct. Each and every one was made to render an account of his stewardship, depending upon his opportunities and previous educational facilities.

The correctness of the foregoing principles, which were formulated by the permanent artillery board; the advantages arising from the establishment of foot-battery schools of instruction; the fairness of the proposition that each should be held to a standard high in proportion to the advantages he has enjoyed, the benefits, in an educational point of view, he has been the recipient of from the Government,—all seem manifest; and they were partially adopted in the scheme for instruction at posts and that for the school of practice, soon after promulgated. The salient points of the former have been given when treating of that subject, (p. 119, *ante;*) the latter was provided in General Orders No. 99, Adjutant-General's Office, November 13th, 1867, and, with slight modifications, continues in force. The number of batteries stationed at the school for purposes of instruction was five—one from each artillery regiment. It was provided, also, that brevet second lieutenants assigned to the artillery arm should serve one year before being sent to their proper batteries, (an objectionable feature, already remarked upon,) and such number of young and intelligent recruits, for the foot batteries, as would keep the five instruction batteries full. The course was similar in scope to that adopted in 1858.

There was this marked difference between the former and present schemes, so far as the instruction batteries were concerned, viz.: formerly their stay was temporary, now it is permanent.

Both Mr. Calhoun and Mr. Davis favored passing all artillery companies in rotation through the school. Which is the better plan may be an open question; permanent instruction batteries are at present in favor, and there is no doubt but that the expense attending constant removals was a serious difficulty which has been overcome by keeping the batteries permanently at the school.

Sending intelligent recruits to the school of practice for an advanced course of instruction has proved scarcely more than a visionary scheme, of little practical benefit *except to the permanent school batteries*, whose ranks the recruits have served to keep full; to the service at large it has been of no real benefit. For commissioned officers, however, the school has proved to be of the greatest service. Facilities for study and practice combined are here offered, to be found nowhere else in this country. The course in artillery is kept up with the progress of the age—the practical as nearly so as the matériel now provided by the proper department will permit; and, although opinions differ as to the wisdom of certain branches pursued and the methods of instruction, no unprejudiced person acquainted with the work it has done and is doing will fail to acknowledge that the school has been, and now gives promise of being, highly beneficial to the artillery arm. It is the only institution maintained by the Government which serves in any manner to unite the artillery. Scattered as the latter is in this country, without a head to direct its affairs, with no bond of union connecting the batteries with the headquarters even of their respective regiments, it is a fortunate circumstance that Fortress Monroe brings the latter together at one point, where an effort is made to impress on the minds of all subalterns of artillery the fact, that only by moving forward can they tread the pathway leading to professional honor.

Circumstances, however, are such as to prevent this school attaining fully the purposes for which it was instituted and is maintained. As recently announced by the authorities, its objects are to secure (1) professional advancement, and (2) unity of method in the artillery arm of service.

Nothing could bring out in bolder relief the inadequate system of instruction, either throughout the artillery arm or at this school, than the fact that, although the first object of the latter is *advancement*, still there have been found here in the same class, pursuing the same studies, the élève of West Point, fresh from the academy, and the graduate of twenty years' experience, including that of a four years' war. Certainly no such spectacle as this, where men of middle age and striplings are placed and maintained on the same footing, can be found at any other military school in any land. If such an union be proper, it requires no professional eye to discern either that there has not been much progress as a result of those twenty years' experience, or that the course at the school is illy adapted to its pupils.

It is one of the cardinal principles of our military system that, *though our army be very small, its officers are trained and efficient*, the small force thus forming a perfectly-appointed nucleus, capable of ready expansion into a large and effective army in time of national danger. If this premise, upon which are based all arguments in favor of our present army organization, be not false, then the joining together of youth and age in the same course of study is unwise. Nor does the incongruity stop here: the graduate of the artillery school returns to the institution years hence, and again finds his classmate to be a youth fresh from college or the military academy.

It is very true that, were the course of study and practice at posts of the artillery what it should be, but what it is not and never will be without a progressive system, *enforced by an efficient inspectorship*, there would be no excuse for this state of affairs. But this would not wholly mend the difficulty.

To insure the attainment of what is said to be the first object of the school of practice—advancement in professional knowledge —the course should be differently arranged. Provision should be made for an advanced class of pupils—officers who are competent to pass a prescribed examination, which should be a prerequisite to entering the class. This is the common practice in other countries. Ambitious officers would keep up their studies, with the hope and reasonable expectation of having their acquirements recognized. The examinations should be rigid, both preliminary and those subsequent to admission.

This is done in the department of artillery studies at Woolwich, England, which, it is said, has accomplished more than all other influences combined to raise the intellectual standard of the artillery of that country. The same remarks are true with regard to the higher artillery and engineer course in Austria and Germany, the Michael artillery academy of Russia, and similar schools in other States of Europe.

Another step in the same direction would be the introduction of the study of modern languages; if possible, both French and German; certainly the former. No one who compares the curriculum of this school with that of similar institutions in Europe but will remark upon the absence of all attention to languages in the former, and contrast it with the reverse practice in the latter. Education can in no way be made a more powerful agent to efficiency with the average artillery officer than by giving him a ready translating knowledge of the French language. It is not meant that he be merely able to stumble through his sentences, guessing at half of them; on the contrary, that he be able to convert French into English, and *vice versa*, with accuracy and facility. It gives him command, either directly or indirectly, of the best military literature of the world. The sooner this fact is recognized, and a practice inaugurated in accordance therewith, the better will it be for the school, the officers who go there, and the artillery arm. Let room be made for this most important and practically useful addition to the course. It may interfere with the convenience of individuals; it is not, however for the personal interest of any one, but for the benefit of an honorable arm of the public service, that this school exists, and the practice should be in accordance with this idea.

Too much importance is not here attached to the mere fact that in other countries advanced courses of study are given officers possessing certain qualifications, without at the same time considering the appropriateness and feasibility of inaugurating the same thing in our own school. No greater mistake can be made than to blindly follow the example of others without considering whether it is or is not suitable or proper in our case. It is grasping form without considering the more important matter—substance. Remembering and giving due weight to this, it yet appears plain that providing such a course as has been indicated, for selected pupils at the artillery school, is not only in keeping with the practice of other nations, but, under existing circumstances, is advisable here. Indeed it seems the only means by which that school can be made to meet the first object for which it was instituted.

The second object is also imperfectly attained; but this is no reproach to, or fault of, the school. Unity of method throughout the artillery cannot be secured when, in the case of at least two-thirds of the officers, instruction in that particular method begins and ends with the school of practice. There are at Fortress Monroe appliances for mechanical manœuvres and experiment — to be found on a plan equally elaborate at no other one place garrisoned by artillery troops. This fact, of itself, would make it difficult to extend and make uniform the methods of instruction there pursued. But even in those matters wherein there might exist the desired uniformity there is no efficient outside effort made to secure it. Were there a well-digested plan of instruction, progressing at equal pace with science and the mechanic arts,—or, if this be impracticable, then a scheme adopted which would at least insure the use, to the utmost practicable extent, of all mechanical appliances pertaining to artillery matériel actually supplied to each post,—then not only would it appear proper, but it would be entirely feasible to make the methods of the school uniform in all parts of the artillery service.

The objects of the school are theoretically correct, and in any other of the great nations of the earth would be practically so. That it does not insure the progress of artillery subalterns to a degree that is possible, is partially due, as has been pointed out, to a course of studies which, in some important particulars, does not rise to the plane of mediocrity; but that it fails so generally to make itself practically what it is theoretically, is due to the fact that the rest of the foot artillery is not organized and operated in unison with, but far below, the artillery school standard; therefore the results of its workings are to a great extent dissipated.

Practically speaking, it is an institution where, unless prevented by political influence or official favoritism, young officers entering the artillery receive a combined theoretical and practical knowledge of their branch of service, and to which they periodically return to brush away from their intellectual horizon the gathering shadows which threaten to obscure the vision when they pass beyond its threshold into a world of professional twilight or darkness.

Let not these remarks be interpreted as an attempt to disparage the school, but the reverse. Aside from the field batteries, it is the one great and good feature of the artillery in the important matter of instruction, theoretical and practical. It is properly regarded as the conservator of professional knowledge and traditions; the good it does extends with impaired yet strongly felt, invigorating, and genial influence to the extremities of the disjointed body of the artillery arm, separated as the latter is into sixty batteries, with scarcely any bond of union between them. Such an institution deserves to be nurtured and sustained by the strong arm of authority and of law. It must be cherished for the good that is in it, while its faults, if any appear, should be corrected as they become manifest. Situated as the artillery is in this country, it is of the first importance that its one common school of practical instruction be built up by the united efforts of the artillery itself and of the Government, for the credit of each of which it is maintained, and whose interests it subserves.

INSTRUCTION AT SCHOOLS: (D) FIELD BATTERIES.

Soon after the mounting of a company as field artillery in each regiment, in pursuance of the general plan of instruction formulated by Mr. Calhoun in 1821, it was decided to make those companies schools for artillery subalterns. The system was initiated by General Orders No. 46, of 1841, Adjutant-General's Office, which' provided that the lieutenants of the four artillery regiments should be passed through the schools of horse artillery in such manner that no lieutenant should serve therein for a longer period than one year. From this rule could be excepted lieutenants who were actually in command of companies, staff lieutenants, and such others as, from accidental causes, might be unable to ride. At this time there were ten companies in each regiment of artillery; consequently it took ten years at least for all eligible officers to pass through this course, which, being found too short to impart the information desired, was shortly afterwards lengthened to two years.

When lieutenants were first thus assigned to the field artillery companies, the armament of each embraced six guns. This number, however, was cut down to four by Special Orders No. 96, of 1842, Adjutant-General's Office, the other two pieces being stored for use when required. To make the instruction company respectably large in personnel, General Orders No. 42, of 1842, Adjutant-General's Office, directed that, in each regiment, another should be associated with the field artillery company. The four selected were (I) of the First, (F) of the Second, (F) of the Third, and (K) of the Fourth. Each of the selected companies remained in charge of its own officers. In respect, however, to exercises and manœuvres as field artillery, the care of batteries, horses, harness and stables, the duties of the two companies were blended, and equalized, under the orders of the senior officer. This plan failed; as, to use the language of one who was at that time an active field artillery officer, "it was a question of constant annoyance to every one concerned where were to begin, where to end, and what really were the appropriate duties of the foot companies which were thus made yoke-fellows to the field artillery."

The practice of having the lieutenants remain only one year with the field companies was found inconvenient, besides being detrimental to service by keeping the officers constantly changing stations. The evil was attempted to be ameliorated by General Orders No. 33, of 1844, Adjutant-General's Office, which made the first lieutenants permanent, as they were in the foot artillery; only the second and brevet second lieutenants, of whom together there were two with each field company, being relieved annually. The first lieutenants thus assigned were selected by the colonels of the respective regiments. Although this order broke up the field artillery schools to a great extent, it furnished these companies when they went to Mexico, in 1846, trained and specially competent first lieutenants; which fact without doubt had its influence in enabling the field companies to make their distinguished records in that war.

Following the cessation of hostilities with Mexico, numerous changes were made in the equipment of the field artillery companies; but, early in 1849, (April 21st and May 12th,) all were ordered to be supplied with their proper arm. Then came (General Orders No. 14, August 24, 1849, Headquarters of the Army,) those rules for the detail of subalterns for field artillery service which are embodied, in substance, in the Army Regulations of the present day. The tour of duty was fixed at two years. Those who could be excepted from the rule were lieutenants in command of companies whose captains were indefinitely absent, adjutants, quartermasters, and those physically unable to ride. The number of subalterns was established at two first and one second lieutenant with each company, the first lieutenants being relieved in alternate years;—this to secure constantly with each company at least one instructed subaltern. The rule here established, reaffirmed by Special Orders No. 141, of 1870, Adjutant-General's Office, continues essentially that by which lieutenants are at present detailed for this duty.

The caprices of those in authority, particularly of the various Secretaries of War, during the following years rendered the field artillery companies extremely uncertain schools of practice. This will appear when we examine the records between the close of the Mexican and the beginning of the Civil war. During that period (K) of the First Regiment was the only company which was not dismounted; it was given a field artillery equipment after its return from Mexico, and has kept it unmolested. Of the others, (A) of the Second, (C) of the Third, and (B) of the Fourth were, in the interval mentioned, each dismounted and remounted once; (I) of the First and (E) of the Third were dismounted twice and remounted twice; (G) of the Fourth was dismounted three times and remounted twice; while (M) of the Second was dismounted three times and remounted as often in the same interval. In fact, although from 1849 to 1851 eight companies were authorized, but seven were actually equipped as field artillery; and on March 31st, 1851, in a paroxysm of economy, the number, in violation of the law of March 2d, 1821, was cut down to two—(K) of the First and (C) of the Third Regiment; but the Secretary, having apparently awakened to the illegality of his action, remounted, September, 1852, one company in each of the other two regiments. Three companies were remounted in May, 1853, but the Secretary of War stationed them on the Indian frontier, and, as a result, in three years the number of mounted companies was again reduced to four.

Immediately upon the assumption of the duties of his office by Secretary Floyd, the question of remounting the field companies came up for consideration. General Scott approved the measure, and, to secure the carrying out of a more elaborate system of instruction, he suggested they be stationed in pairs at posts particularly well adapted to the purpose. This was the attempted beginning of the plan of field artillery posts for batteries of that arm exclusively—a plan upon which the school at Fort Riley, Kansas, was organized in 1869, and of which more will be said hereafter.

But General Scott was not able to carry out his views. It is true that by April, 1858, when Mr. Floyd had been Secretary of War one year, three of the dismounted field artillery companies were again properly equipped; but the Mormon disturbances in Utah had scattered them at different points *en route* to that territory. After their services were no longer needed there, far from concentrating them, they were, as has been mentioned, by General Orders No. 10, of 1859, Adjutant-General's Office, distributed over the western country, with the object of putting into execution an elaborate but, as it proved, a visionary scheme of artillery instruction which embraced both foot and field artillery, and, for the latter, it was substantially as follows: The companies were stationed, (C) of the Third at Vancouver, Washington Territory; (E) of the Third at Fort Ridgely, Minnesota; (K) of the First at Fort Clark, Texas; (I) of the First and (A) of the Second at Fort Leavenworth, Kansas; (B) of the Fourth at Camp Floyd, Utah; and (U) of the Second at Fort Brown, Texas. (G) of the Fourth was not then mounted. In every instance from three to five companies of foot artillery were stationed at the same post with a field company, and all the officers at the post, each in his proper sphere, either commanded or exercised with the field artillery in accordance with the following rule: On Fridays, Saturdays, and Sundays the officers of the field company exclusively served with it. During the remaining days of the week lieutenants for that company were furnished by a roster which embraced every subaltern at the post. During four days out of every twenty-eight, namely, on a Monday, Tuesday, Wednesday, and Thursday, the company was commanded by a captain of one of the foot artillery companies. If the field artillery captain was senior to the foot captain, he superintended the field artillery drill of the latter.

The time during which it was attempted to put in practice the provisions of this order was not long, it is true, but sufficiently so to demonstrate its impracticability. The primary defect was of the same general nature as that which rendered abortive the attempt to combine companies in 1844 for the performance of field artillery duties, viz., the mixing up of commands, placing the field artillery company under command of another captain than its own, and, finally, the impossibility of so adjusting the complex machine as to determine what were the precise functions of its parts. It was attempted to obviate the difficulties by supplementary orders from the War Department, but to no purpose; the whole plan, after a few attempts to make it a working reality, was in a fair way to pass by common consent into contempt and oblivion. Such was the state of affairs when the precipitation of the Civil war swept the artillery officers into a more improving and attractive school of instruction.

While the field artillery companies had, from their first organization in our army, been looked upon as schools of instruction for the subalterns, their captains were always considered as permanent until very recent times. By General Orders No. 96, of 1882, Adjutant-General's Office, the tour of service of captains with light or mounted batteries was fixed at three years,* that of lieutenants remaining as before—two years. To avoid complaints of injustice and to insure uniformity of instruction, the captains are detailed by roster, the senior eligible for detail being designated first.

This practice can only be regarded as an experiment. Whether it will be for the best interests of the service, time must determine. The traditions and experience of the arm lead to contrary anticipations. The old field artillery companies were organized and for years nurtured under the eyes of selected officers—captains and lieutenants—who brought them, spite of many discouraging circumstances, to a high state of excellence. The proud records of these companies in the first war succeeding their organization was then attributed to the fact that they fought under their veteran commanders, even the first lieutenants being then permanently attached. ·The loss of prestige of these batteries during the Civil war is to be attributed, in large degree, to the fact that their old officers were absent; the batteries were often commanded by inexperienced lieutenants who changed frequently. If the principle of having captains rotate be for the good of the artillery, it will prove itself so; and this is the standard by which it will be judged.

---

* Changed by recent orders to FOUR years for captains, (General Orders No. 86, of 1884, Headquarters of the Army.) This is a long step in the right direction. It only remains now to complete the good work by *selecting* the most capable captains, and either give them command of the field batteries permanently, or for a lengthened period, say six years.

If, indeed, it be true that this is the only means by which favoritism can be prevented, it may be conceded to be a wise measure; but if there be not in the military system sufficient virtue to prevent such a state of affairs being brought about, it may well be questioned if the distinguished career of the field artillery be not a thing of the past.

In most European armies the field artillery—mounted and horse—is entirely separate from the foot or fortress artillery, promotion being distinct in the two services. In the English army there is an exception, all the artillery belonging, theoretically at least, to one regiment; but it is in fact a corps, as that term is used in the United States service—not a regiment. *Officers for the horse batteries are selected for their special qualifications*—a principle which has brought that arm to the first rank' in European artilleries. When our field artillery companies were first mounted the same rule was followed here; and as a result, although laboring under disadvantages, (infantry pay, the lukewarm aid of doubting friends, and the hostility of enemies,) the field artillery demonstrated during the Mexican war the superiority of the system of selection by which its officers were appointed. It cannot be denied, however, that it opens the door to favoritism, than which nothing more quickly breaks down military spirit, and that in some instances this operates to the detriment of the service both at home and abroad; but whether the detail of captains for a brief tour is destined to improve matters, may well be questioned. It cannot be claimed, nor will it be conceded, until an experience yet to be acquired has demonstrated its wisdom.

FIELD ARTILLERY POSTS AS SCHOOLS OF INSTRUCTION.

By General Orders No. 6, Headquarters of the Army, Adjutant-General's Office, February 18th, 1869, four of the field artillery batteries were, in pursuance of a *projet* of the Secretary of War, assembled at Fort Leavenworth for the purpose of establishing a field artillery school something similar to that recommended by General Scott in 1857. The post fixed upon was Fort Riley, Kansas, whither the batteries were accordingly sent, to remain, however, as it proved, for two years only, being by General Orders No. 17, of 1871, Adjutant-General's Office, returned to their respective regiments.

Judged alone by the brief term of its existence, the school was a failure. Yet the objects to be attained and which led to its organization were excellent. Much good must accrue to the artillery arm and to the service generally by such a school as this was intended to be, placed and maintained upon a proper footing.

Its failure resulted not from any defect in the fundamental principles of the establishment, but from other causes. Some of the objects for which the school was organized were: (1) To introduce into the field artillery uniformity of practice in all that pertained to instruction and manœuvre. (2) By a well-established system of competitive drills and firings to weed out everything which was not of practical utility, and at the same time develop and suggest improvements in the guns and projectiles, that by timely advances they should keep pace with improvements in small-arms. (3) To study the horse and to determine the best classes and breeds for the light artillery service. (4) To serve as a school of practical instruction for officers, where would be taught not only the duties of the battery as an artillery unit, but also those of the artillery brigade, that administrative and fighting body which has superseded the battery for war purposes, not only in our own experience, but in the practice of every nation of continental Europe. (5) To enable officers to acquire a knowledge of the mounted service required for siege and mountain artillery, parks and convoys; the course at Fortress Monroe not admitting of this instruction being given.

The utility of a school of this character, and its importance to the artillery, can scarcely be overestimated. *If it be desirable to maintain the field batteries, it should be on the footing of highest attainable efficiency consistent with a proper economy.* This the field artillery school would have rendered possible had it been supported as it deserved, and as would have been the case had it remained under the management of its projector, Major-General Schofield. Before systematic organization could be effected, however, the troops were diverted from their proper duties to serve as cavalry on the frontier; the men were taken as teamsters; the horses (draught), not intended for this kind of service, were broken down; finally, the commandant was kept away indefinitely at a time when his presence with the command was indispensable to insure a proper beginning for the institution. In a word, the field artillery school was strangled in its infancy. That which, if properly nurtured, gave promise of fair proportions, bringing strength, symmetry, and a high order of excellence to the field artillery, was cast to one side, to be even now almost forgotten, without an intelligent effort being made to develop what there was good in it.

If the improvement of this branch of service be an object worthy the solicitude of the Government, it is eminently proper and desirable that the batteries be assembled at schools of instruction similar to that contemplated at Fort Riley, Kansas. Aside from the salutary results following honorable emulation when troops serve in large, well-organized commands under the eye of a capable and impartial commander, there are other reasons which make such schools desirable for the field artillery. It is, as compared with other troops, expensive to organize and maintain. In all armies, therefore, no more is kept equipped during peace than proper economy justifies; but what portion soever of the military establishment this may be, sound reason, justice to the Government which bears the expense, and true military policy all demand that it be kept in a high state of efficiency. With competent commanders, a step towards the attainment of this desirable end will be the arranging of the batteries into artillery brigades. This is the organization in which they will fight in a great war; it was adopted by both belligerents during the Rebellion, and has the sanction and practice of all civilized nations. In January, 1861, the field batteries, under a false idea of instruction, were scattered as they are now. By the end of that year, when war had wrought its practical changes, they were grouped together in brigades of four batteries each.

The desirability of assimilating our peace organization to that of actual war, as nearly as practicable, seems self-evident. More particularly is this true when increased efficiency of administration and economy of both money and matériel are thereby insured. Remember the favorite article of our military creed, that, *though our army be small, it is commanded from top to bottom by well-trained officers.* If it be intended to make this a reality rather than an empty boast, it will, for the light artillery, be most surely attained through the instrumentality of the schools in question. The assignment by recent orders of captains to the command of batteries for a limited period of years has but added cogency to the reasons before existing for assembling them into brigades under energetic field officers.*

In other armies, the objects here sought to be attained by the proposed field artillery schools are in various ways secured to that branch of service. So far as is known, however, there is not in Europe a single school of practice equal in scope to that projected at Fort Riley. In Germany the artillery brigade is the administrative unit in peace as well as in war, having in this respect supplanted the battery. There is at Berlin a gunnery school, to which officers and men are sent by detail annually from the field batteries, horse and foot. The course has for its object to teach the use of different kinds of guns, wagons, ammunition, fuses, and the tactics of artillery under all the circumstances of actual war.

England has her gunnery school at Shoeburyness, the object being essentially the same as in Germany. Batteries attend this school in rotation, as was the case with us formerly at Fortress Monroe.

Austria has similar institutions, and at Vienna there is the central artillery riding school, the object being to secure uniformity in riding, in stable management, the government of unruly horses, and the training of riding-masters for the artillery.

The same remarks are true with reference to the other countries of Europe; each puts forth, in one way or another, every energy to improve this branch of the service. Their annual practice firing is in every way worthy of imitation; at known and unknown distances; with good, bad, and indifferent ammunition;

---

*Since the foregoing was written, it is observed that the correctness of the views here expressed on the general subject of field artillery schools are confirmed by Major-General Hancock in his annual report of 1883.

After observing that the four field batteries of his geographical division were stationed, one at Washington Barracks, District of Columbia, one at Little Rock Barracks, Arkansas, another at Fort Adams, Rhode Island, and the fourth at Fort Hamilton, New York Harbor, the general proceeds: "I take occasion to reiterate what I have heretofore said, that I do not think the light batteries are fulfilling a useful purpose as at present located. A light artillery school under one of our best artillery field officers, where all, or at least four or five, of the light batteries could be concentrated, would, in my judgment, best fulfill the object of their organization. Scattered as they are at present, and associated with foot troops, and required often to perform kindred duties, the specialty of their arm is apt to be lost sight of."

battle and all other firing likely to be of use is practiced, *competition between the batteries engaged being the soul of the exercise.* Afterwards, careful notes, covering every important fact elicited, are worked up and given to the army for the information and benefit of all concerned.

Much has recently been said and written in this country on the subject of target practice with small-arms. It is of the first importance; and no one who has labored honestly in this field, has seen the gradual improvement of the men, has remarked the feeling of conscious power manifesting itself as they learned the capabilities in their own hands of the weapons they carry, can for one moment doubt that this practice vastly increases the effectiveness of our infantry.

Every argument that can be advanced in favor of small-arm target practice and battle firing (skirmish infantry target practice is that,) proves still more strongly the necessity that exists for artillery target and battle practice. In Europe artillery firing receives much more careful and conscientious attention than does small-arm firing in this country; there is more system about it; the actual results, the *facts*, are more *guardedly determined* on the spot; and nothing is left undone to turn them to the greatest possible advantage of the artillery arm. In the United States the reverse of this is true; but it should not and need not be; and the proposed field artillery schools, similar to that organized at Fort Riley, would afford, among other things, the means of supplying our deficiencies in this particular.

PRACTICE FIRING FOR ARTILLERY.

Rules and regulations governing this useful branch of artillery instruction were first promulgated in War Department Orders No. 21, April 1st, 1842. They provided in brief for fixed batteries: (1) That a post record-book be kept, wherein for each mounted gun there should be placed all data as to calibre, weight, material of gun, the carriage, and the field of fire. (2) That all the surrounding country and waterways be reconnoitred and thoroughly studied. (3) That every material fact as to the character of shot thrown, and its flight, be noted in the record-book. (4) Each company with a fixed battery was annually allowed one hundred cartridges, with seventy-five shot or shell. (5) Companies equipped as field artillery were allowed annually two hundred blank cartridges and one-third that number of shot or shell. (6) All commanders were directed to keep registers of their practice, so that not a shot should be thrown for instruction without distinct objects; such as range, accuracy of fire, number of ricochets, bursting time for shells, &c. (7) Full reports of results were to be sent to the adjutant-general for the information of the War Department and of the general-in-chief. The general objects to be attained by this practice were to impart to officers and men knowledge of the ready and effective use of batteries, to preserve on record for their benefit the more important results, and to ascertain the condition of both guns and carriages. These rules first appeared as part of the Army Regulations in 1847. In the edition of the Regulations promulgated in 1857 they remained almost unchanged, except that the general-in-chief was not given the results of the practice, they being worked up for the information of the War Department only; and the allowance of ammunition for a field artillery company was changed to five hundred blank cartridges and one-third that number of shot or shell annually. These allowances were cut down in the Regulations of 1861–'63, the field batteries being deprived altogether of either shot or shell for target practice, and blank cartridges given in such quantities as were necessary for instruction and drill. There was not allowed, therefore, by Army Regulations, during the Civil war, a single shot for experimental or target practice, to the fifty-six batteries of regular field artillery which during that contest were equipped and served with the various armies.

Paragraph III, General Orders No. 67, of 1866, changed the annual allowance, for each artillery company serving by itself at a post with a fixed battery, to fifty cartridges and twelve projectiles for sea-coast guns, with twenty projectiles for calibres below 100-pounders; while, for each additional artillery company, there was given one-half this number; all the cartridges and projectiles being equally divided among the companies firing. This was reducing the practice firing to about one-third what it was in 1842, when the system was inaugurated.

At no time subsequent to 1861, until the promulgation of General Orders No. 83, of 1867, Adjutant-General's Office, were the field batteries authorized to expend projectiles for practice; but by that order each was allowed twenty-five rounds, which, for smooth-bores, were one-half shell or case shot, one-quarter solid shot, and one-quarter canister; for rifle guns, (with which half the field batteries were equipped,) three-quarters were shell or case shot and one-quarter canister; while for instruction and drill purposes as many blank cartridges and friction primers were authorized as the battery and post commanders deemed necessary. The allowance to a battery at permanent works was also changed again by this order, each being given twenty-five blank cartridges, with twelve projectiles for calibres above and twenty for those below 8-inch, and the necessary blank cartridges; for each additional battery serving at a post, one-half this number, the whole number being equally divided among the batteries firing; besides, there were allowed annually not exceeding two hundred friction primers to each battery for drill purposes. The condition was added, that the ammunition should be taken from the serviceable yet longest on hand at the post.

General Orders No. 14, Adjutant-General's Office, series of 1876, promulgated existing orders relating to artillery target practice, with the following additional instruction:

"Commanding officers of forts and light batteries will transmit direct to the adjutant-general, for the chief of ordnance, on forms to be supplied by the ordnance department, reports of each and every shot fired from field, siege, or sea-coast guns and mortars. Each gun should have its recorded history. Every shot fired should be recorded and reported, with all the circumstances and incidents attending it. It is of the greatest importance that the whole number and character of rounds to which a gun has been subjected in practice be at all times known."

The official who comes prominently into view here is the chief of ordnance, placed thus in the position of chief of artillery of the army, a rôle never before openly assumed. The next year (1877), upon his recommendation, the above order was modified, omitting an enumeration of the character of ammunition to be used by field batteries, and providing that reports of each and every shot fired, not only in target practice, but in *actual service against the enemy*, should be tabulated for the information of the chief of ordnance; thus adding strength to the functions he had assumed as head of the artillery arm of service—chief of the artillery staff.

When the practice firing of artillery was begun, in 1842, reports were made for the information of the general-in-chief;

but in 1857 he dropped out of sight, and his place has at last been assumed by the head of a non-combatant bureau.

It may not be uninteresting, in this connection, to recall the position in which the new head of the artillery and his department posed at this time before Congress and the public *outside* of the army.

In a printed argument to demonstrate the impolicy of reuniting the artillery and ordnance, the new chief of artillery remarked:

"It [ordnance department] is not the staff of the artillery in any sense; *its duties are defined by law*, and consist in providing, preserving, distributing, and accounting for every description of artillery, small-arms, and all the munitions of war which may be required by the fortresses of the country, the armies in the field, and for the whole body of the militia of the Union. The functions of the ordnance department will thus be seen to be entirely distinct from those of the line of the army in any of its branches; its duties would remain the same whether the peace establishment be large or small, or be entirely abolished."

Where, may we ask, in the organic or any subsequent act, defining the duties of this department, is there any warrant for this assumption, by its chief, of the supervision of the artillery in a matter which belongs essentially to that arm alone? If, indeed, it be found that these *duties defined by law* circumscribe its proper sphere of action, and the nature of things requires that the chief of ordnance should assume charge of one of the most important duties of the artillery arm—collating the results of its target practice—it is time to consider seriously the question thus forced upon us, viz.: *Is not, after all, the uniting of the present ordnance and artillery under one head the natural and proper plan of organization?* Here is a department which, when the question of merging is raised, loudly proclaims that it is in no sense artillery staff, and yet it seeks to assume those duties and is now actually performing them. Not only has this been done in the matter of target practice and other firing, even to the extent of *every shot used in actual service against the enemy*, but, upon the recommendation of the new chief of artillery staff, artillery officers have been excluded from councils which decided upon the armament of the forts they were to defend, and their proper duties in this respect assumed by the officers of that new staff. The absurdity of depriving artillery officers of a voice (which should be a preponderating one) in determining what proportions of guns of the various calibres should be used in defending our forts, is apparent.* Yet this is what the new chief of artillery staff recommended and had the address to secure being done. The regulations of the army require that commanders of fortified places shall consult their senior officers of artillery, who keep journals, in which, in case of investment, every circumstance of importance is entered. In this, and in the duties of the siege, the artillery is intimately associated with the engineers. The commandant of the former submits to the commanding general his views as to everything affecting the artillery, and advises the general throughout as to the employment of his arm. Still this is the officer who, under the dispensation of the new artillery staff, is to be ignored when the armaments of the forts are being determined upon, and his place at the council filled by a non-combatant, "whose services have no immediate connection with the line of the army, who is separated from that body, and given up to a study of the exact sciences and mechanical philosophy"!

The records show that in 1879, after the ordnance department had thus assumed the duties of artillery staff, there were fired at targets by the troops of that arm, exclusive of those at Fortress Monroe, ten 10-inch Rodman, eighteen 10-inch siege mortar, one hundred and fifty-five 8-inch siege mortar, seventeen 8-inch howitzer, seventy 4½-inch siege rifle, fourteen 12-pounder smoothbore, three hundred and eighty-three 3-inch rifle, and three thou-

---

*The recent attempt, through the provisions of a fortification bill, to organize a board, advisory to the Secretary of War, for the determination of all questions relating to the fortification and armament of our most important sea-boards, without having an artillery officer thereon, is another of those efforts to push bureauocracy to the front at the expense of the fighting arms of service and of the public weal, and one to which Members of Congress unwittingly, it is believed, lent themselves.

Why any should be selected for this duty who, during the four years' war for national existence, never heard a hostile shot fired, while artillery officers who faced the enemy on every battle-field, and will do it again if the coast be attacked, are ignored, is one of those questions that cannot be answered.

Why those who will command the sea-coast works in case of invasion, upon whom will devolve the duty of upholding the honor of the flag and the country, should not have a voice in this advisory board, is not apparent; but the shortsightedness of that policy which would exclude from its councils the very officers who ultimately have more responsibility in the premises than any others, or all others combined, is apparent enough.

Fortunately for the security and honor of the United States, Congress promptly relegated to the oblivion it deserved this endeavor to hold up to contempt the

sand Gatling projectiles. No attempt is made by the artillery staff to turn the results of target practice to the advantage of that arm, or of the army at large. The tabulated statements are filed away for the information of the chief of ordnance and nobody else. The general-in-chief knows nothing of them, or at least he has disappeared from view in this connection. No opportunity is given different commands to compare results; and, except in the lowest grades of duties, those of the gunner, it would be difficult to point out in what manner the artillery is benefited by this annual expenditure of ammunition. While large sums are being expended in target practice with the infantry weapon, prizes and honors being showered upon the successful contestants, the artillery is left to languish under the withering influence of official neglect.

It is not so in any of the other first-class nations, for in every other the efficiency of the infantry and artillery, in fighting power, advances with equal pace. There is no feature of their army organization more complete than the firing schools, for the practical benefit of officers and men; and in the artillery, in addition, to test

---

capacity, intelligence, and professional attainments of the officers of that particular arm of service, upon which has heretofore, and will hereafter, devolve the defense of the maritime frontier, while favoring those who are "invincible in peace, invisible in war." [Fortification Bill, section 2, Majority Report, House of Representatives, first session, Forty-eighth Congress.]

Paragraph 1023, Revised Regulations of 1881, (No. 490, of 1863,) directs that the senior officer of engineers, of ordnance, and the departments of the general staff serving at the chief headquarters in the field, shall transmit to the bureau of his department at Washington, at the close of the campaign, and at such other times as the commander in the field may approve, a full report of the operations of his department, and whatever information to improve its service he may be able to furnish.

The artillery is excluded here. Hence, neither during the Civil war, before that, nor since, have commanders of artillery had any means of placing needed information before any authority whatever, let alone the War Department. This being ignored, has proved a heavy and grievous load for the artillery to bear. Thus this most complicated of all arms has been left, in the field, to its own devices. *As artillery* it has never had any standing at the War Department. The head of a bureau non-combatant in war, in peace fiercely combatant, acts as chief of the artillery arm, but without, of course, knowing anything of its needs in campaign. This is but another reason why the ordnance and artillery should be either united under a single head, or the arm given a chief of its own to represent it at the War Department councils.

the guns, carriages, caissons, and ammunition, in order that the theoretical knowledge acquired from books may be made complete by practice, skill acquired, without which the lessons of the school-room are of secondary importance, and to some officers a positive detriment. The annual allowance for each battery is from three to five hundred rounds of ammunition, good, bad, and indifferent in quality, depending upon the particular lessons to be taught. Every effort is made by competition and otherwise to excite the deepest interest in the practice, and when completed to turn its results, carefully noted, to the greatest advantage of the artillery arm.

With us the practice is the reverse of this. The allowance of ammunition is insufficient, and, being selected from "serviceable yet longest on hand," is generally wretchedly inferior in quality. As illustrating what can be done with this kind of ammunition, the firing does, perhaps, very well; but to show the actual power of our artillery, under favorable circumstances, it is of no value whatever. The truth of these statements; their exact accord with the facts as regards quality of ammunition, is abundantly borne out by the marginal remarks on the tabulated records from the various posts. Neither have the officers of the new artillery staff, separated as they are from the line of the army, absorbed in study of the exact sciences, given up to philosophical reflections, time nor inclination to withdraw themselves from these congenial pursuits to work out practical deductions from the results of our annual artillery practice. The artillery officers with troops have not the records, hence they cannot do it; and, as a result, no attempt is made to follow up to its logical consequences the information acquired, thus defeating, in great measure, the objects for which the target practice of the artillery arm is authorized.

CHAPTER VI.

ADMINISTRATION—DUTIES: TECHNICAL.

The Artillery Branch of Service has to a degree, at some times more than others, been intrusted with those technical duties of the laboratory, the workshop, and the arsenal which in other countries are considered as appertaining to the peculiar functions of that arm, but at present, with us, are assigned to the ordnance department.

Knox was the active agent, under the orders of the commander-in-chief, for devising ways and means for manufacturing or otherwise securing, within the colonies, munitions of war, particularly cannon and small-arms, with powder and projectiles. He wished, in regard to technical matters at least, to establish our own upon the plan of the Royal Artillery of England, himself occupying the position of master-general of ordnance. He was never able, however, to fully carry that point, although himself practically performing the duties, not only of the master-general but of his board of ordnance as well, in addition to those appertaining to commander of the artillery arm. This state of affairs was interrupted for one year only, while the plan on which the department of commissary-general of military stores was being tested. The commander of artillery, except during that year, determined upon the models for guns and carriages, and the kinds and quantities of warlike stores to be supplied. Although many cannon of various sizes and kinds of metal were procured abroad, no carriages, tumbrils, ammunition wagons, or other wheeled artillery vehicles were purchased; all were manufactured in the colonies.

In general terms it may be stated that the commander of the artillery controlled everybody and everything connected with that branch of service, both personnel and matériel. He did not make contracts for supplies; that, Congress reserved the right to do, and generally through its cannon committee, the board of war and ordnance, or the finance department. To the board of war and ordnance, appointed June 12th, 1776, was given by Congress the duty of keeping account of all artillery, arms, and warlike stores, and preserving such portion as might not be in use. The next year these duties were extended to embrace the building and management of laboratories, arsenals, foundries, and magazines, thus relieving Knox of a burden which force of circumstances had placed upon him in the earlier stages of the war.

The facts attending the establishment of the department of the commissary-general of military stores, from their direct bearing upon the technical affairs of the artillery at this time, should be understood, and will be narrated.

Soon after assuming command at Boston, in 1775, General Washington recommended to Congress the appointment of a commissary of artillery. This appointment he was authorized to make, at a salary of $30 per month—more than a captain of that arm. The office, purely civil, was first filled by Mr. Ezekiel Cheever; and, in the orders assigning him to duty, the commander of artillery was instructed to place all ordnance stores, not in the hands of troops, in charge of the commissary, who was to see them properly taken care of, and who was in fact made storekeeper for artillery matériel. The number of persons thus employed increased as the war progressed; and one of the recommendations of the commander of the artillery for the improvement of that arm, made to a congressional committee September 27th, 1776, was that, besides the commissaries, there should be appointed deputies—capable, active men—conductors, and clerks, at the discretion of the commander-in-chief.

To meet still further that officer's views, General Washington diverted from its original purpose one of the battalions of artillery the organization of which was set on foot pursuant to authority vested in him December 12th, 1776, and formed it into an artificer-regiment (so called), for labor in the same field of non-combatant duties with the commissaries, clerks, and conductors. (Organization, p. 7.) This was the germ of the department of commissary-general of military stores, or the ordnance department of the Revolution. January 16th, 1777, Benjamin Flower, of Philadelphia, was appointed lieutenant-colonel commandant of this artillery artificer-regiment, with the additional office of commissary-general of military stores. The regiment was recruited from mechanics alone—wheelwrights, blacksmiths, and laboratory men —who never, as soldiers, took the field or fired a gun. The colonel was a capable business man; his subordinate officers were supposed to be master-workmen. The organization, though styled regiment, was never so in fact; it had no staff; its major was a carpenter; the officers of five companies of the regiment were commissioned, while those of five other companies were not. One company was engaged to serve as mechanics for the artillery in the field; all the rest were employed at the laboratories and arsenals.

When the Conway cabal was at its height, in the winter of 1777-'78, several of its members were placed on the new board of war and ordnance, ostensibly presided over by Gates, but really by Mifflin. The faction opposed to General Washington controlled its councils, and, that the commander-in-chief might be struck a blow which at the same time would cement and add to the power of the board of war, it was determined to reorganize the staff departments, place them under orders of that body almost exclusively, and withdraw them to a corresponding degree from control of the commander of the army. The quartermaster's department was overhauled; the inspector's department created, and Conway, against Washington's well-known, publicly expressed wishes, and with the increased rank of major-general, placed at its head; but so ill-timed were these and many other measures undertaken professedly to reform the public service, that they scarcely excited notice, and soon passed into oblivion. It was at this time that, having received the recommendation of the board of war, the department in question—really the department of technical artillery—was placed upon a more elaborate footing, and the control of its officers regulated in accordance with the principle before indicated. In pursuance of this plan Congress, February, 1778—

"*Resolved*, That there shall be one commissary-general of military stores, whose business it shall be to receive and deliver all arms, ammunition, and accoutrements of every species and denomination; to provide and contract for all such articles as may be wanted in this department, according to the direction he shall receive from the board of war and ordnance; to receive and collect returns from all the different States where there are any continental arms and stores, draw them into one general return, and, on the first day of every month, deliver one to the board of war and ordnance. * * *

"All continental armorers shall be under the direction of the board of war and ordnance and of the commissary-general of military stores; the armorers to receive from the said commissary all arms to be repaired, make returns of the state of repairs when demanded, and deliver the arms, when repaired, into his store. * * *

DUTIES: TECHNICAL. 151

"That there be as many deputies, assistants, commissaries, deputy commissaries, conductors, and clerks as the exigency of the service shall require, to be appointed by the board of war and ordnance. * * *

"That for the future no rank be annexed to the officers of this department except they belong to the regiment of artillery-artificers, and then *their rank only to take place as officers of that corps;* the pay also which they receive as officers of that regiment to be included in the pay herein settled for the officers of the commissary-general's department. * * *

"All the artillery-artificers that are or may be employed at any armories, laboratories, foundries, or military magazines, (those employed with the army in the field excepted,) shall be under the immediate direction and subject to the orders and command of the commissary-general, or the officer directed by him to take charge of the same. * * *

"The board of war and ordnance shall transmit from time to time, as the service shall render necessary, transcripts from all returns received from the commissary-general of military stores; also accounts of all ordnance and stores under their care, or belonging to the United States, and the places where the same are deposited, to the commander-in-chief of the armies of the United States, in order that he shall make such requisitions for supplies for the army under his immediate command, or for the separate departments, as he shall think proper. * * *

"The commanding officer of artillery for the time being, in the grand army, with the chief engineer, commissary of artillery, and eldest colonel of artillery in camp, or such of them as are present with the army, shall be a subordinate board of ordnance, under the direction of the commander-in-chief or the board of war and ordnance, for transacting all business of the ordnance department necessary to be done in the field, and to have the care of all ordnance and stores in camp; and in case of sudden exigency the commissary-general of military stores shall be obliged to obey their directions as to any supplies wanted by the army out of the stores not in camp; and the said board shall correspond with and report their proceedings to the board of war and ordnance, from whom they are to receive any necessary assistance."

Colonel Flower was confirmed in the position of commissary-general of military stores, with rations and pay dating back to July 16th, 1776, when he had been appointed commissary of the Flying Camp in New Jersey. He was authorized to augment the number and strength of the companies of the regiment of artificers, the enlisted force of which received every bounty and more pay than the artillery, while the officers received equal pay with those of the same grade in that arm.

The establishment of this department was important in its bearing upon the administrative affairs of the artillery, inasmuch as it materially curtailed the powers of the commander of that arm in the management of technical matters. For the artillery-artificers it proved important also; the clause confining the scope of their military rank to the narrow limits of their own corps placed them in a mortifying position when brought into contact with the rest of the army. They fought hard against this interpretation being given the resolution, but to no purpose; a no less authority than Colonel Pickering, at the time a member of the board of war and ordnance, declaring that it was the intention to confine the operation of the rank of these artificer officers to the limits of their regiment; and as this decision was concurred in by the Secretary at War and the agent for army accounts, the commutation of half-pay for life, given after the war to other continental officers, was denied those of the artillery-artificers. The commissary of military stores department, including that regiment, was considered to be a civil branch of the Government, and the only reason for allowing the officers of the latter organization military rank at all was to enable them to sit on courts-martial to try members of their own corps, and for general purposes of interior discipline.

The career of the new department was neither long nor prosperous. This was due, first, to the fact that the power of the particular board of war and ordnance which brought it into existence was but transitory; second, it withdrew from the commander of the artillery authority which he had previously exercised, and which experience was every day demonstrating he should retain, viz., a deciding voice in determining all questions that arose concerning artillery matériel; third, by far the larger, more intelligent and (excepting the head of the department) influential members among its officials and employés were civilians, the military rank of the artificers, though limited, being still sufficient to beget rivalries, jealousies, and disputes which brought to a stand-still the government workshops.

In so far as the new order of things affected the armies in the field, we may best judge of their workings by the following extract from a letter written to the commander-in-chief by General Knox, and dated artillery park, Valley Forge, June 15th, 1778:

"I feel myself so embarrassed in the duties of my department by the regulations of the 11th February that I send changes for consideration of Congress. I am in the awkward situation of having none of the powers appertaining to the rank of commanding officer of artillery; I am expected to do things, and have no means of doing them. In all considerable armies in Europe a general officer has command and direction of the artillery and the preparation of everything relating to the ordnance department in all its details. He is allowed as assistants commissaries, clerks, conductors, founders, and artificers, all under his immediate control. In the British service the muster-master-general of ordnance or the commander-in-chief of the artillery has a board of ordnance; he presides; and this regulates everything pertaining to the artillery. This board consists of the surveyor-general of the artillery, clerk of the ordnance, storekeeper, and clerk of the deliveries. There cannot be pointed out one instance where the commissaries or clerks are independent of the commanding officer of the artillery, as provided in these regulations. It is necessary that the head of a department should have the direction of all its parts. By these regulations the commanding officer of artillery has no power to give the dimensions or construction of any carriages or cannon, however erroneous they may be; nor directions for making port-fires, fuses, or other matters in which the reputation of his corps is intimately concerned."

The difficulties pointed out led to great inconvenience in the campaign of 1778, and a committee of Congress examined into the subject, heard all parties interested, and then recommended such modifications as amounted in effect to abolishing the department of commissary-general of military stores, in so far as the duties of its head were inimical to the rights, privileges, and powers of the commander of the artillery, as pointed out by Knox. The changes made had the sanction and recommendation of that officer, as well as of the commander-in-chief. They went into effect just one year after the department was organized, when Congress, February 18th, 1779—

"*Resolved*, That the commanding officer of artillery of the United States for the time being shall, under the general orders and concurrence of the commander-in-chief, arrange and direct all business of the ordnance department necessary to be done in the field. The ordnance, arms, and military stores in the fixed magazines to be drawn out only by the orders of the board of war and ordnance, unless, in the course of the service, circumstances should occur in which the procuring such orders from the board would, in the opinion of the commander-in-chief and commanding officer of artillery, occasion improper delays; and in such cases the commanding officer of artillery shall have power to draw from the nearest magazines the supplies wanted for the army; and the different commissaries and directors of the magazines and laboratories shall, in such cases, immediately obey the orders of the commanding officer of artillery, informing the board of war and ordnance of the same. And, that the commander-in-chief and commanding officer of artillery may know, in such cases, where to send for necessary supplies, the board of war and ordnance shall cause monthly returns of all ordnance, arms, and military stores at the magazines in the United States to be made to the commander-in-chief, who will communicate to the commanding officer of artillery the whole or any part of them, as he shall judge the good of the service requires. And as it may frequently happen that parts of the army may be detached to such distances as to render their obtaining supplies, in the circumstances above mentioned, by the immediate orders of the commander-in-chief and commanding officer of artillery, inconvenient, in such cases the commander-in-chief and commanding officer of artillery shall give to the commanding officers of the detachment, and of the artillery annexed to it, proper directions for furnishing the detachment with the necessary supplies of ordnance, arms, and military stores; and the orders of the said commanding officers of the detachment, and of the artillery annexed to it, given pursuant to the said directions, shall be obeyed by the commissaries and directors at the magazines and laboratories as if given immediately by the commander-in-chief and commanding officer of artillery of the United States. * * *"

This was the first point gained under the new regulations, and greatly increased the mobility of the army by placing the ordnance, arms, and military supplies at the command of the general of artillery or his subordinates. But this was not sufficient; a competent machinery was necessary to conduct the commissary duties with the army itself, and to meet this requirement Congress created a new department for this special service by providing—

"That there shall be a field commissary of military stores, to be appointed by the board of war and ordnance, who shall receive and issue all ordnance, arms, and military stores in the field, pursuant to the orders of the commander-in-chief and commanding officer of artillery; all orders for this purpose from the commander-in-chief to be directed to the commanding officer of artillery. The field commissary shall have so many conductors, deputies and clerks, to be likewise appointed by the board of war and ordnance, as, in the opinion of the board, the commander-in-chief, and the commanding officer of artillery, the service shall from time to time require."

And, to show what relation this new department should bear to the rest of the army and the established commissary department, paragraph 5 (*ibid.*) proceeded: "The field commissary of military stores, his deputies, conductors and clerks, shall be independent of the commissary-general of military stores;" and they were instructed to make monthly returns of stores received, issued and remaining on hand, from which a consolidated return was to be made, and a copy sent by the field commissary to the board of war and ordnance, one to the commander-in-chief, one to the commander of artillery, and a fourth to the commissary-general of military stores.

The duty of submitting estimates for ordnance, arms, and military stores necessary for the use of the army was imposed upon the commanding officer of artillery. That the matériel should have that intelligent supervision which the good of the service required, and that the experience of the war might not be lost, it was further provided—

"That, whenever the said commanding officer of artillery shall judge any particular directions necessary for, or alterations and improvements to be made in, the construction or preparation of ordnance, arms, and military stores of any kind, he shall communicate the same to the board of war and ordnance for their consideration, who shall thereupon give such orders to the artificers and laboratory men as they shall judge the good of the service requires."

While the provisions quoted gave the commander of artillery control of all ordnance, arms, and military stores already manufactured, made the field commissary his subordinate, and gave the suggesting of improvements into his hands as his peculiar prerogative, it yet remained to bring the whole field of technical artillery under his supervision. To accomplish this, and thus make the commander of artillery what the name implies in all its plenitude, paragraph 10 provided—

"That there shall be one surveyor of ordnance, to be appointed annually from the colonels, the appointment to be made by the board of war and ordnance, until Congress shall direct otherwise. The officer thus appointed shall retain his rank in the artillery and all the benefits arising from it; but during the time of his surveyorship he shall not, except in extraordinary cases or when called for by the commander-in-chief, perform any duty in the line. His duty as surveyor shall be to examine into the construction, qualities, and condition of all cannon, carriages, arms, and materials for and preparation of every species of warlike stores, and to visit all the different arsenals, foundries, laboratories, and workshops belonging to the ordnance department of the United States, carefully noting every error and defect he shall discover, which, with a general state of the department, he shall report immediately to the board of war and ordnance, as well as the commanding officer of artillery, with his ideas of any alterations or improvements proper to be made thereon. He shall also examine all ordnance and military stores in the field, and report the state of them to the commanding officer of artillery and the board of war and ordnance; and, for the purposes aforesaid, the commissaries of military stores, as well in the field as elsewhere, shall make returns to the said surveyor, and shall expose to his view all the ordnance, arms, stores, and materials for the ordnance department in their custody."

In one word, everything and everybody connected with the department of ordnance, in the field, at the laboratories, foundries, arsenals, or wherever they might be, were brought through this inspectorship, inquisitorial in its powers, to the attention, whether with good or bad report, of the commander of artillery of the United States. The practical effect of this was what Congress intended it should be, and that officer was restored to his position, in fact as well as in name, of commander of the artillery arm. The pay of the commander of artillery was increased $75, that of the surveyor $70 per month, as compensation for the duties imposed, and subordinate officers of the new department received an increase in proportion to their pay in the line.

Colonel John Lamb was, March 6th, 1779, appointed to the office of surveyor. He had from early in life devoted much time and study to obtaining a knowledge of the technical features of the artillery, while a wide experience in the field, in the several grades of captain, major and colonel, had thoroughly informed him of the details of actual service, its needs and defects, and suggested means for overcoming them.

The office of field commissary was conferred upon Mr. Samuel Hodgdon, a civilian commissary of the ordnance department. This gentleman, whose superior as a man of business the Revolutionary war did not produce, had first been appointed commissary by General Knox, February 1st, 1777, and had served in that capacity, principally in the northern department, with Major Stevens' artillery battalion, under Schuyler and Gates. The establishment of his department, the personnel of which were devoid of military rank, was a most difficult matter; but he grappled with the task and was successful. His character was known and appreciated. When Colonel Flower died (April 28th, 1781,) he was appointed commissary-general of military stores, the duties of which office, together with those of field commissary, he performed until the end of the war.*

With such assistants as Lamb and Hodgdon it may be supposed that Knox found his labors greatly facilitated. The appointment

---

* Mr. Hodgdon also performed the duties of assistant quartermaster for the State of Pennsylvania, under Pickering. During President Washington's administration he was quartermaster-general of the army. He filled these positions with conspicuous ability; and notwithstanding a congressional committee held him partially responsible for St. Clair's defeat, December 4th, 1791, public confidence in his great business capacity was not in the least impaired. When General Washington was called to the head of the army in 1798, Mr. Hodgdon was again drawn into the service as superintendent of military supplies and confidential adviser to the Secretary of War.

of the surveyor, however, led directly and rather abruptly to the disintegration of the ordnance department proper. The attention of that functionary was first directed to the extensive laboratory at Springfield, Massachusetts, where, due to misunderstandings between the civil and the military branches of the service, the costly plant was turning out few products, and they inferior in quality. At the same time Governor Reed, of Pennsylvania, reported practically the same state of affairs existing at the Carlisle arsenal. Concerning this the governor remarked: "The iron-work of the carriages was most villainously done. I could run my hands into the joints and cracks in the wood-work, and one 18-pounder carriage that I saw broke down under the first fire."

The reports of the surveyor having been adverse to the management at these and other places, Congress, on August 12th, 1780, razeed the department, retaining only Colonel Flower, one deputy, and one commissary each at Springfield, Carlisle, and the Virginia laboratory, and two or three at places of minor importance. Except the chief, all the principal officers were now civilians. Each company of artillery-artificers was reduced to one officer and forty enlisted men. Lieutenant-Colonel David Mason, of Knox's original regiment, detached for ordnance duty as early as 1776; Mr. Ezekiel Cheever, the first commissary of military stores in the army; Major Eayres, of the artillery artificer-regiment, with the subalterns, almost to a man, were discharged; and although several captains of that regiment were retained as superintendents of harness-makers, carpenters, wheelwrights, armorers, smiths, &c., they were, with scarcely an exception, placed under the orders of civilian commissaries. The next blow was struck by the resolve of Congress of March 29th, 1781, which discharged all the artillery-artificers except two companies. The death of Colonel Flower, and his succession by Mr. Hodgdon, placed now, as had formerly been done by the resolution of Congress of February, 1778, the affairs of the ordnance department, both in the field and elsewhere, under the immediate supervision of a single head; but circumstances were changed, and the whole was entirely under the superior control of the commander of artillery, by virtue either of original powers conferred by Congress, or powers assumed with the acquiescence of the commander-in-chief and the board of war and ordnance. This appears from Mr. Hodgdon's correspondence, covering the minute details of artillery technical affairs at this period.

It only remained to take from it what little of permanency was left, even in appearance, that the ordnance department, as such, should cease to exist. This was accomplished by resolution of Congress of July 24th, 1782, which removed every semblance of stability, by authorizing the Secretary at War to appoint from time to time a commissary of military stores, and, if agreeable to them, to select as many officers of the army to act in that department as the exigencies of service required. Mr. Hodgdon, in a letter to Captain Irish, of the artillery-artificers, concerning this resolution, said: "The department is annihilated. I am retained as commissary of military stores. The Secretary retains you as deputy, with one assistant, one conductor, and one director in the laboratory."

Thus terminated the department of commissary-general of military stores, or the ordnance department of the Revolution. Springing from the inevitable necessities of active service, it was so unfortunate as to receive a distinct organization under the blighting influence of a faction in the army and in Congress, which, seeking to render the department independent of the commander-in-chief and the general of artillery, rendered its successful operation impossible; for the wheels of its machinery, when the army took the field, either dragged heavily or stood still. The rapidly-developed defects caused the organization of a field commissary department, independent of the first. Thereafter it was practically nothing more than a supply corps made up of mechanics, mostly civilians, whose work was supervised by the general of artillery. When the army was disbanded, in 1783, Mr. Hodgdon, with several assistants, was temporarily retained in service. He acted as agent for the Secretary at War, whose duty it was to preserve all military supplies, and was finally discharged July 20th, 1785.

Under resolve of Congress, September, 1782, the field commissary department was readjusted to meet the needs of an army upon the eve of peace. The appointment of the personnel thereafter devolved upon the commanders of artillery in the main and southern armies, acting with the approval of their respective commanding generals. Its existence officially terminated when, pursuant to the proclamation of October 18th, the army was dissolved November 3d, 1783.

The arrangement of a peace establishment was a matter of no little difficulty, although one to which Congress early addressed itself, by appointing a committee, of which Colonel Hamilton was the active member, to consult with the commander-in-chief. Among all the responses to General Washington's request to be furnished with the views of officers, that of General Du Portail, of the engineers, was perhaps most pertinent to the subject now being considered. His counsels derived additional weight from the fact that he was acquainted not only with the experience and practice of European armies, but also of our own. He advised uniting the artillery and engineers, dividing the frontier into sections, placing artillery and engineer affairs in each section under an officer of rank, while over all would be placed a commandant and director-general of artillery and fortification for the United States. To the director-general subordinate officers of the department of artillery and engineers were to be accountable, he to be their commander and the head of administrative affairs, through whom would be transmitted all orders of Congress or the Secretary at War affecting the corps. It was absolutely necessary, Du Portail significantly remarked, to have such an officer, in order that the important branch—the administrative—should be governed by constant principles; for inconvenience, prejudicial to the public interests alone, would follow from having several heads to the department, each independent of the others.

This argument was conclusive with Mr. Hamilton's committee, which recommended the adoption, in the proposed military peace establishment, of the principles here announced; but the unsettled and imbecile Government was incapable of doing anything calculated to secure its perpetuity, and the report of the committee was never heard from after being submitted to Congress.

In the meantime General Knox, retained in service temporarily when the army was disbanded to take care of the interests of the Government in the resulting disorder, wrote the following letter to General Washington, in which was first suggested the advisability of making the Secretary at War commander of the peace army, whatever that might prove to be, and adding to his duties those of master-general of ordnance. He said:

"I have had it in contemplation for a long time past to mention to your excellency the idea of a master-general of ordnance. I beg leave at the same time to remark that, although my expectations and wishes are for private life, yet if any office should be formed upon the broad scale of national policy, I might, if thought worthy, find it convenient to give it my zealous assistance."

General Washington replied:

"I have conversed with several Members of Congress upon the propriety, in time of peace, of uniting the offices of Secretary at War and master-general of ordnance in one person, and letting him have command of the troops on the peace establishment, not as an appendage of right—for that, I think, would be wrong—but by separate appointment at the discretion of Congress. If done, it will make a handsome appointment. My wishes to serve you in it you need not doubt."

Congressional action was such as to meet these views favorably, and was probably the result of General Washington's recommendations, made pursuant to the arrangement here entered into; for although, when Secretary at War Lincoln resigned, it was not expected that his place would be filled, this idea was abandoned, and, by resolution of May 29th, 1784, the proper committee was directed to revise the institution of the War Office, while on the 27th of January following an ordinance was passed to ascertain the powers and duties of the incumbent. Knox was, March 8th, 1785, chosen Secretary at War; his functions were substantially those of the old Secretary, but in addition he was directed to determine "the arrangement, destination, and operation of such troops as are or may be in service, subject to the orders of Congress, or the Committee of the States in the recess of Congress." This made him commander of the forces, and, subject to the limitations indicated, he exercised that authority until the installation of the first President under the Constitution.

In technical artillery matters the powers of the new Secretary were to a degree more limited than those of his predecessor, who had been intrusted with the building and management of laboratories, arsenals, foundries, and magazines; but this resulted from the circumstance that for several years after the war no attempts were made at manufacturing new matériel, the old stock alone being drawn upon for the limited demands of service. It was made the duty of the Secretary at War to see the matériel properly stored and taken care of, to insure which being done the law provided that he should, at least once a year, visit all the magazines and deposits of public stores, reporting to Congress their condition, with the measures taken for their preservation. But the expectation that he would personally inspect these widely-separated depositories proved to be an absurd impossibility, incompatible with a proper performance of his functions at the seat of Government, and by force of circumstances the inspector's duties were devolved on subordinates.

The inauguration of the first President transferred the command of the army from the Secretary of War. In the administration of artillery affairs, however, the functions of the Secretary remained practically as before. He was responsible for matériel, and, at the option of the President, gave orders to the artillery, with other troops.

This was possible in the quiet immediately succeeding the Revolution; but the first symptoms of serious national trouble called for increased administrative facilities. Accordingly, when, in 1794, our relations with England assumed a threatening aspect, leading to the initiating of a plan for the fortification of the sea-board, the raising of a corps of artillerists and engineers, and the providing what was deemed a large amount of cannon and warlike stores, the Secretary of War was given, by act of April 2d, 1794, an assistant in the person of the superintendent of military stores.

This officer's duty was to keep account of warlike matériel, quartermaster and other stores appertaining to the War Department. Practically, however, accountability for public property was but very imperfectly insured. It was not at first considered possible to devise any system by which company commanders could be held responsible for property in their possession, and as late as March, 1800, the superintendent of military stores reported that there was no one whose business it was to make returns for the ordnance in the hands of the regiments. This difficulty was attempted to be met by General Orders issued from the Adjutant-General's Office, War Department, March 17th, 1800, wherein were promulgated regulations for making returns of ordnance and other property. By subsequent orders the military and assistant military agents provided for in the peace organization of March 16th, 1802, were directed, together with all post commanders to whom were issued military and quartermaster stores, to render an account of them to the superintendent of military stores, the agents quarterly and the post commanders semi-annually. Although, no doubt, the surveillance of the superintendent prevented waste and loss, the inadequacy of the system of responsibility may be judged from the circumstance that, in 1809, in response to a direct inquiry of the Secretary of War, the superintendent replied that *there was no system in force which enabled him to know where the Government property was located, or what stores were in existence, as military agents and post commanders exercised their volition about making returns for property in their possession.*

To those acquainted with military affairs, no statement other than this is necessary to prove the utter and entire absence of any proper system of administration. It was a fitting prelude to the enormous losses and misdirection of supplies which marked the movements of the small armies of the war of 1812, and caused commanders to cast a hundred anxious glances to the rear where they cast one towards the enemy.

The office of purveyor of public supplies, created by act of February 23d, 1795, was another of those attempts to improve army administrative affairs which followed when the people, rudely awakened from the dream of universal and everlasting peace which followed the Revolution, were preparing by force of arms, under the vivifying influence of the constitutional Government, to assume and maintain an honorable position among the nations of the world. The duty of the office was to procure all arms, military and naval stores, or other articles of supply requisite for the service of the United States. At first the purveyor was an officer of the Treasury Department only; but by act of July 16th, 1798, when preparations were making for war with France, the contracting for and purchase of supplies for the army was placed in the hands of the Secretary of War, and the purveyor made subject to his orders, thus becoming, at least to this extent, an officer of the War Department.

But it did not suffice that the purveyor should purchase, and the superintendent of military supplies should take care of, artillery matériel; it was found necessary to have an officer act in an intermediate capacity, to examine into the quality of purchases before acceptance by the Government. In a letter dated June 28th, 1798, Secretary McHenry remarked:

"It is with infinite regret the Secretary is obliged to mention that the ordnance of our country is by no means in a position to command respect. Part of it was collected during a season of difficulty and necessity, from different countries, and consequently many of the guns are essentially defective, and those of the same class differ in weight, length, and calibre. The variance in these particulars occasions much trouble and inconvenience, in providing appropriate ammunition, stores, apparatus, carriages, besides subjecting the military service to injurious delays, and the fatal consequences which might result from ammunition and implements being supplied which, in time of need, will be found not adapted to the piece. As there is no established standard, it has also happened, from a defect of knowledge in our founders, or some other cause, that most of the cannon that have been cast within or on account of the United States are defective in very essential points, and exhibit varieties in those cast at the same furnace, and of the same class, with those procured from abroad.

"It is important that some arrangement should be immediately adopted, calculated to give efficacy to a proper system and correct these evils. It is not enough that the President determine upon the size, weight, dimensions, and calibres of the different kinds of cannon, either to be made or imported into the United States, for their use, unless an *inspector of artillery* can be appointed to see that all regulations appertaining to the ordnance department be executed and observed with exactitude."

Moved by these just considerations, Congress, in the bill then pending for the augmentation of the army, and which became law July 16th, 1798, made the appointment of an inspector of artillery obligatory; and, to insure technical knowledge on the part of the person so designated, provided that he should be taken from the line of artillerists and engineers.

Concerning a fit character for this office, President Adams wrote to Inspector-General Hamilton, who had urged the appointment of Major Louis de Tousard, that, while recognizing the professional qualifications of this gentleman, he hesitated to make him inspector of artillery, as there was such a deep-seated distrust of French officers on the part of the people that he expected much trouble. It must be confessed that the President, by promptly dismissing La Rochefontaine, colonel of the corps of artillerists and engineers, and placing the other obnoxious officers under a ban, adopted rather energetic measures to quiet popular apprehension; but, as to Tousard, suspicion was speedily and very justly allayed. He was soon after informally put upon this duty, and May 26th, 1800, appointed lieutenant-colonel commandant of the Second Regiment of artillerists and engineers, with the additional formal appointment of inspector of artillery for the United States. The duties of the office were defined by the Secretary of War in general terms to be—

"First, to take an inventory of ordnance and ordnance stores now on hand, and see that all are placed where they will be properly taken care of; second, to inspect all ordnance and articles of artillery matériel, making report to the superintendent of military stores; third, to prepare and furnish contractors and others proper models for gun carriages and other articles of artillery whenever necessary, and to see that no subaltern officer makes any artillery machine which is not of the model adopted; fourth, to provide lists and models of all necessary utensils and apparatus for artillery at the several laboratories, &c."

The administration of artillery affairs from this time down to 1812 may be summed up as follows: The technical; the Secretary of War contracted for supplies; the purveyor purchased those not procured by contract through the Secretary; the inspector furnished models, and saw that they were strictly complied with, while the superintendent of military supplies received and stored, for distribution on requisitions, what was accepted by the inspector; and as no rigid system of returns was observed, or indeed deemed practicable, an attempt was made to protect the interests of the Government by making it the duty of the superintendent to cut down all estimates for supplies to the lowest limits compatible with public requirements, and of these requirements he was made the judge. Regarding military subordination, the regiment of artillerists, in common with the rest of the army, was, in a general way, under the orders of the Secretary of War, who therefore could be said to administer affairs affecting the artillery, both technical and personnel.

The reorganizing act of March 16th, 1802, was construed to abolish the office of inspector of artillery. Subsequent to the passage of this act, and prior to the organization of the ordnance department in 1812, the colonel of the regiment of artillerists generally performed the duties of inspector, and was the principal assistant to the Secretary on technical artillery matters; in his custody were preserved models for guns, carriages, and machines. Those seeking information on which could be based estimates for the manufacture or supply of matériel were invariably referred by the Secretary to the colonel of the artillerists for details; and in June, 1812, after the department had been authorized by law, Secretary Eustis wrote that officer, then in command of the artillery in New York Harbor: "Until the ordnance department shall be in operation, you will, as far as your other duties may permit, continue to superintend the preparations making therein." Of these duties he was finally relieved by the commissary-general of ordnance a few weeks later. Thus passed from the control of the senior officer of artillery the functions of inspector or supervisor of the technical affairs of that arm.

It thus appears that, from the termination of the Revolutionary war down to the appointment of the commissary-general of ordnance, in 1812, the Secretary of War exercised a very close personal control of technical artillery matters, and there is no reason to suppose that his course would have changed had not the war of 1812 given him other things to think about, and demonstrated the necessity for intrusting minor affairs to subordinates. The fact cited may have been due to the imposition upon the Secretary, under the Confederation, of the duties of master-general of ordnance; and although, prior to 1800, the President himself was supposed to prescribe models for cannon and other matériel, while at that date this authority was transferred to the inspector of artillery, still, the official correspondence covering the period from 1785 to 1812 shows, apparently, that not a carriage was made, not a gun cast, not a single new feature affecting artillery—men or matériel—carried into execution, but that the Secretary of War discussed the measure, raised objections, suggested improvements, and in fine gave as much attention to the matter as though he were chief of the artillery alone.

This was particularly so under Secretaries Knox and Dearborn, both of whom were, from experience, competent judges; and although under the former little new matériel was manufactured, and that of old style, this was not the case with the latter, under whose administration the Gribeauval carriage was brought to the point of being first introduced into our service, a new and excellent system of iron field guns successfully manufactured, thereby greatly increasing the mobility of the field artillery. These, with the equipping of the first horse battery, in 1808, mark what should have been an important epoch in the history of the United States artillery. That no adequate results followed these intelligent exertions was no fault of Secretary Dearborn, and but partially so of the arm itself, many of whose officers were among the ablest and most cultured in service. It followed from lack of a competent head to the artillery—a man who could recognize an improvement when demonstrated to be such—capable of using the good material of the personnel to raise it to its true position as a scientific arm; from changes in the head of the War Department, one tearing down what the other built up; from the depleted state of the treasury and what proved to be false notions of economy; lastly, from the fatal sense of immunity from war into which the Government had lapsed while the reverberation of the *Leopard's* guns yet echoed along the shores of the Atlantic; and although the new system of field artillery proved its superiority over its predecessor in a second struggle with Great Britain, neither it nor the light artillery fully met, owing to the causes mentioned, the anticipations of their projector.

As to the actual professional acquirements of the artillery at this time, (1802–1812,) it may be safely asserted that the mass of its officers knew little or nothing of the higher duties of the profession. Combining, in 1794, the artillerists and engineers had not been productive of the happy consequences hoped for by Mr. Hamilton's committee and General Du Portail. Both La Rochefontaine and Tousard, of that arm, were capable scientific officers, but attention was then turned to the engineering rather than to the artillery duties of the corps; while the former occupied the time of the best educated officers, the latter were turned over to contractors and foundrymen. Artillery officers did not, there is reason to believe, come in contact with practical technical duties, from 1794 to 1800, to a degree that would in the least benefit them.

The embarrassment caused by the Frenchmen when war with France was imminent was a sufficient reason for gradually eliminating them, which process, commenced in 1798, was rendered complete by the reorganizing act of 1802. But, while the country was thus reassured, the artillery was injured in having withdrawn from its ranks its most accomplished members. Nor was this all: that reorganizing act took from the arm its only American officer, above the rank of captain, who was known to be possessed of great abilities and scientific attainments, and placed him at the head of the new engineer corps; while, as colonel of the regiment of artillerists, was retained a respectably practical soldier, with some knowledge of simpler technical affairs, but disqualified by habit and education for the position of chief of a scientific corps. *Here was made a mistake from which the arm has never recovered.* That was the time at which a right direction might have been given affairs; but, being allowed to pass unimproved, through incapacity, the organization of a technical artillery, under capable management if possible, was a logical and inevitable consequence so soon as either efficient readjustment of the army was determined on, or the accumulating responsibilities of war rendered it impracticable for the Secretary to devote a large part of his time to personal supervision of artillery affairs.

Intelligent soldiers, who knew what the deficiencies of service were, had pointed out the necessity for reform of some kind. In the fall of 1811 a board of officers, embracing General Gansevoort, Colonel Williams, and others first in merit in the army, submitted to the Secretary of War, among other recommendations for the improvement of the military establishment, the following for the artillery: First, the adoption of a uniform system of tactics; second, reviving the office and powers of inspector of artillery; third, the appointment of an artillery board, upon which should rest responsibility for determining models, proportions, and metal of cannon of all kinds, in order that system should be established in that department, where, at the time, nothing was definitely determined in regard to these important matters.

Colonel Izard, of the Second Regiment of artillery, (being raised,) likewise addressed the Secretary upon the same subject, urging that active measures be taken for the amelioration of the condition of that arm, the same in substance but more elaborate in detail than that of Du Portail thirty years before. Concerning the professional status of the artillery at the time (1812), this officer, who was perhaps the best informed in that branch of service, remarked:

"The various corps denominated artillery have been such for many years in the United States only in name. The pecuniary advantages which accompany the exertions of American youth in other liberal professions have necessarily deviated their attention from the studies which are indispensable for the exercise of the scientific branches of the military duty, and which require long and serious instruction. It is not to be wondered at, therefore, that the officers of the United States artillery, with but few exceptions, are only acquainted with details of service which are common to every description of soldiers. *With us, contrary to the practice in Europe, it sometimes happens that officers attain to the highest ranks in the army, of corps that are entirely scientific, without being acquainted with the elements which are necessary for the execution of the duties of a subaltern.* How all-important for the public it is to have a remedy for the evil, is proved by the difficulties in procuring those qualified to take the higher commands in the artillery and engineer corps at the present crisis."

The crisis mentioned precipitated what events had predetermined; the technical artillery was given into the hands of those competent to perform its duties; the ordnance department was organized under an able, accomplished scholar and officer; while to the regiments were left the glorious to be sure, yet restricted, duties of the field, to perform which, however, most efficiently and economically, required the technical knowledge of the new department, supplemented by the practical experience of the old. Thus, as a result of the selection of improper personnel in 1802, was the artillery, contrary to the practice of all other armies, separated ten years later into two parts, each in itself imperfect, yet which, properly united, make up a complete and symmetrical whole.

This continued until March 2d, 1821, when, in the reduction and rearrangement of the army, the ordnance department was merged in the artillery and technical duties restored to that arm. The reorganizing act provided that to each of the four artillery regiments should be appointed one supernumerary captain, while the President was given authority to select from the artillery the other necessary officers for ordnance duty.

These were subject, in the execution of their special duties, to the orders of the War Department only; but when companies or detachments of artillery were stationed at arsenals, the commandants of the latter were responsible to regimental and department commanders for the regular returns and reports. In so far as discipline was concerned, officers on ordnance duty were on the same footing as others; and being, in technical matters, exclusively under the orders of the War Department, questions of responsibility to seniors were happily adjusted. On the one hand, they had constantly before their eyes the fact that they were part of the army and amenable to military law; on the other, that, in the performance of the duties to which they were assigned, they were not subject to interference except by order of the Secretary of War.

To insure perfect working of the new department, a special inspectorship was deemed advisable. With this end in view, one of the regular inspectors-general was at first assigned to the artillery arm alone. As to the personnel, his duties, besides those defined by general regulations, embraced reports upon the character, capability, and usefulness of the several officers and agents connected with the artillery, as well as the condition of the posts and troops under their command. Regarding technical affairs, he was instructed to direct his attention to the various depots of stores, arsenals, foundries, and manufactories of arms; the mode of fabrication of the matériel of the army, its quantity and quality. When, afterwards, the order assigning this officer to duty in the artillery was revoked, and the inspectors-general directed to alternate in their inspections without regard to arm of service, it was deemed necessary to have a special inspector for the technical branch at least. Accordingly, a field officer of artillery, assisted by a subaltern, was appointed to subject to proof and critical examination all cannon, shot, shells, &c., at the several foundries, and which were intended for the army and the militia of the United States.

The school of practice at Fortress Monroe was intended by Secretary Calhoun to add to the general efficiency, and, with a proper organization of the artillery, would no doubt have proved to be a powerful auxiliary to that desirable end; but it is not questioned that this school, like all else appertaining to the arm, suffered from want of a central administrative bureau, and, in consequence, but imperfectly attained the object for which it was instituted.

Merging the ordnance in the artillery was done upon the recommendation of Secretary Calhoun, whose clear and logical mind grasped the whole subject of the military establishment in all its details, and, in the duties to be performed, assigned to each its proper part. In a report communicated to the House of Representatives, dated December 20th, 1820, there appeared as his reason for the measure the opinion that, "by uniting the three corps of the ordnance, light artillery, and artillery in one, *appointing one general staff at the head of it*, and making its officers pass in rotation through the three services, the organization of the army would be rendered more simple and the instruction of the officers much more complete."

As the most important step towards putting these views into practice, the Secretary proposed, first of all, that there be appointed for the new corps a lieutenant-colonel commandant, with a staff and administrative machinery competent to give efficiency to the system. But it was a time of reduction as well as of reorganization; officers who had devoted their best years to the service of their country were being razeed in rank or turned out to begin life anew; the struggle for place that ensued was natural. Nor was the legislature insensible to the claims of worthy veterans; personal considerations not unfrequently took precedence of public interests; the artillery arm, under the color of reform, was again, as in 1802, sacrificed to make place for individuals. Instead of being united in one compact whole, as proposed, it was arranged to four distinct regiments, without a bond of union between them. Amidst the disordered body stood the technical artillery—in it, but not of it.

The scheme as attempted was a failure; it lacked every element of strength, while its weaknesses were conspicuous and fundamental. First of all was the omission to place a capable, energetic commandant, with a competent staff, at the head of affairs. This was a vital defect. Nothing in our experience since the foundation of the Government is more clearly established than the fact that, unless there be a single directing mind to set and maintain in harmonious working its delicate and complex parts, no department of the public service can long survive the strains incident to practical and successful operation. The artillery of 1821 proved no exception to this rule.

But this was not all. The regulations established by the War Department restricted, with three or four exceptions, the tours of artillery officers on ordnance duty to one year, a time entirely inadequate to render their services of any substantial benefit to either themselves or the department. Nothing could have struck a deadlier blow at efficiency than this rule of short details. It is very generally believed that four years is the least time that officers detached should serve on this or any other scientific duty. The first year is devoted to obtaining knowledge elementary in character, while, with *faithful* public servants, every additional year adds, in greater or less degree, to the value of a good officer in his specialty. Under the rule adopted, no sooner had an officer become somewhat at home in his new avocation than he was taken away, and his place filled by a new-comer, who must, like his predecessor, spend all his time becoming familiar with mere rudiments.

To the foregoing there must be added, as one of the main elements of weakness, the seeds of dissatisfaction, germinating in intrigue, sown when the ordnance department was *merged, without being absorbed, in the artillery*. The principal officers of that department who were retained under the new régime were placed permanently at the head of artillery technical affairs; but the merging process had cut off their individual prospects of promotion. It were better for them that the newly-organized artillery fail in its mission; return to former practices would be to their advantage; and however much they may have labored, if at all, to build up and sustain the honor of the corps into which they were transferred, their efforts in this direction are not of record; while their schemes for its dismemberment commenced so soon as Mr. Calhoun, the reputed although not the real author of the merging plan, (as actually carried out,) had left his seat in the War Office. No effort of theirs was spared to demonstrate the defects of the existing system; every argument that ingenuity could devise to compass the cherished object in view was pressed upon Congress with a persistency which, had the same abilities, zeal, and industry been directed to making the ordnance department inside the artillery a success, might, spite of adverse surroundings, have partially redeemed the name of the arm to which they belonged and which name they trailed in the dust. Unfortunately, the condition of the artillery, the result of errors of organization and administration which have been pointed out, reinforced and made more apparent by professional apathy on the part of its own disaffected members, furnished a basis for the arguments of the latter; it fell a prey to the weaknesses, inherent or acquired, of the system, and to the parasitic attacks of those who, residing at the seat of Government, had the advantage of personal contact with Congress, while the body of the arm, scattered in regiments to the four winds, without a head to champion its cause or present the true reasons for the existing state of affairs, was compelled to submit to dismemberment, through inability to act in its own defense.

That the promotion to higher grades of those interested was a consideration of the first moment with them, without which the much-sought-for separation was neither acceptable to nor deemed advisable by them, the voluminous papers on the subject with which for six years Congress was deluged give abundant proof. Each was accompanied by a carefully-prepared plan to increase the rank of those who, by virtue of their positions, might expect to be benefited.

Protestations of virtue and disinterestedness in the public service are legitimate objects for suspicion when invariably coupled with conditions for securing personal advancement.

Let not injustice be done the memory of Mr. Calhoun by supposing that a department such as the reorganized artillery of 1821 was his work; far from it. His propositions contemplated reuniting, in a well-proportioned, efficient corps, under the control of one mind, the two parts of what ought to be, and in other armies is, a single service. The organization actually given possessed, with many of its own, every weakness, without a single element of strength, appertaining to the well-considered, admirable plan of the distinguished Secretary.*

---

*Notwithstanding our melancholy experience from 1821 to 1832, the Confederate authorities, to whom the history of those times was familiar, evidently did not, in 1861, deem the union of the artillery and ordnance incompatible with a proper efficiency, but the reverse. They adopted the merging plan of 1821, in form at least.

The Confederate army regulations prescribed that "the senior officer of artillery on ordnance duty is, under the direction of the Secretary of War, charged with the superintendence and administration of the ordnance bureau;" while for field service it was provided that the senior officer of artillery on ordnance duty attached to an army should have charge and direction of the depots of ordnance for the supply of such army. He was to correspond with the chief of artillery through the adjutant-general of that army.

The ordnance officers of the Confederacy, from Brigadier-General Gorgas, chief of the bureau, down, were artillery officers on ordnance duty. The department embraced an ordnance bureau proper, with its officers in the field, at the arsenals and depots, of a nitre and mining bureau; and a bureau of foreign supplies.

It is stated by those familiar with the facts that the workings of this department were eminently successful; that its history, while illustrating the difficulties which lay in the way of supplying large armies under adverse circumstances, demonstrates at the same time that energy and skill, intelligently directed, can surmount every obstacle.

Had the same earnest zeal in the public service characterized the efforts of those who had immediate charge of the department from 1821 to 1832, the result of the merging experiment, which failed so disastrously of beneficial effects, might and probably would have been different.

Since the reorganization of 1832 technical artillery affairs have, under the law, been confided to the ordnance department, then rehabilitated. The act of February 8th, 1815, which the resuscitating act of April 5th, 1832, revived, had been enacted under the auspices of the first and, perhaps, the greatest of its chiefs, Colonel Decius Wadsworth; and it is a model for the concise and clear manner in which the duties of a department may be defined.

Those who labored for the severance of the technical from the combatant artillery, so nearly as political favoritism would permit, now had their reward in the promotion they had sought. Fortunately for the stability of their plans there was placed at the head of the department an officer of ability, education, and long experience in the duties which now chiefly were intrusted to his supervision. The principal assistants were gentlemen of attainments, while among the junior ranks were some of the most approved officers whose names have adorned the rolls of the army—men whose untiring efforts to place upon a firm footing, elevate to and maintain at a high standard their branch of service, challenge the admiration of all who are familiar therewith, or the circumstances under which they were rendered. Their devotion to duty has not been surpassed in the history of the military profession in this country; nor do the members of that profession themselves generally know either the character of their unobtrusive labors, or the full value of the results flowing therefrom.

The personnel of the department has continued to be of a high order of merit. Sweeping at first from other departments and from the line of the army some of the brightest intellects, it has since that time attempted, as a rule, to recruit the commissioned ranks from among those graduates of the military academy standing first in scientific and scholastic attainments; while in these and other respects those appointees from other sources, which a broad and wise policy has admitted, stand second to none.

From the beginning, the department possessed elements of strength which the artillery, except during the Revolution, has lacked, viz., an organization compact and homogeneous from top to bottom, under the direction of a chief, aided by a central system of administration, thus rendering unity of purpose and action easy and practicable. Moreover, it offered opportunity to place and maintain the best, ablest, and most valued officers in positions where their powers and services could be fully utilized,

174 HISTORICAL SKETCH OF THE ARTILLERY, U. S. ARMY.

while the indifferent and incapable were allowed to sink out of sight.

The department inherited much of solid worth from the artillery, and was further fortunate in having early extended to its members, by intelligent and energetic Secretaries of War, unusual facilities for obtaining valuable professional information abroad.

The technical artillery had, in 1830, been placed in possession of all data pertaining to, and had commenced the manufacture of, the new French English-modified style of carriages; that which soon became and has remained the one feature common to all field and siege artilleries of civilized armies. This was of the first importance to any scheme for a reorganized artillery matériel. There were also available and ready, to the hand of him who would use them, the results of deliberations of boards of artillery and ordnance officers convened to investigate the condition of the armaments of the country and report plans for their improvement, at various times from 1818 to 1838. A commission was sent to Europe by Mr. Poinsett, who, with a true genius for military affairs, which took in at a glance, as it were, the requirements of his department, and pointed out what was the one thing necessary to give breadth of thought and exact information to those officers particularly and directly intrusted with the delicate, responsible task of devising and elaborating a comprehensive scheme for a national armament. The knowledge acquired by the commission was of great value, not only in a limited technical sense within the department, but to the rest of the army and to the public, which were thus informed as to what was transpiring elsewhere in these important matters.

Such were the materials from which, under the management and inventive genius of Colonel Bomford, aided by the industry and intelligent perseverance of Major Baker, Captains Mordecai, Huger and others, his assistants, there was evolved the first complete system of artillery matériel adopted in the service of the United States.

How well the department, in its entire work, has met the views and fulfilled the prophecies of those who advocated its establishment, the army and the country will judge; it is foreign to the purpose to here enter that field of controversy. It suffices to remark that at the epoch of the breaking out of the Civil war the United States smooth-bore system of ordnance was not surpassed in excellence by any other. That its rifle system is far behind others is not due to lack either of ability or knowledge of details on the part of the personnel, but to inadequate appropriations, without which improvements cannot be either worked out or practically tested; to the fact that, while adding to its strength politically by making it a compact unit both in offense and defense, the exclusiveness of the organization has a tendency to narrow the minds of its members, to lead them to follow unduly their own fancies to the exclusion of other and better things originating elsewhere, to render them mere theorists after all, through the impossibility of their knowing from experience either the strong points or the weaknesses of their own handiwork, and to cause them to look with suspicion and misgivings upon the suggestions of those who, from knowledge acquired in the field of practical service, are alone capable of judging of the real merits and demerits of artillery or other warlike matériel.

The duties of the department "are *defined by law*, and consist in providing, preserving, distributing, and accounting for every description of artillery, small-arms, and all the munitions of war which may be required by the fortresses of the country, the armies in the field, and for the whole body of the militia of the Union, including the general principles of construction, the details of models and forms of all military weapons." It was expected and intended, when its duties were assigned, that the construction and inspection of all cannon, carriages, implements, apparatus for ordnance, wagons and forges, the inspection and proving of powder, and the preparation of all kinds of ammunition and ordnance stores, would be carried on by that department. The anticipation has in large degree, though not entirely, been realized. The department points to its Wadsworth, Bomford, Mordecai, Rodman, and others since their day, who have stood and now stand in the front rank of scientific investigators; but isolation, self-imposed withdrawal from contact with mankind, must have to no small extent a benumbing effect on the intellectual vigor of any department if its members give way to this habit, while inventive minds elsewhere will not remain idle. Of recent years Congress has taken from the department much that was originally its prerogative, by providing that mixed boards of officers, and sometimes its own committees, should examine into the merits of all improvements and inventions presented touching the particular part of the armament under consideration, whether coming from the small world inside or the large world outside the ordnance department. In the list of improvements and inventions accepted by those boards and committees which have been known to possess most knowledge of the subject-matter of their deliberations, those emanating from the ordnance bureau are conspicuous by their absence.

Why these boards and committees are deemed necessary when they so seriously affect the prestige of the department by taking from it the most important of those "*duties defined by law,*" is known, perhaps, only to the legislature.

It is worthy of remark that, although organized for purely technical duties, the department accepts with reluctance the rôle of artisans, overseers, and manufacturers, which their predecessors, the artillery-artificers of the Revolution, were, and which the "*duties defined by law*" make them. Efforts to escape from this position have been strenuous, long sustained, and have become of interest to the combatant artillery for the reason that they have invariably resulted in trenching upon its rights, privileges, and duties. Seeking the privilege of manning the siege train, the howitzer and rocket battery, by ordnance mechanics during the Mexican war, while regular artillery marched as infantry; organizing an ordnance department in the field during the Civil war, although the laws of April 5th, 1832, and July 17th, 1862, confided that duty to artillery officers; recommending that boards to determine the nature of fortress armaments be organized to exclude artillery officers, while the proper functions of the latter in the premises are assumed by themselves; recommending that the results of all artillery firing, both in peace and war, be tabulated and sent to the chief of ordnance, who thereby becomes, to this extent, chief of artillery,—all these things the department has done, thus usurping the functions of the regimental artillery, and making itself what it insists that it is not, yet which at the same time its assumed and eagerly grasped-after duties make it—artillery staff.

The disposition here manifested to encroach upon the long established rights of the regiments is not, perhaps, to be wondered at; but it cannot be indulged without the utter annihilation of the latter and sweeping away the last pretext for opposing the reuniting, under a proper organization, of the technical and combatant branches of the artillery arm. To gentlemen reared in a school where to seek and fight the enemy is instilled into youth as the highest honor to which the soldier can aspire, this being cut off from all hope of appearing on the field is not agreeable in practice, however it may appear in theory, even though accompanied by increased rank and pay. They cannot indulge the pleasing reflection of having alleviated the sufferings of their fellow-men cherished by the medical, nor that spiritual self-approbation for duty done which buoys up their chaplain non-combatant associates. As a consequence they yearn apparently to escape from a disagreeable situation, supplementing their *duties defined by law* by others *not defined*, yet more soldierly in their nature; and as the functions of artillery as a special arm of service naturally and properly appertain to artillery staff, they are selected. The department thereby gains an eclat which *under the law* it cannot have. In the absence of a chief of artillery at the seat of Government to protect the interests of the arm, this usurpation is all the more easily effected.

When the proposition is made to unite under efficient management the two parts of the artillery, it is earnestly protested by some—with what candor can now be judged—that the ordnance department is wholly absorbed in *duties defined by law*, the proper execution of which requires the combined talent, industry, and business capacity of all its members. No sooner is the danger passed than new inroads are made on the regimental artillery. How long the latter can sustain this undermining process, if continued, it is impossible to determine; its extinction as a separate arm, however, will be the inevitable result, while its prescriptive rights and duties pass to the artillery staff.

That the two corps should be separate is unnatural; and if convincing proof of this were wanting, it is furnished in the continued assumption by the ordnance of the duties pertaining to the other branch of service.

This state of affairs will continue, *the interests of individuals rather than those of the Government be served*, until Congress, with an eye single to the public good, builds up a reorganized artillery service, line and staff together, with a chief and a central administrative bureau similar to that of the ordnance department to-day, and in *which the most meritorious* of that department and of the artillery regiments will be absorbed.

The re-establishment of the ordnance left as before the four regiments of line artillery without aught to unite them. The want of a head to the corps was felt now even more than ever, and the absence of regulations defining its duties, rights and privileges, particularly in active service, binding upon all branches, has operated to the prejudice of its reputation, the misdirection of its powers, the usurpation of its special functions by non-combatants, and has resulted in an increased expense attending its management both in peace and war. There has not been wholly wanting, on the part of the artillery, either appreciation of, or disposition to remedy, the difficulties indicated; but the method whereby relief could best be obtained has not always been clear, or, when known, has not been practicable. Efforts in the right direction have been in the nature rather of isolated attempts than of systematic labors, upon a well-considered plan, looking to the amelioration of the public service.

The superior administrative control of the two branches of the artillery remained the same, after their re-separation, that it was previous to that event, *i. e.*, the technical under the War Department only, while the combatant was under the immediate orders of the general-in-chief, in regard not only to personnel, but the management of its interior affairs. The regiments have always been the military branch of the artillery department, forming part of the army proper, under the military commander. It was so during the Revolution; the periods, intermittent in character, during which General Wilkinson commanded the army; under General Brown and his successors after 1821. The only apparent exception to this was placing, when it was first organized, the command and administrative affairs of the artillery school of practice in 1824 under the control of the War Department. The reason doubtless was that Mr. Calhoun wished personally to supervise measures adopted for carrying into successful operation this experimental school, from which, under proper management, results highly beneficial to the service were anticipated; but whatever may have been the cause of the deviation in this instance from the general rule, it continued in operation but a short time, as by orders of January 26th, 1826, the troops composing that school were placed under the command of the general-in-chief of the army. Order No. 58, Adjutant-General's Office, that year, authorized the commanding officer of the eastern department to exercise the same military control over these troops as over others within the geographical limits of his command; while to the general-in-chief was reserved the exclusive right, under the War Department, to make regulations for the post as a school of instruction and practice. Stated reports and returns were, therefore, made to the department commander. Upon this basis the school was re-established in 1857, while the reorganization of 1867 placed all pertaining to the institution under the orders of the general of the army, subject of course to that general supervision exercised by the Secretary of War over all branches of the service. This is the status, as it should be, of the administrative affairs of the school at present.

In the regular artillery, the prerogatives of colonels in their own regiments, either of administration or command, are very limited. They do not control a battery beyond the particular posts at which they are serving, and it not unfrequently happens that captains command a larger portion of the regiment than the colonels themselves. Information as to the personnel is obtained from monthly returns of the batteries sent to regimental headquarters, which set forth the strength of each, with the changes since the last return; while quarterly reports make known the instruction received by officers, commissioned and non-commissioned, and the state of the battery funds. The authority of the colonel is exhausted when he has required these returns and reports to be made out as prescribed by orders; he cannot, even in the important (if properly attended to) matter of instruction, take one step with a view to making personal inspection beyond the limits of his own post. The regiment of twelve batteries, two of which at this time are equipped and serving as field artillery, is scattered over one or more military geographical departments, embracing several States, the field officers frequently at garrisons of a single battery, while their juniors have commands larger than this. The colonel may, and often does, know but little of the mental, moral, or physical qualifications of his officers through personal contact, nor they anything of him—a circumstance which operates to the detriment of all, who are thus deprived of those advantages ever flowing from an interchange of ideas between intelligent professional gentlemen, and that confidence resulting from a thorough knowledge of those upon whom, as coadjutors, reliance must be placed in times of danger.

The unfavorable conditions here mentioned are not of recent

growth, but are those under which, in all its mutations of organization, the artillery has labored from the beginning. Regiments have never been kept together. In Revolutionary times, aside from the companies attached to brigades and those making up the reserve at general headquarters, many were scattered at various posts and forts, particularly along the Hudson River; but in those times, unlike the present, artillery officers of rank, except those with the army in the field, exercised command over large districts, embracing numerous detached portions of their own arm of service.

With the artillery, as with other portions of the army, concentration in peace is conducive to discipline, economy, and general efficiency. The evils of dissemination, often a necessary incident of service, have been recognized, and measures have been taken, in a degree at least, to counteract them; as, witness the artillery school of practice of 1824; the camp of instruction at Trenton in 1839; the re-establishment of the former in 1857, and again, after the Civil war, ten years later; the elaborate scheme for practical and theoretical instruction combined, promulgated in General Orders No. 10, of 1859; and, finally, the Fort Riley light battery school of 1869. Of these, the school of practice at Fortress Monroe alone remains. The field batteries are isolated from one another, and, *as schools of practical instruction, their utility reduced to a minimum;* the war battalion formation, in which alone that arm now manœuvres with a large army, being entirely ignored, and officers but partially, and that in a an indifferent manner, taught the duties they will be called upon to perform during the first week of active campaign.

The tendency of late has been towards an abandonment of small posts and a concentration of batteries, and is in the right direction; but, if artillery is to be such except in name, these points of concentration must be supplied with the guns and other matériel to enable the troops to practice their specialty. To do otherwise is to neglect the obvious import of one of the most important lessons that recent wars have taught the arm, viz., that untrained artillerymen are incapable of rendering formidable in attack or defense the refined and complicated machinery they are required to use, and knowledge of which cannot be acquired by even long practice at the manual unless accompanied by study of the powers and capabilities of modern armaments, and of their proper use in active service. It is true that but few of our artillery troops have an opportunity to exercise with modern guns; but practice with those at hand, if accompanied by a wise course of instruction, could not but prove of great utility in preventing professional stagnation and decay. If a system of inspection were established, each colonel for his regiment, a degree of knowledge, theoretical and practical, commensurate with the facilities offered at each post, could be required of officers, and which to some degree would keep them abreast with the progress of the age. To station them where there is no artillery, or by an indifferent system of administration make the use of what they have a matter of accident, depending upon the caprice of garrison commanders, is, particularly if our sea-coast forts are to be defended, a fitting prelude to the necessary embarrassment, confusion, and possible defeat, with its attending disasters, that must inevitably follow.

The service of heavy artillery, under modern conditions, is eminently the field of practical scientific labor for that arm; but here labor alone will lead to excellence or skill, either of which can only be acquired through devotion to duty and long-sustained, intelligent use of every means at the command of its members. The truth of this will be demonstrated should this country be brought face to face with an enemy deserving to be called formidable.

Except for *conduct* in war, let appointments to the artillery in time of peace be made only from those graduates of the military academy recommended by the academic board; in case of other graduates and appointees from the ranks and from civil life, only after having passed an examination pronounced satisfactory, and before a board drawn from the staff of the artillery school. Let captains and lieutenants be divided into two classes: first, those who have been commissioned for *conduct* in the field in war; second, all other appointees; and, as in the ordnance, the medical department, and the engineers, make examination a condition precedent to promotion up to the grade of field officer; the character of examination to vary for the classes, but to be the same for members of each class; that every individual, no matter whence he comes, may be justly, equitably, yet firmly called to account, the fact kept ever present to his mind that to hold a commission sufficeth not; to retain, he must be prepared to prove that he is worthy of it; if he cannot do this, he must, as he deserves, cease to be an officer.

In addition to these measures, taken to insure a solid foundation in excellence for the commissioned personnel, let the batteries be grouped together at posts, three, four, or a greater number at each, under their field officers, where the best armaments furnished by the Government are now or may be made available for their use; make the colonels responsible for the discipline and efficiency as artillerists of their regiments; subject the colonels themselves to a surveillance which regards not persons, but keeps in view the good of the public service only, and the artillery will enter upon a career marked by a higher tone and an increased professional knowledge on the part of its officers, who will better be prepared to vindicate a claim to being capable defenders of their country's honor.

To render this or any other plan for the amelioration of the artillery permanently effective ; to make it a living reality instead of an inert theory; to cause to flow therefrom advantages lasting in nature and beneficial to a degree proportioned to the time, trouble, and expense involved, will require that the arm be given what it has not now, and yet the want of which is admitted by all familiar with its history to be its principal organic defect—a chief.

There is every reason for this ; and if proof irrefragable were needed it is found in the fact that, while the artillery struggles along without one in time of peace, no sooner does war arise, requiring the resources of the Nation to be put forth with power and organized with intelligence, than each division, corps, and army in the field is given an officer acting in that capacity.

The artillery of the Revolution was organized to more successfully meet the special requirements of its service in war than it has been since. Disregarding the first year of that struggle, in which experience was teaching the novices—from commander-in-chief down—the rudiments of a newly-practiced art, it is to be remarked that the defeat of Long Island and the retreat through New Jersey placed before the eyes of all, in no uncertain light, the unwelcome truth that the only hope of successful revolution rested on the ability of Congress to raise and maintain what, in contradistinction to militia and short-service men, was styled a *regular army*. The efforts put forth to accomplish this are familiar matters of history. Before the end of the year 1776 one hundred and four infantry regiments, three thousand light horse, a corps of engineers, and four regiments of artillery were authorized by Congress, to form the regular establishment.

Artillery affairs were then fortunately given a proper direction by appointing a young and active colonel, Henry Knox, to be brigadier-general and commander of that arm. He was assigned a staff proper to his rank, and gradually gathered around him an adjutant-general, inspector, aids-de-camp and clerks, wherewith to keep the administrative machinery in order. The companies were scattered, it is true, (for only in the most highly-wrought organizations of modern times are artillery regiments kept together;) but there was one head to supervise them all, attend to their wants, supply deficiencies, keep up the character of matériel, and cultivate a proper *esprit de corps*, thus making the artillery service one its members were proud of, and which challenged the approbation of General Washington, the army, and the Congress. It would seem, too, that whether the subject-matter for deliberation were to determine a plan of campaign, the supplying the army either from home or from abroad, or its reorganization, the commander of the artillery was ever present at the council board. It needs no detailed statement of services rendered to evince that a proper commander, so circumstanced, must from necessity have exerted a potent influence for the well-being and honor of his corps. Of the opinion entertained of it at headquarters we may judge by the following observations of the commander-in-chief to a Member of Congress in 1777: "The department of artillery, presided over by General Knox, has been placed, notwithstanding innumerable difficulties, upon a footing that does its commander the greatest honor." While the Marquis de Lafayette, adverting to the same subject, remarked that "the progress of the artillery during the Revolution was regarded by all conversant with the facts as one of the wonders of that interesting period." And from among testimonials to the efficiency of the personnel in action, covering the whole period of the war, may be here recorded that of Charles Lee at Monmouth: "The behavior of the whole army, both men and officers, was so equally good, it would be unjust to make discriminations; but I can with difficulty refrain from paying compliments to the artillery, from General Knox and Colonel Oswald* down to the very drivers." And of Chastellux at York-

---

* Lieutenant-colonel Second Regiment of artillery.

town: "The guns were always well served, and while the enemy marvelled at the exact fire of the French, we marvelled no less at the extraordinary progress of the American artillery, at the capacity and instruction of its officers."

It cannot be supposed, however, that the abilities, professional attainments, or knowledge of affairs of any one man could have brought about such results in those times of revolution. The general of artillery was fortunate in not being left alone to essay the task of placing and maintaining upon a sound basis the arm he had the honor to command. In the field officers, the captains, and to a great extent the lieutenants, he possessed assistants whose efforts alone made that possible; they understood the science and practice of their profession sufficiently well to meet every demand of service; and without their intelligent aid the chief could never have raised the corps, or the services it rendered, above the level of mediocrity.

From the date (February 26th, 1795) of the appointment of La Rochefontaine to be lieutenant-colonel commandant of the corps of artillerists and engineers, until 1798, was a period in which, jointly with the engineers, the artillery had a chief; but it was not a time when, for the latter, anything of practical value was being done. The lieutenant-colonel commandant, a professional engineer, was busily occupied personally on the sea-coast fortifications then being built, after a crude fashion, along the Atlantic. The execution of a design to garrison the new works on the coast with this corps had passed no farther than its incipient stages; a large part was on the frontier against the Indians, and neither time nor circumstances had permitted anything of importance to be done before La Rochefontaine was dismissed the service. As previously mentioned, a regiment of artillerists and engineers was organized in 1798 as the Second, and the corps of 1794 was styled the First Regiment. Both remained a part of the military establishment until 1802; but the lieutenant-colonel commandant of neither regiment commanded the whole, so that, as chief of artillerists and engineers, La Rochefontaine had no successor.

At this time (1798) the late commander-in-chief, General Washington, with the title of lieutenant-general, was again placed at the head of the army. Except the French, who were not, under the circumstances, to be trusted, there were, as at the beginning of the Revolution, no active, well-qualified officers of artillery or engineers in service. General Washington, however, appreciated the necessity for having at least a capable head to each of these departments, and, as there was no one at home available, he looked to Europe, as before, for educated and scientific officers to fill the positions. Of the advisability of the measure, and of the circumstances rendering it necessary, the Secretary of War made the following statement in a communication to Congress dated December 24th, 1798:

"It is deeply to be lamented that a very precious period of leisure was not improved towards forming among ourselves engineers and artillerists; and that, owing to this neglect, we are in danger of being overtaken by war without a competent number of characters of these descriptions. To form them suddenly is impracticable; much previous study and experiment are essential. If possible to avoid it, war ought not to find us unprovided. It is considered advisable to introduce, from abroad, at least one distinguished officer of engineers and one of artillery."

Clearing away the war-cloud that had threatened made unnecessary a completion of the measure; the foreign officers were not engaged; but that a head to each of these branches of service was deemed absolutely necessary by General Washington and his contemporaries, there is here abundant proof; as usual, when earnest work was to be done, principles asserted themselves.

The reorganizations of 1802 and 1821, with their influence on the artillery arm, have been adverted to. Notice of them here is unnecessary, further than to remark that the former failed principally, not through want of a chief, but from the inability of the person who virtually occupied that position to rise to the necessities of the occasion; the latter was a melancholy instance of the impotency of any organization springing from considerations of expediency rather than those affecting the public service, and based on makeshifts instead of on sound military principles.

Of the intermediate arrangement of March 30th, 1814, nothing need be said, except that it was imbecile to a degree unrivalled—a grasping after form, while ignoring, through incompetency to comprehend it, the soul of a certain proposed plan of organization. The artillery corps of 1814, made up of fragmental battalions, with nothing to unite them, passed away after a painful existence of seven years, sinking, even in memory, out of sight into deserved oblivion.

That there should be at the seat of Government a centre of administration for the artillery is a fact that has not passed unnoticed. Among other measures proposed by friends of the service, Mr. Shields, in March, 1852, from the Senate Military Committee, introduced a bill for supplying the deficiency. (For report accompanying bill, see Appendix B [2].)

The effort then failed. As a result, the batteries, scattered soon after over the western territories in futherance of an utterly chimerical idea, were not at hand when needed at the beginning of the Civil war. No sooner was this war precipitated than the practices of peace were instantly abandoned. Every army was given a chief of artillery, and for the armies covering the national capital an inspector was appointed, with the rank of brigadier-general.* In war even more than in peace the absence of a chief at Washington was deplored as a misfortune operating in every way to the prejudice of that arm and of the service.

With the hope that the experience of this eventful period, to acquire which had cost so much, might not be lost, but turned to advantage in after years, the permanent artillery board (Appendix B [3]) was in 1866 organized by the lieutenant-general commanding the army. The subject of instruction received, among other things, the serious and earnest consideration of the board during its brief, active life; but, in the absence of the general of the army, in the fall of 1866, it was adjourned, never to be reassembled. This was the last attempt to give the artillery a perma-

---

* "Special Orders No. 210.—Adjutant-General's Office, Washington, August 28th, 1862.— * * * II. Brigadier-General William F. Barry, U. S. volunteers, is assigned to duty as acting inspector of artillery, and will report to the chief of ordnance." * * *

"Special Orders No. 242.—Adjutant-General's Office, Washington, September 15th, 1862.— * * * III. Brigadier-General W. F. Barry, U. S. volunteers, inspector of artillery, his assistant and staff, are assigned to duty in the city of Washington, D. C., to date from the 1st instant." * * *

This officer occupied an anomalous position. He belonged neither to the artillery nor the ordnance, but in a degree to both. The necessity for such a functionary was one of many evidences, ever recurring both in peace and war, of the inadequacy of either the ordnance department or the artillery arm as now organized to fully act a part as an important branch of the military service. Proof here exists that the former called to its assistance one of the most experienced and capable artillery officers for the performance of those duties of inspector connected with artillery matériel equipping for the field, which "the functions of its own officers, entirely distinct from those of the line of the army in any of its branches, involving a familiar acquaintance with the exact

nent representative at the War Department competent to advise on its affairs.

. The remedy for this evil will be applied when the efficiency of that branch of the public service becomes a subject for earnest remedial action in either the councils of the War Department or the halls of Congress, and may be applied, with various degrees of efficacy, in the following ways:

(A) Consolidating into a new corps of artillery, and under such restrictions in personnel as will insure efficiency, the present regiments and the ordnance department.

(B) Giving the present regiments a chief, with a competent staff, as contemplated by Mr. Shields. (Appendix B [2].)

(C) Detailing an officer to act as chief, at the War Department, from among the present personnel of the artillery arm.

If placing the service on an enduring basis, rather than the convenience of individuals, be an object worthy the solicitude and corrective power of Government, the relative merits of these plans is that of the order in which they are enumerated. To strike at the root of existing evils and effect an adjustment as permanent as the present methods of organizing armies, (A) should be chosen; but it must be as indicated heretofore, for otherwise would only be repeated the disastrous experiences that have always attended such attempts. While not so thorough in its

---

sciences and with mechanical philosophy," and not extending to any of the practical duties of armies in campaign, had rendered them incompetent to perform. On the other hand, here was the spectacle presented of an artillery arm impotent to discharge its obvious and legitimate duties except under the surveillance of a department made up of manufacturers and theorists, scientific and philosophical students, who, if they kept their places *assigned by law*, could by no possibility ever hear a hostile shot fired.

The inspector of artillery had charge of all the artillery connected with the defenses of Washington and all the field batteries at Camp Barry, which were constantly being changed, dismounted, remounted, &c., as they came from and went forward to the armies.

He was responsible for the condition of these transient artillery commands, regular and volunteer, while at Camp Barry and when starting for the front. They were inspected under his supervision, and all questions relating to the fitting out of artillery for the lines were *supposed* to be referred to him for decision.

He had a regular post system. Morning reports were daily submitted and consolidated at his office.

operations as (A), the second (B) will give that desideratum first of all in importance—unity of purpose and method in the conduct of artillery affairs—and is preferable to (C) in that the chief would be permanent.

Though least desirable, and having within itself fewer facilities for improving the condition of the artillery, (C) could not but redound to the great advantage of that arm, and has the recommendation, if facility of execution be counted a merit, that a War Department order is all that is needed to put it into operation, while both (A) and (B) will require an act of Congress.

Without enumerating the duties of chief of artillery under (A), it suffices to state that they would extend the authority of the chief of ordnance and make him as well commander of the artillery. The following are some duties the chief of artillery would very properly be called upon to perform under (B) and (C):

(1) Principal adviser to the Secretary of War and the general of the army on all artillery matters.

(2) President *ex officio* of the permanent artillery board constituted by General Order No. 6, of 1866, before mentioned, and which has never been dissolved; also of such boards as that assembled by General Order No. 39, of 1881, "to consider the recent changes in guns, harness, and equipments for light batteries."

(3) To see that the armaments of the forts are properly repaired and kept in good order, causing for this purpose careful inspections to be made of all ordnance, stores, carriages, and ammunition in the forts once a year, or oftener if necessary.

(4) Ascertain the degree to which instruction has been carried on in every battery or artillery command; whether it has been given in accordance with the prescribed text-books or existing orders.

(5) To ascertain what appliances for practical instruction are at the artillery posts, to have these appliances distributed, and to see that every use is made of them for imparting practical knowledge to the commands.

(6) To visit the artillery school at Fortress Monroe and the field battery schools which should be established for the general purposes indicated in (4), and to see further that they are fully meeting the end for which they are organized.

CHAPTER VII.

ADMINISTRATION—DUTIES: AS AN ARM OF SERVICE.

The artillery of the Revolutionary army was early in its history officially assigned a place (which the arm has retained) in what was technically known as "the line,"* *i. e.*, that portion of the armed force destined to take position in line of battle, and the functions of which were strictly military. The resolution of Congress (February, 1779) readjusting artillery and ordnance affairs, for instance, provided that the commanding officer of artillery of the United States should be allowed $75 per month extra for his services as head of the ordnance department in the field, while the commanding officer of artillery in any detachment should have a proportional allowance in addition to his pay in the line. In the resolution of September 25th, 1780, establishing the inspector's department, it was provided: "There shall be one inspector to the corps of artillery, to be taken, when the service will admit, from the colonels or lieutenant-colonels, who shall be allowed, in addition to his pay, $7½ per month and forage for three horses, including what he is entitled to in the line of the army;" while in the reorganization of the following month was the provision that the four artillery regiments, among others, should be retain-

---

*It is not overlooked that military men may criticise the arrangement of the artillery to the line of the army. It properly belongs to the special arms of service. In well-organized armies, where the artillery is assigned its natural function—the combined duties of our ordnance department and artillery regiments—there would be no difficulty in classifying it as a special arm of service only. It suffices to state the fact that in this country, from 1775 to this time, the artillery has always, by the laws, been assigned to the line. It is not intended here to enter into a discussion of the propriety, or the reverse, of the arrangement; nor attempt to revise our military nomenclature, the unsatisfactory condition of which is pointed out in various other places in this work. The artillery will, therefore, be here considered as of the line, as it conforms to facts, however repugnant it may be to the rules of a strict technical language. It will also be necessary in some instances to refer to it as a special arm of service. To belong to the line, and at the same time be a special arm, is a contradiction in terms; but this contradiction exists, unfortunately, in the position of the artillery in our military establishment.

ed, the States selecting from the line of the army a proper number of officers. The artillery officers arranged to these regiments were all selected from among those commissioned in that arm.

In the mother country this was not so. There the artillery was regarded, not as part of the line, but, with the engineers, as a special arm. In fact, however, the sphere of duty of artillery officers in our own was as circumscribed as in the British service. Lieutenant-Colonel Carrington was indeed made quartermaster of Greene's army in the south, and Knox, after his promotion to major-general, was given command of the post and environs of West Point, then regarded as the key to the country; but these were the most conspicuous, if not the only, assignments of artillery officers to important duties disconnected from their immediate profession. The rule was to confine them to those duties, either as commanders of artillery in the field, or in the various military geographical departments.

The nature of the duty it was called upon to perform rendered it necessary that the artillery should serve in detachments, only the rarest occurrences bringing all the companies of any regiment together, even in winter quarters. The armies in the field, the various posts and forts to be garrisoned, required the active services of every trained artilleryman, and as a result the arm was almost exclusively confined to its special duties. As to personal arms, the officers carried swords, while, theoretically at least, the rank and file carried fusees or muskets, after the prevailing fashion in Europe at the time. When Captain Lamb, advancing against the gates of Quebec, found it impracticable to drag his guns, they were left by the road, and the company moved on to the assault with fusees alone. When Proctor's artillery regiment (the Fourth regulars) was organized it was supplied with small-arms, belts, and cartridge-boxes. The resolution of Congress authorizing Harrison's regiment (First regular artillery) explicitly directed that it should be armed with muskets and bayonets.

In actual service small-arms proved to be an incumbrance, being always in the way; and Captain Stevens, in his pioneer work on artillery tactics, published in 1797, asserts with a confidence based on long experience that small-arms were found to answer no useful purpose whatever, except to mount guard. It would seem that this or some other cogent reason led to their partial disuse with the artillery, if we may judge from the following exhibit, taken from General Knox's returns: "Harrison's regiment, 72 muskets, 44 bayonets; Lamb's regiment, 90 muskets, 36 bayonets; Crane's regiment, 84 muskets, 31 bayonets; Proctor's regiment, 77 muskets, 72 bayonets." These doubtless represent the number of small-arms retained for guard duty, the remainder of the original quantity received having been turned in for issue to other troops. The artillerymen had apparently determined to make their guns defend themselves.

In the period immediately following the disbanding of the Revolutionary army the whole of the small force kept in service was employed against the Indians in the Northwest Territory. All, both infantry and artillery, were armed in the same manner, and performed substantially, if not identically, the same kind of service, with the sole difference that there was imposed on the latter the additional duty of serving the guns in the forts and those taken against the hostiles.

The threatened war with Great Britain growing out of unsettled boundaries, and the attacks of that power on American commerce, opened up in 1794 a new field for the service of artillery, viz., the defense of the sea-coast. The possibility that such use might have to be made of some portion of the national forces seems to have received but little attention; and it is a singular fact that, in all the various plans for the organization of a peace establishment submitted to Congress by prominent officers at the close of the war, not one had seriously considered the subject of the defense of the maritime frontier; nor was the elaborate report of the congressional committee on the same subject, written by Colonel Hamilton, less open to criticism. This apparent obliviousness to the existence of a very vulnerable point in the national armor resulted doubtless from the circumstance that the whole attention of the Government had been directed, during the Revolution, to defeating the enemy's forces in the field, thus leaving the coast to be defended by the States whose territory was threatened. From necessity it followed that they were scarcely defended at all.

The prospect, however, of war with our old and powerful naval foe, and the growing commercial importance of the harbors on the Atlantic, determined Congress to take measures for the safety of the coast. Accordingly, in March, 1794, the act was passed providing for fortifying twenty of what were considered the most important points between Portland, Maine, and St. Mary's,

Georgia; and, to serve as at least a partial armament, the purchase was authorized of one hundred each of 32-pounder and 24-pounder cannon, their carriages, implements, and other necessary matériel. To construct these fortifications and to defend them required both engineers and artillerists, of which, at that time, we had neither; for the battalion of artillery, equipped as infantry and in the Indian country, could scarcely be considered as artillerists in any proper sense, and of engineers there had been none since the Revolution. Such were the considerations which led to the passage of the act of May 9th, 1794, authorizing the raising of a corps of artillerists and engineers, into which the then existing battalion of artillery should be incorporated. The President was authorized to have such portions of the corps serve in the field, on the frontiers, or in the fortifications on the sea-coast, as he deemed consistent with public interests. The reorganization of 1802 permanently severed the engineers from their yoke-fellows, the artillerists.

Meantime the gathering war-clouds had been dissipated. Jay's treaty and Wayne's victory over the Miamis had deferred the conflict with Great Britain, while the ascendency of Napoleon had restored amicable relations with France. The artillerists and engineers were not called upon to measure strength with the enemy; but attention had been pointedly drawn to the necessity that existed for troops skilled in the practice of sea-coast armaments and capable of defending permanent works. The principle, which has not since been entirely lost sight of or undervalued, had been initiated of assigning this as the legitimate, proper, and important duty of a portion of the regular military establishment.

The splendor which attached to the service of horse artillery in Europe was not without its effect in this country. Tousard, who was personally familiar with the circumstances attending its adoption by Frederick the Second, its subsequent brilliant career under that great master of the art of war and the greater Napoleon, prevailed on Secretary McHenry to warmly advocate its introduction into our army. This the Secretary did in a communication to the President bearing date January 5th, 1800, and by the latter transmitted to Congress. Together with a statement of the military necessities of the country generally, a scheme for the reorganization of the army and the establishment of military academies, the letter contained a brief and spirited review of the services of horse artillery abroad, while the advisability of its adoption as a part of our military force was urged with that earnest eloquence and felicity of expression which characterized Mr. McHenry's writings. Nothing was done at that time. It was reserved for the rival (politically) administration of Mr. Jefferson, eight years later, under the advice of the veteran soldier, Secretary Dearborn, to prevail on Congress to lend legislative sanction to the raising of the first light artillery regiment of the United States army. It was, indeed, a crude attempt at legislation. No horses were provided, neither increased pay nor allowances to officers or men. To belong to this regiment was an expensive luxury; yet the service was in high favor with the first young men of the country, and the personnel, when the companies were first raised, was superior to that of any other regiment. Active measures were at once taken to practically test the new style of troops, in which both the Secretary and Mr. Jefferson took great interest. Although the act authorizing the light artillery was passed in April, the celebration of the thirty-second anniversary of our National Independence, three months later, was signalized by the parade though the streets of the Capital of the first completely equipped so-called horse-artillery company.

Though it was intended to mount the whole regiment, this was the only company so equipped prior to the war of 1812; the others were armed as infantry. The experience of this company was as brief as its position was unique; the succeeding administration, as before mentioned, for economical reasons, sold the horses, stored the guns, and reduced the horse artillery to the same footing with the other companies.

Such was the state of affairs at the beginning of the war of 1812, which precipitated the inevitable second war with Great Britain. The light artillery, raised amidst a flourish of trumpets, was carrying muskets; some of its companies had disappeared even, through consolidation or other natural causes. The old artillerists of the 1802 regiment, scattered in small detachments along the frontier from Maine to New Orleans and Mackinac, were never during the war concentrated; its members, as had been the usual practice with the artillery since the Revolution, served the pieces of ordnance wherever they might be stationed, and in addition, when occasion required, fought as infantry; most of its field and many of its line officers were detached as district commanders, adjutants-general, or staff officers of other departments.

As artillery proper, the services of the Second and Third regiments, organized pursuant to act of January 11th, 1812, were very unsatisfactory. At first Colonel Izard, of the Second, fully expected that his regiment would be equipped as field artillery. Writing to the War Department in October, 1812, he remarked: "The work I have on hand at Philadelphia, besides my duties as recruiting officer for this district, is important; a small train of artillery, consisting of 6-pounders and howitzers, has been preparing under my direction, and will be complete in a few weeks;" while one month later he informed the department that "a train of sixteen pieces of field artillery, with Wurst caissons, [used in some parts of Europe with horse artillery,] implements, and harness complete, will be ready very soon. I hope the whole will be in a state to march in a fortnight. Of the two parts of companies here, a detachment might be formed to escort them to the north. The officers are all anxious to proceed; the pieces might be distributed to the companies on the frontier, and the whole compose the germ of a battalion of artillery." Izard's ambition, however, to have his regiment properly equipped was but partially realized. Two companies, under Captains Towson and Baker, left Philadelphia in September, 1812, for Dearborn's army; these and several other captains of the regiment, Archer, Hindman, Biddle, and others, were wholly identified with the field artillery in that quarter during the war. But the companies of the regiment were never concentrated; and, while most were employed in their special duties in the field, some of them served in garrison on the South Atlantic coast, particularly in the forts of Charleston Harbor, South Carolina.

The Third Regiment, under Colonel Alexander Macomb, served wholly on the New-York frontier, and principally as infantry; although the following, selected from many orders bearing on the subject, show that in some instances it performed the duties of artillery:

"SACKETT'S HARBOR, N. Y., *February 20th*, 1813.

"Captain Crane, Third Regiment, is placed in charge of the ordnance department of this command. He and his company will do nothing but exercise their pieces, take charge of the elaboratory, and mount guard over the guns at the magazines and the batteries."

While in April following it was announced from the same headquarters:

"To enable the commanding officer of the artillery brigade (Colonel Macomb) to practice his men in the art of gunnery, and give him an opportunity to instruct them in the other parts of their duty, that brigade will be exempt from detail until further orders, except guards necessary for the brigade and forts. The pieces will be properly manned, and worked until the men are perfect."

The intention of the War Department, when the war became a foregone conclusion, was to equip the light artillery regiment as horse artillery. Although companies were serving with muskets, orders were given in May, 1812, to provide swords and pistols for the whole regiment. In February, 1812, instructions were issued from the War Department to incorporate the two light companies at New Orleans, and the detachment *en route* to join them, with the companies of the First Regiment of artillery at that city. General Hampton was directed to send the light artillery officers of the incorporated companies to report to the adjutant and inspector-general at Washington. It will not be amiss to note that some of the companies of the First artillery, thus recruited, were themselves equipped and served as field artillery. General Wilkinson, who succeeded Hampton, reported to the Secretary of War, in March, 1813: "I have here [New Orleans] a charming light train of thirty brass pieces, with harness and implements. Our field artillery, to be useful, must be horsed for rapid movements, and will require at least one hundred and twenty horses broken, trained and disciplined, which I have ordered to be purchased." To this Captain Woolstonecraft, of the First artillery, adds his testimony in a report to the inspector at New Orleans, in May, 1814, that his company had helped take care of these horses, which, with the field pieces, he had exercised during fine weather as light artillery.

Colonel Porter being temporarily engaged on artillery duties elsewhere, the task of preparing the light artillery regiment for the field devolved on Lieutenant-Colonel Fenwick, who was at the seat of Government. In June, 1812, Captains Gibson and McIntosh, under Fenwick, marched from their rendezvous at Lancaster, Pennsylvania, for Albany, New York. Each company was full; each was completely equipped as horse artillery, with four guns, their caissons, and the necessary baggage wagons. These officers went to the front with all the ardor of men proud of the arm to which they belonged The appointments, in every respect, of their companies were such as to inspire them and the authorities with confidence.

That no results commensurate with this elaborate preparation followed, cannot be laid at the door of the light artillery companies themselves, as they were, by superior authority, disintegrated before they reached the enemy; but rather must responsibility rest upon those generals who had no knowledge of the proper use of the arm, who had no chiefs of artillery to assign a proper place to that branch of the combatant forces, husband its resources, direct its energies, and develop its fighting powers. Lieutenant-Colonel Fenwick was, it is true, sent forward at once from Albany to General Van Rensselaer with part of Gibson's company and a supply of ordnance, but only in time to be wounded and taken prisoner at Queenstown. Colonel Porter, of the same regiment, was dispatched to take Fenwick's place as commander of all the artillery on the New York frontier, and an effort was made to place an efficient light artillery at his command; but, from the first, the embarrassments attending the procurement of the essential article of forage even were such as to neutralize every exertion put forth to make the horse artillery formidable. The inadequacy of the staff supply department was nowhere else felt more than by this species of troops, who no sooner reached the vicinity of the enemy than they had to scatter to keep from starving.

Writing, October 21st, 1812, to General Van Rensselaer's successor, Dearborn said: "A fine company of light artillery, all mounted, will follow Colonel Porter to the front as rapidly as possible to replace those lost at Queenstown. On their arrival it will, I presume, be expedient to send the greatest number of the horses back to some place where forage may be conveniently obtained." One week later he continued: "Colonel Porter left this place [Greenbush, opposite Albany] on the 24th instant with one hundred light artillerists, all mounted, and well appointed in every respect."

Meanwhile, every company of Porter's regiment that could be spared from their old stations were concentrated at Greenbush. Major Eustis, of that regiment, equipped three of these as horse artillery, and took two of them to Plattsburg with him. It will thus be seen that within six months of the time war was declared

—June 18th, 1812—at least half of the light artillery had been equipped with their appropriate armament. These companies were speedily followed by the others, either as field or horse artillery.

No service is of record commensurate with these preparations. The light artillery seldom manœuvred as such, and then in driblets, in face of the enemy. No action like that which signalized Ringgold's horse battery in its first battle at Palo Alto distinguished the career of that arm during the war of 1812.

If it be asked why this was so, the answer can be easily given. Disregarding the miserable fiascos on the northern frontier in 1812, disgraceful to the American arms, humiliating to every patriot, filling with shame and indignation the breast of every soldier, and involving in dishonor alike all branches of the military service, there were particular and sufficient reasons why the light artillery disappointed the expectations of its own officers, its friends in the service, and the Government. First of all came Mr. McHenry's erroneous theory of having the light artillery horsed in time of war only, and which, since Peter's company had been dismounted in 1809, had been strictly put in practice. Its effect could not but prove disastrous, and especially so at that time, when light artillery was a new institution, an experiment, in this country. None of the officers of the regiment knew from experience in war anything about it. Except Gibson, who had been Peter's subaltern, every captain, when his own was fitted out in 1812, saw, for the first time in his life, perhaps, a properly equipped company of light artillery. Several of the companies were also composed of raw recruits.

These were unquestionably drawbacks, but they were neither all nor the greatest. Before he reached the frontier, Captain Gibson wrote to the Secretary of War that his company had been broken up, many of his horses taken from him, and his command well nigh annihilated. He adds: "It is very discouraging to me to raise a company, have the labor and expense of mounting it, and then have it treated in this manner." No sooner were they in the presence of the enemy, where they felt they could be of some service, than the distinctive feature of the arm—the horses—was taken from all the light artillery. It was said to be a case of necessity. Van Rensselaer, as early as September, 1812, complained of the difficulties attending the feeding of the flying artillery horses. The quartermaster was directed in general orders to furnish forage regularly, but it was in vain; and against the earnest protests of Colonel Fenwick his light artillery was not only unhorsed, but disarmed. The wretched straits to which the army was reduced for means of subsistence paralyzed every effort to render the corps efficient.

When General Wilkinson, in 1813, assumed command in the north, he wished very much to rehabilitate the light artillery regiment, and with this end in view he, while in Washington *en route* to the Niagara frontier, requested of the Secretary of War "authority to equip the whole of the horse artillery, as contemplated by law, because the arm will be found all-important in every combat which may ensue." The Secretary (Armstrong) replied: "The dragoons and light artillery corps shall be made efficient; horses may be bought for both; average price not to exceed $120 each." The records fail to show that the project here authorized was put into execution. The general, like his predecessors, found that to properly organize his army on the eve of a campaign was impossible. To meet the popular demand and the expectations of the administration, he must win victories with the material in hand, and that, too, without delay. Some horses were purchased, but they were of no service practically; as, in the attempted descent on Montreal, the troops, the guns and artillery matériel moved in boats, separated from the horses, which were driven across the country; thus rendering it necessary, when light artillery was needed on several occasions, to dismount dragoons, that the necessary teams could be procured to drag the pieces.

Nor were the fortunes of the regiment more propitious in other fields of action. When Izard assumed command at Plattsburg, in May, 1814, he wrote to the Secretary of War that the three companies of light artillery at that post had but one officer each, and altogether had but forty horses, scarcely enough to haul their guns and ammunition. The Secretary replied: "The light artillery with you will do the duty of heavy artillery, and need not be mounted. I need not tell you the reason for mounting light artillery. With us this reason does not and will not exist until we have masses of cavalry with whom they can co-operate, and until our *champ de bataille* is an open and level plain." In pursuance of these views General Izard, July 1st, 1814, issued the following general order: "It is the pleasure of the President that the regiment of light artillery shall serve as field artillery on this frontier. The commanding officer of that corps will, in consequence, make returns for their equipment with small-arms and accoutrements, and cause them to be duly instructed in the manual exercise and infantry manœuvres, which are indispensable for their service in the field."

In some instances, however, the shifting fortunes of the war were more favorable; for instance, at Sackett's Harbor, in June, 1814, the commanding general directed "that all horses heretofore attached to the artillery of this command will, until further orders, remain under the orders of Lieutenant-Colonel Mitchell, who will cause such numbers as he may deem proper to be placed under Captain Melvin, of the light artillery, the whole to be kept and trained for light artillery purposes; and all the artillery will be exercised at their guns every day, either in their batteries or in the field, from reveille until an hour after sunrise."

Although some of the companies, acting in detachments, still occasionally performed the duties of horse artillery in small expeditions and other light duty, this service was but temporary and unimportant; its prestige as a strong auxiliary arm had gradually disappeared; yet, spite of every discouraging circumstance, the excellent material of which the regiment was composed asserted itself on all occasions. The inspector-general of the northern army remarked in his report dated December 31st, 1814: "The light artillery regiment had just got together when General Izard left. Colonel Fenwick and Major Eustis are with it. It surpasses any regiment in this army in discipline and evolutions." But every distinctive feature appertaining to the light artillery service faded away with the campaign of 1814, at the end of which nearly if not all the companies were equipped as infantry.

Thus terminated the service in its proper sphere of the light artillery regiment of 1808, of which much was expected, yet which, in its special functions as horse artillery, accomplished little. Its successor, the field artillery of the present regiments, has been more fortunate; this, because circumstances, adverse though they have been, are more favorable with the latter; for in intelligence, professional pride, and zeal in their calling, the pioneer light artillery has not been surpassed by any corps of the United States army.

If we scrutinize the instructions of the Secretaries of War—

Eustis, Armstrong, and Monroe—who at various times controlled affairs during the war of 1812, examine their orders and those of the general officers, we find among the mass but a single systematic, properly-founded plan proposed for the organization of the artillery during either peace or war. Turning to what existed, it is seen that this arm, which, to be efficient in the field of active service, at least, requires careful organization, had none save that given by accident. The proposed system referred to originated with General Izard, and embraced a thorough reorganization, which would have united the present duties of the engineers, the artillery, and the ordnance in a single department, with an *efficient personnel*, and would have resulted, had it been adopted, in a vast saving of money to the Government, together with a more complete and efficient service. (Appendix A, [29].)

In active service Izard seems to have been the only general officer who understood the functions and proper distribution of the arm; his order assigning one company to each brigade, while the rest of the artillery, properly equipped, was placed as a reserve under command of the ranking officer of artillery present, is the only instance of which record has been found of any proper and intelligent effort having been made during the war of 1812 to organize that arm in the field.

The active service of the artillery subsequent to the war of 1812, and prior to that with Mexico, was performed almost wholly as infantry, and embraced participation in the Indian hostilities of that period, particularly the remarkable struggle with the Florida Seminoles, which, with varying fortune, covered the period beginning 1835 and ending 1842. Owing to the fact that the companies directed (by the act of March 2d, 1821,) to be equipped as light artillery had never been placed upon a proper footing, they were not prepared to act efficiently in that capacity; and though a few guns and ammunition wagons were taken into the Indian country,*

---

*Paragraph 12, General Orders No. 68.—Headquarters 2d Division, Army of the South, Camp on Jupiter River, January 27th, 1838.—"Captain Washington's Company, [(B), Fourth Artillery,] serving as artillery, with its pieces, caissons, ammunition wagons, and travelling forge, will move with the column, carrying the necessary supplies of ammunition in addition to that in the hands of troops."

Companies (B) and (H) of the First, united, served some light artillery in the Seminole war; and doubtless other artillery companies did the same; but it was of little consequence.

the service they rendered was of little importance either against the enemy or in giving the officers practical experience as light artillerymen. It was during the progress of the Seminole war (1838) that the number of companies in a regiment of artillery was increased from nine to ten. This number was, owing to the defenceless condition in which during the Mexican war the sea-coast fortresses were left, temporarily increased to twelve companies in each regiment. The two additional companies were afterwards made, as they have continued, part of the regular military establishment.

At the date of the campaign in the valley of Mexico there were, therefore, forty-eight companies of regular artillery. Eight of these, under the acts of March 2d, 1821, and March 3d, 1847, were authorized to be equipped as field artillery. Other companies, as Captain Steptoe's of the Third, served temporarily as field batteries. Company (G) of the Fourth served both as field and heavy artillery, its captain (Drum), with his lieutenant (Benjamin), falling by the side of their guns before the gates of the Mexican capital. Other companies and detachments were, upon occasion, equipped as field artillery, only to be again relegated to the position of infantry, in which latter capacity three-fourths of the artillery companies served during the whole war.

While this was the case, there were equipped and serving against the enemy a siege-train and a howitzer and rocket battery, officered and manned by the ordnance department.

This the artillery arm felt to be a deep wrong. It seemed strangely inconsistent then, and no less so now, that a branch of service which had maintained that its exclusive function was to manufacture matériel, whose enlisted men were designated in the laws as mechanics, should seek to exclude from its duties in the field a combatant arm of service, and to appropriate those duties to itself. To understand this unique affair, wherein the ordnance department appears as the first and foremost exemplar of the maxim "the makers should be the users," which on some occasions it affects to deprecate, it will be necessary to take a retrospective glance at the position in the army of the suddenly belligerent department.

It was formally established under our present form of government by the act of May 14th, 1812, for the better regulation of the ordnance. It followed in the footsteps of the revolutionary "department of the commissary-general of military stores," resolved upon by Congress February 11th, 1778. The duties were essentially the same. In the parent organization the chief, styled "commissary-general of military stores," had the rank of colonel; most of his assistants and employés were civilians, the only branch, and it the least important one, of the department having a semblance of military organization being the so-called regiment of artillery-artificers. In the newly-created department (of 1812) the head had also the rank of colonel, and was styled commissary-general of ordnance. His assistants had military rank, but the rest of the personnel—the wheelwrights, carriage-makers, blacksmiths, and laborers—were civilians. In military features, therefore, the Revolutionary department had the advantage, as the presence in its ranks of enlisted artificers made it at least military in appearance.

That the artillery-artificers were not, however, military except in appearance there is abundant proof. When the few officers of this corps who remained in service until the end of the Revolutionary war applied for commutation of the half-pay for life which Congress promised those honorably discharged from its service, they were refused, for the reason that the artillery-artificers had not been a military organization, and because Congress "intended to restrict that grant to officers of the army who could be considered military, whereas commissions were given the artificers for the sole purpose of rank in their own corps, and to hold courts-martial; they belonged to nothing more than a civil branch of the ordnance department." This was equally true of the department organized in 1812. The general duties of each were, first, to manufacture warlike matériel; second, to enforce a system of accountability therefor. These duties, in themselves, are wholly civil in their nature—a fact not in the least affected by the circumstance that since the reorganization of 1815 the rank and file have been in part, as during the Revolution, enlisted men; they remained, as formerly, armorers, carriage-makers, blacksmiths, or other skilled laborers, and were, in contemplation of law, as strictly non-combatants as their associates, the civilian employés.

Colonel Decius Wadsworth, the first chief of ordnance, and in ability second to none, strongly advocated restricting the department to objects defined by law. Upon this subject he remarked: "The duties of the ordnance department should be limited to providing for and supplying the different armies, forts, posts, magazines, and arsenals of the United States. It is incompatible with the other duties of the department to take charge of ordnance and ordnance stores in the field. The responsibility of the department should cease with the act of delivery from the arsenal or magazine."

Regarding the true status of the enlisted men, Colonel Bomford, the worthy successor to Wadsworth, remarked to one of his subordinates: "Enlisted men of the ordnance department are to be considered as mechanics and laborers, and not, of course, to be employed as soldiers, except in case of emergency, when you are justified in equipping any portion of them as a guard." And again: "A guard of ordnance men has never been contemplated by the laws or regulations, which have all been formed on the presumption that these men are always to be employed as laborers and mechanics, saving only on certain occasions of emergency requiring a guard for a short time."

The appearance of these non-combatants in the field, to the exclusion of the artillery, whose functions they performed, was a spectacle which, in view of the foregoing facts, was well calculated to excite criticism.

The immediate steps by which this was brought about are now well known, and can be told in a few words. It is necessary to premise, by observing that Colonel Bomford was absent from the seat of Government at this time, absorbed in those experiments which resulted in the development of a new and improved system of guns—the Columbiad. He had nothing to do with the transformation scene in question, whereby non-combatants were temporarily converted into artillerymen.

In a communication to the Secretary of War early in 1845, the acting chief of ordnance used the following language: "An increase of the enlisted men [of the department], by the addition of one hundred and fifty to the present number, is earnestly urged. This may be done without additional expense to the Government, as it will save the employment of that number of *hired* men. It will also have the advantage of giving the control of a description of *labor* not always readily found when wanted, but indispensable to the proper care and preservation of munitions, and *cheaper*, as well as better, than the *hired labor* now devoted to such purposes." When hostilities had commenced on the Rio Grande, the acting chief of ordnance renewed his recommendations in yet more urgent language, remarking that "the law now provides two hundred and fifty men to be enlisted in the corps. These are not sufficient. To increase the number to meet the needs of service will involve no expense whatever. On the contrary, it will be a measure of economy. The enlisted men would merely take the place of men who are now hired at these ordnance posts, and their pay would be less than that paid to hired men." Influenced by these specious representations, and believing that an increase in the number of enlisted men was directly in the line of economy, and would reduce the number of higher-priced civilians, Congress, by act of June 18th, 1846, authorized the senior officer of the ordnance department to enlist as many armorers, carriage-makers, blacksmiths, and laborers as the public service, in his opinion, under the direction of the Secretary of War, might require.

The time for throwing off the non-combatant mask had now arrived. A large number of men were enlisted under authority of this act. No sooner had this been cleverly effected than the acting chief of ordnance submitted a proposition to the Secretary "of War" to gather at Fort Monroe Arsenal, partly by drafts from other arsenals and by enlistment of laborers of ordnance, a sufficient number of men to man a battery of mountain howitzers now at that post, and also form a brigade of rocketers. Under the law, any number deemed necessary may be provided. They will of course be commanded by ordnance officers." This was followed by flaming posters calling for recruits, and stating that "in pay, provisions, and clothing this corps will be superior to any yet raised, and, from the kind of arms, will be constantly in the advance when the hardest fighting may be expected." Ordnance officers in command of posts were directed to send to Fortress Monroe any suitable and spare men to man the before-mentioned batteries, and, in addition, a siege-train there fitting out by the ordnance department. The places of the enlisted men so detached were authorized to be filled by *hired* men.

Here, then, was the act of duplicity complete! Congress is assured that, in the interests of economy, hired men should be replaced by enlisted mechanics. No sooner are these carriage-makers and blacksmiths secured than they are armed and sent to the field equipped as artillery, while at the ordnance posts their places are supplied by that higher-priced labor to avoid the employment of which was the chief and oft-repeated argument urged for increasing the enlisted force of the department.

Candid men will draw their own conclusions. The character of the transaction is easily understood. Comment is unnecessary, further than to observe that no such systematic deception for the purpose of aggrandizing a non-combatant department at the expense of a fighting arm of service can be found elsewhere in the history of the army.

The reason given by the acting chief of ordnance for usurping the functions of the artillery, viz., that the latter were unacquainted with the duties of their own arm, was as wanting foundation in fact as the methods to build up his department were questionable. The part acted by the artillery in Mexico does not demand defense here or elsewhere; it is written in the history of every siege and battle of that war. It was given no opportunity to use the rocket battery, that duty being entirely usurped by the ordnance department, in violation not only of the law, but in disregard of the decision of the Secretary of War (Mr. Poinsett) in 1838 that this service in the field should be intrusted to the artillery.

In his annual report dated November 30th, 1847, the adjutant-general of the army, adverting to this subject, made the following pertinent remarks:

"It may not be irrelevant to state in this place that, while probably not more than ten companies of the four regular artillery regiments are serving with their appropriate arm—the other thirty-eight companies are armed and equipped as infantry—there are two batteries with the main army in Mexico served by *ordnance men* (with several officers) and one by the Maryland and District of Columbia volunteers. The men of the ordnance department are enlisted as artisans and laborers, and receive a *higher rate of pay* than is allowed by law to soldiers of the light artillery. At the last session of Congress an increase of the ordnance corps was authorized, because the number of officers was deemed inadequate to the wants of that branch of service. It would seem, therefore, peculiarly proper to confine officers of the ordnance to the defined objects of that department. * * * Economy as well as military propriety requires that all the harnessed batteries be transferred to the artillery; and it is respectfully recommended that the transfer be directed accordingly. No corps in service has been more distinguished in the present war than the artillery, and they are justly entitled to be equipped with the arm which they have proved themselves capable of using so efficiently against the enemy."

It is not an uninteresting fact, but one over which artillery officers may do well to ponder, that there is nothing in the relative position of their arm and that of the ordnance department to-day to prevent a repetition of this experience, when they may find themselves marching as infantry supports to batteries commanded by ordnance officers. There is now just as much reason for this as there was thirty-seven years ago.

Following the Mexican war, although the artillery was still, as before, taken equipped as infantry into the field against the Indians, the practice was somewhat abated. This was perhaps due to the service therein of the light companies, which turned the attention of the artillery to the necessity and advantage of being properly equipped and trained in its special duties; but the policy affecting it was as variable as were the Administrations, one tearing down what the other built up. It was during this period that the artillery school was re-established, through which, every ten years, all the companies, except those mounted, were expected to pass, thus receiving, each in its turn, a good practical course of instruction in foot artillery duties, while the field companies were scattered over the western country, each associated with several foot companies (aggregating more than half the whole number in the army), and forming for the latter at each post the nucleus of a field artillery school.

As in the Seminole war it had been found necessary to increase the number of companies in each artillery regiment by one, and in the Mexican war by two, so, when the Civil war broke out, an additional regiment of field artillery was rendered necessary, owing to the scattered condition of the field companies, as just mentioned, and the impossibility of concentrating them where they were needed. This increased the number of artillery companies and batteries in service to sixty. During that war fifty-six of the sixty served for longer or shorter terms as field batteries, and of these about twenty-two were horse batteries. In some instances two and even three distinct organizations were united to form a complete battery. The other four regular companies were, by accidents of service, assigned to duty in the permanent defenses of the country, from which it was not found advisable to move them. The attention given to the subject of field artillery subsequent to the Mexican war, and the strenuous efforts, under adverse circumstances, of the general-in-chief and of the field company commanders to keep these organizations mounted, now bore fruit in the number of officers the regular artillery could turn out acquainted with the rudiments, at least, of field artillery duty, and who were invaluable in the emergency that had arisen.

The large increase, at the close of the Civil war, of the number of infantry and cavalry regiments has obviated the necessity almost entirely of using the artillery, equipped as infantry, on the interior frontier against the Indians. Its employment in this manner has been rare, and for a pressing emergency, when the batteries have returned to their appropriate stations and duties.

The principle of National defense, first recognized in 1794, by authorizing the raising a corps of artillerists and engineers— viz., that for garrisoning the sea-coast fortifications certain troops should be set apart—has ever since been acknowledged as an important feature of the military policy of the Government. The wisdom of this cannot be questioned. It is admitted by all thinking men that there is no branch of the military service requiring more careful preparation to render it efficient than modern foot artillery. The duties of the sea-coast garrison are undeniably the field of scientific research pre-eminent above others. *The refined armaments of modern times are useless in the hands of novices.* The importance, therefore, of maintaining this species of troops at the highest state of efficiency that can be attained with the means at hand or within reach of the Government can scarcely be overestimated. So far as is consistent with other public interests, they should be kept in this condition. True economy and a proper administration alike forbid their diversion to other purposes, or their being deprived of facilities for both theoretical and practical instruction in their special, and now more than ever scientific, duties.

CHAPTER VIII.

DUTIES OF THE CHIEF OF ARTILLERY IN THE FIELD.

A question of importance in the proper administration of artillery affairs in the field is that of the true status of the chief of artillery, *i. e.*, whether he be commander of the artillery in the army, corps, or division in which he is chief, or whether he be a staff officer simply, with authority to issue orders only in the name of the commanding general. The subject gave rise to much discussion and to diverse practices during the Civil war. It was not generally understood, and confusion of ideas operated to the disadvantage of the arm. There is no law defining the duties, rights, and privileges of a chief of artillery; the very designation is of comparatively recent introduction into our service; but it is necessary that it be determined whether he be a commander or not, and, in the absence of positive law, this can only be done from custom (common law) and the regulations.

If we recur to the revolutionary period, we find that General Knox was commander of all the artillery of what was designated by Congress as the regular army—the war organizations. This is manifest from the orders and correspondence of the times—seems never to have been questioned, but, on the contrary, to have been fully recognized by both the army and the Congress. The orders issued by him to artillery officers in armies other than the main army, with which the general served in person, establish beyond question that he occupied towards them the position of commander. These officers were also subject to the orders of the general with whom they served; and just how conflict of authority was avoided in every case it is not possible here to state. From what has been gathered on the subject, the inference is that the orders of the general of artillery were sufficient to cause his views to be everywhere executed in his department of service. The instructions given to officers of artillery commanding during campaign the companies attached to divisions and brigades evince the perfect control exercised over them by the general of artillery; the preservation of both personnel and matériel, the exercise of both, were carefully provided for, and regulations therefor were delivered *direct* to the officers concerned by the general of artillery. The authority of division and brigade commanders over these artillerymen would naturally soon become a question to be determined; and to pointedly set the matter right, in some respects at least, General Washington issued the following order, dated Orangetown, August 15th, 1780:

> "The officers and men of the artillery corps attached to the divisions and brigades are not to be furloughed by division and brigade commanders, as it is irregular, and interferes with the internal arrangement of the corps."

This order makes manifest that at the date of its being issued the artillery serving with divisions and brigades was on the footing of troops attached for service, but belonging permanently to a central and distinct command, which in the order is called the corps.

The trial of General McDougall, in 1782, resulted partially from misunderstandings which arose from this dual responsibility of artillery officers. In January, 1782, General Heath, commanding the Department of the Highlands, with headquarters at Newburgh, assigned Colonel Crane, of the Third Regiment, to the command of all artillery in the department. He was enjoined to pay particular attention to the ordnance and ordnance stores at the posts, and at all of them to place the artillery in position as he deemed best. Major Perkins, of Crane's regiment, was placed by the same order in charge of the artillery at West Point, under the orders of both Colonel Crane and of General McDougall, commanding at that important post. This position of Major Perkins, it is important to remark, is, in the matter of responsibility to superiors, that prescribed by paragraph 1022 of the existing army regulations for artillery commanders at all headquarters.

It so happened that Crane, for the time being stationed at West Point, although commander of the department artillery, was ordered by McDougall to make certain dispositions of artillery matériel at the post. This Crane refused to do, justifying himself by orders received from General Heath, department commander. McDougall insisted upon being obeyed, and was court-martialed for his actions in the premises.

There are two facts clearly established by the correspondence growing out of this court-martial, and which are pertinent to an elucidation of the subject now under consideration: (1) that Major

Perkins, McDougall's artillery officer, was in technical affairs under the orders of the commander of artillery of the department; (2) that the latter officer was answerable only to the commanding general of the department. It would seem there should have been no trouble about the latter point, but it required the court-martial of a major-general to set the matter right. In the positions occupied by Major Perkins and Colonel Crane, as before indicated, we see put into practice the principle of a direct chain of subordination connecting the commanders of artillery at general with those at subordinate headquarters, afterwards embodied in Scott's, and at this time recognized (ostensibly) in paragraph 1022, regulations of the army, edition of 1881.*

Following the Revolution was what may be called the dark age of our army; and, as tending to throw light upon the subject of artillery command, nothing appears until the regulations springing out of our experience in 1812. We may except General Wilkinson's order, dated Sackett's Harbor, N. Y., October, 1813, when preparing for the descent on Montreal, and which assigned the command of all artillery troops, the care and custody of all artillery matériel, without exception, to Brevet Brigadier-General Porter. This officer at that time, and afterwards Major Eustis, his successor, exercised command as much as any brigadier with the army; neither thought of using the name of the general of the forces in matters affecting the artillery, any more than did the brigade commanders in giving orders to their regiments.

The regulations of September, 1816, promulgated pursuant to act of April 24th, same year, provided for the stationing a commander of artillery at the headquarters of an army, and of course wherever at subordinate headquarters the presence of an artillery officer might be necessary; and further, that "the conductors of stores will keep the senior officer of the corps of artillery *in command* acquainted with the state of the ordnance of their respective divisions. Besides the ordnance, ammunition, and stores appro-

---

*The modification of paragraph 489, regulations of 1863, which appears in paragraph 1022, regulations of 1881, is a plain violation of the law of June 23d, 1879, authorizing the codification of the " regulations of the army and general orders " then in force. The unauthorized change consists in substituting the word *officers* for *commanders* where the latter was used with particular significance.

priated to each division of artillery, the senior officer of that corps *in command* with the army will apportion to the respective divisions, according to his judgment, the spare arms, ammunition, gun-carriages, equipments." [The divisions here referred to were those of artillery, viz., a company having six pieces of ordnance, with the requisite stores.] (Appendix C, [1].) "The conductors of stores will, from time to time, as opportunities may offer, and under direction of the senior officer of artillery *in command*, disincumber the division of the empty ammunition wagons and carriages needing repairs."

In the first complete code of regulations supplied the army, and drawn up by Brevet Major-General Scott, were laid down with great care, and, considering the times, with great precision, the functions of artillery commanders. These regulations were written after much experience, research, and reflection on the part of the compiler. There is a singleness of purpose manifest throughout the work, desirable in any system of regulations, resulting from the fact that the compilation was the product of one man's judgment.

As bearing on the subject now under consideration, we quote from paragraph 14, article 44, Scott's Regulations: "The number and description of staff officers, as adjutants-general, inspectors-general, &c., at the disposal of the War Department, for any particular army, will depend on creations made by Congress; but, of the staff officers who may be assigned to an army in the field, the commandants-in-chief of the * * * artillery * * * will be attached to general headquarters, for the direction or administration of their particular departments of service." This plainly contemplated that the chief of artillery was to be also commandant of his corps with the army; and, to clearly set at rest the possible vexed question of double responsibility of subordinate chiefs of artillery, paragraph 15, *ibid*, provided that "the superior officer of artillery serving with one of the army corps, a detached division, or a brigade will receive the orders of the commandant thereof, to whom the said superior officer of artillery will communicate any orders he may receive from his own particular commandant-in-chief attached to general headquarters." And to show the chain of subordination connecting these various artillery officers, it was provided in paragraph 3, article 45: "A colonel, who occupies that position in a division, will have a direct authority over a major, chief of one of the brigade staffs, in the same division, independent of the commander of the division; but in this example, should the colonel give an order to the major incompatible with the duties of the latter towards his brigade, such order would not be obeyed until communicated to the brigadier-general for his approbation." It will thus be seen that the position of these commandants-in-chief of artillery was in a measure that of staff officer, but with this distinction—that they *commanded* in their own branch of service.

Paragraph 14, article 44, Scott's Regulations, appears in the edition of 1841; the others quoted had by that time disappeared. The term "chief of the artillery" now (1841) for the first time made its appearance, although that of commandant-in-chief was also retained, thus by the context showing that these designations were synonymous. It was enjoined in these regulations, also, that all communications relating to ordnance supplies, when in the field, should be transmitted to the ordnance officer in charge of the depots, through the adjutant-general or the chief of the artillery with the army.

The war with Mexico elicited apparently neither interest in nor information on the subject of the proper functions of chiefs of the artillery. They were charged with duties relating wholly to supply; the batteries were considered as exclusively under the control of division or brigade commanders; in battle the chief of artillery of an army had nothing more to do with the management of the batteries than other officers on the staff of the general, *i. e.*, he acted only on the orders of the general.

In the edition of 1857 there first appeared paragraphs 1021 and 1022 of the present regulations of the army. They represent what is left of that portion of Scott's Regulations of 1821 before quoted, after they had been pruned in the interests of a certain staff bureau. Such was the status of the question under consideration when the Civil war broke out.

When the Army of the Potomac was being organized, in 1861, the question early arose whether the chief of artillery should have command of that arm, or whether his functions should be purely administrative. A board of officers was assembled to take the subject into consideration, and reported as a result of its labors that the practice varied in different armies. Owing to the peculiar situation of the artillery arm, General McClellan determined to make the functions of his chief of artillery administrative only; and, as the cavalry was similarly situated, the following order was issued, applying equally to both these arms of service:

"HEADQUARTERS ARMY OF THE POTOMAC, *March* 26*th,* 1862.
"[General Orders No. 110.]

"I. The duties of the chief of artillery and cavalry are exclusively administrative, and these officers will be attached to the headquarters of the Army of the Potomac. They will be required to inspect the artillery and cavalry whenever it may be necessary, and will be responsible that they are properly equipped and supplied. They will not exercise command of the troops of their arms, unless specially ordered by the commanding general, but they will, when practicable, be selected to communicate the orders of the general to their respective corps. All requisitions for officers and men, and for supplies for artillery and cavalry other than the regular supplies furnished by the staff departments on ordinary returns, will be sent to the chiefs of artillery and cavalry, to whom will also be rendered, in addition to those rendered to general headquarters and division commanders, such reports of artillery and cavalry practice, marches, actions, and other operations pertaining to these arms as may be necessary to enable them to judge of the efficiency both of men and material." * * *

General William F. Barry, at the time chief of artillery of the army, pointed out the disadvantages under which he and his arm labored in consequence of the provisions of this order, but to no purpose. It has been said that the peculiar situation of the arm as regards field officers was held to render it necessary that, in the first instance, their duties should be supervisory rather than of command. That situation was as follows: Comparatively few artillery officers, and those mostly of the lower grades, had been instructed in field battery duties; not half a dozen of them had commanded artillery in battle. In the volunteer regiments field officers were wholly inexperienced, and it was deemed proper, in the first months of active operations, to give to the officers who had been instructed the command of the batteries in the field. The duties of the field officers, or chiefs of artillery, were made purely administrative, they being all, except the chief of artillery of the army, from the volunteers. The batteries were assigned to divisions, then about 10,000 strong, giving four batteries—one regular and three volunteer—to each division, the captain of the regular battery, an experienced officer, commanding the four. The object was to so organize the artillery as best to develop its fighting powers, and this was attained by allowing field officers of volunteer regiments first to learn something about handling artillery before taking command according to their rank. Under authority granted by the act of August 5th, 1861, several artillery officers from the lower grades were appointed additional aids-de-camp, and assigned according to their staff-rank to command in the artillery,* to meet the practical difficulty existing of having with the army uninstructed volunteers who would command them. As time passed, battles were fought, the regular captains were, in great measure, promoted and removed from the artillery, the volunteer officers became conversant with their duties, the divisions were reduced in strength, half their batteries were withdrawn and formed, agreeably to the original plan of organization, into corps reserves, some of which were under the command of the volunteer field officers, the chief of artillery of the army commanding the whole. (Appendix A, [51].) This was during the Peninsula campaign, after the termination of which General Barry was removed to other duties, and was succeeded, as chief of artillery, by the late commander of the general artillery reserve.

The position of the chief of artillery of the Army of the Potomac under the various generals who, in rapid succession, were appointed to its command during the following months, cannot better be described than is done by the former in the official report of the operations of his arm at Chancellorsville. He says:

"Command of the artillery, which I held under Generals McClellan and Burnside, and exercised at the battles of Antietam and Fredericksburg, was withdrawn from me when you assumed command of the army, and my duties made purely administrative, under circumstances very unfavorable to their efficient performance. I heard after the movement [preliminary to the battle] commenced that when the corps were put in motion to cross the river they left part of their artillery in their camps. No notice of this was given to me, and it was by accident that I learned that the batteries so left behind were afterwards ordered to join their corps. As soon as the battle commenced, I began to receive demands from corps commanders for more artillery, which I was unable to comply with, except partially, and at the risk of deranging the plans of other corps commanders. Being ordered to proceed to Bank's ford, I was recalled by telegraphic instructions on the night of the 3d [Sunday, May, 1863], when I was ordered by the commanding general at Chancellorsville to take charge of all the artillery of the army."

As a result, although there was sufficient artillery during the first periods of the battle, it was not at the places where needed,

---

* A similar device was resorted to by General Hampton in 1813.

and no one had authority or knowledge of affairs sufficient to supply the demands of corps commanders for guns and ammunition, as, in the language of an eye-witness, the "woods seemed alive with artillery" in a state of utter confusion. This was in marked contrast with the artillery of the Confederates, which, according to one of their first authorities, "in spite of the difficulties of the Wilderness, here co-operated with the infantry in a manner never excelled in promptness and vigor."

When, from want of a directing hand, the artillery was in the condition above described, the general commanding reinstated his chief of artillery in the position of which he had deprived him, that order might be brought out of this chaos which the commanding general had himself created. We thus see a general, when the battle was bearing hard against him, when it was a question whether or not anything could save his army from disaster, abandoning his speculative ideas, and placing his chief of artillery *in command*, in order that the batteries might be assembled and directed against the enemy. No circumstance of the Civil war more forcibly illustrates the necessity that exists for understanding the functions of, and placing in his true position, the chief of artillery of an army, than does this of Chancellorsville. Whatever may or may not have been the views of the commanding general regarding the distribution and command of the artillery, the fact remains that on the field, when pressed by the enemy and disaster seemed impending, he was constrained to forego them, and recall the officer whom he had deprived of that command. Further remark is unnecessary. Armies are organized and maintained to beat the enemy; and that system which, overriding every prejudice, is resorted to when armies meet, is the true one.

It may be said that General Hooker was only returning to the system instituted by General McClellan in General Orders No. 110, Army of the Potomac, 1862, before quoted. While this may be true, the reasons for the order having been issued originally seem either not to have been understood or to have been ignored; and while the letter of the order, so far as it affected the chief of artillery, may have been observed, the spirit of it was entirely lost sight of.

After the battle of Chancellorsville, when the occasion which rendered it necessary had passed, the command with which he had been temporarily intrusted was again taken from the chief of artillery. This was the state of affairs when, on the 28th of the following month—June—the army once more changed commanders, on the eve of the great battle at Gettysburg. The chief of artillery, during the preliminary movements leading to that event, was directed by the new commanding general "to see to the position of the artillery, and make such arrangements respecting it as were necessary," which order was interpreted by the officer receiving it as vesting in him all the powers of *commander* of that arm for the particular occasion.

To every reflecting mind it must appear strange that the duties, powers, and rights of command of so important a personage as the chief of artillery of an army having 364 field-guns, served by 8000 men and 7000 horses, should have been changed from day to day, and, above all, that his status in his own arm, when battles were being fought, was one thing, while in the intervals between it was altogether different.

The necessity for organizing the artillery as a special arm of service is recognized by every nation. It is, as a rule, auxiliary to the cavalry and infantry, though by no means always so; for in siege operations and the forced passage of rivers it becomes the principal, the others the auxiliary arms. But artillery is expensive to organize and maintain in a state of efficiency; therefore only so much is provided as is necessary for the actual wants of the army, and such special rules adopted for the service as will make it available, whether directed in mass by its own superior officer with the army, commonly called the chief of artillery, or whether it be attached to the smaller tactical units—corps and divisions—for fighting purposes. In all armies, therefore, it has been found necessary to regulate the management of this arm, to define the functions of its principal officers in their own corps, and their relations to the other arms of service.

General Meade, the new commander of the Army of the Potomac, appreciating this fact, together with the anomalous and unsatisfactory basis on which the matter at that time stood, proceeded, in the following order, to clearly define the position of the chief of artillery:

"HEADQUARTERS ARMY OF THE POTOMAC, *August* 21*st*, 1863.
"[General Orders No. 82.]
"The duties of the chief of artillery of this army are both administrative and executive. He is responsible for the condition of the artillery wherever serving,

respecting which he will keep the commanding general fully informed. Through him the commanding general of the army will take the proper steps to insure the efficiency of the artillery for movement and action and its proper employment in battle. All artillery not attached to other troops will be commanded by the chief of artillery. He will, both personally and through his staff, maintain a constant supervision and inspection over the personnel and material of the artillery to insure the instruction of the former and completeness of the latter, as well as the discipline of the artillery not attached to other troops.— In battle he will, under the instructions of the major-general commanding, distribute and place in position the reserve artillery, and, when so directed, select positions for the batteries attached to troops, conveying to the commander of the troops the directions of the commanding general. He will give such directions as may be necessary to secure the proper supply of ammunition and to furnish it promptly to the batteries when in action. He will give no orders that will interfere with the military control exercised by the commanders of a corps or division over the batteries attached to their troops, nor will he withdraw batteries from a corps, or transfer them from one corps to another, unless directed to do so by the general commanding the army. Commandants of the artillery attached to troops will be responsible to the chief of artillery for the condition and efficiency of their batteries so far as relates to equipments, supplies, and instruction, and will be governed with respect to orders received from him by paragraph 489, Revised Army Regulations of 1861."

This order sets forth the powers of the chief of artillery of an army in a manner clear and precise, and not equalled in these particulars by any other orders and regulations of our service. Analysis will evince that this officer commanded the artillery reserve and such unattached batteries as were awaiting assignment; that, for purposes of equipment and supply of matériel, and the instruction of the personnel, he commanded every artilleryman and every gun in the army; but, for disciplinary and fighting purposes, the artillery attached to corps or divisions was exclusively under the orders of the immediate military commanders; with these matters the chief of artillery had nothing to do, except when directed by "the general commanding the army." The order very nicely balances the various parts of a delicate machinery, the disjointing of which had caused serious inconvenience. It continued in force until the close of the Civil war, and deserves to be preserved among the valuable contributions to our code of regulations resulting from experience then acquired.

Although little precise information has been obtained touching the subject under consideration, enough has been gathered to indicate that the provisions of the general order just quoted embody the fundamental ideas which in the main, if not exactly, govern in European armies. (Appendix B, [4] and [5].) And although army reserves, made up of a large proportion of the artillery, and under the immediate command of the chief of artillery, are nowhere at this time maintained as in the Army of the Potomac when this order was issued, its provisions are of almost universal application, the absence of the Reserve only lessening the immediate command of the chief of artillery, without in the least affecting the principles governing the employment of the arm or the duties and rights of its officers, either in their own corps or as affecting the army at large.

In this connection, the experience of the Confederate army will be found to be interesting; and although it may be stated that their orders on the subject never so completely covered the ground as did our own, still the practical results at which both armies arrived were almost identical. Prior to the Peninsula, and even during that campaign, their artillery had no organization worthy of the name; there was, however, a large and well-appointed artillery reserve, commanded by the chief of artillery of the army, the batteries of which were afterwards, in 1863, distributed to the army corps. Before the second Manassas a great improvement had been effected in the artillery organization by arranging the batteries in battalions, under field officers, and attaching them to divisions; at that battle the efficiency of the artillery battalion organization was fully demonstrated. When army corps were organized artillery was attached to each corps, under its own chief. Following this came General Orders No. 7, Richmond, January, 1863, providing that—

"Hereafter all field artillery belonging to any separate army will be parked together under the direction of the general, or other chief officer of artillery having control of the same, to be distributed, when required, according to the judgment of the commanding general of such army."

This order may be considered as another step in the plan of concentration which had been commenced as soon as the mistakes of organization were made manifest by experience, and by which plan of concentration the artillery was gradually withdrawn from control of the subordinate (brigade and regimental) commanders and placed under generals of divisions, corps, and armies; but it is believed that the order just quoted went farther in this direction than has been done in any other modern army, and it may be doubted if it was ever given practical effect in the Army of Northern Virginia; this will become manifest when we examine General Lee's order issued pursuant to the provisions of that under review. General Lee directed that—

"All the battalions of each corps will be under the command of and will report to the chief of artillery for the corps. The whole, in both corps, will be superintended by and report to the general chief of artillery."

A question would immediately arise as to the meaning of the word *superintend* in this order. Is it synonymous with *command?* If it were so considered, then why not use the latter in the order? It would have removed ambiguity by terms, the significance of which is well known to every military man. The inference is that if it had been intended to give the chief of artillery command of that arm the order would have said so. He was not, therefore, a commander, but a superintendent, the functions of whose office must have been confined to matters of administration. It may, indeed, have been, and doubtless was, true that the chief of artillery of the army commanded the few batteries unattached to corps, which either by accident or design accompanied the army at various times after the general reserve was broken up in 1863. These unattached batteries, however, formed no proper command for a general officer; and hence the chief of artillery was confined from necessity to a general superintendency of the equipment, supply, and instruction of his arm, the command of the artillery attached to troops being expressly vested in the chiefs of artillery of the various army corps.*

It will be conceded without argument that the position and authority of the chief of artillery of an army, *i. e.*, whether he act the part of an administrative officer simply, or whether he be commander of the artillery, is a matter the correct determination of which is of the first consequence to the proper service of that arm.

In approaching the consideration of the subject, the importance of which, as affecting the efficiency and credit of the artillery, cannot be overestimated, it is to be remarked that this is a case wherein a great mistake might be made by attempting to apply an inflexible rule, without taking into account the varied circum-

---

* For information concerning the organization of the Confederate artillery, Army of Northern Virginia, I am indebted principally to General E. P. Alexander, late C. S. A., and at one time chief of artillery of Longstreet's corps.

stances under which the armies of different nations are organized and maintained.

Of this we may be reasonably certain: Unless the question of the true position of the chief of artillery be happily determined, much cannot be expected from that arm. If the duties of those at the head of affairs be not defined, how is it possible for them to direct those lower in the scale? The hand which should control being palsied, the machinery either works heavily, wastes its power in a useless friction of its parts, or stops altogether.

In the carefully-organized and highly-trained armies of continental Europe each piece in the machine has a well-ascertained function. Its appointed sphere of action in the complete working of the whole is determined beforehand and known to all concerned. The result is this: As each knows perfectly what he is to do, there is less need for supervision by those in chief authority. Each commander of both divisional and corps artillery, (Appendix A, [52],) from study, reflection, and the annual and other exercises in time of peace, knows his duty under any and all circumstances. To him the management of his batteries in war is different from that in peace in this only: that the former gives opportunity for putting in practice those principles with which peace has made him familiar. In these thoroughly disciplined and equipped armies there may be no objection to the distribution of the entire artillery to army corps. The functions of the chief of artillery of the army would in this case be administrative. As the artillery of each corps has its commander, and as all the artillery is distributed to corps, there is no direct artillery command—*i. e.*, of troops—left for the chief of artillery of the army. It is understood that, under the orders of the commanding general, he can at any time assume those functions, and whenever the various corps artilleries are massed for any purpose he would assume command of the mass. Except on these rare occasions, his duties would be purely advisory and administrative. This, it will be found, is the rôle assigned in the field to the chief of artillery of the principal armies of continental Europe. As to the special arm—artillery—its tactical units form permanent parts of the divisions and army corps, and for fighting and disciplinary purposes they are wholly under the orders of the division and corps generals. The establishment of an *imperium in imperio* is in this manner rendered impossible.

Is this system best suited to our service?

If our artillery took the field under similar circumstances as to practice and discipline; if the armies which the Government would send forth in case of war were veterans, well organized; if the duties of each, from the highest to the lowest, were well understood and executed with facility, there would be left no room to doubt about it; we could not in that case do a wiser thing than adopt a system which, amidst the surroundings indicated, has led' to splendid results elsewhere. It may be assumed, however, that the large armies which the United States will send out will not be of this description. They certainly have not been. Veterans are not recruited directly from the walks of civil life. With present practices the artillery which will accompany these armies cannot be expected to be well versed in their special duties, for during peace the regulars received no instruction, administrative or tactical, in the management of that organization—the artillery brigade—into which, when war calls them to action, they will at once be formed; and as for the volunteers, they will have everything to learn.

In armies such as ours would be it is doubtful if the existing methods of European armies are the best, even if they be practicable. There should be a closer bond connecting the detached portions of the artillery scattered throughout the army than the European system recognizes. This will be secured by a code of regulations having for its foundation-stone the two following principles: First, a chief of artillery is commander of that arm; second, batteries or other artillery organizations assigned to divisions and corps are on the footing of troops attached for service. It is to be understood that artillery will be neither attached to, nor taken from, these commands without the authority of the commanding general of the army; and, when so attached, it is for disciplinary and fighting purposes, exclusively under the orders of the division and corps commanders. Batteries and other artillery organizations not attached to military commands will be under the direct orders of the chief of artillery; this to include the artillery reserve, if there be one; also the ammunition columns. For purposes of supply, instruction, and inspection, all artillery, wherever serving, should be under the orders of the chief of artillery of the army.

In the cantonments of winter season, when hostilities are suspended, it would, when compatible with safety, add to the efficiency of the artillery to withdraw it temporarily from divisions and corps into one body, for more thorough and uniform instruction and equipment, and with a view to the batteries being returned in a replenished condition at the opening of a new campaign. This was the plan pursued with the artillery of the main army during the Revolutionary war; and, not because of its ancient origin, but rather of its excellent features, it deserves careful consideration.

If the management of our artillery in campaign be based upon the principles before announced, it would insure all being done that a correct administrative system could accomplish to render the service of that arm efficient, to impart unity of purpose and action to its dispersed members, without in the least impairing military discipline, and open a certain pathway to its honorable career in the field. This done, the prestige and glorious traditions of the arm would be intrusted to the guardianship of the personnel, in which, more than ever before, character, professional attainments, and abilities will be found to be absolutely necessary.

CHAPTER IX.

MATÉRIEL.

The term "system of artillery," as used generally, is synonymous with "system of guns;" but this is not always so, as illustrated in the Gribeauval, the most complete in all its parts of any system of artillery ever devised, embracing not only guns, carriages, and their appliances, but the organization of the personnel as well, the last being as important a feature as any other. The *division* of Gribeauval formed the *first* distinct artillery *tactical unit*, whence sprang the present *battery*, with the men, their pieces and the horses inseparably connected.

Vallier's system related only to the calibres of guns to be used; the stock-trail system to the carriages alone, the calibres of the pieces and the organization of the personnel remaining unchanged.

As the organization of the United States artillery is elsewhere treated of, the *matériel* of the system will here exclusively receive attention.

CARRIAGES.

It has been naturally but erroneously supposed that the Gribeauval carriage was introduced into the American service during the Revolution; instead, the English was then used, and it remained during the eighteenth century the only style known practically to the American artillery service. Many cannon and other military stores were procured in France, and the conclusion was drawn that the carriages accompanied them, and that in effect the whole Gribeauval system was transplanted to American soil. There is no proof, however, that this was the case. On the contrary, the existence of the system seems scarcely to have been known, and only during the later periods of the war. No reference to the system by American officers while the war was in progress has been found; and even those Americans who served with Rochambeau's army seem to have been entirely ignorant of the fact that the French set up claims to special merit for their artillery, if indeed at that time they did.

In Captain Stevens' "System for the Discipline of the Artillery" (1797) there is no reference to the Gribeauval system, except in a foot-note, the purport of which confirms the view here taken. Following the exercise of the field-piece by the American (English) plan, he remarks that "students, as a matter of curiosity, may like to contrast this with a practice the manuscript for which was given General Knox at Yorktown by Lieutenant-Colonel Nadal, director of the French artillery park." This proved to be the manual for the Gribeauval field artillery—a fact of which, farther than supposing it was the system adopted by the French army, Stevens, in 1797, was apparently profoundly ignorant; as he was also of the further fact that such a person as Gribeauval had ever lived. We are justified in drawing this inference, for, had he been aware of the existence of the great artillery reformer, nothing would have been more natural than for him to have mentioned his name when he was dealing with his system of artillery. General Knox did not take the trouble to have Nadal's manuscript translated—a task which, several years afterwards, the American author found great difficulty in having accomplished; not, he remarked, that there was any trouble in having ordinary French converted into English, but because the technical artillery terms were almost unknown. So far was Stevens from conceding special merit to the unknown system that he, in true English style, took just the opposite view, remarking triumphantly, and without thought of having the assertion brought in question, that "to clearly establish the superiority of the American (English) method over the French, one had only to study their respective manœuvres as they were here contrasted."

Beaumarchais, who furnished large quantities of stores to the Americans during the Revolution, including cannon and other matériel, did not, so far as can now be ascertained, send over a single carriage.

It is easily understood why the American artillery adhered to the English system as nearly as possible in everything. First, they were familiar with it, both through inheritance and the fact that Muller's *Treatise*, with its plans and tables for artillery constructions, was in every workshop and foundry which turned out this species of matériel; second, they deemed it superior to every other; and the reason they supplemented home products by importations from France was, that the brass-foundry art being in its infancy in America, the ordnance yielded was not, particularly during the first year of the war, entirely satisfactory, nor was it easy to procure the copper and tin necessary for brass castings.

There was every reason why they should not look with favor on the Gribeauval or French system. The Du Coudray affair had disgusted them with anything that had the semblance of it. They felt that they had been compelled to show that they could take care of themselves, not with the assistance, but in spite of French artillery officers; and it was impossible for them to separate the personnel from the system of matériel it represented.

General Knox, commanding the artillery, stamped on all appertaining to that arm the impress of an active, well-balanced mind, stored with both theoretical and practical knowledge. That he considered the English artillery the best in the world there is abundant evidence; when, in 1776, urging upon a committee of Congress the advisability of establishing for our artillery an academy similar to that at Woolwich, he observed that it was confessedly to this institution that the enemy owed the superiority of their artillery to all that had opposed it; and in recommending to the commander-in-chief the organization of additional regiments, about the same time, he remarked that we were safe so long as we followed the example of the English in this and all other particulars touching the management of the artillery arm, either the personnel or the matériel. The standard set up by the Royal Artillery Regiment was good enough for him; he used the French guns just as though they had come from Turkey, or elsewhere, in happy ignorance of the fact that they belonged to and were the exponents of a system destined soon to become famous, and, except by the English, to be adopted with but slight changes into every artillery of the world, including the American. There is no reason to doubt that, had Du Coudray succeeded Knox as general of artillery, the Gribeauval system, in its entirety, would have followed him to our shores. General Gribeauval himself was perhaps the staunchest of Du Coudray's friends; but the utter and humiliating failure of that scheme proved the American artillery to be strong enough in every way to bid defiance to outside interference. It was intellectually, and in all that goes to make up an efficient arm, the peer of any other in the Revolutionary army.

So far as is known, Professor Muller's work on gunnery was

the only text-book for artillery constructions extant in this country prior to 1797. That it was extensively used by those having charge of artillery technical affairs is well known. With this book in the hands of a superintendent, there was no reason why skilled artisans should not produce English guns and carriages of the most approved patterns. The carriages that Stevens describes as having been used during the Revolution and down to the time at which he wrote were Muller's. The American edition of Muller's treatise, published in Philadelphia in 1779, was dedicated (doubtless without the author's consent*) "to Generals Washington and Knox, to Colonel Proctor, and the officers of the continental army." The typographical and artistic execution of the work was rough, yet sufficiently exact for practical purposes. Contemporaneous testimony establishes the fact that the tables of construction and the drawings therein contained were extensively made use of, while there is no evidence to show that any other than this style of carriage was known. It was called the "bracket," as the Gribeauval was called the "flask," and its successor, the present style, the "stock-trail" system.

The "travelling carriages" were used to transport the heavier pieces which accompanied troops; "field carriages," to carry the lighter pieces. In both cases the material used was wood, except for bolts and bands required to hold the wooden parts together. The cheeks of the traveling carriage flared outwards towards the trail, and were joined together by three transoms—trail, centre, and breast. Firmly mortised into the cheeks was a piece of wood, upon which rested a wedge for elevating or depressing the gun. The inside of the cheeks between the trail and centre transoms was cut away considerably to lighten the trail, while immediately in rear of the centre transom was placed a locker for carrying tools. The field-carriage did not differ materially in design from the other; wooden axles were used for all; but in the field-carriage the wedge was suppressed and the elevation given by means of a screw. The traveling gun-carriage wheels for all calibres—3, 6, 12, and 24-pounders—were of the diameter of field artillery carriage-wheels of the present day—fifty-eight inches; but the

---

*It could not be expected that the preceptor to H. R. H., the Duke of Gloucester, would view with entire approbation this wholesale purloining by unrepentant rebels of the fruits of his brain-work.

field gun-carriage wheels were only fifty inches in diameter. Except for the 3-pounder gun, where they were but forty-five inches, the limber-wheels for all gun-carriages were forty-eight inches in diameter. From this it appears that there was not that disparity in the size of limber and carriage wheels—twelve inches—which characterized the Gribeauval system.

The horses were attached to the carriages of the pieces in single-file. There was no ammunition chest on the limber. That a few rounds might be at hand when the pieces came into action, two side boxes, placed one above the other, the upper for cartridges, the lower for projectiles, were attached to either side of the bracket-trail stock in rear of the axles. When the piece was "in battery" the side boxes were placed on the ground three paces in rear of the end of the trail handspike. The ammunition in the side boxes made the piece in a measure independent of the ammunition wagons. When the British started out on the expedition which terminated in the affair at Lexington, in 1775, they carried with them none other than twenty-four rounds per gun in these side boxes, which therefore served the same purpose as the small-trail ammunition-box of the Gribeauval, and the limber chest of the stock-trail carriage; and it is worthy of remark that, after having been universally suppressed about the beginning of the nineteenth century, when the Gribeauval and block-trail had supplanted all other systems of carriages, the side box is again coming into use, not only with some of the mitrailleurs, but also in the most recent patterns of improved metallic field gun-carriages.

Aside from that carried in side boxes, ammunition was transported in tumbrels, carts, and ammunition wagons. The wagon had four, the tumbrel and cart each two wheels, which were all of different sizes, and unlike either the limber or gun-carriage wheels. The inconvenience resulting from this multiplicity in the sizes of artillery wheels must have been very great, and it is hard to understand why it was tolerated. To the British artillery belongs the credit of having first corrected this evil, by making interchangeable the wheels of limbers and gun-carriages, an important step in the simplification of artillery matériel, which their offspring, the American artillery, did not imitate for many years, nor until, with many doubts and misgivings, the Gribeauval system had first been adopted, and then discarded.

Secretary McHenry was the first to move against the ancient

and honored system of the fathers. He had drawings purchased of carriages of the German horse-artillery system, concerning the power of which he had an exalted opinion, and with a view to having it introduced into the United States army. An elaborate report on the subject was made to Congress, which body did not, however, partake of the Secretary's enthusiasm; and so during the latter part of Mr. Adams' administration the matter dropped out of sight.

Modifications of the old system were begun by Secretary Dearborn almost as soon as he was installed in office, March 5th, 1801, but not in the manner contemplated by his predecessor. The introduction of horse artillery was held in abeyance, even as a measure to be advocated before Congress, and improvements in

---

NOTE—The enlisted men of the artillery did not drive the teams; that was done by civilians, employed sometimes by contract for a certain time, as a year, and at others hired for temporary service. The artillery soldier served his guns and prepared his ammunition. To make a driver of him was considered a degradation. Horses for the artillery were sometimes purchased for that arm alone, but generally the demands of service required the transfer of horses from that to other branches, and the reverse. During the latter years of the war the impressment of horses became quite a common practice, those belonging to Tories being levied upon when possible. The following warrant given Colonel Pickering, quartermaster-general, when Lafayette's detachment was about to march for Virginia, illustrates the manner of procuring means of transport in an emergency: "HEADQUARTERS, NEW WINDSOR, *February* 16*th*, 1781.—Whereas I have ordered a detachment to march from Peekskill on the 19th instant, on a service that may not admit of delay resulting from an observance of the usual forms of procuring teams and forage on the route, you are hereby authorized by yourself or deputy (whenever it may be necessary) to procure those articles by military impress in the country through which the detachment marches, for which this shall be your warrant." This was signed by the commander-in-chief. The "usual forms of procuring forage and teams" here alluded to was by making requisitions for them on the civil magistrates. There was often no money with which to purchase; levies on Tories were not always practicable; and as owners refused to hire their teams when pay therefor was so uncertain, there was nothing to do except to invoke the aid of authority, either civil or military. The former was appealed to preferably, but when prompt action was necessary, as in the instance cited, the vigor of military impress alone sufficed.

Benedict Arnold introduced the use of oxen for transporting heavy artillery, and in this Colonel Pickering followed his example. He has left on record the statement that without oxen there could not have been assembled at Yorktown the necessary siege artillery, and that to their extensive employment might be attributed the success of American arms in that decisive campaign.

the existing but ancient system of matériel became the order of the day.

The translation in 1800 of De Scheel's Treatise on the Gribeauval Artillery paved the way for these innovations. This work, which consisted of a text accompanied by a volume of plates, contained all the information necessary to the proper construction of the Gribeauval carriages. It gave the first information to the army and the public in an available form concerning the particulars of the (to them) new system of artillery; for, though there were many officers of artillery who were cognizant of its existence and its merits, they were those versed not only in the French language, but also in French military literature. This number was very small, and, as they never imparted their knowledge to the community, it availed the latter nothing.

De Scheel's treatise dealt wholly with matériel; hence it for some time longer escaped the attention of the authorities that Gribeauval's completed system extended to the organization of the personnel.

Secretary Dearborn retained in some degree the prejudice against foreign importations which he had imbibed during the first years of the Revolution, when many incompetent officers who sought service in the forces of the colonies were given positions, because of their supposed knowledge, over more deserving Americans. So great had been this abuse that a reaction set in naturally enough, yet as unreasonable as the practice it was intended to correct, and which for some time left even the gallant De Kalb knocking in vain at the doors of Congress for admission into its army.

But although Dearborn deprecated the practice of servilely copying that which was European, he had the practical sense which enabled him to recognize a good thing when he saw it; nor were his prejudices so great as to deter him, through mere sentiment, from adopting, if not the exact form, at least the substance of the Gribeauval carriage improvements. This will explain how it was that, while he did not hesitate to appropriate the new system piece-meal, he could not make up his mind to adopt it bodily. He desired to secure a lighter and more mobile carriage for his new system of cast-iron field-guns, and for this purpose was anxious to secure whatever there was of merit in the Gribeauval; but he determined to make no change until the wisdom of the measure was established to his satisfaction. He relied on his own judgment, instead of being guided by the counsels of other men. By failing to appreciate the importance of having the same parts of all carriages precisely alike and interchangeable, the *soul of the Gribeauval system* was passed by without recognition; but by taking up one after the other its most striking features, the manœuvring power of the field artillery was greatly increased. Thus by degrees the American carriage was brought to the point where but one step was necessary to make it the Gribeauval in its entirety; and this step was taken by Dearborn's successor within a month of the time he was established in the war office.

It will be interesting to trace, as they were successively made, these changes from the old bracket-trail carriage. First of all, the weight was cut down in 1801 about thirty per cent., taken pretty evenly from every part except the axle. The wooden axle next gave way to one of wrought-iron, incased in wood, with composition boxes. Driving teams tandem was discontinued, the shafts of former days being replaced by the pole. These alterations had all been made before 1807, and the year following both traveling as well as firing trunnions were adopted for the heavier field-gun carriages. Thus, during Dearborn's incumbency, and under his directions, four of the most prominent features of the Gribeauval carriage were adopted: First, the carriages reduced thirty per cent. in weight; second, wrought-iron axles with composition boxes replaced those of wood; third, the pole supplanted the shafts; fourth, firing and traveling trunnions were used for the heavier calibres. Except the last, which was a very inconvenient arrangement, these changes have stood their ground for three-quarters of a century, attesting the sterling worth of him who, in that dark age of our army's history, discerned their advantages, and was not deterred by a sense of his exalted position from seeing to it that their merits should be tested, and, when demonstrated to be such, that the improvements themselves should be adopted in service.

The pent-house ammunition box of the Gribeauval system was not made part of the new carriages. Its advantages over the old-fashioned English side boxes were not clearly established; it carried no more ammunition than they, and its manipulation was equally difficult. But it will be seen that the new system had been pushed to the verge of the French without having, however, become identical with it.

It was the intention of the Secretary of War to equip all the companies of the light artillery regiment raised pursuant to the act of April 12th, 1808, with the new carriages and the new system of cast-iron field guns, which also been perfected during his administration of the War Department. Every effort was made to supply the requisite matériel, but, as has been mentioned, the expense that would attend the measure caused its abandonment, except for a single company.

During the Revolution, Americans had accepted the English artillery as the standard of perfection. Time had, however, wrought changes in the artilleries of both countries. Both had abandoned their old and honored system for a new one. Though in many places their lines of research and improvement had been parallel, they had on the whole diverged, until, in 1809, their respective systems were diametrically opposed to each other. The Americans had partially copied, and were now about to adopt, what was considered by all, except the British, the finest system in the world. The English artillery had wrought out a new system for itself—one as much superior to the Gribeauval as the latter was superior to any that had preceded it, and which was destined in a few years to sweep all rivals from the field.

Secretary Eustis was appointed March 7th, 1809. On the 18th of the following April he ordered the military agent at Boston to construct for the light artillery regiment some gun-carriages of the Gribeauval style, without modifications, adding the injunction that, "*as these are the first of the kind on this plan, it is particularly desirable that they should be made in a proper manner and of the best materials and workmanship.*" This is the date at which the Gribeauval system of carriages, pure and simple, was introduced into the American service.

Other carriages of this pattern had, however, been manufactured, and others still had been turned over to the United States authorities at New Orleans in 1803, after the Louisiana purchase; hence those which Eustis ordered to be constructed were not the first seen in this country. In his letter of instruction to the agent, before mentioned, the latter was directed to accept as a model in his constructions a carriage that had already been made by a mechanic of Boston and approved of by competent judges.

The New Orleans artillery—received from the French—consisted of four 12-pounder, four 8-pounder, eight 4-pounder guns, and eight 6-inch howitzers, with the most approved Gribeauval carriages, caissons, and equipments complete. In the fall of 1809 two of these carriages were by the Secretary's order sent to Washington city for examination, and to serve as patterns for others.

The Wurst wagon, which at that time was the French light (horse) artillery caisson, was not introduced, or even manufactured, until 1812, after the declaration of war against Great Britain. Colonel Izard, of the Second Artillery, was the first to construct a few of them for the equipment of part of his regiment fitting out for the Canadian frontier; but, so far as can be ascertained, they were not issued to any part of the army. That portion of the light (horse) regiment which, in the first months of the war, took the field, was equipped as horse artillery proper, with the ordinary caisson.

As the war progressed and the construction of many new carriages became necessary the Gribeauval system was gradually extended to embrace all calibres—3, 6, 12, 18, and 24-pounders—the most noticeable improvement being that the tire, instead of being put on the wheels in sections, as in the Gribeauval, was made into a hoop.

Although the Americans met in the field the new English system of artillery during the war of 1812, the events of the war were not of sufficient magnitude to demonstrate its superiority, which seems to have escaped the attention of all except one man—

NOTE.—It has been stated that the complete Gribeauval system embraced two parts: (1) matériel; (2) personnel. The former included (a) guns; (b) carriages. Of these, (a) was never adopted into the United States service. The manner in which (b) was adopted has been narrated. This left (2) to be accounted for, to take in the completed Gribeauval system.

The laws had organized the personnel of the United States artillery into companies and regiments. The *division* of Gribeauval found no place in the strictly legal organization. It was given one by regulations. After Secretary Armstrong assumed control at the War Department (January 13, 1813), the artillery, on paper at least, was distributed for field service, under the regulations of May 1st, 1813, into divisions or half divisions. This was simply copying the Gribeauval system. It left the adoption of the guns (a) to make that system complete; but this step was never taken. [See Appendix C, (1).]

Colonel Decius Wadsworth, of the ordnance department.* This officer was attracted by the peculiarities of the English field-carriages, and, having given careful attention to their construction, became convinced of their many advantages, particularly as to the increased mobility thereby insured. He was at the time engaged, under the authority and requirements of the act of February 8th, 1815, in devising a complete system of artillery matériel, which he hoped to have adopted by the War Department. Among other things, he proposed a field-carriage in principles of construction very much like the English block-trail. But the idea was novel; it was departing, almost as soon as adopted, from the system of Gribeauval, with its glorious associations, and which, save by the British artillery, had been everywhere accepted as superior to all others. It was natural, therefore, that Secretary Calhoun should hesitate to approve this new and unique field-carriage; and, as the safest course, he proposed that a board of officers should examine and report upon the merits of the Wadsworth system of matériel. The personnel of the board was selected by Colonel

---

* Writing, in 1869, concerning the attempts of Colonel Wadsworth to improve the style of gun-carriage after the war of 1812, Mr. William Wade, who was at the time (1812–1821) an ordnance officer and a co-laborer with Wadsworth, remarked: "In 1817, Colonel Decius Wadsworth, who had been chief of the ordnance department since its first establishment, in 1812, devised a field-carriage of a model entirely different from any hitherto known to our service. Its leading features were similar to the carriages used by the British army in our war of 1812. One of the British carriages captured at the battle of Plattsburg in September, 1814, was sent to the Washington arsenal. It was of the *stock-trail* kind, which coupled with its limber by means of a pintle-hook fastened upon the rear of the limber-axle body. The limber had, instead of a single pole, three thills or shafts, designed for the use of three horses abreast. One of the shafts was movable, to be displaced or attached at pleasure. A large ammunition chest was placed upon the limber-axle body, upon which six men could ride, and seats for two men were placed on the carriage, thus carrying eight men in all upon the carriage. This was the first field-gun carriage of the stock-trail model that I ever saw or heard of, and was doubtless the first ever known in the United States.

"Colonel Wadsworth, in constructing his carriage, modified this English model by substituting the single pole for the three shafts, and by using two bent cheeks instead of the stock-trail, and also by supporting the limber ammunition chest on springs, instead of fixing it upon the axle, as in the English carriage. By bending the two cheeks so that they came nearly together at the trail ends, he retained all the advantages of the stock-trail for wheeling

Wadsworth, and embraced Colonel Porter and Captain Towson of the light artillery, Captain Archer of the corps of artillery, Lieutenant-Colonel Bomford and Captain Wade of the ordnance department. Convened by general order from the adjutant and inspector-general's office, July 28th, 1818, the board was directed to meet on the 1st of the following September "to examine the patterns and models of cannon, howitzers, and mortars; of field and fixed carriages; of caissons and other appendages of the artillery, and such other subjects as may be referred to it, with a view to the establishing of a permanent system of uniformity in relation to that branch of the service. The board will report its opinion on all subjects referred to its consideration." Porter was excused, because of ill-health, from attending. Towson was made paymaster-general in 1819, so the board was soon reduced to its three junior members. It was the pioneer in the field of artillery boards, of which more recent years have been so prolific.

In the acrimonious correspondence that ensued when the board reported adversely to his system the colonel of ordnance showed

---

the carriage on a curve of short radius. I constructed several of these carriages, the first one under the personal supervision of Colonel Wadsworth, in 1817. I made several trials at Pittsburg with one of these carriages in 1818, with as many men mounted upon it as were needed to serve the piece, driving over rough roads, the horses at full gallop, then suddenly halting and firing the gun. I rode myself on the limber with the men that I might observe any defects. This test was as complete as could well be made with untrained horses and men, and was quite satisfactory, and I am now of opioion that if Colonel Wadsworth had continued in authority, with health and other favoring circumstances, he would have effected an entire revolution in the old [Gribeauval] system, and have made important improvements."

There was another particular, not noticed by Mr. Wade, in which Wadsworth deviated from the British system, viz., he proposed that while the limber wheels for all field-carriages should be of the same height, they should be different from the gun-carriage wheels; and the latter differed among themselves, those for the 6-pounder being 4 feet 6 inches in height, those for the 12-pounder, 4 feet 9 inches. During the Peninsular war all limber wheels of the British artillery were of the same height as the gun-carriage wheels—an improvement that Wadsworth had done well to copy, as likewise the block-trail, instead of the two bent flasks. It is evident that, by placing the ammunition box on the limber, carrying on them a number of men sufficient to serve the piece, making practically a stock-trail of the two flasks, Wadsworth had struck the key-note to the modern British artillery system, which he recognized, contrary to the opinion of his contemporaries, as being superior to any other.

himself a master in the polemic art as well as an artillerist of true genius. Referring to the field-carriage before mentioned, and the reception it had received, he remarked:

"The board have thought proper to criticise the carriage constructed under my direction. Whether or not I have succeeded in improving our field carriage, let unprejudiced, intelligent men decide. They say in one place that mine are the only carriages which have not been altered for the worse from the French; in another, that mine are in every way inferior to the latter.

"My carriage has some improvements that will stand their ground. The arrangement of the elevating screw is superior to anything of the kind that has yet appeared. I stake my reputation upon that. The 6-pounder carriage proposed by the board carries fifteen rounds; mine twenty-nine rounds. The limbers of my carriage admit of being employed in time of action as tumbrels to convey ammunition from the caissons to the pieces, thereby permitting the former to remain out of range of the fire. The explosion of a British caisson at Chippewa by a shell from Towson's battery, if it did not decide the fate of that action, at least contributed greatly to its success. If a better plan than mine can be devised, let it be proposed.

"The 6-pounder carriage of my construction permits a number of men sufficient to serve the gun to ride upon the limber and carriage; and, as it is limbered and unlimbered with the greatest facility, which is even partially acknowledged by the board, changes of position may be effected with it in inconceivably less time than with carriages of the French construction."

He appreciated the fact that the Gribeauval was inferior to the English system, the latter of which he proposed essentially to adopt. In that opinion he stood without support; but events have vindicated the keenness of his perception and the soundness of his judgment. Remarking upon the disposition to blindly adhere to the French system, without examining its value, when compared with others, he continued:

"The making of wheel carriages is well understood in this country, and we should lose a great deal and expose ourselves to derision in the minds of those who know how carriages ought to be built to servilely copy French patterns invented fifty or sixty years ago. It is a mistake to suppose the French system of artillery is the most perfect in existence. The British artillery has been greatly improved within the last twenty years. In the construction of carriages, in the celerity of their movements, in the facility of their manœuvres, in the excellent quality of their ammunition, and the convenience with which their pieces are supplied in time of action, the British artillery is now superior to what the French ever was. It is in vain for us to try to underrate it. We shall be obliged sooner or later to contend with it, and a knowledge of its perfections and power ought to stimulate us to greater exertions to bring our own to a point of excellence—to equal, at least, if we cannot surpass it. The

British artillery has been brought to its present state by gradual improvements, made under the direction of men of intelligence and experience, equally versed in the theory and the practice of their profession. The Government has spared no expense to attain the object in view."

This statement of the relative merits of the two opposing systems, considering the time at which it was made, is remarkable. The colonel of ordnance only, of the artillerists in this country, took in at a glance, as it were, though he had carefully studied it, the great superiority of the English system—something that the French Government, with every proof before it, did not acknowledge until ten years later. Wadsworth did not live to see the justness of his views established, the English sweep the Gribeauval and all other systems before it, to become, as it has remained, without change in principle and but few in minor details, master of the battle field. He discerned what others, bound by that strange spell—a name—could not see. It is due the memory of this truly great man to place on record this narrative of his labors. The opposition he encountered, and principally from within his own department, was like that which for a time baffled Congreve, Gribeauval, and other artillery reformers. He combined the learning and sense of Muller with a power of analysis equal to Gribeauval himself. Ill health impaired his usefulness and frustrated his plans, though it did not for one moment cloud his clear intellectual horizon. He lived before his time. Twenty years afterwards his associates and opponents acknowledged that he had been right. He retired from the service in that struggle illustrating the survival of the *physically* fittest—the reduction of 1821. Had he remained at the head of the technical artillery, there is no doubt that he would, with proper support, have overturned the system finally (in 1819) determined upon, and which, almost as soon as established, went down before that other, the advantages of which Wadsworth alone of his cotemporaries had pointed out to the army.

The contest between the Gribeauval and the Wadsworth systems was an unequal one. The former was backed by the memories of a brilliant career; the latter, unknown and without honor even in its own country, was considered as merely an experiment, which, however successful it might be, could produce nothing having merit equal to that of its world-renowned rival.

The board reported adversely to the proposed system, and, acting under instructions from the War Department, it then proceeded to digest another, complete in all its parts, embracing every branch of the artillery service, and which would strictly conform—except as to the calibres of the ordnance and the metals used in the construction thereof—to the latest and most improved patterns of the Gribeauval. After much labor, prolonged experiment, and patient investigation, the board submitted a system for the approval of the Secretary of War, embracing three general features: First, cast-iron as the gun-metal for all calibres; second, cast-iron as the matériel for gun-carriages of all fixed batteries; third, the most recent patterns of the Gribeauval for field, siege, and garrison artillery carriages. The proceedings of the board were approved by Secretary Calhoun, and the system of artillery recommended by it was adopted for the service of the United States.

The French system, now definitely determined upon, after a vigorous effort to obtain a better one had failed, retained undisputed sway until, in 1829, there were deposited with the technical artillery department complete and accurate drawings of carriages—field, siege, garrison, and sea-coast, all, except the last, based on the English plan, which Colonel Wadsworth had championed ten years before. The construction of model stock-trail carriages was at once begun. The first stroke of the hammer sounded the death-knell of the Gribeauval régime.

We will briefly notice the career of the system—English block-trail—which, after twelve years of rigorous experiment, had, despite national prejudice, and at the sacrifice of the cherished idol of a half century, forced itself upon the French artillery, and was now to be retransplanted into our own.*

Captain Congreve broke ground against the bracket-trail system as early as 1776, and the following year experimental carriages, having the ammunition-boxes on the limber-axle, were made at his suggestion. He pointed out the advantage of having the limber and the gun-carriage wheels of the same size, and interchange-

---

* The facts here given concerning the gradual introduction of the salient features of the English stock-trail system of carriages were furnished the author by the late General Tyler, who, through the courteous assistance of Major Hime, Royal artillery, and perhaps others of that service, was enabled to establish their correctness from the official records at Woolwich.

able. The associate of Congreve in these improvements was De Sagulier, who, in 1778, constructed carriages with interchangeable limber and piece wheels, and in 1779 introduced wrought-iron axles for 3-pounder and 1-pounder gun-carriages. The substitution of a block of wood for the bracket-trail seems first to have occurred to De Sagulier, who, in 1778, proposed block-trails for heavy 3-pounder carriages. By 1794, due to the joint labors of these officers and of others, perhaps, wrought-iron axles with composition-boxes, the block-trail, the pintle-hook, wheels for limber and gun-carriage interchangeable, with ammunition-chest placed on the limber-axle, were generally recognized improvements which, one after another, had become leading features of the English field artillery matériel. Having taken these steps, it was but making another in the same direction to convert the clumsy caisson into a carriage built upon the same general principles, thus enabling it to turn upon the same ground as the piece. The forge and battery wagon were similarly affected by this spirit of change, which had so thoroughly accomplished its work that when Wellington began his Peninsular campaigns the artillery matériel of his army was the same in principle, and almost the same in detail of construction, with that adopted by the French in 1827, and concerning which, in 1829, the United States War Department received its first information.

The superiority of the new English system could not but have attracted the attention of the veteran artillerists who had to contend against it. They saw that its mobility far exceeded what it was possible to attain with their own. After the fall of Napoleon, when the allies were encamped in the environs of Paris, the simplicity of this unique system and the facilities of its manœuvres attracted the attention, awakened the interest, and challenged the admiration of not only the artillery, but of all the principal officers in that vast assembly of the armies of Europe. Following the Restoration, when the Congress of Aix-la-Chapelle had freed France of the allies, the question whether or not the English system should be chosen to supersede the time-honored Gribeauval attracted the serious consideration of the French military authorities. Boards of experienced officers were appointed to examine into the subject in all its bearings. After years of careful investigation, aided by the severest and most elaborate series of experiments, and including many futile attempts to modify the Gribeauval, reports were made in favor of the proposed change. To accept the system of a victorious, exultant, and insolent enemy drove the iron to the soul of the French artillery. Many, blinded by national predjudice, held out against it, but, to the honor of those upon whom the responsibility rested, be it remembered that they had the courage of their convictions ; and placing behind them as unworthy of consideration whatever of professional pride they felt which might bias their judgment in a matter affecting the well-being of the State, they united in recommending, regardless of its origin, the adoption of a system of artillery which in every point of view added strength to the military power of the Nation.

Several copies of the able and dispassionate report of the committee which finally determined the matter, and upon which report the French Government ordered, July, 1827, that the stock-trail system of artillery should be adopted, were among the valuable papers furnished the United States authorities through the untiring labors of Lieutenant Tyler during a few months' stay in Europe.

The principal changes made in the English system by the French were as follows : (1) The iron axle, encased in wood, was replaced by a single piece of iron without any support. (2) A pole replaced the shafts of the limber. (3) The height of the wheels was diminished a little more than an inch, to better adapt them to the draft of the French horses. (4) The elevating screw, which in the English system was bolted to the knob of the cascable and worked in a movable bed, was given a fixed seat, with the breech of the piece resting on the head of the screw. (5) The limber was given a movable splinter-bar. (6) In place of the two small ammunition-boxes, side by side on the limber and the caissons, and secured by cords, a single ammunition-box was substituted, retained in place by iron fastenings. (7) In the English ammunition-boxes the apartments were made to carry the ball and cartridge separately; in the modified chest the apartments were for fixed ammunition.

The drawings which the lieutenant placed at the disposition of the Department were of the latest models. By July, 1830, the preliminary work was begun looking to the construction of some of the field carriages based on these drawings, from which was derived the only information possessed concerning the new system.*

The young officer, to whose intelligent and almost unaided exertions the artillery arm was indebted for this important acquisition, deserves to be remembered among those who have contributed

---

*The following letter, written by Major Alfred Mordecai, late of the United States ordnance department, dated September 27th, 1872, confirms in the most positive manner the claim here put forward, that to this officer, and to him alone, is due the credit of having introduced into our service a full knowledge of the stock-trail system of artillery. Major Mordecai was a lieutenant of engineers in 1832, and was appointed a captain in the ordnance department organized that year. * * * "My actual service in the ordnance department began on the 1st of January, 1833, when I joined Captain Symington at Washington arsenal, and soon after succeeded him in the charge of that post. He had then constructed the first of the field gun-carriages and caissons of the present system, adopted from the French, and in doing so he used as models the drawings of the French system which Lieutenant Daniel Tyler had obtained in France and deposited in the ordnance office. I made at that time from the same drawings the first drawings, and translated the tables of construction for the field forge, which was afterwards modified, I think at Watervliet arsenal, by a slight change, perhaps, in the bellows, and covering it with a roof. At the same time Symington was just finishing the first of the barbette carriages, which were also copied from the French system, knowledge of which in detail was obtained also from drawings deposited by Lieutenant Tyler in the ordnance office. The first of these barbette carriages was sent in the winter or spring of 1833 for the armament of Fort Moultrie on account of the political disturbances in South Carolina. I can have, therefore, no hesitation in saying that the first full knowledge of the French system, which we copied in the field, siege, and barbette carriages, was derived from the complete drawings and tables of construction which were furnished by Lieutenant Tyler to the ordnance office." The writer of the above (Major Mordecai) was one of the officers who labored most intelligently and with greatest effect to secure to the artillery a complete system of matériel. From 1835 to 1860 his name was intimately associated with every effort to build up an efficient national armament. From 1835 to 1840, to his exertions more than to those of any other, and, so far as can be seen, from 1840 to 1850, to his industry and perseverance more than to those of all others united, the vast mass of data on artillery subjects which had been collected was systematically arranged, published, and placed in the hands of the army in the "Artillery of the United States Land Service," text and plates, 1849, and in the "Revised Ordnance Manual" of 1850. No other testimonial to the work that Lieutenant Tyler performed could be wished than is here given by this accomplished scholar, profound thinker, and scientific artillerist.

most to its advancement. With no wish to make invidious comparisons, it can be claimed, without risk of being successfully controverted, that none others of the many who have been dispatched by this Government to Europe have secured, either in so short a time or at so great pecuniary sacrifice, such a variety of useful information, or made it so directly available to his associates of the military profession. After a few months' sojourn in France, there appeared, as the result of his labors: (1) 300 lithographed copies of a translation, accompanied by plates, of the whole system—field, seige, garrison, and sea-coast—of the Gribeauval artillery tactics. (2) Many lithographic copies of the report (translated) of the French committee, which discussed the relative merits of the ancient and the modern systems of artillery matériel, and finally decided the question between them. (3) Most important and useful of all, complete copies of the working drawings and tables of construction, perfect in every particular, of the latter system, as modified and adopted by the French Government. All this was done at the expense of the young military enthusiast. In addition, he obtained and rendered promptly available to the Government (4) valuable information concerning the most improved patterns of small arms used abroad. For the pecuniary outlay incurred he received but a tardy and most inadequate return.

Disappointed at the lack of a just appreciation of his services in building up the technical artillery, in which field he was at that time the most prominent and advanced laborer, disgusted that merit should remain unrewarded, while in some instances mere political favorites were promoted into this branch of the artillery, now organized as the ordnance department, he resigned his commission to seek and receive in the open competition of civil life that recognition of great talents and business capacity, and the rewards of indefatigable industry, for which in the army he had hoped and struggled in vain. Death, in 1882, terminated a life of activity and usefulness that may well serve as a model for the emulation of the youth of his native land. Full of years and honors, he has been gathered to rest, but the work he did lives after him. In the light artillery system of the present day, with its distinguished career in peace and war, in the bivouac and on the battle-field, there stands an enduring monument to the memory of Lieutenant Daniel Tyler, of the First regiment of United States artillery.*

The system of artillery prepared by the board of 1818, although it had been adopted after what were deemed sufficient tests, was not found to be adapted to actual service. A half battery, composed of Wadsworth carriages and the long 6-pounders of the adopted pattern, was sent to the artillery school of practice at Fortress Monroe in 1827 for trial.† The guns burst under cir-

---

*The author experiences great pleasure at being authorized to insert the following tribute to the memory and later services of this distinguished officer, written by Senator Joseph R. Hawley, of Connecticut, late major-general U. S. volunteers, who received his first lessons in the military art under General Tyler's instructions in 1861, when, although sixty-four years of age, the gallant patriot and soldier, abandoning lucrative civil pursuits, buckled on the armor and went forth to do battle for the maintenance of the Union with all the fervor of a youth of twenty-five:

"General Tyler's name is remembered with the warmest gratitude in Connecticut. Of the best blood of the Revolutionary era, he was every inch a soldier. His residence and business connections in the South as well as the North gave him a very thorough comprehension of the temper and purposes of the conspirators against the Union. Like General Sherman, he was misunderstood, and believed to be magnifying the coming war. The moment Sumter was fired upon he placed himself at the service of the good war governor, Buckingham. The first regiment of three-months volunteers was raised in a very few days, and Captain Tyler, as he was then called, was made colonel thereof. The other two three-months regiments followed quickly, and Colonel Tyler was made a brigadier. These three regiments he took into camp at New Haven, thoroughly equipped in every respect, and put them under the severest drill for two or three weeks before they started for Washington. Several hundred of the officers and privates of these three regiments became officers of the three-years regiments raised immediately after. General Tyler infused into all under his command a spirit of severe, exact discipline, a determination to master speedily the details of a soldier's duty, and a blazing patriotism that made no measure of its devotion. Without doubt his influence was most beneficially felt during the four years of, and among the 54,000 troops Connecticut sent to, the war. Some people, doubtless, thought him unduly impetuous, but he was—physically, morally, and mentally—to those under him the model of a chivalrous, fearless gentleman and thorough soldier."

† Why Wadsworth's rejected carriages should have been selected for these important experiments with the new field-gun is not known. The fact that they were so used is established. After that officer had left the army, it is possible, and altogether probable, that his note of warning concerning the superiority of the English carriage, on which his was modeled, began more

cumstances which destroyed all confidence in them and their system, and the attention of the department was at once drawn to the fact that a new one, for the field artillery at least, was absolutely necessary.

Without any accepted pattern of field-piece, and with the attention of the department divided between the Gribeauval going out and the stock-trail system coming in, it is not to be wondered at that Secretary Cass should have reported, in 1831, that the matériel of the artillery was in an unsettled state. He also announced that a board would be appointed to examine into the matter and definitely settle upon some permanent system. Accordingly, by Order No. 74, Headquarters of the Army, December 24th, 1831, instructions from the War Department, dated December 8th, 1831, were promulgated, instituting a board, consisting of Generals Macomb commanding the army, and Scott commanding the eastern department, Inspector-General Wool, Colonel Eustis commandant of the artillery school of practice, and Lieutenant-Colonel Bomford on ordnance duty, "to take into consideration the establishing of a uniform system of operations in the ordnance department, both as regards the models and patterns of arms, carriages, and equipments of every species, as well as all kinds of supplies furnished by that department." It was further directed to report, for the examination and decision of the War Department, such a system for the government of the ordnance department as should appear proper and necessary. This board first met March 28th, 1832, when Colonel

---

and more to attract the attention of those who had been his colaborers, and who had remained in the artillery service. The desire would naturally arise to give the carriage a fair trial, that its merits, if any it had, might be found out. Had this been the reasoning of those having such matters in charge, the result would have been just what happened—the occasion for more severely testing the new guns was seized on as a proper one for similar experiments with the carriage. As, however, the guns failed so signally, (being only rivaled in this respect by the "conversion system" of 1881,) the carriage, with the pieces, seems to have been permanently relegated to the obscurity whence it had, for a temporary purpose, emerged. There was no further opportunity given to test the Wadsworth, as, before another pattern of field-gun was decided on, the Government was actively engaged in constructing the latest model of stock-trail carriage, of which Wadsworth's was at best but an inferior copy, made before the original of the system had been brought to its present state of perfection.

Gratiot, of the engineers, relieved Scott, and the labors, which, after many mutations of the personnel—caused by changes in the boards which one after another took up the work, here given the original in charge—were finally to result in giving a definite system of artillery to the United States army. The Macomb, officially designated the "ordnance board," continued in existence until June 22d, 1837, when the duties of its members, consequent upon the Florida war, being such as to prevent their giving that attention to the subjects intrusted to it which their importance demanded, another board was convened to take up the duties of the former. The relieving board was assembled pursuant to General Orders No. 41, Headquarters of the Army, agreeably to instructions from the War Department of June 21st, 1837, and was composed of Brevet Brigadier-General Eustis, president; Colonel Cutler of the infantry, Lieutenant-Colonel Crane of the artillery, Major Craig and Captain Baker of the ordnance, members; Captain A. Mordecai, ordnance, secretary. By Special Orders No. 45, June 26th, 1837, Lieutenant-Colonel Talcott, ordnance, relieved Major Craig; and on July 4th following, the board met at West Point, and proceeded to take up the thread of the armament investigation where it had been left off by its predecessor. The same causes, however, which had rendered a dissolution of the original board advisable now operated to prevent the reassembling of its successor, thus seemingly, but not in fact, retaining matters relating to the procurement of an efficient artillery matériel *in statu quo*. But this was not true. On the contrary, some of the most important measures looking to the solution of the armament problem, and which had been inaugurated by the Macomb board, were being successfully prosecuted, and had led to the procurement of a large amount of matériel, with more in process of manufacture. The results of this labor were placed at the disposition of a board convened by General Orders No. 20, Adjutant-General's Office, July 2d, 1838, and used by it to definitely settle upon a system of field, seige and garrison, and sea-coast artillery, which was approved by the Secretary of War, as announced officially to the army in 1839. The board of 1838 was composed originally of Colonel Fenwick and Captain Erving, of the artillery; Lieutenant-Colonel Talcott and Captains Baker and Mordecai, of the ordnance. The unique spectacle was presented of a civilian—Paymaster-General Towson—sitting, at the special request of the Secretary of War, as an honorary member of this military board, and partaking of its deliberations. When the question of the sea-coast armament was being determined on, Colonel Totten, the chief of engineers, was, by Special Orders No. 93, Adjutant-General's Office, December 24th, 1838, also added to the board.

In the meantime the board appointed by Order No. 50, Adjutant-General's Office, August 24th, 1835, which was practically, though not altogether in personnel, a branch of the Macomb board and acted the part of a committee of the latter, had, in pursuance of the general plan, made its important contribution to the stock of information being acquired in the line of field artillery. The members were Inspector-General Wool, Colonels Gratiot and Eustis, all of the "ordnance board," with Lieutenant-Colonel Talcott, Major Worth, and Captain Mordecai, of the ordnance. By Special Orders No. 63, Adjutant-General's Office, September 12th, 1835, Captain Huger, ordnance, was appointed an additional member of the board, with the proceedings of which, because of some difficulty regarding relative rank, Major Worth refused to have anything to do. The board was instructed to examine into, prove, and report upon the merits of new field-guns, carriages, harness, and equipments which had been manufactured in pursuance of the resolutions of the ordnance board, of which General Macomb was president. Its proceedings, therefore, were in strict conformity with the general plan of operations mapped out by the latter at its first session, and they form a most important link in that unbroken chain which connects the labors of the ordnance board of 1831 with those of its successors of 1837 and 1838, and which, the succeeding year, resulted in the adoption of those calibres of ordnance, the models of their carriage and equipments, which constituted the main features of a new and improved system of artillery.

Much had been done, but the work was not complete; a mass of valuable data was collected in these years of research and experiment, which had either to be systematically arranged and published, or lost to the public service; besides, the question of a proper metal for field-guns was still undecided; in a word, the task of naturally and methodically putting in order the accumulated materials brought together through the intelligent labors of so many boards, all directed to the same end, had yet to be performed. The particulars as to metals, models, and dimensions of the adopted ordnance, to a considerable extent, remained to be determined.

It was now that Secretary Poinsett, placing before it all information thus far acquired, devolved on a committee of ordnance officers the onerous duty of putting the last hand to the work begun by the ordnance board of 1831. This committee, consisting of Lieutenant-Colonel Talcott, Major Baker, Captains Mordecai and Huger, was appointed, April 16th, 1839, for the purpose, as announced by the Secretary of War in his letter of instruction, "of devising and arranging a uniform system of artillery and other supplies of every kind furnished for the military service by the ordnance department." The result, as immediately affecting the artillery, was the gradual perfecting, and ten years afterwards the adoption, of a uniform system of matériel, the most minute particulars of which were carefully worked out, and which in its leading features has remained to this day essentially unchanged.

The labors of this committee were but a continuation of those of its immediate predecessors, the ordnance boards of 1831, 1835, 1837, and 1838. Each acted its part for the attainment of the grand object kept steadily in view. Without the contribution of each, the result would have stopped short of success; the connected efforts of all produced the perfect system.

Upon the ordnance department was placed the responsible duty of digesting, reducing to method, and publishing to the world the outcome of the ten years' investigations of the mixed boards, supplemented by much valuable information acquired through a commission of its own officers sent to Europe, and the original researches of the ordnance committee. This committee performed well the part allotted it by the Secretary of War; but, while conferring this, its just meed of praise, it will not be lost sight of that it had, as a foundation on which to base its inquiries, the accumulated knowledge resulting from the efforts of many hard-working, conscientious, and intelligent boards of officers, without which the triumph which crowned its protracted labors would have been much more difficult of accomplishment and much less complete.

The calibres and natures of the standard ordnance, the system of carriages and their equipments, the nomenclature of every part, with the principles to be observed in preparing the whole for active service, were definitively settled upon before the appointment of the ordnance committee of 1839, nor were they afterwards modified in any essential particular. The efforts of that committee were directed, not to tearing down what others with so much laborious care had built up, but rather, by rounding off angles and filling in vacant places, adding not so much strength as beauty and symmetry to the structure, the frame-work of which had been placed, already joined together, in its hands.

Notwithstanding the very generally-conceded superiority of the stock-trail, it did not formally and entirely supersede the Gribeauval for several years after its first introduction into the service. It was no doubt deemed unprofessional to discard an old, faithful, and valued servant for one comparatively unknown, and of the merits of which, from personal experience, we knew nothing. Such seemed to be the view of the ordnance board of 1831; and one of the first questions to the determinate settlement of which it addressed itself was that of the relative merits of these two systems of carriages. Among other resolutions adopted by the board at its first meeting, were the following: " * * * 3. That the chief of ordnance be required to procure from Europe the best models of French and English * * * artillery, * * * including guns and carriages of field-artillery, and models of sea-coast and garrison guns and mortars, with their carriages, for the use of the board. * * * 5. That a committee of the board be appointed to consider the proper calibres and models for guns and carriages of field artillery, the materials of which they should be made, to report its opinion on the subject, and prepare a plan for carrying its views into effect."

The next day it resolved: "1. That the Secretary of War be requested to send to Europe one or more officers of the army for the purpose of carrying into execution the third resolution of yesterday." This being approved by Secretary Cass, Inspector-General Wool, a member of the board, and of course conversant with its views, was dispatched to Europe with the necessary funds and instructions to purchase one English 6-pounder and one 4-pounder, one 12-pounder, and one 5½-inch howitzer of the French system, with their carriages, caissons, and equipments complete; also *models* of the French siege and sea-coast mortars, with their beds, and *drawings* of the rest of both the English and French systems of artillery. The inspector-general started on his mission with alacrity, and no doubt, as a matter of personal gratification, it was eminently successful; but, so far as the objects of the ordnance board and the interests of the Government were concerned, it was devoid of any useful results. He brought back eight swords and belts!

The committee appointed under the fifth resolution of the board before mentioned was composed of Colonel Eustis and Lieutenant-Colonel Bomford. They were met at the threshold of their investigations by an absence of proper facilities for conducting the experiments which that resolution necessitated being made. This fact was reported to the board by the committee in February, 1834, accompanied by a request to be furnished with the necessary ordnance, mounted in equal proportions on the Gribeauval and on the stock-trail style of carriages, to enable the committee to execute the duty devolving upon it. The request received the approval of the Secretary of War, and measures were taken to have the iron guns and the stock-trail carriages procured, but it was not given to the committee to pursue the investigations; this duty was devolved on the ordnance board of 1835, before mentioned, and which met for the first time September, 1835, at Watervliet arsenal. The Gribeauval carriage was not experimented with, as it was doubtless considered that nothing which was not well known could be developed concerning it; but the stock-trail carriages were day after day put to the severest tests possible with the ample facilities placed at the disposition of the board, which, September 22d following—

"*Resolved*, That the system of carriages for field artillery, recently adopted after much trial and minute investigation by the Government of France, is the best hitherto devised for the service of the United States, and that it ought to be received, with no further alterations than may be found necessary for the adoption of the respective carriages to our guns and roads."

Before the board adjourned, September 26th, following, similar resolutions were passed concerning all carriages appertaining to the field-train of the French system. After the usual number of references from one department to another, this report was approved by Secretary Cass July 8th, 1836, who directed that the money appropriated for the purpose by Congress at its last session should be expended in carrying into execution the measures proposed in the resolutions of the board.

We are not, therefore, left in doubt as to the date at which, or the circumstances under which, the stock-trail system of carriages was adopted into our service. Its position has never been questioned since. Time has served to only more fully develop its merits, and while alterations in a few of the details of construction have been made, the underlying principles have remained unchanged; the system itself, taken as a whole, seems incapable of improvement. The harness and all equipments making up the complete French matériel were adopted at the same time, with but slight and generally unimportant modifications.

Recent attempts at improvement have been directed, not at the system on which they are constructed, but towards the securing a better material for the carriages, limbers, caissons, and wagons, replacing the wooden frame by combinations of wood, steel, and iron, each placed so as most advantageously to perform the work thrown upon it.

Attention began to be directed to the subject of metallic carriages soon after the Civil war. At that time wrought-iron was the only metal thought of. The advantages which it was supposed would result from the change were—1. Lightness and cheapness. 2. By placing the pintle two feet in rear of the limber axle-tree the trail of the gun-carriage would act as a counterpoise, relieving the wheel horses of the weight of the pole. 3. By bringing the trunnion-beds nearer the axle-tree the liability of the carriage to overturn while traveling would be diminished. 4. By allowing no part of the limbered carriage to project below the plane of the axle-trees the breaking of implements in passing over stumps, stones, and other obstacles would be prevented. 5. A more convenient method of carrying rammers and the trail handspike would be secured. 6. By placing thimbles in the trunnion holes for the larger, when the smaller calibred guns were being used, one carriage would be made to suffice for all calibres of field guns.

A few wrought-iron carriages were made and issued to the artillery for trial, but they were heavier than was necessary, of rough construction, and were pronounced unsatisfactory. It would seem, however, that they were not intended to exhibit what the department could do, but were made for preliminary tests merely, and to indicate in what line of investigation the carriage of the future would be found. Strong and not very clumsy cannoneer seats were placed between the wheel and the gun; but its excessive weight, and an awkward angle to the trail, which caused undue labor in limbering and unlimbering, with other defects, caused the carriage to be rejected as inferior to that already in use; and, as there was a large stock of wooden carriages on hand, the subject of metallic ones dropped out of sight, while the inventive and mechanical ingenuity of the country was taxed to the limit in endeavors to devise a heavy armament equal to the necessities of the nation, and has but recently come up again for serious consideration.

Steel has invaded this as it has all other fields of improvement in modern ordnance. In the more recent constructions the prominent features consist of (1) a trail formed of steel flasks, strengthened by flanges and bolted together; (2) steel axle-tree, so strengthened by steel plates as to resist shock of discharge; (3) wheel with wooden spokes and fellies, steel tire, and brass boxes; (4) a brake for changing the wheels from rolling to sliding friction; (5) a tool-box placed in rear of the elevating screw between the trail flasks. The last was one of the devices which characterized the Wadsworth carriage of 1818. The flasks are assembled very much as in the old bracket-trail, but the principles on which the carriage is constructed are strictly those of the stock-trail system.

A new departure has been taken recently in regard to the method of eliciting information on artillery subjects, which bids fair to lead to the better construction of carriages as well as of other field artillery matériel. Pursuant to General Orders No. 39, Adjutant-General's Office, series of 1881, a board of artillery officers was convened to consider recent changes in guns, harness, and equipments for field batteries, and to recommend any deviations from existing methods which to their experience and judgment seemed fit. The recommendations of the board were in the direction which has been marked out as that taken with reference to gun-carriages, but they embraced, besides, changes in the caissons, battery-wagons, and forges, for not only field but magazine guns, and were, for the former, in substance as follows: 1. *All wheels* to have eight fellies, sixteen spokes, and to be interchangeable throughout the field-gun system. 2. *Gun-carriages* (*a*) to be of *steel* in *two parts;* that on which the gun rests to have a small movement, independent of the other, cheeked by an elastic buffer, and by which means the shock received by the trunnions may be progressively and with diminished force transmitted to the second part; (*b*) two axle-seats between the gun and wheels, so cannoneers face towards the muzzle; (*c*) brake to be operated if on the march by cannoneers on axle-seats; (*d*) cheeks and elevating apparatus to admit of curved fire with reduced charges; the angle of depression to be six degrees; (*e*) single elevating screw, with slot and side-screw, to prevent its running down when gun is fired; (*f*) trail handspike of hollow metal to fold back securely on stock; (*g*) trail-box for implements between cheeks. 3. *Limber:* (*a*) pole of wood; (*b*) frame-work, steel or iron; (*c*) limber-chest of steel, projectiles placed horizontally therein, cartridges in waterproof apartments above projectiles; two drawers, one exclusively for implements, the other for friction primers; the back to let down to horizontal position by means of hinges at the bottom, exposing rear of chest; (*d*) canvas boot in front of limber-chest for men's knapsacks; (*e*) pintle to project in rear of chest, securing longer lever-arm for the weight acting as counterpoise to pole, which, unless rendered absolutely necessary by other details of construction, should not bring more than eight pounds pressure on the neck of each wheel horse. 4. *Caisson:* (*a*) limber similar to and interchangeable with that of piece; (*b*) frame of caisson body to be of iron or steel; (*c*) one *steel* chest, lid movable, projectiles placed therein on end, cartridges in trays above projectiles, the chest so placed as to serve as counterpoise to pole; (*d*) common lever brake. 5. *Battery wagon:* (*a*) framework, iron or steel; (*b*) box, iron or steel, rectangular in shape, longitudinal strip along roof, to which two sloping lids can be hinged. 6. *Forge:* (*a*) frame-work and box-like battery wagon, with drawers for the safe and convenient transport of stores and tools. 7. *Wagon for ammunition columns:* (*a*) this to be of easy draught, good capacity, for transportation of spare ammunition; (*b*) have a wooden instead of a canvas cover; (*c*) carry two spare wheels for field-artillery carriages. 8. *Carriages for machine guns:* (*a*) to be of steel, similar in construction to field gun-carriage; (*b*) axle-tree ammunition-boxes to hinge so as to fold to front if necessary; (*c*) no style of caisson, properly so called, recommended, there being probably better arrangements for meeting the same end; (*d*) forge and battery wagon similar to those for field-artillery train; (*e*) steel two-wheeled cart for ammunition of 45-calibre Gatling gun, *short.*

Field-gun carriages must fulfill two conditions, which are incompatible, and their construction in the most approved form will be a compromise: First, they must be light; second, their recoil must not be excessive. As the shock producing recoil is expended principally in communicating motion to the carriage, it is evident, if condition second is to be insisted upon, that condition first cannot be, and *vice versa*. With the large charges and heavy projectiles of the present field artillery, the problem of how best to adjust the opposing conditions becomes the more difficult.* The result has been that, contrary to what at the first blush might seem possible, and what was expected, the field gun-carriage has not been diminished in weight to any extent, whatever other advantages may be claimed for the metallic construction.

The appointment of the light artillery board of 1881 was a move in the right direction. Under the present imperfect system officers of the ordnance department cannot acquire experience with their own handicraft; that, so far as artillery matériel is concerned, is reserved for artillery officers alone. In the United States two separate departments are the custodians of a knowledge which, in the first armies of the world, is entrusted to a single, and, therefore, a much more perfectly equipped artillery service than our double one is or may hope to be.

The deliberations of the board covered as completely as it was practicable for them to do the matters referred to it, and in its recommendations it traversed the whole subject of light artillery matériel. But, because of our dual artillery organization—one part for constructing things, the other part for using them—it is impossible for the board to see its recommendations followed out to their legitimate consequences, except through the agency, and perhaps the interference, of a distinct bureau. It is understood, however, that in the matter of carriages and caissons its recommendations are being favorably acted upon; their manufacture has been begun. Referring to this board and its work, in his annual report of 1882, the chief of ordnance remarks:

"The action of such a board I deemed of the first importance, as little had been done in that direction for some years. The board made a preliminary report to enable this department to manufacture samples of carriages, harness,

---

*Recent experiments with the spring recoil check indicate that, as at present applied, it will be impracticable elsewhere than on the proving ground and with guns of position. A lock which requires the gun-carriage to be halted and *backed* at the foot of a declivity is worthless for service purposes.

&c., embodying its views, so as to present to a subsequent board the articles or improvements recommended, that action might be taken on practical results. The preparation of a metal field-carriage, limber, and caisson has been greatly delayed by the difficulty of procuring suitable material in proper shapes, but it is confidently believed that we will be ready for the action of an artillery board at an early day."

We may hope, therefore, that the labors of this board will yet be productive of good, by stamping on the field artillery matériel the impress of a certain knowledge only to be derived from officers of practical experience. If so, this may be the precursor of an era marked by a closer relationship between two departments which, when a proper organization becomes the order of the day, will become one; but until that time arrives, and while an unnatural divorce renders them independent of, yet dependent on, each other, it is of the utmost importance, though working separately, that they should be directed, not only in their aims, but in their methods, towards a common purpose—an increased efficiency of the public service.

SIEGE, GARRISON, AND SEA-COAST CARRIAGES.

The same general principles which have governed with the field have been observed in the construction of siege and garrison carriages. In early days the heavier were denominated "traveling," in contradistinction to the "light field" carriages which were to manœuvre with troops on the field of battle. The former term was not, however, applied to the carriages of any particular calibres, as there were both *light* and *heavy* guns for every calibre in the service, the latter being used in siege or garrison, or forming, on the line of battle, guns of position. Traveling carriages were used to transport every species of heavy gun, and therefore were as necessary with the heavy 6-pounder as with the heavy 24-pounder.

The systems of siege and garrison carriages have conformed to those of the field service. First came the bracket-trail; then the Gribeauval; finally the stock-trail; but the fact that equal mobility cannot be attained with siege and garrison as with the field-carriage has modified the construction of the former. For instance, ammunition-boxes have never formed a feature of the heavier carriages—ammunition, as well as implements and tools, being transported in wagons, and when taking the road, the pieces are now shifted from their firing to what in effect is the Gribeauval traveling trunnion-beds. Nor have they, until quite recently, been made of any other material than wood; but, following as usual the lead of the field, a few of the siege gun-carriages have of late been made of various kinds of metal; and it has been announced that metallic constructions will in the near future replace entirely those heretofore in vogue.

It was not until after 1800 that a gun heavier than the 32-pounder was mounted in the sea-coast defenses. The carriages for these guns were, as a rule, wooden frames, mounted on four heavy wheels, although there were also in vogue those made up of two parts—a chassis and an upper carriage; the former, fastened to a front pintle, and supported in rear on wheels, was capable of being traversed, as in the barbette carriage of the present, through an angle approximating 180 degrees.

Except slight attempts at improvements, there was no change made in these carriages—the only iron work in which appeared to be bolts and traverse-wheels—until Wadsworth, in 1818, projected his system of artillery. In this, cast-iron was contemplated for all carriages to be used in the sea-coast defenses; and in this one respect, as the views of his antagonist, the ordnance board, coincided with his own, the measure was adopted. Cast-iron sea-coast carriages, to replace those of wood, began to be extensively made. The former were at the time in favor abroad, and the experiments of the ordnance board were considered to have demonstrated their general superiority. They cost less and lasted longer than the wooden carriages; in fact were as indestructible as the guns themselves. From 1819 to 1839 they continued to be manufactured, the appropriations for the armament of fortifications at times being almost entirely used in their purchase.

With more extended experience, however, their superiority was brought in question; and among other matters referred to the Macomb board, was the determination of the relative merits of these two rival systems of heavy gun-carriages. That board did not make a report on the subject, which was then referred to its successor—the board of 1838. In its final report of January, 1839, the latter embodied a resolution condemning cast-iron for gun-carriages as being for this purpose inferior to wood, neither was it suited for general use. It recommended that no more be purchased, but that the cast-iron carriages on hand be distributed for service, and that transoms of this metal be no longer procured for casemate or barbette carriages, until by proper trials the relative cost and efficiency of the iron and wooden transoms be certainly known. These recommendations having been approved by the Secretary of War, cast-iron carriages, except to use up the stock on hand, may from that time be said to have become a thing of the past. After a trial of twenty years, resort was had again to wood, which remained for fifteen years longer the favorite material for all classes of fixed carriages.

Meanwhile in Europe wrought-iron was forcing its way to the front. Officers who had inspected foreign armaments reported that for sea-coast carriages this metal was superior to any other. The matter was brought formally before the ordnance board by letter of September 12th, 1856. Drawings of some of the European patterns had been procured by the commission of 1855, and the board recommended that wrought iron be tried for carriages, both barbette and casemate. Finally, in April, 1859, it recommended their definitive adoption—one style each for the 10-inch and 8-inch Columbiads, en barbette; one for 42-pounder and 32-pounder, en barbette; one for the 24-pounder and smaller calibres, en barbette; one for 8-inch Columbiad and 42-pounder casemate; one for 32-pounder and 24-pounder casemate,—altogether six different kinds. When guns of different calibres were used on the same carriage, trunnion-plates to fit the smaller were to be adjusted to the permanent trunnion-beds of the larger calibres.

The wisdom of changing to wrought-iron has been vindicated. In the United States it is to-day the sole material used for sea-coast carriages. Its superiority over all others and its adaptability to the object in view has been more completely demonstrated by time and experience; and though in some styles of German coast-carriages the upper part, which works on the chassis, is made of cast-iron, it is exceptional—the use of wrought-iron for this purpose being almost universal, not only at home, but abroad.

The material for construction having been definitively settled, the remaining problems connected with the securing a suitable heavy gun-carriage were—first, to take up the recoil; second, to depress the gun *en barbette* behind the parapet after being fired, and while being loaded; third, to manœuvre the carriages by mechanical means alone, thereby economizing the labor of cannoneers.

The first has been very happily solved by the use either of the English hydraulic or the American pneumatic buffers, which not only take up recoil, but relieve both carriages and platforms from danger of being broken to pieces by the shocks to which they are subjected.

The solution of the other problems has not been so satisfactory. Several models of depressing carriages have been proposed, and Major King's has been experimented with. The results were favorable, but the carriage is apparently complicated, and for twelve years it has not been heard of among the measures brought forth to improve the sea-coast armament. For simplicity, an elegant adjustment of parts, and an exact compliance with mechanical principles, Lieutenant-Colonel Buffington's model leads the others ; but, so far as is known, no carriage of his design has been constructed and practically tested. Until that be done, the question of its merits will remain a matter of speculation.

The manœuvring of carriages by mechanical appliances is a problem as far from solution as the other. While abroad the aid of the steam-engine has been successfully brought to bear, the sole attempt in that direction in this country is Benton's apparatus, consisting of ropes and a windlass, by which means the piece is run from and into the battery, traversed to the right or left, the muzzle raised or depressed. To a limited extent, and under favorable circumstances, it has been tried, and found to work well.

The buffers serve their important office without in any degree complicating the machinery to be manœuvred. This is not true of either the depressing or the manœuvring apparatus. Each of the latter, as experimented with in the land service, is complex, making the result of accidents a more serious matter than with the simpler machine it is intended to supersede. Moreover, the advantages to be derived from either depressing carriages or manœuvring appliances are, it is believed, generally overestimated. The increased immunity from danger is questionable. The whole matter seems for the present to be held in abeyance. Questions concerning the carriage are overshadowed and lost sight of in presence of more important problems affecting the gun it is intended to carry.

CHAPTER X.

MATÉRIEL: METAL.

From 1775 down to the close of the eighteenth century brass was, in the American service, the metal almost exclusively used for ordnance, the largest calibre (the 32-pounder) alone being always made of cast-iron. Though more expensive than iron, there was not the same danger from the guns bursting; besides, brass guns were at that time more generally used abroad, which naturally caused them to be looked on with favor in the colonies. This is evinced in the resolutions of Congress instructing its cannon committee to procure certain calibres of guns; as, for instance, August 21st, 1776, that committee was ordered to purchase six 6-pounders, six 12-pounders, four 8-inch and four 6-inch howitzers, and six Coehorn mortars, *preferably of brass;* but if that were impracticable, then of iron. The 19th of the following November, on General Washington's recommendation, Congress directed that there should be procured for the field service of the United States one hundred 3-pounders, fifty 6-pounders, thirteen 18-pounders, and thirteen 24-pounders, *all of brass*. These instances, from among many that might be cited, are mentioned to show that brass was the favorite metal, iron being resorted to only when the other was not to be obtained.

Some of this ordnance was manufactured in the United States, some in France. Castings of this nature began to be made in the colonies before the war; and, from evidence elicited by the Duke of Richmond, November 10th, 1775, it appears that large quantities of both brass and iron cannon were at that time being turned out by the foundries of Philadelphia.

The brass was substantially what was afterwards, and is now, known as bronze. Muller called the alloy gun metal, also brass, and stated that its constituents were copper and tin. In Martillier's "Observations on Casting," published in 1790, and quoted by Tousard, the mixing of a little zinc with the copper and tin was recommended, in proportions depending upon the nature of the gun, and with the object of increasing the endurance of the resulting alloy. The brass gun metal of Woolwich at that time was made of sixty-eight parts copper, fifty-two parts brass, and twelve parts tin. Stevens gave as the mixture of different metals: for 4,200 pounds, $3,687\tfrac{11}{11}$ copper, $204\tfrac{11}{11}$ brass, and $307\tfrac{11}{11}$ tin.

Some of the bids for supplying ordnance that have been preserved prove that at this time copper and tin alone were the constituents of the gun metal, the founders covenanting that none others should enter into the products of their manufactories.* It appears, also, from various sources, that this continued until after 1800, when Secretary Dearborn began to have extensive experiments made to test the suitableness of cast-iron for the construction of field guns, as for some time it had been exclusively used in the construction of heavy ordnance.

In the United States, as in Europe, the cheapness of cast-iron ordnance, as compared with brass, had caused the former to be looked on with favor, which was only counter-balanced by the supposed superiority of the latter. During the Revolution there was neither time nor opportunity to test the question here raised; but when peace was restored, the attention of founders began to be directed to cast-iron as the metal from which the heavier natures could be not only more cheaply but more serviceably made. We find, therefore, that the commissioner of revenue, in all contracts

---

*In a bill rendered to the Government by Daniel Foy, superintendent of ordnance, Philadelphia, 1778, are the following items and memorandum: "For making alterations, improvements, and proving cannon, as per orders of cannon committee of Congress, $, viz.: (1) Boring and proving new brass 3, 6, and 12-poundered guns, 5½-inch and 8-inch howitzers, $. (2) Boring out Hessian 3-pounders to 6-pounders, $. (3) Drawing draughts and altering plan of brass ordnance, which were much approved of, $. (4) To drawing draughts and calculating proportions of wrought-iron cannon, from 3 to 12-pounders, $.

"N. B.—Not one of Mr. Bird's cannon that were made before I got the plan altered stood the proof, nor was any of the brass ordnance sound until my advice was taken."

The field commissary issued this new ordnance to the artillery at White Plains in the fall of the same year. It may be interesting to know what was considered a full equipment for a brass 6-pounder, on this occasion: Ready shot, 80; grape, 70; case-shot, 35; tubes, 35; tube-boxes, 3; sponges and rammers, 2; coils, slow-match, 6; portfires, 24; portfire stocks, 2; lint stocks, 2; hammers, 4; pairs pincers, 4; priming wires, 6; gimlets, 2; sets drag ropes, 4; gunners' belts, 2; sheepskins, 2; sponge tacks, 20; powder-horns, 3; budge barrel, 1; wagon with gears, 1.

for supplying the first heavy ordnance, which under the constitutional government Congress authorized for a sea-coast armament, stipulated cast-iron as the metal of which these 32-pounder and 24-pounder guns should be constructed; 12-pounders and 18-pounders were also included in the list, and from this time on a bold effort was made to push cast-iron to the front. But the little encouragement given to founders by the Government, as well as lack of skill on the part of the artisans, for some time delayed the success of the scheme, and brass held its own in public favor against the constantly increasing strength of its rival until about the year 1800.*

The career of the coming metal was not without reverses. In a report to Congress, December 12th, 1795, on the measures which had been taken to replenish the magazines with military stores, Secretary of War Pickering remarked:

"The casting of cannon has not been attended hitherto with the expected success. The foundries, which formerly succeeded very well in the casting of small guns, were not well adapted to the casting of 24 and 32-pounders. A French gentleman, of some knowledge and experience in cannon foundries, has

---

*In 1793 Secretary Knox reported that at Springfield, Massachusetts, there were being cast thirty brass guns and twenty howitzers. This was the Government foundry; and however trustworthy the products of private establishments were, it would seem from the following extract from the New York State "arms commissioner's" report (1795) that those cast at Springfield were not to be depended on implicitly: "The field pieces to be cast by Mr. Byers were to be proved as were those made for the United States. On September 3d, 1794, the deputy commissary of military stores at Springfield certified that he had proved twelve 3-pounders, and October 22d, 1794, eight 3-pounders and four 6-pounders, all of brass. Nevertheless, certain persons deemed it expedient to further prove the pieces before mounting them on carriages. Of twenty-three thus proved thirteen burst. Another 6-pounder, proved in presence of the maker, the commissioner, General Lamb, Colonel Stevens, and Colonel Beauman, burst also. The pieces were then recast into fourteen guns, (the number burst,) all of which, except one, stood the test at Springfield."

Some attempts were made to make wrought-iron guns during the Revolution, the principal manufacturer being Mr. Samuel Wheeler, of Philadelphia. The congressional cannon committee ordered several to be purchased, and Tousard says that one of them, with the artillery at Brandywine, gave very satisfactory practice, but it was captured by the enemy. Due to difficulties of welding, perhaps, but certainly to some cause, this metal was not used to any extent, though Tousard favored giving it an exhaustive trial. From the Revolution down to the time when the Macomb board commenced to experiment with various gun metals, wrought-iron dropped completely out of sight.

lately been employed to amend the process of casting and to improve the machinery for boring; but in an undertaking so important, and at the same time so expensive, it was desirable to obtain a complete cannon founder. Measures have accordingly been taken to procure one from the first foundries of Europe."

We may infer, however, that the evil was not at once remedied, for Secretary McHenry, in 1798, when war with France seemed to be a foregone conclusion, expressed himself on the same subject in a clear and forcible manner. (See page 163, *ante.*)

The reasoning of the Secretary appealed so favorably to the sense of the Legislature that an inspector of artillery was at once authorized, whom Mr. McHenry immediately set to work superintending the construction and proof of cast-iron field-guns. The results were encouraging; and upon Secretary Dearborn entering the war office, he proceeded to follow up energetically the path thus marked out, and which gave so much hope of leading to important practical results. He at once stopped the casting of brass guns, and directed that no more should be manufactured until either the practicability or the reverse of the successful casting of iron field-guns was demonstrated. It was at this time (1801) that cast-iron for field artillery supplanted brass. Great deliberation was used in every step. The best advice the country afforded was sought in determining the proportions of the guns and all details of construction. The pieces were cut down to fourteen calibres in length, and the weight reduced to that of brass guns of the same calibre.

The new departure was considered by many of the best-informed artillerists as a doubtful experiment. The example of the world was against it. But Dearborn was a man who depended more on his own judgment, deliberately formed, than upon the opinions of others. Having made up his mind to the advisability of the measure, he never faltered in its execution. The price of brass was five or six times that of iron. The country produced the best iron-ore, but as yet only a small quantity of copper, and no tin. There were two important reasons why cast-iron should be experimented with until a definite conclusion could be arrived at as to its adaptability for field-guns: First, economic considerations; second, that we might depend on our own resources. Success the most complete crowned the Secretary's efforts. The excellent character of the 6-pounder field-guns then introduced was proved in the war of 1812. They were referred to in terms of highest praise by Colonel Wadsworth, and by every board assembled for the amelioration of the artillery down to that of 1838, And, as will be seen hereafter, it was to these guns that Secretary Poinsett, in his controversy with the committee of ordnance officers in 1840, referred as establishing, in the manner most convincing of all—in actual field service—that efficient, trustworthy cannon could be made of cast-iron.

The change from brass to iron was not effected without opposition. No sooner was Dearborn gone than an effort was made to bring the department back to former practices. A few orders were given by his successor for brass guns, one of March, 1812, being for twenty-four 6-pounders and twelve 12-pounders. But so complete was the triumph of the other that an officer of the ordnance department, who, in the year 1813, fitted out the field artillery sent to the armies operating against Canada, has left on record the statement that during that time he did not see a single piece of brass ordnance.

Practically speaking, the use of brass ceased in 1801, and was not resumed until 1836, upon a recommendation of the ordnance board of 1835. That brass guns, &c., in limited quantities were manufactured during this period of thirty-five years, which may properly be called the "iron age" of our ordnance, is true; but it was apparently in deference to the wishes of individual States or private corporations; the policy of the Government was against it.

In the first system of land ordnance formally adopted by the War Department—that promulgated in the regulations of 1816—cast-iron alone appears as a gun metal. While in the style of carriages and the disposition of the personnel for field service we followed the Gribeauval system, this was not true of the guns. Except the Napoleon gun, the French ordnance has had no footing in the United States artillery since the Revolutionary war. While the French used brass, we used iron; while they adhered to 4 and 8-pounders, we clung to 6 and 12-pounders. Neither in Colonel Wadsworth's system nor in that of the ordnance board of 1818 was the use of any other metal than cast-iron contemplated.

Notwithstanding this, however, and the fact that cast-iron, after great deliberation, had been definitively adopted and used for several years, one of the first acts of the Macomb board was to throw wide open the door for investigation and experiment, with a view to returning to the employment of brass for all kinds of field ordnance.

This action of the board was due to one cause—a lack of confidence in cast-iron. The want of confidence in its turn was due to the complete breaking down, in 1827, of the field-gun system of the board of 1818, which, after enduring what were deemed satisfactory tests prior to adoption, went to pieces in a most unaccountable manner. Besides, in Europe, whence we have drawn most of our ideas concerning military supplies, brass had remained the generally accepted material for field service.

It may be asked, Where were the Dearborn guns now? They had been pushed to one side in that desire for change which characterized the proceedings of the ordnance board of 1818—to have their places filled by an inferior system. When the Macomb board began its labors, this inferior system attracted very little attention. On the other hand, reference was constantly made in the most eulogistic terms, by those who were cognizant of the facts, to the great endurance and the excellent record in action of the cast-iron guns of 1812. After brass returned to the field as a competitor with cast-iron, it had a long, precarious, and uncertain struggle for supremacy, during which its opponent based its claim to favor upon the Dearborn system, tried by the ordeal of battle, and not upon the "walking-stick" system of 1818.

The old brass guns on hand not being considered reliable, and it not being practicable to purchase any abroad, as contemplated by the board of 1831 (Macomb), the comparative tests directed by this board to be made could not be at once instituted; and when the board of 1835 met at Watervliet, it found awaiting trial none other than cast-iron ordnance, which it proceeded to dispose of in what was no doubt meant for a very deliberate, but in fact was a very summary, manner. After subjecting the 6-pounder and 12-pounder pieces to what they considered a proper trial, the board resolved unanimously that none of them were such as should be received as models for the field service of the United States; that the howitzers were not worthy the labor and expense of proving them; and finally, that *iron was not a proper material for field ordnance, which should be made wholly of bronze.** It

---

*This is the first instance in our records in which the alloy commonly called *brass* is officially designated *bronze*.

then proceeded to enumerate the natures, weights, and dimensions of the bronze ordnance which should form the field armament of the United States; and, continuing, observed: " If, however, the Government, rejecting the experience of the warlike nations of Europe and the opinions above expressed by this board, determines to adhere to the system of iron guns for field service, the board is of opinion that neither the 6 nor the 12-pounder should be less than fifteen calibres long, the former weigh not less than 850, the latter 1800 pounds." This report was approved by the Secretary of War (Mr. Cass) July 8th, 1836, which is therefore an important date in the history of our artillery matériel, marking as it does the formal introduction of the stock-trail system of carriages and the authorization of brass as a material for field-guns.

The contest between brass (bronze) and iron now began in earnest. The struggle was not unlike that at present going on in this country—the iron-founders on one side, the most respectable professional artillerists on the other.

July 13th, 1836, a contract was entered into with the Ames Manufacturing Company, and in October, 1837, ten bronze guns were turned over by that company to the ordnance department. The competitive trials which the Macomb board had resolved to make were now commenced. Malleable cast-iron, as well as cast-iron, entered the lists as a disturbing factor, and for a time threatened to sweep all else before it, eliciting from the colonel of ordnance the remark, that by this process guns could be made lighter and stronger than brass, and that the trials then being prosecuted promised to establish the great superiority of this species of ordnance. In this, however, he and the other adherents to iron were disappointed. The malleable burst like all the other cast-iron guns, and, though they tested well, their good qualities was not conspicuous.

The diversity of opinion entertained by artillerists in this country concerning the proper material for field-guns was nowhere more manifest than in the proceedings of the ordnance board of 1838. At first the cast-iron element seemed to predominate, and a resolution was adopted to the effect that, while this metal, as ordinarily manufactured, was unreliable, still, as had been shown in the field-guns of the late war (1812), it was possible to make iron guns of such patterns as would endure successfully every strain incident to service.

For horse artillery the board recommended both malleable cast-iron and bronze; but under instructions from the Secretary of War to choose between these two metals, they took the latter. At this time Ringgold's horse-artillery battery was being mounted and equipped with its proper arm.

The bursting of both the cast-iron and the malleable cast-iron guns and howitzers which were being tested but increased the uncertainty of the board regarding the merits of the several metallic contestants. The result was to leave undisturbed the bronze field-gun system of *1835*, except the suppression of the 9-pounder. Regarding the seige, garrison, and sea-coast armaments, they were wholly of cast-iron, except the bronze Coehorn and the 16-inch Stone mortars.

Thus the matter of gun metal stood when was assembled the committee of ordnance officers appointed by Mr. Poinsett April, 1839. Experiments with bronze, cast-iron, and malleable cast-iron had been industriously carried on, but without any definite result. The best metal for a field armament was as far from settlement as ever; each had its partisans.

This was one of the first questions to the determination of which the committee addressed itself. The interesting correspondence which ensued between the committee and the Secretary of War—the former advocating bronze, the latter inclining to cast-iron—led directly to the sending of the first "armament commission" to Europe to study on the ground and from the masters in the art the practical details of gun-casting, to which we were in a measure strangers. (Appendix C, [2].) This correspondence makes clear the fact that to Mr. Secretary Poinsett more than to any other of the many who contributed to that end is the artillery indebted for the elegant and complete system of 1849. It will be readily admitted that he had a much clearer perception of what was needed, and the proper methods to attain it, than the ordnance committee. He rejected all temporary expedients. What he wanted, and determined to have, was a system of artillery based on correct principles. The first step was for those into whose hands the working out of details was intrusted to acquire knowledge of their business. These considerations led to sending the commission of ordnance officers to Europe in 1840. This strengthened and fitted the department for its work. The information acquired abroad by the members of this commission gave dignity and importance to the deliberation of the committee, now become the "ordnance board." From the return of the commission the work of arranging details of the proposed system went straight on without break or hindrance, other than those properly incident to the service. There was no halting, no thought of meeting by temporary devices an assumed present demand which did not exist. The foundation of the new system was deep laid in experience, knowledge of the practices of the old nations, and professional lore, and it was permanent.

The commission, consisting of Major Baker, Captains Mordecai and Huger of the ordnance department, with Mr. Wade, a practical founder, (formerly captain of ordnance,) spent about nine months in Europe, visiting the principal arsenals, cannon foundries, and armories. It had seen enough to have its views concerning field-gun metal confirmed, and, January 2d, 1841, the ordnance board again unanimously recommended bronze. This was approved by Mr. Poinsett. From this time, therefore, we may date the undisputed ascendency of bronze over cast-iron of all kinds.

Nor were wrought-iron guns more successful. They had been urged as a last resort by the friends of iron, but neither those experimented with in 1832, nor those of improved manufacture tested in 1839 and 1840, gave results that inspired confidence in this method of gun making. The first difficulty was to weld the parts; the next and greater was to determine whether the welds were perfect. Wrought, with all kinds of cast-iron, notwithstanding the persistent efforts of the founders, at last for twenty years gave way to bronze. It may be stated, therefore, that in 1835 bronze became the favorite. The next year its use was authorized. In 1841 it was officially and permanently recognized as the metal for field ordnance—a position which it retained, with none to dispute its title, until 1861. Except the Stone and Coehorn mortars, the former of which was abandoned in 1861, the heavy ordnance—siege, garrison, and sea-coast—continued to be made of cast-iron, the quality of which, in all that went to make up first-class gun metal, was second to none in the world.

The Civil war inaugurated a revolution in this as in every other feature of gun construction. Although the French rifled field-pieces used in 1859 were of bronze, experience showed that this metal was not adapted to the strains and wear of guns constructed on the rifle principle. In 1860 a board of officers had recommended that the bronze guns then in service, or at least fifty per cent. of them, be rifled. The latter recommendation was ordered to be put in execution ; but scarcely had the work of conversion begun, when it was found the altered bronze pieces were too weak, and the scheme was abandoned; thus forming a fitting prelude to the fate of the conversion heavy-gun system of 1881.

As, however, it was necessary to have rifled guns, the Secretary of War (Mr. Cameron), June 22d, 1861, ordered three hundred wrought-iron field-guns to be purchased. Two-hundred of these were rifles. But the use of wrought-iron was not looked upon with favor. The ordnance board passed a resolution giving their sanction to its employment as a temporary expedient only and to supply the pressing demands for rifled ordnance of the armies in the field. Notwithstanding this, wrought-iron has not only held its ground, but at this time has driven bronze before it, and it will surrender only to steel. During the Civil war it had as competitors in the field armaments bronze, cast-iron hooped with wrought, and steel; but as a representative of the Government department, wrought-iron for rifled guns stood alone. The 3-inch wrought-iron rifle, called the "ordnance gun," although made upon a plan devised at a private foundry, was recognized from the date of its first appearance, in 1861, as *the* Government gun. After a quarter of a century it maintains that position.

In larger natures of ordnance the use of wrought-iron first began in 1861, when the plan of hooping large cast-iron rifles at the breech, which had been suggested to the ordnance board in 1858, and rejected by it, was successfully put in practice by Captain Parrott. This was known as the "Parrott system," and it furnished the only large rifled ordnance which appeared during the war. Thus, after having been uniformly rejected whenever it knocked at the door for admission into the list of gun metals, from 1777 down, wrought-iron, in 1861, forced itself to the front, where it has, for field artillery, retained the position then acquired. The want of confidence expressed by the ordnance board in 1861 has not been justified by events.

Since the close of the Civil war, and down to this time, the problem which has engrossed attention, to the exclusion of every other connected with a public armament, has been the building up of an efficient system of heavy ordnance. The most perplexing element entering into the determinate solution of this problem has been the selection of a proper gun metal. So long as the smooth-bore held its own against the rifle, the racking stood up in the presence of the punching system of fighting, cast-iron alone was used. That contest was short. It ended, even in the opinion of the most enthusiastic supporters of the old system, about 1871. The struggle between cast-iron and other metals for purposes of rifled-gun construction had been going on for some time prior to this. The former was that of which, excepting the Parrott guns, American heavy artillery had alone been made. Cast-iron was part and parcel of the smooth-bore system; but it did not follow that the two elements were inseparable. Large smooth-bore guns had elsewhere been made of other metals than cast-iron. On the other hand, it was hoped that this metal could be manufactured into efficient heavy rifles. Although intimately associated, the smooth-bore system and the metal of which it had been built were to be considered separately, each to stand by its own merits or fall from its own weakness. The fate of the smooth-bore will be considered elsewhere. Attention will for the present be directed to cast-iron (1) as a gun metal, pure and simple; (2) in combination with other metals.

1. The excellent character of the cast-iron of the United States ordnance, which was second to none in the world, even if it did not lead all others, together with Rodman's method of cooling the molten mass from the interior, gave rise to the hope, which in some influential though not official quarters has not yet died out, that this metal might prove equal to all the demands of heavy rifled ordnance. In 1861 a cast-iron 12-inch rifle—experimental gun—and in 1862 an 8-inch, both on Rodman's plan, were constructed. This number was increased in 1868 by another 12-inch rifle. The result of the experiments instituted with these guns was not favorable. The chief of ordnance, who was the firm friend and champion of cast-iron, in his report of 1870, remarked on this subject:

"The principal nations of Europe, fully aware of the necessity of having heavy rifled guns for their coast defense, have spent millions in search of a reliable rifle gun. We have confined our experiments to one or two cast-iron rifled guns. The results obtained do not warrant me in recommending that any cast-iron rifled guns be procured for arming the forts. We must try some other material for heavy rifle guns."

Nothing could be plainer than this: cast-iron had been weighed in the balance by its own zealous advocates, and found wanting. Just at this juncture, however, hope was revived by two experimental facts: First, the expanding metallic sabot, which replaced the buttons of rifle projectiles, had made it possible to secure uniform results (action in the bore) with the latter; second, the increase in size of powder-grain, and the successful manipulation of the ingredients, had rendered it possible to greatly increase the initial velocity of the projectile, with a diminished pressure on the walls of the gun. So favorable were these to the metal just discarded, that, in 1873, the chief of ordnance recommended that an appropriation of $75,000 be asked of Congress for the manufacture and trial of 12-inch cast-iron rifles. The money was not appropriated. The test of heavy rifled cast-iron guns under the new conditions of projectile and powder has not been made. Nevertheless, in the opinion of the most experienced military authorities of the world, the views of the chief of ordnance, as expressed in 1870, relative to the fitness of cast-iron, are as sound to-day as they were then; nor have the new and supposed favorable conditions raised it in the scale of relative merit. Neither the board of officers assembled pursuant to act of June 6th, 1872, to designate models of heavy ordnance, nor that assembled pursuant to the act of March 3d, 1881, for the same purpose, nor has any other board of officers since 1870, recommended that cast-iron, except when combined with other metals, be used for heavy-rifled guns; but, on the contrary, it has been uniformly proscribed. It, however, is not dead. Private founders having failed to secure recognition from the military profession, have appealed their case to a non-military but more powerful tribunal—the Congress of the United States—and with better success. The result is that while others, after the most exhaustive trials, have given up cast-iron, we are to-day making experimental guns with this metal. The outcome will be looked for with great interest. Fortunately, the experiments by which these souvenirs of a past age in gun construction are to be put on their trial will be conducted under the surveillance of officers actuated by the sole desire to arrive at truth, regardless of the interests of individuals or corporations.*

---

* The cast-iron guns now being made, one of which is tubed with steel from the breech to a point just in front of the trunnions, are "in lieu of" the new Americanized Krupp 12-inch rifles, which, although contracted for, were,

Happily for the safety of the country—in great degree dependent on its sea-coast armament, standing sentinel, grim-visaged, at the portals of the Nation—the character, professional and scientific attainments of those who control in the councils of the present ordnance board, the consciencious attention to duty evinced in the modest, yet thorough, painstaking, and able reports which have of late emanated therefrom, leave no room for doubt but that these representative of an elsewhere-discarded heavy gun metal will be tested without "fear, favor, or affection," and with an eye single to the good of the public service.

2. *Cast-iron in combination with other metals.*—The first constructions on this principle were Parrott's guns, which, in 1862, formed the most powerful rifled system in existence. The experience of the Civil war was not favorable to this type of built-up gun, which, after its close, seems to have passed out of notice, while attention was being directed to other systems.

In the next attempt to combine wrought with cast-iron, the order of metals was reversed, the wrought-iron being placed as a tube *inside* the cast-iron body of the gun—a plan which, in the conversion of old smooth-bore guns into low-power rifles, is still practiced.

The armament board of 1867 having decided that the rifled heavy-gun system of the United States should consist of 10-inch and 12-inch rifles, it became a question for the ordnance board to decide what should be the construction of these guns and the metal used therein. Among other types, this board recommended the building up of cast-iron guns with *steel tubes*. There was not, however, spite of all these resolutions as to calibres, metals, and modes of construction, a single built-up rifle gun in the United States, except Parrott's, until after the board appointed pursuant to act of June 6th, 1872, made its report. Congress had appropriated $270,000 for experiments and tests with the models of heavy ordnance to be selected by this board, half of which, as it proved, viz., the converted smooth-bores, the Thompson and the Sutcliff types, were combinations of a cast-iron body, with either a steel or a wrought-iron tube.

---

after the failure of the "system" in 1881, not constructed. They may be considered as in some degree compensating the cast-iron founders for the expense and trouble they were put to in taking the preliminary steps looking to the manufacture of the subsequently abandoned guns.

Of these, the Thompson and the Sutcliff have never been tested beyond a few preliminary shots. Every attention was given, every nerve bent, to the development of the *conversion* system, and with such success that the manufacture of new constructions on the same general plan was determined on, and carried into execution in 1877 by the building of a 12.25-inch cast-iron gun with wrought-iron tube.

In the system of standard ordnance promulgated by the ordnance department in 1880, the only built-up heavy guns are combinations of cast and wrought-iron. The friends of the conversion system were, however, doomed to disappointment; the system itself, brought up with so much care, and to the exclusion of everything else, "burst to pieces," not figuratively, but literally—a fact to which, in the Fall of 1881, testimony was amply borne by the fragments of its guns scattered everywhere over the Sandy Hook proving ground.

Meantime the board of officers convened pursuant to act of March 3d, 1881, had been at work. As a result of its exhaustive researches, and in the guns recommended by it, wrought-iron, in combination with cast, was replaced by steel. Ten varieties of heavy ordnance were deemed by this board to be worthy of trial. Five of these were built-up guns embracing two metals in their constructions and in all of them the metals were steel and cast-iron.

The recommendations of this board, whether they be carried into execution or not, will stand their ground against adverse criticism. Private interests may, through political influence, frustrate the legitimate results that should flow from the labors of the board; the spectacle be presented of the United States going backward while other nations go forward in the grand march towards the securing an efficient national armament; but whatever deviations may be made from the course marked out by it, those who are familiar with the subject will not expect them to make easier of attainment that great desideratum—the object of years of patient labor and experiment—a heavy gun system which will guarantee security to our shores and consideration before the nations of the world.

Wrought-iron.

Except when used in combination with cast-iron, either as bands or as tubing, this metal has received but little consideration during the last fifteen years. For independent heavy-gun constructions, while not ignored, it has been pushed completely out of sight by its more popular and powerful rivals.

As with steel, the practical difficulty that lay in the way was the inadequacy of foundry facilities to forge or otherwise prepare large and homogeneous masses, and the other alternative which has been seized on with steel, viz., to build up a wire gun, was not practicable with wrought-iron.

In 1868 the chief of ordnance recommended that a wrought-iron 12-inch gun be constructed to be tested, in a series of comparative trials, with a cast-iron rifle of the same calibre. The proposition met with the approval of the Secretary of War, but neither of these proposed rifles has been manufactured. Notwithstanding that armament boards met and decided on the calibres of the ordnance that should be used, and ordnance boards followed with plans and specifications, embracing the metals, their combination, and their distribution in the completed gun, nothing was done until the board of officers appointed pursuant to act of June 6th, 1872, had completed its work. Among other designs approved of by the board was that of Mr. Hitchcock for a wrought-iron 12-inch rifle, built up by welding rings end to end; and although the inventor was given every facility he asked, and personally superintended the preliminary arrangements, the difficulties were so great and the promised results so unsatisfactory that he abandoned the project in despair.

The result of these failures has been, taken in conjunction with the successful manipulation of other metals, to remove wrought-iron from the list of even possible materials for efficient heavy-gun constructions.

Steel.

The career of steel has been, in the long run, diametrically opposite that of wrought-iron; as the latter disappeared, the former came more boldly into view—first as an auxiliary in the shape of tubing to cast-iron, then for both wrapping and tubing, and finally for the building up independently of the heaviest calibres. Down to the time that *conversions* became the rage, the two metals—wrought-iron and steel—were about equally favored as a tubing material, in which form alone, practically speaking, either had entered as a factor into the gun problem. In the muzzle-loading conversions, wrought-iron linings were supposed to have quickly established their superiority. The tubing metal of the standard gun system, as appears in the report of the chief of ordnance of 1880, was wrought-iron alone. Indeed, steel does not appear in any manner in the heavy-gun armament there presented.

From this state of utter exclusion, steel quickly recovered, not only regaining from wrought-iron the ground thus lost, but driving out the latter, and springing by a single bound into the first rank of gun metals. Nor is this a temporary victory. Steel in some form, either in masses or wire, or both combined, is conceded by all artillerists to be the metal of the future as well as of the present.

This reaction, which from the first impulse has gone on gaining strength, until to-day all competitors have been passed, began in this country when breech-loading conversions won their way to favor. The board of 1872 had recommended, among other things, that a Krupp 12-inch be procured as a representative, (1) of a breech-loading system, (2) of a system of gun construction. The gun was not purchased; instead, the attempt was made to graft the Krupp breech-loading mechanism upon the conversion system of rifled guns. The jacket, breech-block, and breech-band for the members of this new departure in the scheme of conversion were of imported steel. The pioneer gun was manufactured and on the proving ground by July, 1878, and by 1880 the record was such as to justify the ordnance board in the following conclusions:

"The endurance of this system of gun construction, and the endurance as well as the successful manipulation of the breech mechanism, in the opinion of the board, have been satisfactorily established, and, in its judgment, the department is warranted in their adoption for future new constructions as well as in future conversions of smooth-bore into rifled guns."

At the same time that the breech mechanism was being thus successfully tested, another important element was added to the system by the introduction of the chamber, which, without any bad effects, had increased the power of the 8-inch muzzle-loading converted rifle thirty per cent., and led the board to the following conclusions and recommendations:

"This experiment shows that, with pressures entirely within the limits of safety, the increased velocity due to chambering has increased the power of the

8-inch rifle about one-third, and that the increased power has been accompanied by an increased accuracy of fire. The area of bore incident to the higher charge with the one hundred and eleven rounds fired seems no greater than that in the unchambered gun with the 35-pound charge. The board, therefore, recommends the adoption of the system of chambering in all future conversions or new constructions of this and of 11-inch calibres. In higher calibres the system has already received the approval of the department."

The conversion system had now reached the summit of its prosperity, whence, through the untoward events which followed, it rapidly descended. The successful application separately of the breech-loading and the chamber principles to the conversions led, very naturally, and under the preceding resolutions of the board, to the next step, which was to combine the two in the same gun; but the overstrained system broke down completely, the pieces bursting one after the other as they were subjected to trial. The system, passing its limit of safety, fell at once into disfavor, and work on the 12-inch rifles of the new Americanized Krupp models, contracts for which had been let, was immediately stopped.

Without waiting to inquire into the causes of this hopeless collapse, it is a fact that the prestige of steel as a metal for gun constructions was not thereby impaired, but the reverse. When the Americanized Krupp system went to wreck amidst the débris from its own exploded members, the board appointed pursuant to the act of March 3d, 1881, was pursuing its investigations. It recommended that nine different models of guns and a rifled mortar be constructed, all on the built-up plan. Five of the guns were to be constructed wholly of steel, the remaining four, as has been previously mentioned, of steel and cast-iron combined; the latter being mere make-shifts, as "they can be readily and rapidly produced in this country without the delay of sending abroad for large masses of forged steel."*
With us, therefore, as abroad, steel, either by itself or combined with other metals, has supplanted wrought-iron in the construction of heavy armaments; and although quacks may still advocate others, the masters turn to steel as that material which alone gives promise of meeting successfully the crucial tests of modern gunnery.

---

* One of these 12-inch guns, concerning the endurance of which there was not even "the suggestion of a doubt," went to pieces, with the rest of its type, on the Sandy Hook proving grounds.

Investigations and experiments having in view the selection of proper materials for siege and field ordnance, under the modern conditions of increased weight of metal thrown and larger charges of powder, have of recent years attracted comparatively little attention pending the solution of that infinitely more difficult problem—the construction of an efficient sea-coast armament.

For siege guns cast-iron retains its place, although in the proposed 4½-inch rifle a body of this material is both hooped and lined with steel; and, like all others of the recent models for the land service, the breech-loading mechanism is a prominent feature. Both steel and wrought-iron 4½-inch guns were recommended by the ordnance board of 1868 to be tested for power and endurance with those of cast-iron, and which during the Civil war did excellent service, but they have not been constructed.

In the line of field artillery there has been greater activity; more experiments have been made, and a greater variety of metals have been tested. The Moffatt steel breech-loader, the Dean bronze muzzle-loader, (with metal around bore hardened by compression,) and several 3-inch wrought-iron rifles converted to 3.20-inch breech-loaders by screwing on a breech block of steel, have all received attention. The latter is apparently a most excellent field piece, forming by far the most successful attempt that has been made at converting old into new and more powerful guns.

In siege and field equally with sea-coast artillery the tendency has been towards the use of steel, and it seems to be simply a question of time when this metal will supersede all others.

CHAPTER XI.
MATÉRIEL: SYSTEMS OF ARTILLERY.

The great variety of calibres presented by the artillery during the Revolution may be judged from the array set forth in a general return of the commissary of military stores at the end of that war. In this there were enumerated as being on hand, mounted and ready for service: Of guns, 1, 3, 4, 6, 9, 12, and 24-pounders; of mortars, 4½, 5½, 8, 10, 13, and 16-inch; of howitzers, 5½ and 8-inch, all of brass; and of iron, 1, 2, 3, 4, 6, 9, 12, 18, 24, and 32-pounder guns, 18-pounder carronades, and 3½-inch howitzers.

It must not be supposed, however, that all these guns, howitzers, and mortars accompanied each army to incumber it; or even that, in all the ordnance, both field and garrison, used actively against the enemy, this great variety of calibres could be found. It would be just as reasonable to assume, because an ordnance return of the present day took account of many varieties of ancient and antiquated models, that these formed part of the present artillery system. Fortunately, the records do not leave us in doubt on this point; they reduce the calibres and the natures of ordnance which were habitually used to narrow and well-defined limits, making it for practical purposes as easy a matter to fix upon what was the Revolutionary system as though it had been formally announced in orders.

In an official report submitted January, 1778, General Knox mentioned the following as the artillery which it would be necessary for the main army to have during the ensuing campaign:

"Brigade artillery, seventeen brigades, with four guns each, sixty-eight pieces, to be 3, 4, or 6-pounders; with the park, two 24-pounders, four 12-pounders, four 8-inch howitzers, eight 5½-inch howitzers, ten 3 or 4-pounders, ten 6-pounders; for the *reserve*, to be kept at a proper distance from camp, thirty 3, 4, and 6-pounders, two 12-pounders, one 24-pounder; all the foregoing brigade, park, and reserve guns and howitzers *to be of brass*. In addition, twelve 18-pounders, twelve 12-pounders, battering pieces, on traveling carriages, together with two 5½-inch and twelve 8, 9, and 10-inch mortars; the battering pieces and mortars to be of *cast-iron*."

When preparing for the eventful and decisive campaign of 1781, the general of artillery estimated that, to accompany the main army into the field, there would be necessary, three 24-pounders, seven 12-pounders, twenty each of 3 and 4-pounders, thirty 6-pounders, five 8-inch howitzers, and six 5½-inch howitzers. From which it will be seen that he had concluded, for active field duty, to dispense with the heavy 32-pounder gun and discard mortars entirely. When, however, soon after, preparations were making to lay siege to New York, the train collected for this purpose embraced 12, 18, 24, and 32-pounder guns; 5½, 8, 10, and 13-inch mortars; 5½ and 8-inch howitzers. Finally, there were taken on the march to the southward when the siege was abandoned, and were present with the army before Yorktown, of field artillery, two 12-pounders, four 3-pounders, six 6-pounders, three 5½-inch howitzers; of siege artillery, two 8-inch mortars, ten 10-inch and six 5½-inch mortars, and three 8-inch howitzers, all of brass; and of iron, three 24 and twenty 18-pounders.

The ordnance which accompanied others than the main army was of the same character as that which made up the armament of the latter. It were useless to particularize concerning it.

It is seen from what precedes that the field artillery embraced—of guns, 3, 4, 6, 12, and 24-pounders; of howitzers, 5½ and 8-inch, all of brass. Of these, the 3, 4, and 6-pounder guns habitually, and the howitzers occasionally, were attached to the infantry brigades; while the 12 and 24-pounders were held for guns of position. The siege artillery embraced (in addition to the field) *iron* 18, 24, and 32-pounder guns, with the 13-inch mortar; of *brass*, the 5½, 8, and 10-inch mortars.

The field system included five different calibres of guns and two of howitzers; for the siege there were added two distinct calibres of guns and four of mortars, or seven calibres of guns, two of howitzers, and four of mortars—total, thirteen. Thus, instead of the Revolutionary army being loaded down, as were those of Europe a few years before this time, by an almost endless variety of guns, mortars, and howitzers, it was not incumbered at all. Thirteen different calibres will not appear a large number when we recall that the field and siege train of the Army of the Potomac before Petersburg in 1864 numbered seventeen different calibres of guns, mortars, and howitzers, and that the complete system of ordnance of 1850 embraced eighteen different calibres.

MATÉRIEL: SYSTEMS OF ARTILLERY. 277

Subsequent to the Revolution, and prior to 1800, there was no change worthy of note made in the calibres of artillery constructed for either field, siege, or sea-coast armaments. The 32-pounder continued the heaviest gun. The act of March 20th, 1794, providing for the manufacture of sea-coast guns, directed that they should be 24 and 32-pounders. Men longed for and dreamed of peace. Though brought to the verge of war in 1794, and again in 1798, we had escaped it. The danger passed, retrenchment brought to a stand-still every measure looking to the building up of the artillery system.

The new century ushered in a new era in gun making. The 42-pounder was added in 1801, the 50-pounder Columbiad in 1811, while in 1819 these, as well as 100-pounder guns, formed part of the sea-coast armament. But we are forced to the conclusion that the utility of each and all of these larger natures was not apparent at the time, as, in the systems for the land service as announced by the War Department both in 1816 and 1821, the 24-pounder was the largest calibre prescribed, the contingency which would require heavier guns being so remote that it was not considered necessary to provide against it.

If we examine the calibres of the artillery in use at the close of the War of 1812 we will find that, except the addition of the 42-pounder and the Columbiad, and replacing the field 8-inch howitzer by the 24-pounder howitzer, there had been no change since the Revolution. No inconvenience was experienced from the multiplicity of calibres; but there were very many varieties of each calibre, due to the fact that the guns were not cast upon any exact plan, and this led to interminable confusion in the construction of carriages.

Colonel Wadsworth's service in the artillery, the engineers, and finally in his position as head of the ordnance department, gave him opportunity to observe the evils resulting from this state of affairs. From the time of his appointment as colonel of ordnance until his muster out of service in the reduction of 1821 he labored faithfully and intelligently to correct them, and to secure for the artillery a uniform, practical, and permanent system of matériel. Dearborn had done much for the artillery, particularly the field artillery, by making it lighter, and otherwise increasing its mobility; but his improvements seem rather like disjointed efforts, all tending towards the desired end, it is true, yet lacking that important characteristic—*method*—without which no extensive, consistent, and lasting amelioration could be effected. With Wadsworth the case was different. He had the benefit of the labors of those who had gone before. He carefully surveyed the ground, saw what the difficulties were, proceeded promptly, yet deliberately, and upon a matured plan, to the work of reformation. Whatever may be claimed for others, to Colonel Wadsworth is due the credit of having first worked out upon proper principles the details of a complete system of artillery matériel. Commencing his administration of the ordnance department when the armies were taking the field, in 1812, he found time amidst the turmoil that involved his own as well as every other branch of the public service to develop a plan for placing the artillery upon a sound basis. (Appendix C, [3.]) As a result, the system of artillery for the land service of the United States was first formally announced by authority of the War Department, in the regulations of 1816, as follows:

"To insure greater simplicity and uniformity in future in the calibres and patterns of cannon, &c., the cannon, howitzers, and mortars to be provided hereafter for the land service will be as follows:

"For the field: Cannon—light 6-pounder, light 12-pounder, and medium 18-pounder; howitzers, 24-pounder, 8-inch.

"For sieges (including also field pieces of the foregoing descriptions): Cannon—heavy 24-pounders; mortars—8-inch, 10-inch, and 13-inch.

"For fixed batteries on the seaboard and forts in the interior (including also field pieces of the foregoing descriptions): Cannon—heavy 24-pounders; mortars—10-inch and 13-inch.

"All ordnance to be provided hereafter of any of the natures and calibres above expressed are to be *invariably of the same pattern;* and it will be the duty of the ordnance department to adopt proper measures for insuring uniformity in the ordnance hereafter by gradually abolishing and replacing the guns of other calibres than the foregoing which have been introduced into the service, as well as guns of patterns different from those which have or may be established, so as eventually to bring all the guns of any one calibre to a uniform pattern."

A comparison of this list of ordnance with that proposed by Colonel Wadsworth in May, 1813, (Appendix C, [3]) the language of the regulations, together with the views of the colonel of ordnance as there expressed, will at once evince that the system adopted was on the recommendation of that officer.

The 3-pounder which in 1813 had been proposed as part of the field train, was suppressed in 1816, as Wadsworth had intimated that it might be, thus reducing the total number of calibres to eight instead of nine. Following Napoleon, (Appendix C, [1],) the 6-pounder had supplanted the 4 and 8-pounders of Gribeauval.

Having thus secured the limiting to eight—the number of calibres that should constitute the land armament—the next step was to devise patterns therefor, together with models for the carriages on which they should be mounted. This work was completed and submitted to the Secretary of War in 1818, and constituted our first complete system of artillery for the service of the United States, the details of which had been worked out in the minutest particulars. The main features of the gun system proposed were: First, the retention of all calibres then prescribed by regulations; second, increasing the power of the guns by diminishing the windage. For carriages, the main features were: First, the adoption of a modified English block-trail in place of the Gribeauval for field service; second, a reduction in the number of carriages by mounting different pieces on the same carriage; third, the replacing wooden by cast-iron carriages in all fixed batteries. It was the patterns and models of this system which were referred by the Secretary of War to the ordnance board of 1818 for examination, and upon which that board reported adversely.

Having rejected Wadsworth's, the board proceeded, under the instructions of the Secretary of War, to devise another. Its action regarding carriages has been mentioned. For the guns it proposed a new system, built upon a plan of its own. For field artillery the weight was cut down to the proportion of 100 pounds of metal to one pound of shot. This, together with the length of the 6-pounders (18 calibres of bore), gave the 6-pounder field-guns recommended the popular name of "walking-sticks." The medium 18-pounder was abolished, thus reducing the field artillery to 6 and 12-pounder guns and the 24-pounder howitzer. The 8-inch and 13-inch mortars were abolished; a 15-inch Stone mortar introduced, as were also battering 12 and 18-pounder guns. The siege artillery embraced, therefore, heavy 12, 18, and 24-pounder guns, the 8-inch howitzer, the 10-inch mortar (light), and the 15-inch stone mortar. The sea-coast armament embraced the heavy 24-pounder and the 10-inch mortar (heavy). Thus the entire system as proposed embraced four calibres of guns, two of howitzers and two of mortars, the same as Colonel Wadsworth's.

While the 6-pounder had the same length as the French, it weighed only two-thirds as much. The 12-pounder did not weigh two-thirds as much as the French, and was but fifteen and one-half calibres, while the French 12-pounder was eighteen calibres long. The howitzers proposed by the board were both longer and heavier than the French, and intended for larger charges. The 24-pounder battering-gun weighed 5,500, the 18 pounder, 3,700 pounds—not differing from the English guns of corresponding calibres. In one word, so far as can be discovered, the board followed no rule in devising its system, which, excepting the 15-inch mortar, was, however, in 1819, adopted for the land service of the United States.

It will be noticed that the heaviest calibre was a 24-pounder. In 1829 a 32-pounder was added and in 1831 a 42-pounder. With these two exceptions, and that of the 15-inch Stone mortar mentioned, the system of the 1818 board remained without change until replaced by that devised by the Macomb board of 1831—a list of the calibres of which appeared in the army regulations of 1835. This was as follows:

For field service: 6, 9, and 12-pounder cannon (light) and 12 and 24-pounder howitzers (long).

Siege and garrison: 12, 18, and 24-pounder cannon, 8-inch howitzer (light), and 8 and 10-inch mortars (light).

Sea-coast: 24, 32, and 42-pounder cannon, 18, 24, 32, and 42-pounder carronades, and 10-inch mortars (heavy).

The changes from the system of the 1818 board, besides those already mentioned, consisted in the addition to the field system of the 9-pounder gun and the 12-pounder light howitzer; to the siege, the 8-inch mortar, which the 1818 board had discarded, while the sea-coast was increased by the carronades. In fact, however, the carronades never, except on paper, became part of the land armament. None were manufactured. The colonel of ordnance reported, in 1837, that the only knowledge he possessed regarding them was derived from the British regulations; and the following year they were dropped out altogether.

This ordnance was iron throughout. But the whole subject of a land armament being then in a state of transition, the preceding list of calibres could only be considered as temporarily indicating what, in the opinion of the board, the artillery system should be.

From 1835 until 1839, when the ordnance board of 1838 made

its final report, which was approved by the Secretary of War, there was constant change either being attempted or being made in the field artillery; the siege and the sea-coast remained comparatively undisturbed. This change was inaugurated by the board of 1835, which, rejecting *in toto* the iron field-artillery system presented to it for trial, recommended the following as a substitute therefor, and to be made wholly of bronze.

Nature of Piece.	Length in Calibres.	Weight. (lbs.)
6-pounder gun.	15.669	672
9-pounder gun.	16	1,350
12-pounder gun.	16	1,800
12-pounder howitzer.	10 (not exceed.)	700 (fit 6-pounder carriage.)
24-pounder howitzer.	11 (not exceed.)	1,260 (fit 9-pounder carriage.)

—the 9-pounder and 12-pounder guns and 24-pounder howitzers to have square handles, like the French patterns.

As the recommendation was approved, the manufacture of bronze guns and howitzers was immediately begun. The brass ordnance enumerated became an authorized field system of the United States, and, excepting the 9-pounder, which fell into disfavor from the first, these calibres were only retired from that system, by order of the Secretary of War, in 1868.

But it seemed impossible to settle permanently anything connected with the artillery. Nothing ought to have changed the field system after it had been definitely fixed upon by competent authority. Yet this was exactly what was done. When the ordnance board of 1838 met, the instructions given it plainly indicated that nothing appertaining to the national armament was considered as determined. This state of affairs was probably due to two causes: First, a change of administration; second, the persistent efforts of the iron founders to gain back for their metal the ground it had lost. The result was that the field system of 1835, (excepting the 9-pounder,) while it eventually triumphed, had to fight its way at every step, and victory was not assured until after the return of the ordnance commission from Europe, and its recommendation that bronze be adopted definitely as the metal for field artillery.

The board of 1838 retired the neglected 9-pounder from service, recommended the substitution, in lieu of the 9-pounder and 12-pounder bronze guns, of a malleable cast-iron 12-pounder, and the replacing for horse artillery of the 6-pounder of 1835 by one fourteen calibres in length. This action did not make any impression further than to rid the service of the 9-pounder. So far as is known, the 12-pounder malleable cast-iron gun was not made, or, if made, not issued to troops; and though a few short 6-pounders were cast, they seem to have been looked upon as parasites, clinging to without having a place in the system, and they soon disappeared.

To siege artillery the board added an iron 24-pounder howitzer, the Coehorn and the 16-inch Stone mortars, both of bronze; to the sea-coast armament, iron 8-inch and 24-pound howitzers and a 13-inch mortar; while the carronades were abolished.

Secretary Cass had, in 1836, added the French mountain howitzer to the field system through a belief, which events confirmed, that this gun would be of practical utility against the Indians, with whom at that time we were commencing the tedious and not very glorious Seminole war. The various calibres composing the land artillery, as determined by the joint labors of the ordnance boards of 1831, 1835, and 1838, and as announced by the War Department in 1839, were as follows:*

For the field: 6 and 12-pounder guns (light), 12 and 24-pounder howitzers, and the 12-pounder mountain howitzer.

Siege and garrison: 12, 18, and 24-pounder guns, 8-inch and 24-pounder howitzers, 8 and 10-inch mortars (light), and Coehorn and 16-inch stone mortars.

Sea-coast: 24, 32, and 42-pounder guns, 8-inch and 24-pounder howitzers, and 10 and 13-inch mortars (heavy).

This was the condition of affairs when the ordnance committee of April 16th, 1839, was appointed. In commencing its labors this committee laid down as a principle not to change any piece of ordnance so that the carriage already made for it could not be

---

* In October, 1838, Mr. Poinsett informed the board that it was advisable to introduce rocket service into the army, and it was directed to report whether, in its opinion, the service of rocket batteries should be given to the artillery arm, or whether a separate brigade should be organized for that purpose. The board gave as its opinion that this service should be committed to the artillery troops. This view was concurred in by the Secretary of War. This was the origin of the "rocket battery" which was taken to Mexico in 1847, manned, *not* by the artillery, but by the mechanics of the ordnance department. From 1838 to 1847 information concerning rockets had been carefully guarded by that close corporation. What the artillery learned was picked up in spite of this secrecy.

utilized. After the return of the commission from Europe the committee suggested slight changes in the models of the 32 and 42-pounders, the 6-pounder gun and the 24-pounder howitzer; but the field pieces were not altered as recommended. The remainder of the system, as received from the board of 1838, was left untouched.

In 1843 a 32-pound howitzer was added to the field service as a shell-gun, to be used in conjunction with the heavy 12-pounders.

At this time Colonel Bomford was making experiments with heavy ordnance, which resulted in the development of the Columbiad, only to make way for the stronger Rodman system. The 10-inch sea-coast howitzer and the 8 and 10-inch Columbiads recommended by him were added to the land system, the former in 1841, the latter in 1844. This model of Columbiad was, in 1858, pronounced too weak for the work expected of it, and these guns were then degraded to the position of shell-guns using reduced charges.

In 1850 the system embraced the following calibres:

Field service: 6 and 12-pounder guns, 12, 24, and 32-pounder howitzers, and 12-pounder mountain howitzer, all of bronze.

Siege and garrison: 12, 18, and 24-pounder guns, 8-inch and 24-pounder howitzers, and 8-inch (light) and 10-inch (light) mortars, of iron; Coehorn 24-pounder mortar, and 16-inch stone mortar, bronze.

Sea-coast: 32 and 42-pounder guns, 8 and 10-inch Columbiads, 8 and 10-inch howitzers, and 10 and 13-inch (heavy) mortars, of iron.

Six different calibres of guns, two of Columbiads, five of howitzers, five of mortars, or eighteen altogether—an increase of four over the system of 1839, and principally in the larger natures—the precursor of that ceaseless struggle for an efficient heavy armament which from that day to this has gone ever forward, guided by the inventive genius of the Nation, inspiring hope that the grand object kept steadily in view is at last to be realized.

Rodman's plan of casting by cooling from the interior was a conception of true genius. It raised the American artillery, in 1861, to a leading position among the heavy-gun systems of the world.

Lieutenant Rodman began the investigations which led to the development of his theory, about 1845, when superintending the construction of the Columbiads. In 1849 two guns—an 8-inch and a 10-inch—were cast upon this principle, and in the tests to which they were subjected vindicated completely its correctness. Other experiments were carried on at various times, in all with six pairs of guns, the results only confirming the conclusions first arrived at regarding the great practical advantages of this method of casting. The six solid-cast guns endured 772 rounds altogether, while the hollow-cast fired 5,515 rounds, and remained unbroken. Upon the evidence here afforded of its superiority the War Department, in 1859, directed that thereafter all the larger natures of ordnance should be cast on Captain Rodman's plan.

So early as 1855 experiments were made at Fortress Monroe with a grooved gun—the forerunner of the rifled cannon that was speedily to follow, and the development of which has given increased interest to every question appertaining to field, siege, and sea-coast armaments, of armor and of land defense. But, though bearing evidence of intrinsic merit, the rifle principle, the workings of which as illustrated in the performances of the Lancaster guns were not altogether satisfactory, could only be considered as foreshadowing great possibilities. Experiments were, however, pursued in a small way to develop the new principle, and with encouraging results. By Special Orders No. 144, Adjutant-General's Office, 1860, a board of artillery and ordnance officers was appointed to make more elaborate trials of the rifled cannon and projectiles. The report of this board was submitted November 1st, 1860. Regarding the method of rifling and of constructing projectiles to be used therewith presented to it for trial, the board remarked:

"It is admirably adapted to the various calibres of guns now in use, requiring only that they be rifled (which can be done at the forts and arsenals where they now are) and supplied with proper proportions of rifled projectiles. Another advantage is that these same guns, and without increase of charge, will be enabled to throw a weight of metal about double what they have heretofore fired, with more accuracy, effectiveness, and greater range. The board, therefore, recommends the rifling of all, or at least fifty per cent., of the guns at forts and arsenals."

Thereupon fifty per cent. of the guns, as here recommended, were ordered by the War Department to be rifled on the James plan. But this attempt to secure an efficient artillery by converting old guns on hand, like its antitype, the conversion system of 1881, was a total failure. After a brief yet more extended experience than that of the board the project was abandoned, as the increased weight of projectile, when fired with a proper charge of powder, strained the conversions of 1860, as it did afterwards those of 1881, beyond endurance.

The War Department had been put in possession of drawings of the 12-pounder Napoleon or gun howitzer, designed by Napoleon III, and intended to increase the power of the light, reduce the weight of the heavy, and render but one field-gun necessary. As in the Dearborn gun and those recommended by the board of 1818, the weight of metal per pound of shot was fixed at 100. This gun was adopted in 1857, and still forms part of the field system. It was a most efficacious weapon—proved to be such on many battle-fields of the Civil war, where the heavily-wooded and broken surface of the country together with the inferior small arms of the enemy caused the severest fighting to be done at short ranges, where the gun howitzer, with its heavier shell and case-shot, was often found to be more destructive than the light 10-pounder rifle gun.

The Civil war gave an impetus to the manufacture of all kinds of artillery matériel. The talent and mechanical skill of the country at large were given remunerative employment in this branch of the public service. The result was that private manufactories alone, unaided by the military authorities, gave to the armies operating in the field their first systems of rifled ordnance. As the sources from whence the guns came were numerous, the varieties of calibres and types were very great. Some idea may be formed of the complexity of the resulting armaments from the fact, cited at random from among many similar instances that could be mentioned, that the field artillery with Rosecrans' army, February 8th, 1863, was made up of thirty-two 6-pounder smooth-bores, twenty-four 12-pounder howitzers, eight 12-pounder light Napoleons, twenty-one James rifles, thirty-four 10-pounder Parrotts, two 12-pounder Wiard steel guns, two 6-pounder Wiard steel guns, two 16-pounder Parrotts, and four 3-inch rifle ordnance guns.

Of all private corporations to which the Government was indebted for prompt and efficient aid at this time, without which the Union armies would have been equipped with a field armament worthy at that time only the semi-barbarous nations of Asia, the Cold Spring foundry may perhaps lay claim to pre-eminence. The specialty of this foundry was the Parrott gun, upwards of seventeen hundred of which, with three million projectiles, were procured by the War Department alone during the war. From a report made November, 1861, of a board of officers upon the rifled guns of the Army of the Potomac, this system appears to have embraced, among others, 10, 20, and 30-pounder Parrotts, all of which had been tested with satisfactory results before the 3-inch (10-pounder) ordnance gun made its appearance among the field batteries of that army.

The decade from 1850 to 1860 had been signalized by experiments which laid the foundation for changes that now followed each other in quick succession. The original 8-inch and 10-inch Columbiads having been previously turned into shell-guns, were finally suppressed in 1861, their places supplied by others of the same calibre, but strengthened at the breech to withstand the shock of heavy charges. The 42-pounder gun and the 16-inch stone mortar were suppressed. In February, 1861, a 15-inch Columbiad, of the type afterwards known as the Rodman gun, was adopted. In the same year new modeled 8 and 10-inch siege mortars, 10 and 13-inch mortars and an 8-inch howitzer for sea-coast service, were adopted. These were all distinguished, as were the Rodman guns, by an absence of ornamental mouldings. In the line of rifled ordnance, the 4½-inch siege and the 3-inch field were adopted in 1861. The changes which have been noted established the artillery system in the Fall of 1861, when the Civil war had been fairly inaugurated, so as to embrace the following:

Field: Wrought-iron 3-inch rifle, bronze 6 and 12-pounder guns; 12-pounder Napoleon, 12-pounder mountain, and 12, 24, and 32-pounder howitzers.

Siege and garrison: Cast-iron 4½-inch rifle, 12, 18, and 24-pounder guns, 24-pounder and 8-inch howitzers, and 8-inch and 10-inch mortars; Coehorn mortars (bronze).

Sea-coast: 32-pounder gun, 8, 10, and 15-inch Columbiads, 10 and 13-inch mortars. The total embraced seven different calibres of guns, three of Columbiads, four of howitzers, and four of mortars, or eighteen altogether—the same as in 1850.

In 1861 the smooth-bore system of the United States was certainly excellent. In quality of cast-iron used and its manipulation during manufacture it has been claimed, and with reason, that our ordnance department led all others. If not the first upon the ground, the department was among the pioneers in heavy modern armaments, as was shown by the casting successfully in that year what at the time was the most powerful weapon known—a 15-inch Rodman gun—followed, in 1864, by a similar but 20-inch smooth-bore, throwing a shot weighing 1,080 pounds. This was a grand stride, and placed the American artillery in no secondary position in the array of national armaments at that time developing.

The power of these smooth-bore guns developed the 'racking' as distinguished from the rifle-gun 'punching system' of attack on iron-clads, and enabled the former for several years to hold its own against the latter. To bring about this result was a task of no mean magnitude. Its accomplishment redounds immeasurably to the credit of those to whose labors success was due. It was a new thing for a system of artillery, distinctly American, to command the serious attention and respect of the military nations. The disabling of numerous iron-clads, however, by shots from exemplars of the 'racking system' placed beyond question its efficiency when brought to bear on the armor-plated vessels of that day.

But the contest which sprang up between the two systems proved to be an unequal one. The 'racking,' after a gallant fight, went down before its opponent. This followed naturally the successful application abroad of the principle of rifling to heavy-gun constructions. In the United States men's minds were too busily occupied with the paramount duties of the hour, growing out of the Civil war, to fully take cognizance of—as they had not time to investigate—the great advantages of the rifled cannon. Seasons of active hostilities are not favorable to well-considered changes of armament. The study—the deliberate experiment which must precede alterations based on correct scientific principles—can only be secured in time of peace. Napoleon, at St. Helena, while complaining that the Gribeauval system was too heavy, and otherwise objectionable, took care to observe that, though he had appreciated these facts, yet he had been too busily engaged to apply, except imperfectly, the remedies, as this could only be done when quiet and opportunity for experiment enabled intelligent investigation to work out its methods of reform.

This was eminently true in the United States during the Civil war. The development of the smooth-bore system went on naturally and as a matter of course; it involved no principle not already understood; it was but unfolding one after another the principles of a system the foundations of which were laid by the labors of Bomford and Rodman years before. Under the circumstances it was to be expected that the smooth-bore would, and it was right that it should, receive more attention than the rifle. Nor was this due to a disposition to ignore the importance of the latter. In the report of the armament board appointed December, 1861, it was remarked that "at present it is not deemed expedient to recommend placing any large rifled guns in our forts, but at an early day it is anticipated that guns of this nature may take the place of an equal number of those in the tables of armaments prepared by the board. In the meantime, we recommend that unremitting experiments be made to settle this point."

But, as Napoleon had found, due attention to the enemy in front left little time for experiments in the rear. Only one 8-inch and one 12-inch cast-iron Rodman rifle were placed on the proving ground down to 1865. The result was that at the end of the Civil war the only rifled guns of large calibre that had been tested in service were the sole products of private foundries, where plans for their construction had been matured prior to the commencement of hostilities.

From 1861 to 1867, therefore, the heavy armament of the United States was made up of smooth-bores, except in so far as the purchased products of private foundries were put in requisition to add a rifle element of secondary importance.

Meanwhile the punching system—rapidly abroad, at home slowly—had advanced in favor. It had begun to be doubtful as to how long the racking could hold its own against the punching system. That the rifle should longer be excluded from the sea-coast armament seemed suicidal. Accordingly the armament board of 1867* was instructed to determine, not only the calibres of the ordnance for the forts, but also the proportion of rifled guns which should be procured. This was a recognition officially of the necessity that existed for supplementing (as in that light it seemed to be viewed) the power of the smooth-bore by that of the rifle. The board recommended the purchase of

---

*Convened per Special Orders No. 29, Adjutant-General's Office, January 18th, 1867.

equal numbers of smooth-bores and of rifles; but it seemed to discern the handwriting on the wall which foretold that the days of the smooth-bore were numbered; for, after having made the recommendation indicated, it adopted a resolution practically stultifying itself, but no doubt expressing its views truthfully as to the rifle-gun problem, to the following effect: "From the fact we are now dealing with a *new and greatly more powerful gun,* and as the emplacements, traverses, and platforms in fortifications *will all undergo change from the use of rifled artillery,* we can express no determinate opinion as to the relative number of rifled and smooth-bore guns which should go to make up our armaments." From this time on, however much the gospel of the 'racking system' might be preached by its disciples, its glory had departed. Thenceforth the most that could be hoped for was that the smooth-bore might share honors equally with its more promising competitor. The postponement of the inevitable—the relegation of the smooth-bore to the position of a mere auxiliary—was due to the fact that it was not practicable to procure a proper metal for the rifle gun. Our cast-iron, indeed, was unsurpassed, but such had been the experience with it that the chief of ordnance reported in 1870 that the results obtained did not warrant him in recommending that any cast-iron rifle guns be procured for arming the forts, and followed it the next year by the remark that, with our knowledge of their construction and the metals of which they should be made, he was not willing to recommend the purchase of any rifled cannon, but adding, "as our smooth-bore Rodmans are regarded as reliable and perfectly fit for service, I shall continue to recommend their purchase."

From 1867 down to 1871, therefore, the smooth-bore, due partly to the fact that efficient rifles seemed beyond our manufacturing facilities, and partly to the reluctance of its devotees to acknowledge that it had a superior, was in assumed relative importance kept side by side with the rifle. The year 1871 saw it fall to the rear in spite of the efforts of its friends and admirers. That which had happened in every other artillery happened here—the smooth-bore took its proper and secondary place. This event, which had been foreseen by the armament board of 1867, was officially announced by the chief of ordnance in his report of 1872. After recommending the purchase of more smooth-bore cast-iron guns, he remarked of their accuracy that "within a mile distance it is fully equal to that of rifled guns, and in many of our exposed positions within easy range of hostile ships would be entirely effective. To solve the problem completely, rifled guns with great accuracy and long ranges and great penetrating power must be provided." Although the smooth-bore was still clung to, the insignificant part it was considered competent to act may be judged when we reflect that, standing outside the range at which it was claimed to be efficient, a modern iron-clad with even third-rate rifles could crumble to pieces the foundation on which rested its helpless and impotent adversary.

But even reduction to this unimportant rôle could not long save the once formidable smooth-bore system, which was to receive no rest until retired permanently from respectable modern armaments. The chief of ordnance, it is true, continued as late as 1873 to urge the purchase of more smooth-bores; but the only result was to add to the already generous array of antiquities that garnished the defences of our extended sea-board. The reign of the smooth-bore was ended. Congress, by act of June 6th, 1872, had appropriated $270,000 for experiments and tests with *heavy-rifled ordnance.* This was the last nail in the coffin of the racking system, confessedly worthless as it was for purposes of defense against even second-rate armor-plated vessels of modern construction. The lid which shut out forever the remains from view was firmly yet decently closed by the hand of that faithful advocate and friend, the chief of ordnance himself, who, December 14th, 1874, in an official letter or report calling the attention of the authorities to the importance of building up the sea-coast armament, remarked:

"Rifle guns ranging from eight inches to twelve inches in calibre, with power sufficient to penetrate at considerable distances the armor of iron-clad vessels, must be provided. *The heaviest rifles are the guns of the present, as they will be of the future;* and *while smooth-bores may for some time to come play a secondary part, for want of a more powerful weapon, they must inevitably yield to the rifle in every important juncture* as the old smooth-bore musket has given place to the breech-loading rifle in the hands of the soldier."

In the United States, therefore, the final and overwhelming triumph of the heavy-rifle gun dates from 1874. While the smooth-bore remains in our list of standard ordnance, it is simply for the utilization of material on hand; the system is as obsolete as anything can be; and, amidst the interesting questions that now absorb the attention of the artillery world, it is, except as a relic of the past, almost forgotten.*

At the same time that the question of smooth-bore against rifle was being decided, that of breech against muzzle-loading was receiving attention.

The proposition to construct heavy-rifle guns on the breech-loading principle received little serious consideration until, in 1872, the importance of the measure was so convincingly presented to Congress that special appropriation was made to enable breech mechanisms to be tested experimentally. Previously, however, the subject had been discussed and reported on favorably by boards of officers; but, except to fire a few shots on the proving ground with the Mann cast-iron rifle, nothing in the line of testing the breech-loader was done until about 1879. The ordnance board of 1868 and the mixed board of 1870 recommended the construction of 12-inch breech-loading cast-iron rifles, but the chief of ordnance announced that he disapproved of and would oppose the measure, until it was determined whether or not a successful muzzle-loading rifle of large calibre could be manufactured.

The act of June 6th, 1872, providing funds for experiments and tests with heavy-rifled ordnance, stipulated that the money should be used to procure at least three models, to be designated by a board of officers appointed by the Secretary of War, and to include both classes—breech and muzzle-loading cannon. Of the seven different models selected by the board as worthy of

---

*The truth of what precedes is in nowise impaired by recent apparent attempts to galvanize into life the corpse of the obsolete system and the report of the ordnance board, as a result of experiments, that : " With our improved powders and projectiles the projectile energy of this gun [15-inch smooth-bore] has been increased to an extent which renders it not only an efficient weapon for secondary defense, but even formidable as a primary gun for racking in many of our harbors."

We have three hundred 15-inch smooth-bore guns distributed to the sea-coast forts. The effort (a most laudable one) seems to be to prevent their being a total loss on our hands without having fired a shot. The best we can hope from them is to prevent a contemptible enemy approaching our shores with impunity. But no amount of experiment, nor yet the profoundest reverence for the racking system, will save the fort defended by these guns from being knocked to pieces by even low-power rifles held beyond the range at which the smooth-bore is claimed to be efficient.

trial, four were breech-loaders, viz.: (1) Krupp's, (2) Sutcliff's, (3) Thompson's, and (4) French and Swedish; and, contingent upon the appropriation proving sufficient, the Mann and the Lyman multi-charge guns were recommended for trial.

Of these systems Krupp's alone had a well-established reputation; and the board was led to recommend the purchase of a 12-inch gun of this pattern. No purchase, however, was made of the 12-inch or any other Krupp. Instead, as is elsewhere mentioned, an attempt was made to build up an American-Krupp system, by attaching the Krupp breech-loading mechanism to the converted 8-inch and the cast-iron 12-inch rifles of new construction. As a final result, the intentions of the board of 1872 have been entirely frustrated. Neither the *conversions* nor the new constructions could in any proper sense be said to test either the Krupp breech mechanism or that system of gun-making. In the attempt to build up a breech-loading American system the principle of the breech mechanism was held entirely subordinate to the absorbing desire to develop successfully the *conversion idea*, which for years monopolized the time and attention of the authorities to the exclusion of all else. Yet experiments made in pursuance of this plan were so satisfactory as to lead the ordnance board in 1880 to conclude that "breech-loading systems must supersede muzzle-loading;" and immediately contracts were entered into for the construction of four new 12-inch breech-loading rifled guns, appropriation for the manufacture of which had been specially made by Congress. Fortunately, before work had far progressed, the breaking down of the American-Krupp system, upon which they had been projected, enabled their construction to be arrested before the Government had been put to the expense of adding four more to the number of pieces in its weak and inefficient heavy-rifle armament.

The other breech-loaders recommended by the board of 1872 were duly manufactured; but, except the Lyman multi-charge, they had not, save to fire a few rounds each, been experimentally tested. Until the conversion mania had subsided, by the blowing up of the system in 1881, there was neither time nor money available for other purposes. Other systems were placed to one side, while the favorite went boldly on to its natural and legitimate end—complete failure. But ere this time had arrived the idle guns—in the presence of that new and powerful element of gun construction, steel—had joined the ranks of systems past and gone; nor had their peculiar breech mechanisms any advantages over that of Krupp, already thoroughly tested, not only on the proving ground, but in the more trying practice of active service.

To summarize, we see that, until 1868, the muzzle-loader alone was thought of. The few shots fired from the Mann before this had led to no practical result whatever. From 1868 to 1872, the breech-loader, while it had entered the lists, was kept subordinate to the other; but it gradually gained ground, until, in the latter year, the two systems about equally divided the attention and favor of our authorities. The breech-loader kept straight on in its course, passing its competitor, which, under the announcement of the ordnance board that breech-loading systems must supersede muzzle-loading, finally, in 1880, retired from the field. The appropriateness of this act was confirmed by the unanimous voice of the board appointed pursuant to act of March 3d, 1881, not one of the constructions recommended by it being a muzzle-loader. The venerable and venerated associates—the smooth-bore and the muzzle-loader, full of years and honors—were together laid quietly away to rest. The latter has, however, been dragged temporarily forth to fill the obscure niche cut out for it in the system of 8-inch rifles converted from 10-inch smooth-bores. But all new constructions are breech-loaders, which system is therefore, for all practical purposes, master of the situation, without a rival worthy of the name.

Among improvements in modern gun construction, each of which acts an important part in the perfect machine, is the chamber. Although experimented with abroad before that time, the first test of the principle in this country, so far as known, was made with a muzzle-loading 3.17-inch wrought-iron gun at Sandy Hook in 1879. In reporting on the results, the ordnance board remarked:

"It will be seen that the advantage of chambering is fully established, as the results attained are most excellent, and fully equal to any developed abroad. It is, therefore, of the highest importance, in the opinion of the board, that further experiments be made by applying this principle to higher calibres, and practically establishing the extent to which it can be used in our sea-coast armament."

The results of the experiments here recommended have been

elsewhere mentioned. They, in 1880, established that the chamber was an indispensable feature of all gun constructions—field, siege, and sea-coast.

Regarding siege artillery, there is little to say. No gun, except the 4½-inch rifle, adopted in 1861, has been added to that armament. The same general principles of construction which affect the heavier calibres must have their influence on the siege and field-guns. The 12, 18, and 24-pounder smooth-bores have disappeared from the list of siege pieces; and in proposed constructions, steel as the metal, and the breech-loading and chambering principles, appear as prominent, absolutely necessary, features.

There has been greater activity in the province of field artillery. The 3-inch wrought-iron rifle of 1861 was pronounced too light, in weight of metal thrown, by those who used it extensively during the Civil war. Since then the effort has been to secure a gun which will correct this evil. This caused the adoption, in 1868, of a model for a 3.5-inch rifle of wrought-iron firing a shot weighing 16.75 pounds with three pounds of powder. While the weight of the projectile would be an important point in its favor, it is not likely this gun will ever appear in the field. With all other wrought-iron muzzle-loaders it must give way before the breech-loading steel guns, which alone at this time and prospectively will make up first-power field armaments.

Experiments have been made with Moffatt's 3.07-inch breech-loading steel rifle, Sutcliff's breech-loading mechanism applied to an ordinary 3-inch rifle, Dean's 3.5-inch muzzle-loading rifle, made of bronze with hardened metal around the bore, and with several 3-inch rifles converted into both muzzle and breech-loaders of various models. The result has been that all interested have settled down to the belief that a breech-loading steel gun is the field-piece, not of the future only, but of the present. Of the conversions, the 3.20-inch, consisting of the original 3-inch wrought-iron gun reamed out and a steel breech-receiver attached, seems to solve very efficiently the problem as to what disposition shall be made of the present stock of 3-inch rifle muzzle-loaders.

In the United States, as in most countries, much attention has been given, since 1870, to machine guns. In 1874 the .45-calibre Gatling was adopted as an auxiliary for flank defense and for all other parts of the national armament. By 1880 the 1-inch and

.5-inch Gatlings, the 1.45-inch Hotchkiss revolving cannon, with the 1.65-inch Hotchkiss breech-loading rifle, the latter for mountain service, had been added to the field system. The part that these guns are to act in war remains to be determined. Their chances, if brought against the longer range and more powerful field-gun of the present day, would appear to be slight, and their employment has been rejected by some of the first artilleries of the world. Still, for flanking purposes, and in positions where they can be protected from the projectiles of the rifle-gun, they are very formidable, and in their effects on human life terribly destructive.

The latest views on the subject of field artillery are contained in the report of the board convened by General Orders No. 39, Adjutant-General's Office, April 28th, 1881, which, in treating of the field armament, proceeded as follows:

"After a careful examination of the various field-guns tested by the ordnance board, we recommend for immediate adoption the converted 3.20-inch calibre breech-loading gun with the round-back wedge fermeture, and that a sufficient number to equip the five field batteries, for purposes of instruction and for service generally, be prepared and issued as soon as practicable. Although not in all respects such a gun as the board would suggest in a new construction of the same calibre, the gun we have recommended satisfies nearly, if not quite, all the conditions sought for in a light gun. Additional reasons render this gun suitable for adoption, and they may be briefly stated as follows:

"1st. From the trial reports of the ordnance board it appears that this gun compares favorably with any other field-gun of the same calibre in velocity, accuracy, range, and weight of metal in the shell. In the simplicity of the breech mechanism, and the facility with which it can be worked and handled, it possesses undoubted advantages over any other gun presented or known to the board; in this respect it is not inferior to any other field gun now manufactured.

"2d. It is a tested and approved construction of the ordnance department far superior to any field-gun now in our service.

"3d. As it is a converted gun, it is comparatively inexpensive, and, if adopted, will enable the Government to advantageously and speedily dispose of the old 3-inch muzzle-loading guns.

"4th. The only change recommended by the board in this gun is that the position and direction of the vent and action of the fermeture shall be such that the gun cannot be fired until the breech is closed and locked.

"The board is of opinion that for a permanent field system there should be steel guns of two calibres, having weight and length of bore sufficient to give a muzzle velocity of not less than 1,600 feet—the lighter gun to throw a shell of about thirteen pounds weight, and the heavier a shell of about twenty-two pounds weight; both guns to be modeled on the 3.20-inch gun recommended by the board.   *   *   *   *   *   *   *   *

"In determining the most suitable gun for field service, the board has not lost sight of the value of vertical fire in all field operations, and the likelihood of its greater development in consequence of the influence of intrenchments, rifle-pits, forts, and other temporary covers to which troops resort when confronting each other. To provide for this kind of fire, the board recommends a short rifle steel howitzer or mortar of not less than 5½-inch calibre, and of a weight not to exceed 1,000 pounds, the same to be mounted on an iron or steel carriage, so arranged that it can be attached to a limber, and when unlimbered be ready for firing. Such a piece would find its use in reaching an enemy sheltered by intrenchments, rifle-pits, or other cover, and in such temporary siege operations as might take place.

"In fact, the usefulness of such batteries would be very great; and while the board is in doubt whether the service of such a piece does not more properly belong to the heavy than the field-artillery branch, its importance in future field operations may be given as the reason for alluding to it."

The board commended the 1.65-inch calibre Hotchkiss mountain rifle as an excellent gun for mountain and Indian service.

Concerning machine guns, the board made the following recommendations:

"1. That the Hotchkiss revolving cannon, calibre 1.5 inch, be adopted for field service.

"2. That the Gatling gun be retained, and that the calibre .45 gun have the side-action crank and the improved rear adjustment.

"3. That the improved Gardner gun be adopted for service.

"4. That all guns, calibre .45, intended for field service be made to take the cartridge of 70 grains powder and 500 grains bullet."

In conclusion, it will not be uninteresting to notice in detail the measures which, since 1860, have been taken to secure a proper system of artillery. First, there was the armament board of 1861,* and which was instructed " to regulate and fix the number and calibre of the cannon to be mounted *en barbette* and in casemates in each of the permanent fortifications of the United States, and also the number and descriptions of guns to comprise field batteries." This board recommended the adoption of a 13-inch smooth-bore as an intermediate calibre between the 10-inch and the 15-inch then in service, and that both 20-inch and 30-inch smooth-bores, on the same plan as the 15-inch (Rodman's), should be constructed. Except for the 30-inch gun, these recommenda-

---

* Appointed pursuant to Special Orders No. 314, Headquarters of the Army, November 26th, 1861.

tions were carried into execution, the first 20-inch being cast in 1864.* The armament board of 1867 added a 15-inch mortar and 10 and 12-inch rifle-guns to the list of calibres, and expressed the opinion that the Gatling gun, or one of similar character, might be advantageously used in flank defense in place of the 24-pounder howitzer of 1839.

The calibres of guns, mortars, and howitzers having been determined upon by the armament board, a board of ordnance officers was assembled to determine the best mode and metal for their construction. The latter was the first board to recommend the construction of lined cast-iron rifle-guns. Among others, this board also made the recommendation that the 8-inch howitzer, without preponderance, supplant the 24-pounder flank defense, the latter to be abolished. Further, it presented the following as a list of the standard ordnance; and as this part of the proceedings was approved by the Secretary of War, it exhibits the authorized artillery system of 1868:

Field service: 3 and 3.5 inch rifles, wrought-iron; 4.62-inch smooth-bore (bronze) Napoleon; 4.62-inch smooth-bore mountain howitzer; and 1-inch and .5-inch Gatling guns (on trial).

Siege and sea-coast: 4.5-inch rifle, cast-iron; 8-inch smooth-bore howitzer, cast-iron; 8-inch smooth-bore mortar, cast-iron; and 10-inch smooth-bore mortar, cast-iron.

Sea-coast: 10-inch rifle, cast-iron; 12-inch rifle, cast-iron; 13-inch smooth-bore, cast-iron; 15-inch smooth-bore, cast-iron; 20-inch smooth-bore, cast-iron; 13-inch smooth-bore mortar, cast-iron; and 15-inch smooth-bore mortar, cast-iron.

---

* The committee of the armament board of 1861, upon which was devolved the duty of determining the number and kinds of guns for field batteries, was composed of General Barry, Colonel Hunt, and Captain Rodman. The report of this committee, which was adopted by the board and approved by the Secretary of War, was in substance as follows. In the light of subsequent events it will not be uninteresting. They recommended (1) that mounted batteries be composed of eight pieces; horse-artillery batteries of six pieces; (2) that but one calibre, smooth-bore or rifled, be used in any battery; that for the time being those calibres be 12-pounder Napoleons and 3-inch rifles, and that horse-artillery batteries be equipped exclusively with 3-inch rifles.

"However, as to mounted batteries, we have not yet sufficient experience with the rifled field-gun to fix their composition definitely, but, so far as practicable, but one kind of gun should be used in any battery.

"The description of guns for each battery and the proportion of each in mixed batteries must be determined by the nature of the service to be performed and by other circumstances."

This list embraced no model of a date previous to 1861, except the 12-pounder Napoleon.*

The 10-inch Rodmans, since become famous through the efforts to build up thereon a system of 8 and 9-inch rifles, are omitted from this table. In so far as the heavy-rifled guns were concerned (10 and 12-inch), it would appear that they were standard ordnance in name and on paper only, as, in 1873, the chief of ordnance, in his report, remarked that "no rifle of large calibre has yet been adopted for our service."

As a result of the recommendations of the board convened pursuant to act of June 6th, 1872, and the exertions of the ordnance department in the same line of action, the converted system of rifles was added to the list of heavy ordnance. Between 1874 and 1880 the machine guns and the 1.65-inch breech-loading Hotchkiss rifle, as previously mentioned, were added to the field system.

The modifications here mentioned changed the list of 1868 to that of 1880—the last published system of United States artillery—which is:

Field service: 4.62-inch (12-pounder) smooth-bore, bronze; 3.5-inch rifle, wrought-iron; 3-inch rifle, wrought-iron; 1.65-inch rifle (breech-loader), steel; 1.45-inch revolving cannon, steel; .45-inch Gatling (both long and short), and 4.62-inch smooth-bore howitzer, (mountain service.)

Siege and garrison: 4.5-inch rifle-gun, cast-iron; 8-inch smooth-bore howitzer, cast-iron; 8-inch smooth-bore mortar, cast-iron; 10-inch smooth-bore mortar, cast-iron; and 5.82-inch Coehorn mortar, bronze.

Sea-coast: 12-inch rifle, cast-iron; 12-inch rifle, cast-iron, with wrought-iron tube; 10-inch rifle (converted), cast-iron, with wrought-iron tube; 8-inch rifle (converted), cast-iron, with wrought-iron tube; 20-inch rifle (smooth-bore), cast-iron; 15-inch rifle (smooth-bore), cast-iron; 13-inch rifle (smooth-bore), cast-iron; and 13-inch and 15-inch mortars, (smooth-bore), cast-iron.

---

* The 24-pounder Coehorn was, perhaps inadvertently, omitted from the list.

CHAPTER XII.

TACTICS: GENERALLY.

Introductory to a few remarks on the tactics of artillery, it will be interesting, and tend as well to an understanding of the subject, to mention in their order the various works in this field that have been published for the use of the army.

Only meagre information has been gathered concerning instruction for and manœuvres of artillery during the Revolutionary war. Tousard's Artillerists' Companion, printed in 1809, gives the manual as then practiced, and the simplest exercises of battalion pieces, with their ammunition wagons or tumbrels. But from Stevens' "System of Discipline for the Artillery," we are led to believe that each artillery officer exercised his detachment or company as suited his fancy, according to traditional ideas, as there was nothing written and stamped with the seal of authority for his guidance.

The first treatise on the tactics and discipline of the artillery arm emanating from an American source that has descended to these times was that of Captain Stevens referred to. Prepared for the press as early as 1792, its publication was delayed until 1797. The author had been a captain in Lamb's regiment of Revolutionary artillery. The manuscript was prepared for three volumes, duodecimo. Volume one treated of the formation of a corps of artillery and the duties and practice of light field artillery; volume two, of the theory and practice of heavy artillery in garrison and on board the navy, and furnished an extract on the origin and principles of courts-martial. Volume three treated of laboratory duty, gave a great variety of directions for making compositions, the method of preparing fire-works, and the various kinds of ammunition necessary for different species of ordnance. Thus the plan of the work covered the ground of both theoretical and practical artillery, except fortification, very thoroughly; but in fact only volume one was published.

It is not known whether this system was or was not adopted by the War Department for the regular artillery. There is no doubt as to its adaptability, although the context shows that Stevens had directly in view supplying the wants of the militia artillery, in which he was an officer. In those early days, when the hopeless failure of Knox's utopian plan of militia organization had not become an established fact, it was believed that this branch of the national force could be equipped, prepared for, and placed in the field, as provided by law, which illusion has since been rudely dispelled.

That the System of Discipline was not, however, considered all that was needed by the regular artillery, even if adopted therefor, may be inferred from the fact that Inspector-General Hamilton and Major-General Pinckney had made considerable progress in digesting a system of exercises and discipline for the artillery arm, when, in 1800, the additional army raised in anticipation of war with France was disbanded, and those officers mustered out of service. Their manuscript was left at the War Office, where it was doubtless, in the same year, destroyed by the fire which consumed the Department records.

In September, 1808, General James Wilkinson, then commanding the army, had prepared a complete "modern system of movements and manœuvres for infantry, artillery, and cavalry," translated principally from the French, and was arranging, under the direction of Secretary Dearborn, for its publication; but, so far as is known, the work was never prosecuted to completion, although the Secretary urged that it be given to the army with all possible celerity. The manuscript, like its predecessor prepared by Hamilton and Pinckney, has disappeared, and left behind but the faintest trace of having existed. It is possible that the change of administration, March 4th, 1809, put an end to this measure, as it did to others of great practical utility which Secretary Dearborn had set on foot for the benefit of the army. The result was that a second war with Great Britain found the United States without any recognized system of instruction save Baron Steuben's infantry regulations and a system of horse-artillery manœuvres written at Paris in 1800 by General Kosciusko. The latter had been prepared at the request of an American citizen, who presented it to the Philosophical Society of West Point, New York. Although Kosciusko's manœuvres were written on the supposition that the battery was organized as in France, they could be, with obvious modifications, equally adapted to the light artillery of the United States.

The paucity of materials on the subject of regulations, tactics, and military administration impaired alike the discipline and efficiency of the army, and formed an almost insurmountable barrier to the progress of an officer ambitious to excel in, or even attain a fair knowledge of, the theoretical part of his profession. This fact was forcibly presented to the War Department by Captain Winfield Scott, of the new light artillery regiment, in a letter dated July 14th, 1809, in which he requested to be sent to Europe to collect and compile materials for supplying the army with treatises on military police, discipline, and tactics. Referring to the limited knowledge of officers regarding the proper management and uses of horse artillery, the writer remarked: "The recent introduction of this important corps into the American service, and its peculiar duties and organization, leave it certain that it can be but imperfectly practiced or understood in this country. France is the best school for obtaining a knowledge of it." Captain Scott's proposition was not accepted. It was left for him, six years later, when, as a general officer of the regular army, he visited Europe, to collect the necessary data for the first comprehensive system of regulations given to the regular army, and which, to use General Scott's words, after being "obscured, mutilated, and pirated from 1836 down to 1861, inclusive," forms the foundation on which rest the army regulations of the present day.

War was declared without the Government having at its disposal any system of manœuvres for the artillery except that of Kosciusko. Major Amos Stoddard compiled and hurried through the press a small work on the manual of cannon and the manœuvres of field and horse artillery. It was incomplete in details. The emergency did not permit elaboration; yet it proved sufficient for practical purposes. And as the order formally adopting Stoddard's work furnishes the first instance of the artillery being authoritatively supplied with a general system of instruction, it merits preservation. It is as follows:

"WAR DEPARTMENT, *August 1st*, 1812.

"The 'exercises for cannon and field ordnance,' and 'manœuvres for horse artillery, as altered from the manual of General Kosciusko and adapted to the service of the United States,' are hereby ordered for the government of the several corps of artillery in the said service. Such alterations and improvements as experience may suggest will be reported to the several commanding officers of regiments, and by them to the Department of War."

The Government gave the West Point Philosophical Society $200 for the copyright of Kosciusko's manœuvres thus appropriated. No alterations or improvements in Stoddard's work were announced during the war of 1812. It remained the standard authority until the adoption of Lallemand's system in 1821.

Tousard's Artillerists' Companion, before mentioned, which appeared in 1809, although an exhaustive, scientific, and excellent treatise, was neither a system of tactics nor of instruction. In the language of Colonel Tousard, it was intended to demonstrate, "first, the necessity for both theoretical and practical instruction to officers of artillery; second, that the artillery—one of the most necessary branches of the military profession—requires at the hands of its devotees early, constant, and attentive study; third, the present advantages of improvements, founded on theory and practice; fourth, the advantage of uniformity and regularity in the construction of matériel." We are informed in the preface that the work "was composed in obedience to the wishes of the great George Washington. It was begun as early as 1795. This great man often lamented the absolute want of an elementary treatise on artillery and the scarcity of English books on this branch of military science. He considered such a deficiency as an obstacle to the progress of instruction, which he was very desirous to remove, by rendering the works of authors and officers who had written upon artillery in other languages familiar to the officers of the corps of artillerists and engineers." While well serving the purposes for which it was written, the Companion was too voluminous and expensive for general distribution to the army, though it was long justly considered an authority on the subjects of which it treated.

The only other American work which has covered, equally with the Companion, the whole ground of the artillerists' professional studies, is a "Treatise on Artillery" by H. Lallemand. The author had been general of artillery of the Imperial Guard under Napoleon; and being proscribed by Louis XVIII, July 24th, 1815, sought refuge in the United States, where he died September 15th, 1823. His manuscript treatise was in three volumes. Volume one treated of the organization of artillery, its service in campaign, and tactics ; volume two, of the art of fortification, principally in connection with artillery, and of castramentation; volume three, of the principles of construction to be used in all kinds of artillery matériel, and the relations of the artillery to the other arms of service. Volumes one and two were translated and published in 1820. By orders from the War Department the President directed that, having approved the treatise, so much of the work as was embraced in the exercise of field artillery, school of the battle piece, evolutions of field batteries, school of the mountain pieces, exercise and management of siege, garrison, and sea-coast guns, and mechanical manœuvres, should be adopted for the service of the United States. Volume three, so far as is known, was never printed. It was ready for publication at the time of Lallemand's death, and Mr. Calhoun authorized its purchase, with a view to adoption as a text-book at the artillery school; but as no copy has been found, it is inferred that volume three was not published.

Lallemand's were not so bulky as Tousard's volumes, but were in other respects little better suited for text-books. They formed, as the name indicated, a *treatise* on artillery covering the whole range of professional subjects, with their bearings upon other branches of service, and from necessity were written in a style entirely too general to serve for a system of tactical instruction adapted to the needs of service.

By act of May 12th, 1820, Congress prescribed that the tactics of the regular army should be used by the militia also, but Lallemand's treatise was too elaborate for either. To supply the deficiency for the militia, a mixed board of regular and militia officers was convened in October, 1826, of which General Scott was president, to prepare, among other things, a system of instruction for field artillery. The board made a report in December of the same year, recommending the "*Manual for Artillery of the Garde Royale*," translated by Lieutenant Daniel Tyler, First Artillery. It was subsequently published, and, pursuant to act of Congress, 5,000 copies purchased for the use of the militia, the title being: "A System of Exercise and Instruction of Field Artillery, including Manœuvres of Light or Horse Artillery."

The proceedings of this board early drew attention to the fact that if this work were approved the militia would be furnished with a system of manœuvres for field and horse artillery far more complete than was that of the regular army. It was felt that this was a state of affairs neither creditable to the latter nor to be perpetuated. To meet the difficulty, a board was at first resolved upon to digest a complete course of instruction based on the Gribeauval system of artillery. There was not a single harnessed battery in service. It was conceded that the facilities at hand were not such as would enable the board to take up and push to a successful issue, and in a manner satisfactory to the Government, the work in contemplation. Even at the artillery school of practice, though the matériel was forthcoming, the pieces, when manœuvred, were hauled by men using bricoles. Under these circumstances the plan that gave promise of being most successful was not to convene a board, as had been proposed, but to send an officer to study the adopted (Gribeauval) system on its native soil and at the French camps of instruction. This course was determined on by the Department after more maturely considering the situation. The proposed board was therefore unnecessary, its labors being performed by more satisfactory methods. Lieutenant Tyler was selected for this delicate and responsible duty. His orders, dated War Department, January 3d, 1828; directed him to examine into and report upon the most recent system of French artillery, to translate their tactics and manœuvres with a view to adopting all into the regular service of the United States; and so far as compatible with this, the main object of his mission, he was to take advantage of every opportunity to acquire information on other military matters of interest and importance.

Proud of the honor thus conferred upon him, and anxious to prove himself worthy of it, Tyler, with abundant opportunities for observation, soon translated the whole Gribeauval system of exercises and manœuvres, a lithographic edition of three hundred copies being struck off at Metz, in 1828, under his supervision and at his expense. These were sent to the United States and distributed to the army, supplying a long-felt want, when circumstances to be mentioned, and which had not been anticipated, rendered them valueless. The translation was in three volumes. Volume one embraced the school of the cannoneer, field artillery; volume two, the service of siege, garrison, and sea-coast artillery; volume three, manœuvres of field batteries.

Although Lieutenant Tyler had, in obedience to instructions, made the translations in question—by far the most complete that the army had seen—he soon became convinced that the course of the Gribeauval artillery system was run. The French Government had already, after the most exhaustive trials to prove its efficiency, adopted a modification of the English block-trail system of gun-carriage. Notwithstanding the efforts of that Government to keep everything pertaining to it a profound secret, the young American obtained minutely exact drawings of the new system of matériel. These, upon his return to the United States, were turned over to the technical branch of the artillery, and were at once utilized to manufacture the first of the present style of artillery carriages for field, siege, and garrison guns. (See Matériel, p. 239, *ante*.)

It was at once seen that labor on the old system, if not lost, would be of questionable utility. The new system met triumphantly every objection urged against the Gribeauval, while introducing scarcely any of its own.

Artillery matériel being in this state of transition, it followed that questions of tactics and instruction also remained in abeyance. As a result, Lallemand's *Treatise*, with its recognized imperfections, remained for some years longer the only authority on these subjects issued to the army.

As was the case in France, whence we had directly received our ideas, it took nearly ten years of discussion and experiment to bring out the stock-trail system, which drove all competitors from the field and relegated that of Gribeauval to the back-ground. Simultaneously with this event came the mounting of Ringgold's horse battery and the equipping as field artillery of one company in each of the other artillery regiments. Provisions for instruction moved on with equal pace, and in 1839 appeared Captain Anderson's translation of the French "Instruction for Field Artillery, Horse and Foot," arranged for and adapted to the service of the United States. These instructions were for the stock-trail system what the manual of the Garde Royale and the work of Lallemand were for the Gribeauval, but more complete than either; and so far as field artillery was concerned, it superseded both. The principles upon which this arm of the public service is based were unfolded in a manner at once entertaining and instructive; the arrangement of the subject-matter was systematic, the definitions clear and explicit.

There was, however, one officer who was dissatisfied with the new instructions. This was Brevet-Major Ringgold, of the horse artillery, who had, previous to the appearance of the new, manœuvred his battery in accordance with the English system. For a time the practice of that portion of Anderson's work relating to horse artillery was, by War Department orders, suspended; but this injunction proving only temporary, Ringgold, in 1843, had the address to secure the ordering a board, of which he was a member, for its revision. The result of the labors of this board appeared in the form of a system of "Instruction for Field Artillery, Horse and Foot," which was adopted by the War Department March 6th, 1845. The changes from Anderson's Instruction, which characterized its successor, were adopted at Major Ringgold's suggestion, and resulted in an English-Americanized revision of the French system. The new work appeared just in time for the Mexican war, in which the field artillery sprang at once into the front rank of the combatant arms.

The siege and mountain matériel of the stock-trail pattern having been closely guarded by the ordnance department until taken to the field by its employés, in 1846–'47, and the character of the seacoast armament not having been determined upon, no change from Lallemand's system of instruction for these was necessary, nor was any made, until after the return of the army from Mexico, when, by General Orders No. 12, Headquarters of the Army, July 27th, 1849, a board of officers was instituted to prepare a complete course of instruction for siege, garrison, sea-coast, and mountain service. That for the mountain service was approved by the War Department December 5th, 1850, and that for the heavy artillery May 10th, 1851, which therefore marks the date when, for the first time, all branches of the arm were provided with tactics adapted to the stock-trail system of carriages.

The instructions of 1845, although excellent so far as they went, embraced little more than the manual of the piece and the manœuvres of a battery. The proper organization of artillery for and its management in the field were merely touched upon. Much of Anderson's instruction germane to these important features of any complete system were omitted, thus securing brevity at the expense of clearness and a knowledge of the principles on which the field artillery rested, which made the work very unsatisfactory as a text-book.

The board of officers appointed to supply this deficiency by Special Orders No. 229, Adjutant-General's Office, 1855, for some cause, never met; but its work was taken up and pushed to completion by another board, assembled in 1858, which prepared the "Instruction for Field Artillery," approved by the War Department March 6th, 1860.

This, while embodying the instruction of 1845, went much further, far exceeding in breadth of design and completeness of execution anything of a similar nature that had been given the artillery arm. Its appearance on the eve of the Civil war was a most felicitous event, enabling the volunteer batteries to systematically and thoroughly prepare for the field in the least possible time and most efficient manner.

At the same time with the new instructions there was adopted in service what was a fitting supplement thereto, viz., "Evolutions of Field Batteries," translated from the French by Major Robert Anderson, and embracing essentially the same manœuvres as are comprehended in the "School of the Battalion," present light-artillery tactics. Together, they supplied the theoretical knowledge necessary to organize the regular and volunteer batteries, both singly and in masses, for the great events calling them to action.

The features wherein the instruction of 1860 was superior to its predecessors consisted in articles on organization, matériel, and the service of artillery in campaign, presenting a philosophical and instructive *exposé* of the general principles underlying the formation, discipline, and service, both in peace and war, of an efficient field artillery. To this *rationale* of the subject-matter of instruction there was added the school of the soldier, mounted and dismounted, beginning at squad drill and extending to the exercises of detachments, together with a system of battery manœuvres more complete than any that had preceded it. The first was an important feature, rendering the instruction independent of others, and making unnecessary constant reference to the tactics of infantry and cavalry, as had been the case before; the latter only added to the finished character of the work as a course of instruction. And while the assimilated tactics now in use seek to render the information and experience acquired in one arm of service directly available in others in a greater degree than was formerly attempted, it is equally true that the clear, incisive style of the instructions of 1860 has been obscured in the assimilated edition by transposition, attempts at brevity, and a passion for change, which could only be indulged at the sacrifice of a distinctive, well-defined individuality.

The result of the labors of the board appointed to assimilate the tactics of the other arms to those of infantry were given to the army in 1873. The success with which the work of assimilation has been met in these tactics—a principle the value of which, *if properly put in execution and restricted to its proper limits*, is not underestimated—will be considered hereafter; but protest is here entered against some of the principles laid down for the guidance of artillery in the crucial test of battle.

In the assimilated infantry tactics, it is enjoined upon officers to "cultivate among the men the feeling that they *cannot* be beaten," while with artillery the aim seems to be to create the impression that they *can* be beaten, and that easily; hence they must take care of themselves, even at a sacrifice of bold and decisive movements. It is taught that the safety of the pieces depends upon the advantage that is taken of accidents of the ground; that the increased range and effect of infantry fire has impaired the utility of guns at short ranges, and made cover more necessary than ever for the protection of batteries; that the latter can no longer move up within short range of troops and open fire with cannister—the use offensively of which is entirely ended; that artillery fire is apt to become inefficient at a greater range than 2,500 yards; that if a battery remains within 900 yards of the enemy's infantry the chances are, particularly if there be no cover, that it will be disabled.

So far from these principles being calculated to inspire the artilleryman with the "feeling that he cannot be beaten," which feeling alone can and does render the soldier individually, or soldiers collectively, formidable, they must have the opposite tendency, engendering timidity and pusilanimity; as his only hope to escape annihilation at the hands of his murderous adversary, the infantryman, inspired with the true spirit of the soldier, through the "feeling that he cannot be beaten," is to either seek cover or leave the field. The sole relief from this impression of decadence in the importance of his arm, when compared with that of his more fortunate rival, vouchsafed to the artilleryman, is in the reflection that the value of his rifle-gun fire has been enhanced *at long range*.

This attempt at depreciation is hardly to be looked for, particularly in artillery works of instruction, and must, if followed to its legitimate consequences—undue cautiousness and loss of military spirit—strike at the foundation of honor; is a fitting prelude to disaster, is repugnant to every instinct that animates the soldier, and is at variance with experience, which shows that improvements in artillery and infantry arms have gone on *pari passu*, as have likewise the importance of these branches of service; and, in truth, in Europe to-day more attention is directed to bringing out the powers of artillery than is the case with any other arm, through a well-founded belief, based on the experience of recent wars, that the way is open for the development therein of an increased relative importance.

In the field of heavy artillery tactics,* the edition of 1862, published when the Civil war was in progress, formed the only connecting link between the tactics of 1851 and Tidball's Manual, approved in 1880, for use in sea-coast garrisons.

The heavy artillery tactics of 1851 embraced only the manual, mechanical manœuvres, and the nomenclature of siege, sea-coast, and garrison artillery, with just so much instruction for dismounted detachments as would enable the cannoneers to be marched to and from their pieces. The edition of 1862 differed from that of 1851 in the parading of detachments, which was done as in field artillery, and the addition of a few hints on the service of rifled guns.

---

*Artillery troops are divided into light and foot or heavy. Pieces of artillery are sometimes designated as light and heavy. The latter term, applied to *personnel* as distinguished from *matériel*, is of recent origin in the United States service; but *confounding* the *piece* with the *man who handles it* is not of recent date, nor has it been confined to the heavy artillery branch.

Captain Stevens applied the terms light, field, and heavy to *pieces* equipped for service, *i. e.*, matériel. Light artillery, as used in the act of April 12th, 1808, referred to personnel, being by contemporaneous authorities synonymous with horse artillery; and the latter, as used by both Kosciusko and Stoddard, meant personnel, or its organization, and had no reference to the matériel used.

Stoddard applied the term field artillery to both personnel and matériel, while he used the term cannon to designate larger calibres of guns.

Lallemand divided the personnel of artillery into field, horse (or light), and foot. The latter manned mountain, siege, garrison, and sea-coast artillery.

In Anderson's translation (1839) and the instruction of 1845, the designations horse and foot referred to personnel.

Tidball's Manual of Heavy Artillery is a much more comprehensive work. During the Civil war the whole subject of the proper handling of heavy artillery was in an unsettled state. It was necessary to use such means for the management of the new matériel as circumstances allowed; but from necessity there was diversity of practice, and there was neither time nor opportunity to reduce the whole to system.

The re-establishment of the artillery school at Fortress Monroe in 1867 laid the foundation for this deferred work. Notes on the results of practice at the school in the manual and in the mechanical manœuvres of the most recent siege, garrison, and sea-coast guns in the hands of artillery troops were carefully made, revised, and preserved, to appear in the new Manual, replacing what was old and obsolete. But this was not its only important feature. Breaking from the fetters which, under the *specious plea of assimilation*, would *bind all arms to the infantry, no matter how incongruous their natural elements may make the union*, Major Tidball has given the troops of heavy artillery a system of manœuvres of their own. It is worthy of note that this system, founded on the 'exercise of detachments,' Field Artillery Instructions of 1860, demonstrates conclusively that the present assimilated tactics of all arms rest, through the infantry tactics, upon the same basis, the only difference being that in the Instruction mentioned and in Tidball's Manual the block of eight men is styled a 'detachment,' while in the infantry tactics it is called a 'set of fours.' Aside from the advantages that must

---

As used in the tactics of 1851, the term heavy artillery referred to matériel only.

In the Instruction for Field Artillery of 1860, where the analysis of principles on which the artillery service is founded is presented in a clear manner, the *personnel* of that arm is divided into field and foot—the former serving mounted and horse batteries; the latter, mountain, rocket, siege, garrison, and sea-coast batteries.

Up to this time the term "heavy," in the artillery nomenclature, referred to *matériel* only, and there was no confusion of ideas as to what it meant; but during the Civil war, the designation "heavy" was given several regiments of volunteers raised to serve siege and sea-coast guns. Right here, and under the sanction of the highest military authority of the Government, the practice began of using the same term—heavy—to designate both personnel and matériel. However objectionable this may be, tending to confusion and being unnecessary, it has, for the present at least, fixed itself upon the service.

result from a system of manœuvres adapted to this (heavy) branch of the artillery, the recognition of the fact that this is a distinct part of the military service, subject to rules peculiar to itself, is not only conducive to discipline, but creates and strengthens a pride in their own arm, by reminding soldiers that they are not simply infantry in artillery garb, but that they are in fact *artillerymen*.

The remaining articles of the Manual—(1) Artillery against Armored Vessels and in Harbor Defense, (2) Attack and Defense of Intrenched Positions, (3) Field Intrenchments, (4) Submarine Mines, (5) Salutes and Ceremonies—are important and practically useful, and add to the completeness of the work as a valuable course of instruction.

To the credit of the artillery school let it be remembered that principally through its instrumentality is due the fact that the scope and value of Tidball's Manual, when compared with its predecessors—the various heavy artillery tactics—may be taken to measure quite accurately the interest in and knowledge of their profession, which characterized officers of the artillery at the epochs, respectively, at which they were written and issued for the use of the army.

CHAPTER XIII.

TACTICS: FIELD ARTILLERY.

Except for a few pieces mentioned in Tousard's Artillerists' Companion, no trace has been preserved of the field-artillery exercise of the Revolutionary war. There is the best authority for the statement that there was in this matter no uniformity, either prescribed or practiced. In the introduction to Stevens' System of Discipline, it is remarked:

"Several authors have written on the theoretical part of artillery, but the manual exercise of field-artillery has been transmitted by tradition, which accounts in some measure for the variety in this part of their duty among artillerists. It is therefore absolutely necessary to have a uniformity in the exercise of artillery, there not being any in particular adopted, but every officer teaching the men he exercises according to the traditional idea he forms of this part of his duty."

As Stevens was a captain in the regular artillery during the Revolution, his word on the subject must be accepted as conclusive; but he states that, in 1779, General Knox had the field officers of artillery draw up a plan for manœuvring a regiment of infantry with field-pieces attached, whereby the whole moved and the firings took place by beat of drum. Stevens does not state what these manœuvres were, but Tousard gives those of two pieces attached to and parading with a battalion; from which it appears that in both line and column the guns with their tumbrels were held on either flank. From necessity the exercise was simple in nature; the pieces were hauled by drag-ropes manned by artillerymen, for which purpose there was supplied the requisite number to each piece in excess of those needed for the manual.

For the service of the light brass 6-pounder in action there were required one commissioned officer, one sergeant, one corporal, two gunners, and twelve matrosses. This does not include the drivers, who as a rule were hired with their teams. For the service of the 5½-inch howitzer there were necessary one commissioned officer, one sergeant, one corporal, two bombardiers, and ten matrosses. In the manual of the 6-pounders, numbers 1 and 2 stood in front of and close to the axle, between the wheel and the piece; numbers 3 and 4 supplied number 2 with ammunition from the two side-boxes which, when the pieces were unlimbered, were taken from their axle-seats on either side of the piece and placed three yards in rear of the end of the trail handspike; numbers 5 to 12, both inclusive, manned the drag-ropes; number 1 sponged and rammed; number 2 placed ammunition in the bore; the first gunner (on the right) tended vent and primed; the second gunner (on the left) fired the piece with port-fire and lintstock; the corporal pointed; the sergeant was chief, and took charge of the piece; the commissioned officer supervised the whole, including the supply of ammunition. The commands of the instructor in the manual of the piece were: (1) Attention. (2) Unlimber piece. (3) Secure side-boxes. (4) Man out the piece. (5) From right to left, dress. (6) Advance sponge. (7) Tend vent. (8) Sponge piece. (9) Handle cartridge. (10) Charge piece. (11) Ram down cartridge. (12) Prime. (13) Take aim. (14) Fire. To limber from this position the commands were: (1) Unhook drag-ropes. (2) Mount side-boxes. (3) Limber piece. (4) Shoulder rammer. (5) Carry lintstock. In the manœuvres, unlimbered, three men carried the side-boxes, always keeping in rear of the trail. When prepared for action, the drag-ropes were 'manned out' in prolongation of the axle-tree of the gun-carriage; when moving in advance they were fastened to the washer-hooks of the wheels; when in retreat, to the trail-hooks.

The field artillery of the Revolution could in no sense be termed light. It had little mobility; nor was that prime consideration of the present day deemed necessary. Artillery tactics embraced the manual of the piece, with a few of the simplest manœuvres. The first system that divorced the field-gun from the drag-rope was the horse artillery manœuvres of General Kosciusko. It was in 1808 translated from the French by Colonel Jonathan Williams, superintendent of the Military Academy, and, so far as is known, was the first artillery tactics recognized as authority by the War Department, two hundred copies being distributed to troops and fifty copies being purchased for the use of cadets at West Point. As, owing to this circumstance, the work occupies an interesting place in artillery literature, a brief yet more extended notice of it here will not be out of place.

Written in 1800, but a few years after the introduction of horse artillery into the French army, and before its organization in our own, this system of manœuvres was not properly a treatise on the functions and uses of that species of troops, but rather a short memoir, such as a distinguished soldier could find time in leisure moments to write for a friend, being in some places so obscure that translator's notes were necessary to render it coherent and intelligible. The *movements* were thirty in number; were crudely, often erroneously, illustrated; yet furnished in a manner clear enough for practical purposes all that was necessary to enable a battery to manœuvre in face of the enemy. The habitual formations were not arranged to their three natural orders—line, column, and in battery—as has been the case in all subsequent tactics; but these orders evolved themselves without effort from the manœuvres, which covered what at the time was considered to be the whole science of field-artillery tactics, illustrating as they did how, with the utmost facility and precision, to advance and retreat in column and in line of battle; to fire both while advancing and retreating in line; to form front in any direction, both from line and column; and to change front from line to fire either to the right or left.

The prolonge had now superseded the drag-rope; the Gribeauval had supplanted the obsolete system of the Revolution; mobility had been thereby increased, and yet, when compared with those of the present day, Kosciusko's horse batteries were but little deserving the name of light artillery. Arriving at the field of exercise or in presence of the enemy, the prolonge was fixed and used in all manœuvres. The habitual column of manœuvre was that of a front of two pieces, or double column, formed from line by advancing the centre, though it might be formed by throwing forward either the right or left; but although the double column was preferred, manœuvring in *single* column was likewise provided for equally with the other. Instead of each gun being, in all formations, immediately followed or preceded by its caisson—a practice introduced by Lallemand—the pieces were grouped together, while the caissons formed another and distinct group. Advancing in column and in line, the group of pieces preceded that of the caissons; in retreat, the caissons preceded. The principle of inversions was rigidly adhered to—Anderson, in 1839, being the first to disregard it. The original right and left of the battery retained, therefore, these designations, no matter what the formations might be. In column, the mounted gun detachment marched in single-file on either side of the teams of the pieces; in line of battle they moved in the same order in the tracks of the gun-carriage wheels. There were no horse-holders. When the men dismounted to serve the pieces they gave the reins of their horses to the drivers of the gun-carriage teams or tied them to the limbers. Kosciusko favored the double column on the centre as that of manœuvre, for the reason that it was more quickly formed than any other;. and while this is true, the objection that thereby some of the lieutenants have their commands broken up, has, in the minds of other tacticians, outweighed this advantage. Lallemand did not use it; and though restored by Anderson, and since retained, it has been considered rather in the light of an exceptional movement, to be resorted to only under particular circumstances.

The horse-artillery manœuvres of Major Stoddard were those of Kosciusko, only slightly modified, so as the more readily to adapt them to the American light artillery, and therefore need not be further noticed.

In forming the men dismounted for service at the pieces, Stoddard, as is the case to-day, divided both field and horse artillerymen into *sections*, but the sections were only *gun detachments* in fact, each being composed of one non-commissioned officer and eight matrosses. The non-commissioned officer, styled section officer, was a functionary similar to his successor— the chief of piece, or the present chief of section. The matrosses were numbered in substantially the same way as practiced since, viz., numbers 1 and 3, gunner of the right, and number 5, in the rear rank; numbers 2 and 4, gunner of the left, and number 6, in the front rank. Although in field as in horse artillery, manœuvring with the prolonge was recommended, supernumeraries, numbered from 9 to 14, inclusive, were, in the former, added for the service of each piece, for dragging which, when the prolonge was not at hand, every man of the section carried a bricole. The manual was an adaptation of American drill to the Gribeauval system of carriage, then but recently introduced into the service. The duties of the different numbers were nearly the same as during the Revolution, the only difference being that the small ammunition-box, carried between the flanks of the trail in the Gribeauval system, had taken the place of the side boxes formerly in vogue. Eighteen rounds were carried in the movable ammunition-box, while in the ammunition wagon, which, "in battery," was placed fifty yards behind the piece, there were eighty-eight rounds for the 6-pounder, and one hundred and fifty for the 4-pounder.

Comparing the exercises of 1812, as presented in Stoddard, with those of the Revolution, set forth in a fragmentary manner by Tousard and Stevens, it is evident that the mobility of field artillery had been increased. This was rendered possible by two circumstances: First, the gradual introduction, under Secretaries Dearborn and Eustis, of the Gribeauval system of artillery; second, placing in the hands of troops a system of manœuvres for its proper and efficient management. The drag-rope had given way to the prolonge; the burden had been removed from the backs of men and placed on the backs of horses.

As was natural at a time when knowledge of professional subjects could scarcely be obtained in this country for love or money, the organization and management of horse artillery was, in the early days of the century, clouded in an atmosphere of mystery. One of the services rendered by Stoddard was to clear this away, by showing that the only difference between what were known as field and horse artillery lay in the circumstance that in the latter the cannoneers, to facilitate rapid movements, rode on horses, while in the former they walked by the sides of their pieces. Plain as this now appears, it was then an important point to have established and clearly understood, and it greatly simplified to the artillerymen of that day the whole subject of light artillery manœuvres.

Following this idea, Lallemand made the manœuvres applicable directly to dismounted detachments (field artillery), indicating, in the few instances requiring it, the special movements necessary for the horse artillerymen. This plan has been followed by subsequent authors, and it has greatly facilitated a comprehension of the whole matter, for all the horse-artillery detachment has to do, as a rule, is to follow directly in rear of its piece, while the latter moves in the field-artillery evolutions.

Understanding from experience the value of correct principles of organization, Lallemand paid great attention to this part of his treatise. The company, dismounted, was formed into detachments, each containing a number depending on the service required, but generally consisting of eight men, told off as 1, 2, 3, 4, gunner of the right, gunner of the left, 7, 8. In addition, there were attached to each detachment one non-commissioned officer or artificer, who had charge of the caisson, and another non-commissioned officer who was chief of piece.

The general principles on which the battery was organized for manœuvre were carefully and clearly presented. The duties of each person holding a position of responsibility were minutely set forth. The term 'section,' to indicate two pieces with their caissons, was first introduced. The important post of chief of caissons, intrusted by Stoddard to a sergeant or a cadet, was conferred by Lallemand upon a commissioned officer. Two non-commissioned officers were used as special guides or markers. Upon them, when forming line, the wheel horses of the leading carriages were dressed. In double column, they moved four feet in advance of the leading team of each column of carriages. These special guides disappeared from our tactics with Lallemand's treatise.

When formed in line the pieces, sections, and half-batteries had permanent numerical designations, commencing on the right, which they retained under all circumstances. The principle of inversions, with all its inconveniences, was therefore fully recognized. This converted the battery into what, compared with the battery of these days, might be called a rigid system. Advancing in column and in line, the piece preceded the caisson; in retreat, the caisson preceded the piece. Any formation which inverted the original order of the carriages was considered an inconvenience, to be escaped from as soon as possible.

The formations of the battery in the three natural orders for manœuvre—column, line, in battery—were here first fully elaborated. The processes by which passage was made from one to the other were unfolded in an easy, natural manner, thus enabling the essential features of battery exercise to be taken in at a glance. The single column of pieces was never used for manœuvre; and though column of half batteries was permitted, that of sections, formed by breaking line forward from either the right or left, but never from the centre, was habitually used. Like Stoddard, Lallemand presupposed that the system of artillery employed would be the Gribeauval; but he went a step further, and introduced the French manual of the piece, which was practiced until supplanted by the instructions of 1845. By this, numbers 1 and 2, acting together, handled the sponge and rammer; and while advantageous for large guns or small men, it was not necessary, and, for ordinary field-guns, could by no means be considered an improvement on the old method. Numbers 4, 7, and 8 supplied ammunition; the gunner of the right commanded during the manual exercise; number 3 served vent and primed, while the gunner of the left fired the piece.

Whether the guns should be grouped together, distinct from the caissons, as practiced by Kosciusko, or whether each should be either followed or preceded by its caisson, were questions upon which artillerists at that time were divided. Lallemand adopted the latter plan, which has been followed since. The horse artillery detachment was moved from the place assigned it by Stoddard, placed two paces in rear of the muzzle of the piece, when limbered, and horse-holders were introduced.

Lallemand added to the battery manœuvres 'on right into battery,' closing intervals in line, exercises with closed intervals, the passage of obstacles and defiles. His style of commands was vastly superior to Kosciusko's; but, with the exceptions just noted, his battery exercise was essentially the same as that of the latter.

Considering the reputation and great experience of General Lallemand, it might appear from a casual examination of his work that he paid but little attention to the exercise and evolutions of artillery; but it must not be lost sight of that his was a *treatise* on the art, science, as well as the practice of artillery in all its branches, rather than a tactics in any proper sense of the term: the geometrical problem of the movements of a battery being but an incident, and no doubt in the author's mind a comparatively unimportant one, in the main plan of his work. It was adopted as a text-book, for the reason that, notwithstanding its recognized imperfections, it was the best that could be had. No sooner, however, as has been mentioned, was it apparent to the War Department that the militia, through the translation of the manual of the *Garde Royale*, were about to be supplied with a plan of instruction superior to that of the regular artillery, than efforts were energetically begun to secure for the latter the perfect system of Gribeauval—matériel, tactics, and all—a task, so far as tactics were concerned, intrusted to Lieutenant Tyler, executed by him, and the results given to the army just as that celebrated system had been pronounced obsolete.

Between 1830, when the Government was furnished with drawings of the newly-adopted French system of artillery, and 1839, when Anderson's translation of the field manœuvres appeared, the new had gradually supplanted the old style of matériel. This translation was for the stock-trail what Lieutenant Tyler's translation of the whole French tactics had been for the Gribeauval system, viz., a plain presentation of the principles of organization and manœuvre, by which it was to be prepared for and made available on the field of battle. It embraced the school of the piece, including the manual and the mechanical manœuvres; school of the cannoneer, mounted; school of the driver; school of the battery. As with Lallemand's Treatise, the text was directly applicable to foot (field artillery), the variations necessary for horse artillery being noted as they occurred. No instruction was given in squad drill or that of the soldier dismounted, reference being made for what was needed to the infantry tactics. The school of the cannoneer, mounted, embraced but the simplest elements of cavalry exercise. The system, in the matter of rudimentary instruction, was therefore defective—a remark equally true of all others prior to that given the service in 1860.

The school of the driver embraced (1) exercises of couples unhitched and (2) exercise of several pieces horsed. It was an extension of Lallemand's school of the battle piece, and formed altogether a very admirable preparatory instruction for the school of the battery.

The cannoneers for the service of one piece and its caisson were styled a platoon. They were paraded in two ranks, as at present—numbers 1, 3, gunner of the right, and 5 in rear, and served on the right of the piece unlimbered; numbers 2, 4, gunner of the left, and 6 in front, and served on the left. In the school of the piece, as in Lallemand, numbers 1 and 2, working together, handled the sponge; 3 fired, using port-fire and lintstock; gunner of the right pointed; gunner of the left tended vent; 4, 5, 6 supplied number 2 with ammunition. The practice of dividing the loading exercise into motions, separated by pauses, together with moving the piece, unlimbered, by hand to the front and rear, were here introduced. Changing wheel and carrying piece on its limber were added to the mechanical manœuvres; and, as contemplated in the new style of carriage, provision was made for mounting the cannoneers on the ammunition chests, and for dismounting them. In the school of the battery the double column was, as usual, the habitual column of manœuvre, and under certain circumstances column of half batteries was used, but never the single column of pieces.* Combining the practice of Kosciusko and Lallemand, Anderson (as have his successors) formed the double column from line by moving forward either the centre or either flank.

Anderson's translation introduced several new and important principles of manœuvre. They were—(1) disregarding inversions, thereby causing the designation of pieces to depend, not upon their original, but upon their actual positions in line or column; (2) the passage of carriages; (3) the countermarch; (4) using the movable pivot only, with the guide towards the pivot; (5) dispensing with general or special guides. These principles, which were mostly rendered practicable through the discarding of the prolonge (except for firing in retreat,) greatly added to the flexibility of the mass; and now it could be said with truth that mobility in a correct sense for field artillery was first secured.

The habitual formations—column, line, in battery—were in detail of execution somewhat different from Lallemand. 'In battery' the horses, except when firing in retreat, faced as they do now—towards the enemy. In Lallemand they faced from the enemy. As in other arms of service, both the column and the line were used as a basis of manœuvre. The reciprocal movements of passing from column into line, and conversely, were first explained. This was followed by the formations 'in battery'— first from line and then from column. The passage of carriages, the countermarch, and the disregarding inversions permitted an almost unlimited variation of former manœuvres, while 'right (or left) front into line, faced to the rear,' was added to those already authorized. The intricate changes of front were carefully ex-

---

*Since Kosciusko's time the single column for manœuvring has been either wholly or partially discarded. Lallemand, Anderson, and the 'assimilation' proscribe it. The instructions of 1845 and of 1860 recognize the fact that it might be necessary to manœuvre from single column, and stated how, when necessary, it should be done. Kosciusko was in this matter wiser than those who have succeeded him.

In the United States the single file of carriages is the natural column of march, as the roads and topography, in nineteen cases out of twenty, do not,

plained and illustrated—an example followed by others, until the assimilated tactics, where they are impotently left to be executed according to the whim of each battery commander. The terms 'interval' and 'distance' were introduced, and so calculated that the various changes of formation occupied the least possible space. Another noticeable feature of Anderson was the character of the illustrations, which were numerous, exact, and, compared with any that had preceded them, elegant.

For the field artillery the year 1839 was an important epoch. One company in each of the four regular regiments had been at last equipped as contemplated by the reorganizing act of 1821. The completion and issue to troops of carriages upon the new system had not only increased immensely the mobility of both foot and horse artillery, but the mounting of cannoneers on limbers and caissons, as provided for the former, had practically well-nigh annihilated the difference between them, so far as facility of movement was concerned. Simultaneously with the providing a properly-equipped personnel, there was furnished in Anderson's work a very complete course of instruction, giving the details of field artillery organization for purposes of manœuvre, as well as the manœuvres themselves, thus adding, so far as a course of instruction could do, all that was needed to place this arm upon a proper footing for service.

The circumstances leading to the revision of Anderson's instructions, which appeared in 1845, have been detailed. And notwithstanding the excellence of Anderson's work, if proof were needed of the wisdom of the changes then (1845) made, it is found in the fact that now, after being continuously in use for forty years, they are found embodied almost literally in the light artillery tactics of the present day.

The new instructions (1845) embraced the three schools of the

for any distance, admit of two carriages moving abreast. Hence it almost always happens that the single column is that in which the battery will approach its position on the battle-field. In view of this fact, it is remarkable that the present light artillery tactics, being a revision after the Civil war of the instructions of 1860, and purporting to contain the practical suggestions gathered in that eventful struggle, does not explain the manner of forming *directly* 'in battery' from single column, although, should a battery take the field, the chances are that, if marching at the head of the column, this is the first manœuvre it would be required to perform in presence of the enemy.

piece, the driver, and the battery. The school of the cannoneer mounted of Anderson was suppressed, and, for the preliminary instruction needed in those branches of service, reference was made to the cavalry and infantry tactics.

In the school of the piece, the French manual, introduced by Lallemand and followed by Anderson, was discarded, and that at present in use adopted. Previous to this two gunners had always been told off to each gun detachment. This was so not only in the French, but the old American service. Now one sufficed. Instead of numbers 1 and 2 working together, number 1 alone handled the sponge and rammer. In the manual the movement of detachments to the front, rear, right, and left of the piece limbered were introduced, while dismounting and mounting carriages appeared as a new feature of the mechanical manœuvres.

Aside from the changes indicated, the most important difference between the old and the new systems of instruction consisted in the introduction of the 'actions' (right, left, and front) and the manœuvres depending on them, thus perfecting that mobility which, since the practice of Anderson's new principles of manœuvre, had characterized the movements of field artillery batteries. Pieces could now be brought 'in battery' to the front, right or left, when on the line they were to occupy in action, by the gun detachments simply turning the carriages on their own ground, thus, if desired, effecting an important saving of time at a critical moment. The 'reverse' was for the first time employed, and to facilitate the execution of the manœuvre of coming into 'action' (right, left, and front). Throwing the caissons on the flank of the pieces while in column, with the formations 'in battery' from this position, was now for the first time also authorized.

The style of commands was a great improvement on Anderson, being briefer, yet clearer. As adding to the value of the work as a course of instruction, the careful drawings of the new style of carriage, with proper explanations thereof, deserve notice. Anderson's translation had not given these, which are necessary to any finished work of this nature. The most important improvements, however, wrought by the Instruction of 1845 consisted in the changes in the manual exercise and in the introduction of the manœuvres 'action' (right, left, and for coming into front).

Reference has been made to the circumstances which caused

the preparation of the Instruction of 1860 and to the scope of that work. In the various schools—of the piece, the section, and the battery—the preliminary principles were stated with a clearness and fullness that left nothing to be desired. For exercise without the guns the company in double rank was formed into detachments, of which those charged with the particular duties of the service of the pieces were designated gun detachments. On the left of each gun detachment, when paraded, were the drivers and others appertaining to the piece with its caisson, the whole divided into sets of eight men each, and constituting with that detachment the platoon. Two platoons formed a section. Manœuvring by detachment was, therefore, in all respects similar to the movements by sets of fours, which form the basis of the present infantry and cavalry tactics. This is all the more apparent in Tidball's Manual, where the principles of the artillery instructions of 1860 and the form of the present infantry tactics are blended, the commands 'detachment right,' 'right forward, detachment right,' &c., replacing the movements by fours of the infantry.

In the mere battery manœuvres there was very little difference between the Instruction of 1860 and its predecessor. Bricoles were entirely dispensed with, no provision being made, as had always been the case before, for their use under any circumstances. For short distances the movements by hand, both unlimbered and limbered—the former introduced by Anderson and the latter in 1860—had rendered bricoles unnecessary, while for long distances horses were put in requisition. In Anderson and the Instruction of 1845 the guide, in obliquing, had always been on the side opposite to that towards which the movement was made. For instance, if obliquing towards the right, the guide was left; and *vice versa*. This was now changed, the guide, as it has remained since, being placed on the side towards which the oblique was made. In the school of the battery the guidon was introduced, and his functions made somewhat similar to those of the general guides of Lallemand. Contrary to the practice of Anderson and the Instruction of 1845, the chief of caissons was, in column, placed on the side opposite the captain.

It was more particularly in a clear exposition of the principles on which field artillery rested, both as regards organization and service, both in war and in peace, in campaign as well as on the field of exercise, and in its entire independence of other tactics, that the Instruction of 1860 surpassed all that had preceded it. The equipment of a battery, both in personnel and matériel; and its management, both as a school for subalterns and under all circumstances of war, marches, transportation, encampment, and conduct in action, were fully and clearly laid down with many practical suggestions—the result of experience in the field.

There was, however, in the Instruction of 1860 a defect which has been corrected in its successor, the present assimilated artillery tactics. It was an attempt to generalize too much in the arrangement of details. While generalizations, properly presented, facilitate the understanding of a complex subject, by placing the salient points in bold relief before the mind, they cannot be carried too far without defeating their object, which is, to make easy the ready comprehension of important features, around which naturally, and with little mental effort, details may be left to arrange themselves. There should, therefore, be a direct and obvious connection between the main head and the subordinate heads grouped under it; but this in the instructions in question was sometimes wanting.

Leaving out of consideration the articles on organization, matériel, and service, the subject-matter of instruction was arranged under (1) the 'school of the piece,' (2) 'school of the section,' and (3) 'school of the battery'; but except the last, it was not possible, without examination, to divine what subjects were classified under each. The 'school of the piece,' for instance, embraced (1) cannoneers dismounted, (2) manual and exercise of the sabre, (3) exercise of gun detachment, dismounted, (4) manual of the piece, (5) mechanical manœuvres, (6) school of the soldier, mounted, (7) riding house drill, (8) gun detachment mounted (horse artillery), and (9) school of the driver. With the 'school of the piece' properly speaking, most of these subjects of instruction had nothing directly to do. There was not the relation between them of antecedent and consequent. The impropriety of the arrangement seems sufficiently manifest, and led to a curious error in the contemporaneous heavy artillery tactics, where it is stated that 'the cannoneer, previous to receiving instruction in heavy artillery, should be thoroughly instructed in the school of the piece, field artillery.' By 'school of the piece' is here meant, of course, manual of the piece, for nothing could be more absurd or unnecessary than to require foot artillerymen, as a preliminary to heavy artillery exercise, to learn all that appertained to the 'school of the piece,' field artillery instruction, before enumerated.

The arrangement of the 'school of the section' was almost as objectionable as the other. It embraced the drill of several detachments—(1) dismounted, (2) mounted; (3) exercise (mounted) of several pieces; (4) school of the section, *i. e.*, the school of the section was a sub-head under the more general one, 'school of the section'—than which a more confusing and incongruous classification cannot easily be imagined.

While it is theoretically very well to have the schools of the platoon and the battery distinct, in order that the former may serve as a preliminary to the latter, it is practically objectionable. First, it is unnecessary, the school of the battery embracing that of the platoon; second, because, with beginners, of the constant and annoying references that have to be made to the latter school, that a proper understanding may be had of battery manœuvres. In the assimilated tactics these schools are combined into that of the battery—a change which seems to be conducive to simplicity and convenience.

The assimilated tactics which appeared in 1873 but more fully carried out attempts in that general direction which had marked the labors of military writers for many years. Stevens in his system of discipline based the dismounted manœuvres of artillery troops on the infantry instructions of Baron Steuben—a fact noticed in the introduction, in the following words:

"I must acknowledge myself greatly indebted to Baron Steuben's Regulations for the Discipline of the Army, from which I have received abundant assistance in blending the duty of the artillery with that of the infantry. Where they are connected in the following work I have adopted its principles, and have extracted from it whatever I deemed necessary or useful to my plan."

In pursuance of this idea, Anderson and his successors remarked that "the same general principles regulate the manœuvres of infantry, cavalry, and artillery. As the former, however, makes up the main body of an army, its movements must control those of other arms of service. Hence the infantry forms of command have been adopted for the artillery where the difference between the two services would permit. A battery executes nearly the same manœuvres as a battalion (of infantry), but with less precision, its elements not being susceptible of manœuvring with the same geometrical accuracy as platoons of well-instructed infantry."

The experience of the Civil war showed that an officer might be rapidly transferred from one arm of service to another. The arms themselves were sometimes called upon to interchange their normal duties; the infantry to serve mounted, the cavalry dismounted; the artillery to act sometimes on foot and again on horseback.

Although each arm had an appropriate code of its own, which could not be subordinated to the manœuvres of other troops, it was a recognized fact that the same general principles lay at the foundation of all. Hence, so far as was practicable, the experience acquired in any one should be made available in the others. That this might the more easily and satisfactorily be done, it was peculiarly proper to assimilate the instruction for the three arms, in so far as the tactical elements of each and the character of each service would permit.

In executing this task it was necessary, on the one hand, to make the good of the whole service paramount, and, disregarding mere prejudices or fancies, to render the assimilation as complete as possible; on the other, to avoid indulging a passion for change, which, confounding words with the things they represent, would, under the guise of assimilation, apply general, inflexible rules to elements peculiar to each arm, and which cannot properly be subjected to the same laws. While the blending process went on it was necessary to remember that each arm had a distinct personal identity that could not be sacrificed without injury to not only the arm itself but to the general service.

The evolutions of a brigade, some forms of inspection and review, an article on horses and stable duty similar to that of the cavalry tactics, with others on honors to be paid by troops, and on the service of the mitrailleur, embodied in the assimilated tactics, were either wholly or partially new to light artillery instruction; that on horses and stables being an elaboration of the same subject, as presented in the Instruction of 1860. The remaining portion of the work was a recast of materials, culled mostly from the latter system of artillery instruction and from the established infantry tactics.

First is the school of the soldier (squad drill) dismounted. This is identical, or nearly so, for the three arms, and there is no reason why it should not be. The manual and exercise of the sabre, the manual of the piece, and mechanical manœuvres are essentially as in the Instruction of 1860. In the manual of the piece the only change of consequence was the introduction of 'action rear' for forming 'in battery' in the direction indicated.

The school of the battery dismounted was the counterpart of 'exercises of several detachments dismounted,' instructions of 1860; but it introduced some new and important features of organization which deserve notice. That which before was known as *platoon* was now called *section;* that formerly designated *section* now became *platoon*. The section embraced the personnel for the service of a piece with its caisson; two sections formed a platoon. In the school of the battery these definitions were given a slightly different significance; there a piece with its caisson, manned, horsed, and equipped, being designated a section, two sections forming, as before, a platoon.

The school of the soldier mounted, with that of horse-artillery detachments, was but slightly changed from the work of 1860, whence were also gathered most of the materials for the school of the driver, the only exceptions being in the latter, and embraced the introduction of Lallémand's school of the battle piece, and the exercise of a single unhitched team. In this school (driver) the 'reverse' of former tactics becomes 'left about'; the former 'left about' changes to 'reverse.' Differing also from previous practices in the passage of carriages, that which is passed takes up the gait of the passing carriage; formerly the converse of this was true.

The manœuvres 'school of the battery' are so nearly identical with those of 1845 and 1860 as not to require further notice. The difference between them resulted not from the invention of new manœuvres, but in applying the principles of assimilation. The movements as taken from former tactics are supposed to be performed by commands drawn from the infantry. This, apparently, was the great end to be attained. To a degree the labor was successful. The similarity of commands perhaps enables one versed in the tactics of either infantry or cavalry to more readily acquire those of the artillery. It will not escape notice, either, that rules for the guides, for the movements of the guidon, changes of gait, together with the duties in all formations of each of the battery personnel, are more carefully prescribed than ever before. This gives a more finished school than others had done, for these details are not embellishments—they are essentials in any perfect system of instruction.

It would be useless to recite the various points of difference between the assimilated tactics and those which preceded them. But one principle for giving commands may be mentioned, as its tendency is manifestly in the direction of simplicity. It is this: In other tactics an entirely different command was given when a movement was executed from a halt from that used when the same movement was executed from the march. In the assimilation, the commands are the same, except the addition of 'trot' or 'gallop' in the second case. For instance, being in line at a halt, to break column of sections to the front by the old system the commands were—(1) by section from the right (or left) front into column; (2) march; guide left (or right). Or if the line were advancing—(1) by the right (or left), break sections; (2) march; (3) guide left (or right). In the new system, whether at a halt or marching, the commands are—(1) right (or left), by platoons; (2) march; guide (right or left): if marching, and the movement is to be performed at an increased gait, the command 'trot' or 'gallop' precedes the command 'march.' The principle here illustrated is of general application, and is in accord with the infantry rule. Not so, however, with the commands (1) forward, (2) march, which, in the light artillery tactics, are not given except to move forward from a halt or from an oblique; never after a change of direction—an innovation not in the line of assimilation to the infantry, but the contrary.

The interchange of the designations 'section' and 'platoon,' the movements 'left about' and 'reverse,' was apparently inspired by a consuming desire for varying what had gone before. There is no reason based on true principles of assimilation why the term 'section,' to designate two pieces of artillery with their caissons, should not have been retained. And as with that meaning it was well established in the military vocabulary, while 'platoon' is not, the technical language has been garbled without corresponding benefit.

In the United States service the designation 'platoon' had been applied to a variable number of men in ranks; it had been used in the tactics of artillery, infantry and cavalry, both mounted and dismounted, but the idea of a definite number of units of any kind was never associated with it. On the other hand, from Lallemand down, when a battery was equipped, the term 'section' had been used to designate two pieces and their caissons—a fixed number. In infantry, cavalry, and dismounted artillery, 'platoon' retains its primitive signification; not so, however, when applied to field batteries; there it has come to signify a certain unalterable number. This is a violation of one of the first principles in military organization, which is never, if possible to avoid it, to have the same term applied to things essentially different in their natures, it being of the greatest importance that perfectly distinct names should be used in all armies.

If this change had led towards the goal for which the field artillery tactics were revised—assimilation—it would have been more reasonable; but in truth nothing of the kind resulted. The artillery platoon column is that for manœuvre; in infantry the habitual column of manœuvre is that of fours or of companies; assimilation is not gained here. Moreover, the section of artillery, like the platoon, is a unit which may be used for manœuvre. We have, for instance, 'right by platoon,' and also 'right by section;' and as both are thus retained, why interchange their long-established meaning?

It may be answered that it was necessary to apply a definite term to the piece, taken in conjunction with its caisson, instead of, as formerly, considering them a unit, covered by the term *piece*. While attaching no importance to this, as the old nomenclature had not led to any confusion, it is remarked that, granting this to be true, it had been far better in the assimilated tactics to have given the designation 'platoon' to a piece with its caisson, as the Instruction of 1860 had already given to their personnel, and retained 'section' to mean two platoons; it would have been equally as conducive to assimilation, and would have retained in the artillery vocabulary terms with their proper and well-known signification.

So in regard to 'reverse' and 'left about'; nothing was gained by their interchange. There is no 'reverse' in infantry or cavalry, and the 'left about' with these arms is executed on a fixed pivot, while in field-battery drill it is always executed on a movable pivot. Assimilation was not gained in this instance; therefore the only result was the mixing up of terms before well understood.

The great object kept in view in the work of assimilation seems to have been to render the commands similar to those of infantry. While the new signification given the term *platoon* lends a color of success to this questionable improvement, it is plain that in other respects, notably the rules for guides, the changes have led in the reverse direction. Mere similarity of commands is of itself of little value, which cannot justify the sacrifice of a single principle in the organization or manœuvres of any arm; yet if this similarity in commands be conceded the crowning triumph of the new dispensation, it is about all that can be claimed for it. This has been attained at the expense of technical language, a forced and unnatural parallelism in the treatment of the dissimilar elements of infantry, cavalry, and artillery, and a surrender of artillery (perhaps cavalry) independence, which cannot lead, if allowed to work out its natural results, to other than a conscious self-abasement of that arm, which is made to feel from first to last that its identity as artillery is being impaired, and, so far as possible, destroyed.

APPENDIX.

A [1].

List of Field and Staff Officers and Captains of Colonel Richard Gridley's Regiment of American Artillery, 1775.

Colonel, Richard Gridley; lieutenant-colonel, William Burbeck; first major, David Mason; second major, Scarborough Gridley;* surgeon, William Eustis; surgeon's mates, Samuel Tenny and Elijah Hewins; adjutant, Jeremiah Niles; quartermaster, Thomas Edes; captains, Edward Crafts, Joseph Chadwick, Edward Burbeck, Thomas Waite Foster, Thomas Pierce, Samuel Gridley, John Popkins, Samuel R. Trevett, John Wiley,† and John Callender.‡

Organization of Colonel Richard Gridley's Regiment.

One colonel, 1 lieutenant-colonel, 2 majors, 1 surgeon, 2 surgeon's mates, 1 adjutant, and 1 quartermaster. (2 cadets, 4 conductors, 1 store-keeper, and 2 clerks attached to regimental staff.)

Ten companies, each 1 captain, 1 captain-lieutenant, 1 first lieutenant, 2 second lieutenants (who were also fire-workers), 4 sergeants, 4 corporals, 6 gunners, 6 bombardiers, and 32 matrosses.

---

*Dismissed by sentence of court-martial September 24th, 1775, for misconduct at Bunker Hill. Vacant majority offered December 11th, 1775, to Mr. Thomas Crafts, Jr. (declined.)

† Superseded June 25th, 1775, by Ezra Badlam.

‡ Dismissed July 7th, 1775, for cowardice at Bunker Hill.

NOTE.—The title 'captain-lieutenant' was taken from the British, where it had been introduced in 1720, and where, by Royal warrant, June 22d, 1772, captain-lieutenants of artillery and of engineers were given the rank of captains in the army at large. The title was abolished in the Royal artillery in 1802, and that of 'second captain' substituted for it; and as in 1872 the first captains in that service were designated majors, the second captains dropped the 'second,' and became captains (though not commanders) of the batteries of the Royal artillery. In the American service the title captain-lieutenant did not survive the Revolution, and nothing took its place. So long as it continued, however, the position, although not equal to that of captain, was markedly above that of first lieutenant, the grade next below, and which finally crowded it out. The distinction is well shown in the rate of pay given by Congress pursuant

A [2].

Organization of Fourth Battalion, Royal Regiment of Artillery, 1771.

One colonel commandant, 1 lieutenant-colonel, 1 major, 1 adjutant, 1 quartermaster, and 1 chaplain.

Ten companies, each 1 captain, 1 captain-lieutenant, 2 first lieutenants, 2 second lieutenants, 2 sergeants, 2 corporals, 4 bombardiers, 8 gunners, 2 drummers, and 52 matrosses.

A [3].

List of Commissioned Officers of Colonel Henry Knox's Regiment of Continental Artillery, as Organized Pursuant to Resolve of Congress, December 2d, 1775, and Subsequent Resolves.

Colonel, Henry Knox; first lieutenant-colonel, William Burbeck; second lieutenant-colonel, David Mason; first major, John Crane; second major, John Lamb (appointed chief of artillery, northern department, pursuant to a resolve of Congress, January 9th, 1776, with rank of major; assigned by the commander-in-chief to Knox's regiment); chaplain, Rev. Abiel Leonard; adjutant, Jeremiah Niles; quartermaster, David Bradley; surgeon, William Eustis.

Captains—Edward Crafts, Thomas Pierce, Thomas Waite Foster, John Popkins, Edward Burbeck, William Perkins, Dimond Morton, Stephen Badlam, Eliphalet Newall, William Dana, Ebenezer Stevens, and Jotham Drury.

Captain-lieutenants—Benjamin Eustis, William Treadwell, Benjamin Frothingham, Timothy Stow, Jotham Horton, Edward

---

to resolve of July 29th, 1775. While a captain of artillery received one-third more pay, a captain-lieutenant of artillery received the same pay as a captain of infantry, and the artillery first lieutenant received one-tenth less pay than the latter.

The title 'fire-worker' was also inherited from the British, where it was the name given the lowest lieutenant of the company, who was generally, though not always, promoted from cadet gunners. The rank fire-worker was abolished in the British service in 1771, nor did it long survive in the American. No mention of it is made in any organization after 1777.

NOTE.—The Royal artillery was reorganized in such manner in 1782 as to increase the number of field officers from the ratio one field to twenty-one company officers, to the ratio one field to eight and one-half company officers. The change was for the avowed purpose of removing the stagnation in promotion that had weighed down that arm of service.

APPENDIX. 333

Rumney, David Allen, Winthrop Sergeant, John Johnson, Thomas Seward, Asa Rawson, and Benajah Carpenter.

First lieutenants—Thomas Randall, David Briant, Henry Burbeck, William Stevens, John Welch Edes, Samuel Treat, John Bryant, Isaac Coren, Isaac Packard, Jonas Simmons, David Cook, and John Sluman.

Second lieutenants—Henry Wells, John Lillie, Joseph Loring, Thomas Vose, Thomas Deane, David Preston, Thomas Jackson, James Furnivol, Peter King, Joseph Savage, Joseph Thomas, Samuel Shaw, Daniel Parker, Hardy Peirce, Isaiah Simmons, Oliver Brown, John Chandler, Thomas Machin, Joseph Blake, John Bull, James Steele, Thomas Carnes, Samuel Daggatt, and Jeremiah Freeman.

Organization of Knox's Regiment, 1776.

One colonel, 2 lieutenant-colonels, 2 majors, 1 chaplain, 1 adjutant, 1 quartermaster, 1 surgeon, 1 surgeon's mate, 1 drum-major, and 1 fife-major.

Twelve companies, each 1 captain, 1 captain-lieutenant, 1 first lieutenant, 2 second lieutenants, 4 sergeants, 4 corporals, 6 bombardiers, 6 gunners, 1 drum, 1 fife, and 32 matrosses.

A [4].

List of Commissioned Officers, Battalion of Artillery, Composed of two Companies of Knox's Regiment, Detached March 28th, 1776, for Service with Army Operating in Canada, and given a Battalion Organization by the Commanding Generals, Northern Department.

Stephen Badlam, captain, commander, with rank of major; Thomas Kendell, chaplain, appointed by General Gates; Alexander Stewart, surgeon, appointed by General Thompson; James Gardner, quartermaster, appointed by General Thomas; Ebenezer Stevens, captain; Benjamin Eustis, captain-lieutenant; Asa Rawson, captain-lieutenant; Henry Wells, first lieutenant; David Cook, first lieutenant; Thomas Vose, second lieutenant; Isaiah Simmons, second lieutenant; John Bull, second lieutenant; Samuel Daggatt, second lieutenant; James Gardner, conductor.

NOTE.—These companies were commanded by Captain Stevens while *en route* from Boston to Canada, where Badlam joined them. Although provisionally arranged as a battalion, they remained part of Knox's regiment.

A [5].

Names, Rank, and Dates of Commissions of the Officers of Colonel Charles Harrison's Regiment of Continental Artillery, Organized Pursuant to Resolve of Congress, November 26th, 1776.

N. B.—The data which follows is gathered from proceedings of the Continental Congress, from Saffell's records of the Revolutionary war, and those of the State Department, Washington. As affecting this regiment, the State Department records are only fragmentary, but, so far as they go, they confirm generally the correctness of Saffell's compilation.

Colonel, Charles Harrison, commissioned November 30th, 1776; lieutenant-colonel, Edward Carrington, commissioned November 30th, 1776; major, Christian Holmer, commissioned November 30th, 1776; adjutant, William Camp, commissioned as adjutant June 1st, 1778; adjutant, Richard Waters, commissioned as adjutant September 21st, 1778; paymaster, Ambrose Bohannon, commissioned as paymaster June 1st, 1778; quartermaster, Jervis Adams, commissioned November 21st, 1777; quartermaster, Clement Skerrett, commissioned December 6th, 1779; surgeon, Thomas Chrystie, appointed April 1st, 1778; surgeon's mate, Jonathan Calvert, appointed November 30th, 1776; surgeon's mate, Alexander Lajournade, appointed March 15th, 1778; sergeant-major, John Coale, appointed November 30th, 1776; quartermaster-sergeant, Griffitt Evans, appointed November 30th, 1776; drum-major, Robert Hart, appointed November 30th, 1776; fife-major, Thomas Parr, appointed November 30th, 1776. Captains (commissioned by Congress November 30th, 1776)—Samuel Denny, Nathaniel Burwell, William Pierce, Buller C. Claiborne, Joseph Scott, William Murray, Spotswood Dandridge, Matthew Smith, Sir John Pettus, and William Waters.

The Assembly of Virginia was authorized to appoint the subalterns. Of the captains, Claiborne, Scott, and Dandridge declined, and Congress, February 7th, 1777, appointed Anthony Singleton, John Winter, and Jacob Walker in their stead.

The commissioned officers attached to the various companies on the dates and at the places specified are given by Saffell as follows:

Company No. 1. Valley Forge, June 3d, 1778.—Captain, William Pierce, commissioned November 30th, 1776; captain-lieutenant, William Frazier, commissioned November 30th, 1776; first lieutenant, Thomas Dix, commissioned January 15th, 1778; first lieutenant, Samuel Coleman, commissioned June 15th, 1778.

Company No. 2. Valley Forge, June 3d, 1778.—Captain, Nathaniel Burwell, A. D. C. to Brigadier-General Howe, commissioned November 30th, 1776; captain-lieutenant, John Blair, commissioned November 30th, 1776; first lieutenant, William Camp (adjutant), commissioned November 30th, 1776; first lieutenant, William Stevenson, commissioned June 15th, 1778.

Company No. 3. Valley Forge, June 3d, 1778. — Captain, Anthony Singleton, commissioned February 1st, 1777; captain-lieutenant, Ambrose Bohannon (paymaster), commissioned January 13th, 1777; first lieutenant, William Miller, commissioned January 13th, 1777; second lieutenant, Henry Wallace, commissioned March 1st, 1778.

Company No. 4. Pluckemin, July 16th, 1779.—Captain, Drury Ragsdale, commissioned February 7th, 1777; captain-lieutenant, William Godman, commissioned January 1st, 1778; first lieutenant, Richard Waters (adjutant), commissioned January 13th, 1777; second lieutenant, William Darvil, commissioned February 7th, 1777.

Company No. 5. Valley Forge, June 3d, 1778. — Captain, James Pendleton, commissioned February 7th, 1777; captain-lieutenant, John Prior, commissioned February 13th, 1777.

Company No. 6. Valley Forge, June 4th, 1778. — Captain, John Dandridge, commissioned February 7th, 1777; captain-lieutenant, William Meredith, commissioned January 13th, 1777; first lieutenant, Michael McNamera, commissioned January 1st, 1778; second lieutenant, Walter Richardson, commissioned March 4th, 1778.

Company No. 7. Valley Forge, June 3d, 1778.—Captain, John Champe Carter, commissioned October 30th, 1777; first lieutenant, William Poythress, commissioned November 20th, 1777; second lieutenant, Robert Dandridge, commissioned October 30th, 1777.

Company No. 8. Valley Forge, June 3d, 1778.—Captain, Samuel Eddens, commissioned January 1st, 1778; captain-lieutenant, Lewis Booker, commissioned January 13th, 1777; first lieutenant, Richard Hill, commissioned October 20th, 1777; second lieutenant, Abraham Cole, commissioned November 30th, 1777.

Company No. 9. Valley Forge, June 3d, 1778. — Captain, Thomas Baytop, commissioned February 5th, 1778; captain-lieutenant, William Flemming Gaines, commissioned October 20th, 1777; first lieutenant, Holland Haynie, commissioned November 30th, 1777; second lieutenant, William Stevenson, commissioned September 30th, 1777; second lieutenant, James Tyrie, commissioned April 23d, 1778.

Company No. 10. Valley Forge, June 3d, 1778.—Captain, John Henry, commissioned February 7th, 1777; captain-lieutenant, William Meredith, commissioned January 13th, 1777; first lieutenant, Thomas Fenn, commissioned January 13th, 1777.

By orders of General Washington, May 30th, 1778, the two Maryland companies of Captains Brown and Dorsey were annexed to Harrison's regiment, thus bringing it, in pursuance of the resolve of Congress, May 27th, 1778, up to twelve companies.

Captain, William Brown, commissioned November 22d, 1777; captain-lieutenant, James Smith, commissioned November 22d, 1777; first lieutenant, James McFadden, commissioned November 22d, 1777; second lieutenant, Clement Skerritt (quartermaster), commissioned February 5th, 1778.

Dorsey's Company. Valley Forge, June 3d, 1778.—Captain, Richard Dorsey, commissioned May 4th, 1777; captain-lieutenant, Ebenezer Finley, commissioned July 4th, 1777; first lieutenant, Robert Wilmott, commissioned November 24th, 1777 ; second lieutenant, Nicholas Ricketts, commissioned December 1st, 1777; second lieutenant, Young Wilkinson, commissioned February 25th, 1778.

Organization of Colonel Harrison's Regiment, Under Resolve of Congress, November 26th, 1776, and Other Resolves.

One colonel, 1 lieutenant-colonel, 1 major, 1 surgeon, 1 surgeon's mate, 1 adjutant, 1 quartermaster, 1 paymaster, 1 sergeant-major, 1 quartermaster-sergeant, 1 fife-major, and 1 drum-major.

Ten companies, each 1 captain, 1 captain-lieutenant, 1 first lieutenant, 1 second lieutenant, 1 sergeant, 4 corporals, 4 bombardiers, 8 gunners, and 48 matrosses.

A [6].

Writing to the President of Congress from camp above Trenton Falls, December 20th, 1776, General Washington remarked: "Under the resolution of Congress of the 12th instant, at the instance of Colonel Knox and the pressing advice of all general officers now here, I have ventured to order three battalions of artillery to be immediately raised." These battalions, commanded by Colonels Lamb, Crane, and Flower, subsequently formed the Second and Third regiments of regular artillery and the so-called artillery-artificer regiment of the Revolutionary army.

List of Officers of Colonel John Crane's Regiment (or Battalion) of Continental Artillery as First Organized.

Colonel, John Crane, commissioned January 1st, 1777; lieutenant-colonel, ———; major, ———; adjutant, James Gardner, commissioned January 1st, 1777; quartermaster, Thomas Baker (April 12th, 1777, to November 1st, 1778); paymaster, Charles Knowles, commissioned January 1st, 1777; surgeon, Isaac Spofford, commissioned January 1st, 1777; surgeon's mate, Benjamin Upham, commissioned January 1st, 1777.

Captains (commissioned January 1st, 1777)—William Perkins, Jotham Drury, Benjamin Eustis, William Treadwell, Jotham Horton, David Allen, Thomas Seward, Winthrop Sergeant; and David Bryant, commissioned May 10th, 1777.

Captain-lieutenants (commissioned January 1st, 1777)—Henry Burbeck, Thomas Wells, David Cook, John Sluman, Thomas Jackson, Daniel Parker, Oliver Brown, Isaiah Bussey; and John Gridley, commissioned June 1st, 1777.

Supernumeraries (commissioned January 1st, 1777)—John Callender, Thomas Deane, Joseph Loring, Joseph Blake, and Jeremiah Niles.

First lieutenants (commissioned February 1st, 1777)—John Compston, John George, John Peirce, Eli Parsons, Edward Proctor, Noyes Arnold, Jacob Goldthwaite, Joseph Andrews, and Benjamin Allen.

Second lieutenants (commissioned February 1st, 1777)—James Hall, William Price, Zacheus Dunnell, John Harris, William Andrews, Artemus Knight, Daniel Jackson, Samuel Jefferds, Florence Crowley, Samuel Bass, Abijah Hammond, Joseph Bliss, David Mason, Thomas Bailey, Samuel Cooper, John Cooper, John Hiwell, Benjamin Eaton, Abraham Eustis, Jonathan Clark, David Putnam, John Crosier, ———— Le Brum, and George Hutton.

List of Officers of Crane's Regiment, September, 1778, after the Absorption of Lieutenant-Colonel Ebenezer Stevens' Battalion.

Colonel, John Crane; lieutenant-colonel, John Popkin, commissioned July 15th, 1777; major, William Perkins, commissioned September 12th, 1778; adjutant, James Gardner; paymaster, Charles Knowles; quartermaster, Thomas Baker; surgeon, Samuel Adams, commissioned May 12th, 1778; surgeon's mate, Benjamin Upham.

Captains—Benjamin Eustis, William Treadwell, Benjamin Frothingham, Winthrop Sergeant, Thomas Seward, Stephen Buckland, Nathaniel Donnell; John Winslow, commissioned June 8th, 1777; Henry Burbeck, commissioned September 12th, 1777; Thomas Wells, commissioned May 14th, 1778; David Cook, commissioned May 14th, 1778; John Sluman, commissioned September 12th, 1778.

Captain-lieutenants—John Lillie, William Johnson, Thomas Vose, Thomas Jackson, Samuel Shaw, Daniel Parker, Oliver Brown, Joseph Blake, John Callender, Isaiah Bussey, John Gridley; John Cumpston, commissioned September 12th, 1777.

First lieutenants—Joseph Perry, John Pierce, John George, Constant Freeman, James Gardner, Jacob Goldthwaite, Edward Proctor, Jacob Kemper, Eli Parsons; James Hall, commissioned September 12th, 1777; Jacob Welsh, commissioned September

12th, 1778; Charles Knowles, commissioned September 12th, 1778.

Second lieutenants—Daniel McLane, Zacheus Dunnell, William Price, Artemus Knight, Daniel Jackson, John Harris, Isaac Barber, Joseph Driskill, Richard Hunnewell, Thomas Bailey, William Andrews, David Mason, Samuel Jefferds, Florence Crowley, Abijah Hammond, John Crosier, John Hiwell, George Ingersoll, Joseph Bliss, Samuel Cooper, John Cooper, Samuel Bass, Benjamin Eaton, David Putnam, John Liswell, David Deming; Elias Parker, September 12th, 1777; Isaac Morey, January 1st, 1778; William Downe, May, 1778.

A [7].

Stevens' corps or battalion of artillery, absorbed in Crane's regiment in the fall of 1778, was organized in the following manner: As the terms of service of Knox's two companies, detached as already mentioned to the northern department, were about to expire, the Congressional committee which was sent to investigate the cause of disasters and set matters to rights in that quarter authorized the raising a small battalion of artillery, as appears in the following letter from Stevens to General Schuyler, then in command at Albany:

"TICONDEROGA, *November 25th*, 1776.

"The honorable the committee of Congress have been pleased to determine that a corps of artillery be raised in this department, consisting of four companies, three of artillery and one of artificers; and have been likewise pleased to give me command thereof, with the rank of major."

The next month Stevens was dispatched by Schuyler to Boston for the necessary matériel for the new corps, and also for recruits, neither of which could be obtained at Ticonderoga. From the circumstances under which this battalion was raised, Stevens looked upon his command as an independent organization. At the same time, however, that he was recruiting, Colonel Crane was likewise in Massachusetts raising his regiment, under the authority of the commander-in-chief. The authorities of the State, General Knox, and Colonel Crane all decided that Stevens' corps formed part of Crane's regiment, which, in consequence, was raised with but nine companies, the three of Stevens making up the complement. The controversy led to a bitter personal quarrel between Crane and Stevens, the latter declaring that he would resign rather than yield. This alternative would probably have been forced upon him had it not been for the fact that his battalion served in the northern department, without contact with the artillery regiments, until the fall of 1778, when, a vacancy happening in the lieutenant-colonelcy of the Second regiment,

Stevens was transferred to it, and his three artillery companies formally incorporated into Crane's regiment. That Stevens had practically carried his point, and that his corps was in fact a complete and independent organization, the following roster and data will abundantly prove:

Return of Stevens' Corps, June 20th, 1777.

Major, Ebenezer Stevens, commissioned November 9th, 1776; adjutant, Hezekiah Whetmore, commissioned February 1st, 1777; surgeon, John Stevenson, commissioned April 1st, 1777; commissary of military stores, Samuel Hodgdon, commissioned February 1st, 1777; first conductor, Benjamin Bartlett, commissioned January 9th, 1777; second conductor, Jasper Manduit Gidley, commissioned June 1st, 1777; director of laboratory, John Bull, commissioned June 15th, 1777; captain of artificers, Noah Nichols, commissioned November 9th, 1776; lieutenant of artificers, Nathaniel Call.

COMPANY OFFICERS.

Captains (commissioned November 9th, 1776)—Stephen Buckland, Nathaniel Donnell; John Winslow, commissioned June 8th, 1777 (paymaster, June 1st, 1778).

Captain-lieutenants (commissioned November 9th, 1776)— William Johnson, Thomas Vose, Thomas Barr.

First lieutenants (commissioned November 9th, 1776)—Joseph Perry, Constant Freeman, Jacob Kemper.

Second lieutenants (commissioned November 9th, 1776)—Jacob Welsh, Daniel McLane, George Ingersoll, Joseph Driskill, Isaac Barber ; Richard Hunnewell, commissioned February 1st, 1777; John Liswell, commissioned February 1st, 1777; David Deming, commissioned February 1st, 1777; Andrew H. Tracy, commissioned June 1st, 1777.

The dating of commissions, November 9th, 1776, seems to have been a local arrangement, and perhaps was part of the 'independent corps' idea. Certain it is that the records of the State of Massachusetts do not credit any of these officers with service under these commissions anterior to January 1st, 1777, when Crane's regiment was organized; and those dated November 9th, 1776, when transferred to that regiment formally, were cut down to date January 1st, 1777; and this determined their position in the Third artillery.

The anomalous position of this corps seems to have been due to the fact, in the first instance, that its organization was in effect a private arrangement between a Congressional committee and Captain Stevens, of which no one else knew anything, but which was, nevertheless, acquiesced in by the commanding generals of the northern department. The corps was an independent body, so long as it remained in that department, and was a law unto itself regarding dates of commissions and details of organization. Its isolated position, and the acknowledged ability, high character, and distinguished services of its commander made this fiction of independence a practical reality until the corps joined the main army in the fall of 1778; then a readjustment had to be effected and matters placed on a sound basis. This was done by assigning Stevens to a vacancy elsewhere, and placing his companies in the Massachusetts artillery regiment upon the same footing that would have been conceded them had they served with it from the date of its organization.

Of Stevens it is too much to assert that in ability he was the peer of any officer of the Revolutionary artillery. He only of all started low down, and was carried near the top on merit alone.. He was picked out by Congress and given rank step after step over the heads of others, in disregard of rules of promotion, which were generally treated as sacred. The justness of this statement is in nowise affected by the position of General Knox at the head of the artillery; nor is it intended to disparage either his talents, business capacity, or attainments in his special arm of service. He was selected from civil life, and given command of the artillery because of his youth, great energy, intelligence, and zeal in the service displayed as a volunteer under the eye of the commander-in-chief at a time when youth and energy were in demand. Having gained the first step, his subsequent advancement was both natural and proper; but there were no competitors in the field. With Stevens the case was different. Starting after the general reorganization of January, 1777, with several captains above him, he was breveted major by the Continental Congress May 27th, 1777; was breveted lieutenant-colonel of foot April 30th, 1778, and made full lieutenant-colonel of artillery November 24th, 1778, to date from his brevet of April 30th, Congress at the same time directing that he should be assigned to the first vacancy happening in that grade and arm. General Washington inclosed his commission December 17th following, assigning him, *vice* Oswald, to Lamb's regiment, which he joined on the 22d of that month.

The three artillery companies of which Stevens' corps was composed had each 1 captain, 1 captain-lieutenant, 1 first and 3 second lieutenants, 6 sergeants, 6 corporals, 6 bombardiers, 6 gunners, 1 drummer, 1 fifer, and 28 matrosses. The company of artificers had, when full, 1 captain (Noah Nicholls), 1 captain of cartridge-makers (Nathaniel Call), 1 foreman of smiths (Thomas Patton), 1 quartermaster (Bela Nicholls), 1 lieutenant (Joseph Olmstead), and about 40 enlisted men, all mechanics. This company was attached to the artillery park of the main army when Stevens' corps was broken up.

APPENDIX. 341

A [8].

Roster of Crane's Battalion (Regiment), April 16th, 1780.

Colonel, John Crane, January 1st, 1777; lieutenant-colonel, John Popkin, July 15th, 1777; major, William Perkins, September 12th, 1778; adjutant, James Gardner, January 1st, 1777; paymaster, Charles Knowles, January 1st, 1777; quartermaster, Samuel Cooper, May 9th, 1779; surgeon, Samuel Adams, May 14th, 1778; surgeon's mate, Benjamin Upham, January 1st, 1777.

Captains—William Treadwell, January 1st, 1777; Benjamin Frothingham, January 1st, 1777; Winthrop Sergeant, January 1st, 1777; Thomas Seward, January 1st, 1777; Nathaniel Donnell, January 1st, 1777; Henry Burbeck, September 12th, 1777; David Cook, March 14th, 1778; John Sluman, September 12th, 1778; John Lillie, November 1st, 1778; Thomas Vose, December 2d, 1778; Thomas Jackson, February 22d, 1780; Samuel Shaw, April 12th, 1780.

Captain-lieutenants—William Johnson, January 1st, 1777; Thomas Barr, January 1st, 1777; John Callender, January 1st, 1777; Isaiah Bussey, January 1st, 1777; John Gridley, January 1st, 1777; John Pierce, September 12th, 1778; John George, October 1st, 1778; Constant Freeman, October 1st, 1778; Jacob Kemper, December 2d, 1778; James Gardner, February 22d, 1780; Jacob Goldthwaite, March 6th, 1780; James Hall, April 12th, 1780.

First lieutenants—Charles Knowles, August 1st, 1778; Daniel McLane, September 12th, 1778; William Price, September 12th, 1778; Daniel Jackson, September 12th, 1778; Samuel Jefferds, October 1st, 1778; Florence Crowley, October 1st, 1778; Abijah Hammond, December 2d, 1778; Joseph Driskill, May 7th, 1779; George Ingersoll, June 10th, 1779; John Hiwell, February 22d, 1780; Isaac Barber, March 6th, 1780; Thomas Bayley, April 12th, 1780.

Second lieutenants—William Andrews, February 1st, 1777; David Mason, February 1st, 1777; John Liswell, February 1st, 1777; Joseph Bliss, February 1st, 1777; Samuel Cooper, February 1st, 1777; Samuel Boss, February 1st, 1777; Benjamin Eaton, February 1st, 1777; Elias Parker, September 12th, 1777; Moses Porter, January 1st, 1778; William Moore, September 9th, 1778; Edward Blake, September 10th, 1778.

The organization of Crane's regiment, when raised, was the same as that of Lamb's regiment, authorized at the same time;

NOTE.—Samuel Shaw was brigadier-major (assistant adjutant-general) of the artillery brigade from May 11th, 1777.

but in the former, as has been mentioned, Stevens' corps was considered as furnishing three companies to complete the organization to that authorized by the commander-in-chief. It was as follows:

One colonel, 1 lieutenant-colonel, 1 major, 1 adjutant, 1 quartermaster, 1 paymaster, 1 surgeon, 1 surgeon's mate, 1 sergeant-major, 1 quartermaster-sergeant, 1 drum-major, and 1 fife-major.

Twelve companies, each 1 captain, 1 captain-lieutenant, 1 first lieutenant, 3 second lieutenants, 6 sergeants, 6 corporals, 6 bombardiers, 6 gunners, 1 drum, 1 fife, and 28 matrosses.

It is probable that this organization for artillery regiments was adopted at the instance of General Knox, as it is almost identical with that proposed by him to the commander-in-chief, and mentioned by the latter in his letter of December 20th, 1776, to the President of Congress. [6, *ante.*] This supposition is strengthened by the fact that when, May 27th, 1778, a general reorganization was given the army, including the artillery, Crane's, Lamb's, Harrison's, and Proctor's regiments were all given the organization just mentioned as that of Crane's and Lamb's regiments, January 1st, 1777, with the single exception that while in the latter the adjutant, quartermaster, and paymaster were extra lieutenants, in the organization of May 27th, 1778, these staff officers were made detailable from the captains and subalterns of each regiment.

A [9].

List of Commissioned Officers of Lamb's Regiment as First Organized.

Colonel, John Lamb, commissioned January 1st, 1777; lieutenant-colonel, Eleazer Oswald, commissioned January 1st, 1777; major, ———; adjutant, Isaac Hubbell, commissioned January 1st, 1777; quartermaster, William Fenno, commissioned March 5th, 1777; paymaster, John Dutton Crimshire, commissioned July 1st, 1777; surgeon, —— Hosmer; surgeon's mate, Caleb Austin, commissioned January 1st, 1777; captain of artificers, Anthony Post, commissioned January 1st, 1777; lieutenant of artificers, Garret Brower, commissioned January 1st, 1777; foreman, Samuel Johnson, commissioned January 1st, 1777.

Captains (commissioned January 1st, 1777)—Sebastian Beauman, James Lee, Isaiah Wool, Samuel Mansfield, Samuel Lockwood, Andrew Moodie, Robert Walker, Gresham Mott, John Doughty, and Thomas Theodore Bliss.

Captain-lieutenants (commissioned January 1st, 1777)—Samuel Treat, William Stevens, James Simonds, George Flemming, Joseph Thomas, Joseph Savage, Thomas Machin, Thomas Thompson, William Powers, James McClure, Daniel Ganno, and Jonathan Pearsia.

APPENDIX. 343

Supernumeraries (commissioned January 1st, 1777)—Edward Archibald, Jacob Reed, Cornelius Swartwout, and Ephraim Fenno.

First lieutenants (commissioned February 1st, 1777)—Thomas Sutton, Baxter Howe, Sheppard Kollock, John Miles, Isaac Hubbell, Henry Warring, Clarkson Edgar, James McNair, Samuel Webb, Caleb Brewster, and James Mackinson.

Second lieutenants (commissioned February 1st, 1777)—Elisha Harvey, Peter Nestill, Joseph Ashton, Isaiah Thompson, James Brewster, Stephen Alling, Isaac Guion, Francis Shaw, Peter Woodward, Cornelius Cunningham, John Troop, George Laycraft, Henry Bogart, Oliver Lawrence, William Cebra, James Hughes, William Hubbell, John Waldron, Chilion Ford, Robert Parker, Ezra Patterson, Ezekiel Howell, Samuel Whiting, Samuel Doughty, Alexander Guy, and George Whipple.

List of Commissioned Officers of Colonel Lamb's Battalion (or Regiment) of Artillery, September 12th, 1778.

Colonel, John Lamb, January 1st, 1777; lieutenant-colonel, Eleazer Oswald, January 1st, 1777 (left regiment in July, 1778; place filled December, 1778); major, Sebastian Beauman, September 12th, 1778; adjutant, Joseph Ashton; quartermaster, William Fenno, March 5th, 1777; paymaster, John Dutton Crimshire, July 1st, 1777; surgeon, ———; surgeon's mate, Caleb Austin, January 1st, 1777; captain of artificers, Anthony Post, January 1st, 1777; lieutenant of artificers, Garret Bower, January 1st, 1777; foreman, Samuel Johnson, January 1st, 1777.

Captains (commissioned January 1st, 1777)—James Lee, Isaiah Wool, John Doughty, Andrew Moodie, Gresham Mott, Thomas T. Bliss, Robert Walker, Samuel Lockwood, Andrew Porter, Samuel Mansfield, Jonathan Brown; and William Stevens, September 12th, 1778.

Captain-lieutenants (commissioned January 1st, 1777)—James Simonds, George Flemming, Joseph Savage, Joseph Thomas, Thomas Machin, Jacob Reed, Cornelius Swartwout, Thomas Thompson, Daniel Gano, Edward Archibald, Ephriam Fenno, James McClure, and William Power.

First lieutenants (commissioned January 1st, 1777)—Isaac Hubbell, Baxter Howe, Henry Warring, Sheppard Kollock, John Miles, Caleb Brewster; and (commissioned September 12th, 1778) Isaac Guion, John Waldron, William Hubbell, Francis Shaw, Isaiah Thompson, and Joseph Ashton.

Second lieutenants (commissioned February 1st, 1777)—Elisha

NOTE.—Swartwout and Fenno were considered supernumeraries, being prisoners with the enemy.

Harvey, Peter Nestill, Samuel Doty, James Brewster, Stephen Alling, John Throop, Samuel Whiting (prisoner), George LeCraft, George Hutton, Oliver Lawrence, Chilion Ford, William Cebra, Robert Parker, Ezra Patterson, Ezekiel Howell, Peter Woodward; and William Strachan, commissioned September 23d, 1777.

(For authorized organization of Lamb's regiment, under the orders of the commander-in-chief, to date from January 1st, 1777, and also under the resolve of Congress, May 27th, 1778, see Crane's Battalion, Appendix [8, *ante*].)

List of the Officers of Lamb's Regiment at the end of the Revolutionary War.

Colonel, John Lamb; lieutenant-colonel, Ebenezer Stevens; major, Sebastian Beauman; surgeon, Garret Tunison.

Captains—John Doughty (brigade major of artillery), Andrew Moodie, Gresham Mott, Thomas T. Bliss, William Stevens, George Flemming, Joseph Savage, Joseph Thomas, Thomas Machin, and Jacob Reed.

Captain-lieutenants — Cornelius Swartwout, Ephriam Fenno, Isaac Hubbell, John Miles, Caleb Brewster, Isaac Guion, Isaiah Thompson, Elisha Harvey, Peter Nestle, and James Brewster.

Lieutenants—Stephen Alling, John R. Throop, George LeCraft, Chilion Ford, Robert H. Livingston, Hiel Peck, John Campbell, Michael Wetzell, Peter Woodward, William Strachan, James Bradford, Henry A. Williams, Henry Cunningham, Timothy Mix, William Pennington, Alexander Thompson, John Smith, Alexander Clinton, John Reed, Robert Burnet, William LeCraft, William Morris, Isaac Smith, Peter Tappen, Jonas Addoms, Henry Demlar, and John Shaw.

A [10].

List of Field Officers and Captains of Proctor's Regiment (or Battalion)—Fourth—of Continental Artillery.

Colonel, Thomas Proctor, commissioned February 6th, 1771, resigned April 9th, 1781; lieutenant-colonel, John Martin Strobagh, promoted from captain March 3d, 1777, died December 2d, 1778; Thomas Forrest, promoted, *vice* Strobagh, resigned, October 7th, 1781; lieutenant-colonel commandant, Andrew Porter, promoted from major December 24th, 1782, to rank from January 1st, 1782; served to end of war.

NOTE.—In the list of officers (Lamb's regiment) given above, and which is certified to by Colonel Lamb as being correct, there is no distinction in the grade of lieutenants; *i. e.*, they are not distinguished as first and second.

Majors—Thomas Forrest, from captain, February 5th, 1777 (promoted); Benjamin Eustis, commissioned December 2d, 1778, died October 6th, 1781. [This promotion was made in pursuance of the rule established, that captains and officers of higher rank should be advanced in the artillery line at large. Eustis came from Crane's regiment.] Andrew Porter, from captain, April 19th, 1781 (promoted); Isaac Craig, first major, from captain, *vice* Eustis, to rank from October 7th, 1781; Francis Proctor, Jr., second major, December 24th, 1782, ranking from January 1st, 1782, retired January 1st, 1783.

Captains—Gerard Jacob Dircks, March 3d, 1777, to July 6th, 1777 (resigned); Isaac Craig, March 3d, 1777, to October 7th, 1781 (promoted); Hercules Courtenay, March 3d, 1777, to March 3d, 1778 (dismissed); Joseph Rice, March 3d, 1777, to August 1st, 1780 (resigned); Francis Proctor, Sr., March 3d, 1777, to April 14th, 1778, (dismissed); Bartholomew Van Heer (captain of provost), March 3d, 1777, to June 1st, 1778 (resigned); Amos Wilkinson, March 14th, 1777, to ———; Francis Proctor, Jr., July 16th, 1777 (promoted); Charles Turnbull, July 16th, 1777, to ———, served to end of war; Patrick Duffy, February 29th, 1778, to October 12th, 1781 (dismissed); William Ferguson, April 14th, 1778, to end of war; John Brice, June 1st, 1778, to end of war; Robert Coultman, June 1st, 1778, retired January 1st, 1783; Worsley Emes, September 26th, 1780, retired January 1st, 1783; Andrew Porter, transferred from Lamb's regiment, January 1st, 1787 (promoted); James Simonds, transferred from Lamb's, January 1st, 1787, served to end of war; James McClure (*vice* Porter), April 19th, 1781, retired January 1st, 1783; William Power (*vice* Craig), October 7th, 1787, retired January 1st, 1783; Thomas Douglass, October 12th, 1787, retired January 1st, 1783; and William Martin (*vice* Proctor), January 1st, 1782, retired January 1st, 1783.

The following is the organization of the regiment as authorized by the Pennsylvania Council of Safety, February 6th, 1777:

One colonel, 1 lieutenant-colonel, 1 major, 1 adjutant, 1 quartermaster, 1 paymaster, 1 surgeon, 1 surgeon's mate, 1 sergeant-major, 1 quartermaster-sergeant, 1 drum-major, 1 fife-major, and 12 musicians for a band.

Eight companies, each 1 captain, 1 first lieutenant, 1 second

---

NOTE.—Although the record of the field officers and captains of this regiment is satisfactorily given, it is regretted that no list of the subalterns has been procured.

The grade of fireworker was unknown in any of the regular artillery organizations at this time, and it seems soon to have been discarded in this, and the grade of captain-lieutenant introduced here as elsewhere in that arm. The date of this change is not known, but it must have been immediately after the date of organization, as Courtenay, on March 3d, and Francis Proctor, Jr., and Turnbull, on July 16th. 1777, were promoted to be captains from captain-lieutenants.

lieutenant, 1 lieutenant-fireworker, 4 sergeants, 4 corporals, 1 drummer, 1 fifer, and 60 privates.

Proctor's regiment, with the others, partook of the general change of organization wrought by the resolve of Congress, May 27th, 1778. (See Crane's Regiment, *ante*, Appendix [8].) In fact, however, it was not found practicable to assign Proctor twelve companies, as contemplated by that organization. There were with the army when this change was proposed two companies of New Jersey artillery, the officers of one being Thomas Randall, captain; John Lillie, captain-lieutenant; Eli Elmore, first lieutenant; Seth Bowen and David More, second lieutenants. Of the other, Thomas Clark, captain; Thomas Jenner Carnes, captain-lieutenant; John Vandyke, first lieutenant. It was intended to place these in Lamb's regiment, and take therefrom the companies of Captains Porter and Lee. These latter, with another commanded by Captain Gibbs Jones, then unattached, were raised by no particular State, but chiefly recruited in Philadelphia, Delaware, and New Jersey. It was proposed to attach them to Proctor's regiment. This was not done; and Proctor remained with but eight companies until after the reorganization of October 3d and 21st, 1780, when Porter's and Lee's companies, the latter now commanded by Captain James Simonds, were transferred from Colonel Lamb's to Proctor's regiment, where Porter rose to the rank of lieutenant-colonel commandant.

Under the resolve of Congress, August 7th, 1782, the Fourth artillery was reduced, January 1st, 1783, to a battalion of four companies, still retaining, however, the regimental band. The commissioned roster was as follows:

Lieutenant-colonel commandant, Andrew Porter; major, Charles Craig.

Captains—Charles Turnbull, William Ferguson, John Brice, and James Simonds.

Captain-lieutenants—James Lloyd, James Smith, Robert McConnell, and Jesse Crosley.

First lieutenants—John Stricker, Samuel Doty, Joseph Ashton (paymaster), and John B. Webster (quartermaster).

Second lieutenants—Robert Parker (adjutant), Henry Greer, Ezekiel Howell, Robert Porter, James Gamble (from 4th Pennsylvania), John Humphrey (from 6th Pennsylvania), and John Van Court (from 6th Pennsylvania).

A [11].

The records show that the artillery-artificer regiment of Colonel Flower was a regiment in name only. Its officers, May 24th, 1780, were:

Colonel, Benjamin Flower; major, Joseph Eayres.

Captains—Coren, Jordan, Irish, Wylie, and Chapman.
Captain-lieutenants—William E. Godfrey and A. Dow.
Lieutenants—H. Stroop, George Norris, John Sproules, James Gibson, and Alexander Power.

There was no regimental staff. Flower was commissary-general of military stores. Major Eayres, who was borne on the rolls as a master mechanic, was at the Springfield (Massachusetts) armory. The captains and subalterns before mentioned were all employed in Pennsylvania, either at the armory at Philadelphia or the arsenal and laboratory at Carlisle. The artillery-artificers formed in fact, while an important, yet, when compared with the civil branch, an altogether secondary feature of the ordnance department.

A [12].

SOUTH CAROLINA ARTILLERY REGIMENT.

November 13th, 1775, the Provincial Congress of South Carolina resolved to raise a regiment (more properly a battalion) of artillery to serve not less than six months nor more than two years, and to consist of—

One lieutenant-colonel commandant, 1 major, 1 adjutant, 1 quartermaster, 1 surgeon, 1 surgeon's mate, 1 paymaster, 1 armorer, 1 assistant armorer, and 1 sergeant workman, to attend laboratory.

Three companies, each 1 captain, 1 first and 1 second lieutenant, 2 lieutenant fire-workers, 4 sergeants, 4 corporals, 10 gunners, 1 drum, 1 fife, and 86 matrosses.

The officers chosen by the Provincial Congress were: Lieutenant-colonel commandant, Owen Roberts; major, Barnard Elliott; captains, Barnard Beckman, Charles Drayton, and Sims White; paymaster, Paul Townshend; surgeon, John Budd.

The subalterns were to be selected by the captains with the approbation of the commandant.

June 18th, 1776, this battalion, although not expected to serve beyond the limits of South Carolina, was taken by the Continental Congress into the pay and service of the Revolutionary Government.

A [13].

Organization of the Regiments of Artillery, Regular Army of the United States, under the Resolves of Congress of October 3d and 21st, 1780.

One colonel, 1 lieutenant-colonel, 1 major, 1 adjutant, 1 paymaster, 1 quartermaster, 1 surgeon, 1 surgeon's mate, 1 sergeant-major, 1 quartermaster-sergeant, 1 drum-major, 1 fife-major, and 1 chaplain (to a brigade only).

Ten companies, each 1 captain, 1 captain-lieutenant, 1 first and 3 second lieutenants, 6 sergeants, 6 corporals, 6 bombardiers, 6 gunners, 1 drum, 1 fife, and 39 matrosses.

This remained the established organization until the end of the war.

APPENDIX. 349

A [14].

Troops Provisionally Retained in Service when the Revolutionary Army was Disbanded.

January 3d, 1784, Major-General Knox transmitted to the president of Congress a list of the officers retained, accompanied by a return showing the organization of the troops. As this paper is certified to by Knox as correct, and will prove of general interest, it is inserted here entire:

ARTILLERY.

	Major	Captain	Captain-Lieutenants	Lieutenants	Adjutant	Sergeants	Corporals	Bombardiers	Gunners	Matrosses	Total
	1	1	2	7	1	10	12	2	2	100	138

INFANTRY.

	Colonel	Lieutenant-Colonel	Major	Captains	Lieutenants	Ensigns	Adjutant	Paymaster	Quartermaster	Surgeon	Surgeon's Mate	Sergeant-Major	Quartermaster-Sergeant	Drum-Major	Fife-Major	Sergeants	Drums and Fifes	Rank and File
GENERAL HENRY JACKSON'S REGIMENT.	1	1	1	9	9	9	1	1	1	1	1	1	1	1		45	16	500
Invalids				4	4											2	1	27
Total	1	1	1	13	13	9	1	1	1	1	1	1	1	1		47	17	527

APPENDIX.

List of Officers.

ARTILLERY.

Major, Sebastian Beauman, commissioned September 12th, 1778; captain, John Doughty, commissioned January 1st, 1777; captain-lieutenants, William Johnson, commissioned January 1st, 1777, and Ephraim Fenno, commissioned January 1st, 1777; first lieutenants, William Price, commissioned September 12th, 1778, and Samuel Jefferds, commissioned October 1st, 1778; second lieutenant, Joseph Bliss, commissioned February 1st, 1777; lieutenant and adjutant, James Bradford, commissioned September 12th, 1778; lieutenants, Alexander Thompson, commissioned May 31st, 1779, and John Reed, commissioned June 29th, 1781.

Of the artillery, seventy non-commissioned officers and matrosses belonged to the New York line; fifty-five to the Massachusetts line. One subaltern and twenty-one men were *en route* to Fort Schuyler (Rome, N. Y.) to guard stores there and to take possession of the forts on the western lakes when surrendered by the British. One subaltern and twenty-three men were in New York city to assist in restoring civil government. The rest were at West Point or dependencies.

INFANTRY.

Colonel, Henry Jackson, January 12th, 1777; lieutenant-colonel, William Hull, August 12th, 1779; major, Caleb Gibbs, July 29th, 1778; adjutant, Lieutenant Charles Seldon, March, 1778; quartermaster, Lieutenant Henry Nelson, March 1st, 1782; paymaster, Lieutenant Thomas H. Condy, March 1st 1779; surgeon, John Hart, ———; surgeon's mate, Nathaniel Leavenworth ———.

Captains—Joseph Williams, January 1st, 1777; Isaac Frye, January 1st, 1777; Job Sumner, January 1st, 1777; William Mills, May 11th, 1781; John Hobby, July 24th, 1781; Joseph Potter, October 16th, 1781; Elnathan Haskell, April 1st, 1778; Thomas Hunt, March 1st, 1779; Simon Jackson, April 1st, 1782.

Lieutenants—Patrick Phelon, June 20th, 1777; Thomas Cushing, January 14th, 1778; Charles Seldon, (adjutant), Jonathan Haskell, February 5th, 1779; Thomas H. Condy (paymaster); Ralph H. Bowles, March 20th, 1779; Nathaniel Stone, March 20th, 1780; Joshua Merrow, July 12th, 1780; Gamaliel Bradford, September 3d, 1780; John Adams, October 6th, 1781; Henry Nelson (quartermaster); William Pickard, April 14th, 1782.

Ensigns—Caleb Swan, November 26th, 1779; James Sever, February 1st, 1781; James Sawyer, February 22d, 1781; Elisha Horton, April 2d, 1781; Jeremiah Lord, June 15th, 1781; John Rowe, June 15th, 1781; John Graton, July 16th, 1782; Amasa Jackson, October 13th, 1782; Charles Jackson, February 4th, 1783.

Of the infantry, 461 belonged to Massachusetts and 103 to New Hampshire.

Invalids—Captains, John McGovern, William Williams, Philip Seibert, and Leonard Cooper; captain-lieutenant, William McElhothen; lieutenants, Jonathan Pugh and James McLane.

One hospital mate (Dr. Coggswell) and one steward were, besides those enumerated, retained for hospital service at West Point.

A [15].

Provisional Force Recommended by a Congressional Committee in a Report of May 12th, 1784, to be Enlisted for Three Years, each State furnishing its Quota.

One adjutant-general, 1 inspector-general (both with rank and pay of major of infantry), 1 colonel, 1 lieutenant-colonel, and 1 major of engineers.

Three battalions of infantry, the staff for the whole being 1 colonel, 1 captain quartermaster, 1 captain paymaster and clothier, 1 surgeon, and 5 mates.

Each infantry battalion to embrace 1 lieutenant-colonel, 1 major, 4 captains, 5 lieutenants (including 1 adjutant), 4 ensigns, 16 sergeants, 1 quartermaster-sergeant, 1 music-sergeant, 4 drummers, 4 fifers, and 200 privates.

In addition to the three infantry battalions, 1 battalion of artillery was recommended, embracing 1 lieutenant-colonel, 1 major, 4 captains, 4 captain-lieutenants, 4 first lieutenants, 4 second lieutenants, 1 adjutant lieutenant, 1 captain quartermaster, 1 captain paymaster and clothier, 1 surgeon, 1 surgeon's mate, 1 quartermaster sergeant, 1 sergeant major, 1 music sergeant, 24 sergeants, 4 drums, 4 fifes, 100 artificers, and 100 matrosses.

A [16].

Officers of Artillery Retained in Service Pursuant to Resolution of Congress, June 2d, 1784.

Captain, John Doughty; captain-lieutenant, William Johnson; lieutenants, Samuel Jefferds and James Bradford.

NOTE.—The author is indebted for this list to the researches of Professor A. B. Gardner, judge-advocate, United States army.

Commissioned Officers of the Detachment of Artillery, Composed of Fifty Men, Raised in Pennsylvania Pursuant to Resolve of Continental Congress, June 3d, 1784.

Captain, Thomas Douglass; lieutenant, Joseph Ashton.

Officers of the Pennsylvania Artillery Detachment, as Reorganized under Resolve of Continental Congress, April 12th, 1785.

Captain, William Ferguson; lieutenant, Joseph Ashton.

A [17].

Organization of the Artillery of the Legionary Corps into which the Troops Raised Pursuant to Resolves of April 12th, 1785, and October 20th, 1786, were Arranged under War Department Order of January 30th, 1787.

One battalion—1 major, 1 adjutant, 1 quartermaster, 1 paymaster and clothier, 1 sergeant-major, 1 quartermaster-sergeant.

Four companies, each 1 captain, 2 lieutenants (no distinction as to grades), 4 sergeants, 4 corporals, 4 artificers, 1 drum, 1 fife, and 45 matrosses.

List of Officers of the Artillery Battalion, Legionary Corps.

Major, John Doughty.

Captains—William Ferguson, James Bradford, Henry Burbeck, and Joseph Savage.

Lieutenants—Joseph Ashton, Mahlon Ford, Dirck Schuyler, John Pierce, Moses Porter, William Moore, Ebenezer Smith Fowle, and Matthew Ernest.

A [18].

October 3d, 1787, the battalion organization for the artillery was retained by resolve of Congress, but the personnel of the artillery company, like that of infantry, was 4 sergeants, 4 corporals, 2 musicians, and 60 privates.

As thus modified, the battalion passed, two years later, into the regular army under the Constitutional Government.

A [19].

The President nominated the officers for reappointment in the following message:

"UNITED STATES, *September 29th*, 1789.

"GENTLEMEN OF THE SENATE: Agreeably to the act of Congress for adopting the establishment of troops in the public service to the Constitution of the United States, I nominate the persons specified in the inclosed list to be the commissioned officers thereof. This nomination differs from the existing arrangement only in the following cases, to wit: * * * * Ensign E. Spear, promoted to vacant lieutenancy of artillery * * * * . It is to be observed that the order in which the captains and subalterns are named is not to affect their relative rank, which has hitherto been imperfectly settled, owing to the perplexity of promotions in the State quotas, conformably to the late Confederation." * * * * * * *

Officers of the Battalion of Artillery.

Major commandant, John Doughty.
Captains—[3]* Henry Burbeck, Massachusetts; [1] William Ferguson, Pennsylvania; [4] Joseph Savage, Massachusetts; and [2] James Bradford, New York.
Lieutenants—[3] John Pierce, Massachusetts; [4] Moses Porter, Massachusetts; [5] William Moore, Massachusetts; [2] Dirck Schuyler, New York; [1] Mahlon Ford, New Jersey; [6] Matthew Ernest, New York; [8] Edward Spear, Pennsylvania; and [7] Ebenezer Smith Fowle, Massachusetts.
Surgeon's mate, Nathaniel Heyward, Massachusetts.

A [20].

The act of April 30th, 1790, for regulating the military establishment, gave to the artillery battalion an organization which in no essential particular differed from that prescribed by Secretary Knox, January, 1787, as modified by the resolve of October 3d, same year. That provided by the act in question was:

One major commandant, 1 adjutant, 1 quartermaster and paymaster (each from the subalterns of the line), and 1 surgeon's mate.

Four companies, each 1 captain, 2 lieutenants, 4 sergeants, 4 corporals, 2 musicians, and 66 privates.

A [21].

Legion of the United States, Organized December, 1792, by the President, Pursuant to Authority Vested in Him by Act of March 5th, 1792.

One major-general (or legionary general), with 2 aids-de-camp, 1 adjutant and inspector, 1 quartermaster, 1 deputy quartermaster,

---

*The figures inclosed in [ ] indicate the relative rank of the officers as fixed upon in the President's message of June 2d, 1790. The date of their new commissions was, in every instance, fixed at September 29th, 1789. (See letter of Secretary of War, March 14th, 1792, "Executive Journal, Senate.") No attempt has been made to present the names of artillery officers at any period subsequent to the adoption of the military establishment by Congress, September 29th, 1789, under the provisions of the Constitution. These will be found in the "Dictionary of the Army" and in Registers.

354   APPENDIX.

1 surgeon, 1 chaplain, 1 major commandant of cavalry, and 1 major commandant of artillery.

Four sub-legions, each of 1280 rank and file, arranged as follows:
One brigadier (or sub-legionary) general, with 1 aid-de-camp, 1 brigade (or sub-legionary) major and inspector, 1 quartermaster, and 1 surgeon.

One troop of dragoons, to consist of 1 captain, 1 lieutenant, 1 cornet, 6 sergeants, 6 corporals, 1 farrier, 1 saddler, 1 trumpeter, and 65 dragoons.

One company of artillery, to consist of 1 captain, 2 lieutenants, 4 sergeants, 4 corporals, 2 musicians, and 50 privates, to include 10 artificers.

Two battalions of infantry and 1 battalion of riflemen, each 1 major, 1 adjutant, 1 quartermaster, 1 surgeon's mate, 1 sergeant-major, 1 quartermaster-sergeant, 1 senior musician; and

Four companies, each 1 captain, 1 lieutenant, 1 ensign, 6 sergeants, 6 corporals, 2 musicians, and 81 privates; to the rifle companies, 1 bugler and 81 privates.

A [22].

Act of May 9th, 1794, to organize a corps of artillerists and engineers, to be incorporated with the corps of artillery already in service (entire rank and file 992), to consist of—

One lieutenant-colonel commandant, 1 adjutant, and 1 surgeon.

Four battalions, each 1 major, 1 adjutant and paymaster, 1 surgeon's mate; and

Four companies, each 1 captain, 2 lieutenants, 2 cadets (pay, clothing, and rations of sergeants), 4 sergeants, 4 corporals, 42 privates, sappers, and miners, 10 artificers, and 2 musicians.

It was made the duty of the Secretary of War to provide, at the public expense, under regulations prescribed by the President, the necessary books, instruments, and apparatus for the use and benefit of the corps, which was to serve in the field, on the frontiers, or in the fortifications on the sea-coast, as the President should deem consistent with the public service.

A [23].

Organization of a Regiment of Artillerists and Engineers, Authorized by Act of April 27th, 1798.

One lieutenant-colonel commandant, 1 adjutant, and 1 surgeon.

Three battalions, each 1 major, 1 adjutant and paymaster, 1 surgeon's mate; and

Four companies, each 1 captain, 2 lieutenants, 2 cadets, 4 sergeants, 4 corporals, 42 privates, sappers, and miners, 10 artificers, and 2 musicians.

The act of July 16th, 1798, to augment the army, authorized 1 inspector of artillery (from line of artillerists and engineers), 4 teachers of the arts and sciences, or a less number, as might be necessary for the instruction of the artillerists and engineers (the teachers each fifty dollars per month and double rations).

A [24].

By act of March 2d, 1799, the President was authorized, in case war should break out between the United States and a European power, or in case there was in his opinion imminent danger of invasion of their territory by any such power, to increase the military establishment by * * * one battalion of artillerists and engineers, * * * the authority to cease at the expiration of the next ensuing session of Congress, unless by future law continued in force. The continuation was rendered unnecessary by the general law of March 2d, 1799 (same date), reorganizing the army, and which for the artillerists and engineers gave the corps and the regiment the same organization, viz.:

One lieutenant-colonel commandant; 1 adjutant, 1 quartermaster, 1 paymaster, (extra lieutenants); 1 surgeon, 2 surgeon's mates, and 1 chief and 10 other musicians.

Four battalions, each 1 major, 1 sergeant-major, 1 quartermaster-sergeant; and

Four companies, each 1 captain, 2 lieutenants, 2 cadets, 4 sergeants, 4 corporals, and 56 privates, including 8 artificers.

The increase here authorized for the regiment of artillerists and engineers was held to supplant the necessity that might exist for raising the battalion of that arm authorized by the preceding act of the same date. The reorganizing act prescribed that a "regiment of artillery" should consist of, &c.; but this was construed to mean "regiment of artillerists and engineers," which branch of service thereafter, and until 1802, was arranged to two regiments, styled the First and Second. The First regiment supplanted the old corps of artillerists and engineers of 1794.

Two engineers were authorized, distinct from the officers of artillerists and engineers, with the rank and pay of lieutenant-colonels; also an inspector of fortifications, to be taken either from the army or civil life, and to have the rank of major.

A [25].

Organization of the Regiment of Artillerists, Act of March 16th, 1802.

One colonel, 1 lieutenant-colonel, 4 majors 1 adjutant.

Five battalions, 20 companies; each company 1 captain, 1 first lieutenant, 1 second lieutenant, 2 cadets, 4 sergeants, 4 corporals, 4 musicians, 8 artificers, and 56 privates.

NOTE—This act formally separated the artillerists from the engineers. In the former the grade of second lieutenant was introduced for the first time since the army was disbanded in 1783. [The musicians were intended in great part for a regimental band. The act of February 28th, 1803, provided for two teachers of music for the regiment of artillerists.]

A [26].

Organization of a Regiment of Light Artillery, Acts of April 12th, 1808, and March 3d, 1815.

One colonel, 1 lieutenant colonel, 1 major; 1 adjutant, 1 quartermaster, 1 paymaster, each taken from subalterns; 1 surgeon, 1 surgeon's mate, 1 sergeant-major, 1 quartermaster-sergeant, and 2 principal musicians.

Ten companies, each 1 captain, 1 first lieutenant, 1 second lieutenant, 2 cadets, 4 sergeants 4 corporals, 2 musicians, 8 artificers, and 58 matrosses.

[Act of February 24th, 1812, provided that this regiment should be mounted, in whole or in part, when deemed expedient; and when so mounted, the officers were entitled to forage, or money value thereof, on same terms as the light dragoons; and that one farrier and one saddler should be added to each company. Act of May 16th, 1812, gave a regimental paymaster, (pay and emoluments of captain of his regiment,) and added twelve drivers to each company of light artillery. Act of January 20th, 1813, gave the regiment a second major; to each company a third lieutenant and a fifth sergeant. The act of March 3d, 1815, restored the light artillery to its original organization, *i. e.*, that of April 12th, 1808.]

A [27].

Organization of the Second and Third Regiments of Artillery, Authorized by Act of January 11th, 1812.

One colonel, 2 lieutenant-colonels, 2 majors, 2 adjutants, 1 quartermaster, 1 paymaster, 1 surgeon, 2 surgeon's mates, 2 sergeant-majors, 2 quartermaster sergeants, and 2 senior musicians.

Two battalions, each 10 companies; each company 1 captain, 1 first lieutenant, 1 second lieutenant, 2 cadets, 4 sergeants, 4 corporals, 8 artificers, 2 musicians, and 72 privates. [Act of March 28th, 1812, authorized four conductors of artillery, pay and emoluments of a lieutenant.]

APPENDIX. 357

A [28].

Act of March 30, 1814, arranged the First, Second, and Third artillery regiments into a corps of 12 battalions, with 6 lieutenant-colonels, 6 majors, 12 adjutants, 12 quartermasters, and 48 companies; each 1 captain, 1 first lieutenant, 2 second lieutenants (one to be conductor of artillery for his company, with ten dollars additional per month), 1 third lieutenant, 5 sergeants, 1 quartermaster-sergeant, 8 corporals, 4 musicians, and 100 privates.

The officers of artillery, whether of the corps or of the light regiment, were given dragoon pay.

A [29].

Plan for the Organization of the Artillery of the United States, proposed to the Secretary of War July 19th, 1812, with Remarks thereon by Colonel George Izard.

"It is proposed to substitute for the four regiments, making ten battalions, a regular force, of which all the component parts shall be assimilated to each other; to connect the engineer department with that of the artillery, and thus to place at the disposal of the Government a body of officers and men who, from the nature of the institution, will progressively become more and more useful.

"The establishment will embrace 1 colonel-in-chief, 4 colonels, 1 lieutenant-colonel (adjutant-general of the corps), 8 lieutenant-colonels (commanding battalions), 1 major and assistant adjutant-general of the corps, 8 majors, 10 captains (assistant inspectors), 64 captains (commanding companies), 74 first lieutenants, 148 second lieutenants, 74 cadets, 8 sergeant-majors, 8 quartermaster-sergeants, 8 senior musicians, 320 sergeants, 320 corporals, 128 musicians, 256 fire-workers, 456 artificers, 100 sappers and miners, 1,792 privates of the first class, and 2,560 privates of the second class. The whole arranged to eight battalions, eight companies each, *except* the colonel-in-chief, 4 colonels, 1 lieutenant-colonel, 1 major, 10 captains, 10 first lieutenants, 20 second lieutenants, 10 cadets, four companies of artificers, 50 each, and two companies of sappers and miners, 50 each. Each company of the battalion to consist of 1 captain, 1 first lieutenant, 1 second lieutenant, 1 cadet, 5 sergeants, 5 corporals, 2 musicians, 4 fire-workers, 4 artificers, 28 privates of the first and 40 privates of the second class.

"The proportion between the number of officers and men depends upon the nature of the duties to be performed. In the field service of artillery it is ascertained by experience that the superintendence of more than two pieces in action cannot be executed by one officer well. In the French system a division or company embraces 4 officers and 88 non-commissioned officers and soldiers, including artificers and musicians. Each company is subdivided into four squads, one of which is supernumerary, to supply loss of men in action; each remaining squad has two pieces, commanded by a subaltern. The captain commands the division or company; eight companies are in one battalion; eight battalions make up a corps of artillery.

"It will be asked, Where is the flying or horse artillery in this arrangement? Let me in turn inquire what are the peculiarities in the service of horse artillery which distinguish it from artillery on foot? Is there one circumstance in their manœuvres or in the construction of their gun-carriages and caissons which need vary from those adopted in the latter? Wherefore is the soldier of horse artillery mounted on horseback? Not to do cavalry duty in any shape whatever, but simply to expedite his transportation from one distant point to another. All that it is essential for him to know, which his comrade on foot may dispense with, is to sit upon his horse in moving for an hour or so at a rapid pace."

A [30].

The act of March 3d, 1815, fixed the military peace establishment at not to exceed 10,000 men, of artillery, infantry, and riflemen, in such proportions as the President should deem proper; the regiment of light artillery to be retained as organized April 12th, 1808; the corps of artillery as organized March 30th, 1814.

Under the discretionary authority given him, the President retained in service eight of the twelve battalions into which the corps of artillery was organized by the act last mentioned.

[By act of April 24th, 1816, one paymaster was allowed each battalion of artillery, who was also to be a district paymaster, to be appointed from subalterns or citizens, with pay and emoluments of major. Act of April 20th, 1818, fixed the commissioned officers of a light artillery company at 1 captain, 1 first lieutenant, 2 second lieutenants (one to act as conductor of artillery); of a company of the corps of artillery, at 1 captain, 2 first lieutenants and 2 second lieutenants (one to act as conductor of artillery); while to each battalion of artillery, and to the regiment of light artillery, 1 armorer was attached (with same pay as in ordnance department).]

A [31].

Organization of the Artillery under the Act of March 2d, 1821, to Reduce and Fix the Military Establishment.

Four regiments, each 1 colonel, 1 lieutenant colonel, 1 major, 1 captain, supernumerary for ordnance duty, (repealed by act April 5th, 1832,) 1 adjutant, from the line of subalterns, 1 sergeant-major, and 1 quartermaster sergeant; and

Nine companies, one of which it was directed should be *designated and equipped as light artillery;* each company 1 captain, 2 first lieutenants, 2 second lieutenants, 4 sergeants, 4 corporals, 3 artificers, 2 musicians, and 42 privates. Ordnance department merged in the artillery; officers of artillery to be selected for ordnance duties, and, when so serving, to be under orders of War Department only; the number of enlisted men in the ordnance department to be reduced to fifty-six.

[Act of April 5th, 1832, reorganized the ordnance department with no officer under rank of captain. It authorized the President to select from the artillery such number of lieutenants as might be necessary for ordnance duties. Act of July 5th, 1838, added 1 company to each regiment of artillery, organized as those already in service; reduced the number of second lieutenants for each company to one, and added 16 privates to each. Act of August 23d, 1842, took away these 16 privates, and also 1 artificer from each company of artillery, leaving the enlisted strength of each at 4 sergeants, 4 corporals, 2 artificers, 2 musicians, and 42 privates.]

A [32].

Table Showing the Reorganization of the Artillery, June, 1821, Under the Act of Congress to Reduce and Fix the Military Peace Establishment of the United States, Approved March 2d, 1821.

Organization prior to 1821.	Captains.	Became in Reorganization.
A, Light Artillery	McDowell	A, 1st Artillery.
B, "	Leonard	G, "
C, "	Brooks	C, "
D, "	Wilkins	H, "
E, "	Hobart	G, 4th Artillery.
F, "	Morris	H, 3d "
G, "	Eastman	D, 1st "
H, "	Was broken up	in April, 1821.
I, "	Craig	E, 3d Artillery.
K, "	Bell	A, 4th "

Corps Artillery, Northern Military Division.

A, 2d Battalion	Erving	I, 1st Artillery.
B, 4th "	Read	F, 1st "
C, 3d "	Mountfort	C, 2d "
D, 2d "	Crane	B, 1st "
E, 3d "	Ansart	A, 3d "
F, 3d "	Legate	C, 3d "
G, 4th "	Dearborn	Broken up.
H, 4th "	Stockton	H, 2d Artillery.
I, 1st "	Gates	B, "
K, 4th "	Roach	G, "
L, 1st "	Heilman	D, "
M, 2d "	Beall	A, "
N, 2d "	Churchhill	E, 1st Artillery.
O, 1st "	Pierce	I, 2d "
P, 1st "	Farley	Broken up.
Q, 3d "	Zantzinger	F, 2d Artillery.

Southern Military Division.

A, 3d Battalion	Sands	F, 4th Artillery.
B, 2d "	Wilson	B, 3d "
C, 3d "	Humphrey	B, 4th "
D, 4th "	Fanning	C, 4th "
E, 1st "	Burd	F, 3d "
F, 3d "	Whiting	Broken up.
G, 3d "	Root	D, 4th Artillery.
H, 4th "	Archer	Broken up.
I, 1st "	Mason	H, 4th Artillery.
K, 2d "	Jones	D, 3d "
L, 4th "	Loomis	See C, 4th Artillery (list below).
M, 4th "	Biddle	I, 4th Artillery.
N, 1st "	Payne	E, 4th "
O, 2d "	Allen	I, 3d "
P, 2d "	Lomax	G, 3d "
Q, 1st "	O'Conner	See E, 3d Artillery (list below).

APPENDIX.

New Organization.

Regiment.	Co.	Captains.	Organized From—
1st Artillery	A	McDowell	A, Light Artillery.
"	B	Crane	D, 2d Battalion, Northern Division.
"	C	Brooks	C, Light Artillery.
"	D	Eastman	G, " "
"	E	Churchill	N, 2d Battalion, Northern Division.
"	F	Worth	B, 4th " " "
"	G	Mason	B, Light Artillery.
"	H	H. Whiting	D, " "
"	I	F. Whiting	A, 2d Battalion, Northern Division.
2d Artillery	A	Fanning	M, 2d Battalion, Northern Division, and detachment at West Point, N. Y.
"	B	Gates	I, 1st Battalion, Northern Division.
"	C	Roach	C, 3d " " "
"	D	Heilman	L, 1st " " "
"	E	Nourse	6th Infantry Recruits.
"	F	Belton	Q, 3d Battalion, Northern Division.
"	G	Zantzinger	K, 4th " " "
"	H	Mountfort	H, 4th " " "
"	I	Legate	O, 1st " " "
3d Artillery	A	Ansart	E, 3d " " "
"	B	Wilson	B, 2d " Southern "
"	C	Jones	F, 3d " Northern "
"	D	Stockton	K, 2d " Southern "
"	E	Craig	I, Light Artillery, and Q, 1st Battalion, Southern Division.
"	F	Laval	E, 1st Battalion, Southern Division.
"	G	Lomax	P, 2d " " "
"	H	Morris	F, Light Artillery.
"	I	Baker	O, 2d Battalion, Southern Division.
4th Artillery	A	Bell	K, Light Artillery.
"	B	Humphrey	C, 3d Battalion, Southern Division.
"	C	Burd	D and part of L, 4th Battalion, Southern Division.
"	D	Pierce	G, 3d Battalion, Southern Division.
"	E	Payne	N, 1st " " "
"	F	Hayden	A, 3d " " "
"	G	Hobart	E, Light Artillery.
"	H	Erving	I, and part of E, 1st Battalion, Southern Division.
"	I	Sands	M, 4th Battalion, Southern Division.

NOTE.—The author is indebted for the preceding interesting and valuable table to the researches of Mr. Heitman, Adjutant-General's Office, Washington, who, with the kind permission of Adjutant-General Drum, devoted much time to its preparation. It is with great pleasure that this acknowledgment is made.

A [33].

The legislation affecting the artillery and growing out of the Mexican war was initiated by the act of May 13th, 1846, which authorized the President to increase the number of privates in each company to one hundred [reduced, act August 14th, 1848]. This was followed by the act of February 11th, 1847, giving to each regiment an additional major, to be taken from the captains of the army; and a regimental quartermaster, to be selected from the subalterns.

The act of March 3d, 1847, added to each regiment of artillery two companies, two principal musicians, one principal teamster, and to each company two teamsters. The President was empowered, when he should deem it necessary, to designate four other companies, one in each regiment, to be organized and equipped as light artillery, the officers and men of the light artillery, when serving as such and mounted, to receive the same pay and allowance as dragoons.

The various additions made to the artillery, except the two companies to each regiment, were intended to be but temporary in nature, and to terminate with the war. As to the regimental quartermaster, the principal teamster to each regiment, and the teamsters for the companies, the original purpose was carried out. The majors were, by act of July 19th, 1848, made part of the permanent organization of the artillery regiments, while the principal musicians were allowed to disappear by casualties of service, their places not being filled.

[By act of June 17th, 1850, the enlisted strength of light artillery companies was fixed at 4 sergeants, 4 corporals, 2 artificers, 2 musicians, and 64 privates. By the same act the President was authorized to properly mount and equip such portions of the army as served habitually on foot whenever, in his opinion, the exigencies of the public service might require it. This, of course, empowered the President to temporarily equip as field artillery, or as cavalry, any of the foot artillery companies. Under the provisions of the act of July 17th, 1862, officers when so mounted were authorized to receive cavalry pay.]

A [34].

Organization of the Fifth Regiment, United States Artillery, Raised Pursuant to the President's Proclamation, May 3d, 1861, and Act of July 29th, 1861.

One colonel, 1 lieutenant-colonel, 1 major (to every four batteries); 1 adjutant, 1 quartermaster and commissary, (to be taken from the lieutenants of the regiment); 1 sergeant-major, 1 quartermaster-sergeant, 1 commissary sergeant, 2 principal musicians, 1 hospital steward, and 1 band of not more than 24 musicians.

Not more than 12 batteries, each 1 captain, 1 first lieutenant, 1 second lieutenant, 1 first sergeant, 1 quartermaster-sergeant, 4 sergeants, 8 corporals, 2 musicians, 2 artificers, 1 wagoner, and not exceeding 122 privates, at the option of the President, who was authorized to add to each battery 1 first lieutenant, 1 second lieutenant, 2 sergeants, and 4 corporals.

This was the organization, save in the matter of artificers, of a 6-gun battery on a war establishment, as prescribed in the authorized light-artillery tactics of the time. The Fifth was raised as a regiment of artillery simply. The term 'light artillery' nowhere appears in the act of July 29th, 1861; nevertheless, the personnel of each battery was that, as has been seen, appertaining to field artillery only. This fact has given rise to the general but erroneous impression that the Fifth was organized as a regiment of field artillery.

A [35].

By the act of July 28th, 1866, the four old regiments of artillery were each given the same organization as the Fifth regiment, except that the regimental adjutants, the quartermasters and commissaries were made extra lieutenants. The act of March 3d, 1869, allowed each artillery regiment 1 chief musician, insructor of music. The act of July 15th, 1870, abolished the grades of regimental commissary-sergeant and hospital steward, and the number of corporals in each battery was reduced by it to 4.

Under the provisions of the Revised Statutes the organization of each regiment of artillery is 1 colonel, 1 lieutenant-colonel, 1 major for every four batteries, 1 adjutant, 1 quartermaster and commissary, 1 sergeant-major, 1 quartermaster-sergeant, 1 chief musician, 2 principal musicians, and 12 batteries; each 1 captain, 1 first lieutenant, 1 second lieutenant, 1 first sergeant, 1 quartermaster-sergeant, 4 sergeants, 4 corporals, 2 musicians, 2 artificers, 1 wagoner, and privates, as many, not exceeding 122, as the President may direct.

NOTE.—The President may add at his discretion 1 first and 1 second lieutenant, 2 sergeants, and 4 corporals to each battery.

The actual personnel of artillery organizations under existing orders at this time (1883) is as follows:

	Captains.	First Lieutenants.	Second Lieutenants.	First Sergeants.	Sergeants.
Field battery	1	2	2*	1	6
Foot battery	1	2	1	1	4

	Corporals.	Musicians.	Artificers.	Wagoners.	Privates.
Field battery	4	2	2	1	49
Foot battery	4	2	2	1	26

* At present half the field batteries have 2, the others 1 second lieutenant.

A [36].

[General Orders No. 49.—Extract.]

WAR DEPARTMENT, ADJUTANT-GENERAL'S OFFICE,
WASHINGTON, *November 5th*, 1838.

* * * * * * *

IV. Captain Ringgold having been instructed to organize and equip a company of light artillery, in conformity with the act of 1821, at Carlisle Barracks, the men detailed from the First and Second regiments of artillery for this service will now be dropped from the rolls of their respective companies and be mustered as C company of the Third regiment. Captain Ringgold's former company, now in the field, will be broken up, the men transferred to the other companies of the regiment, and the subalterns will join their company at Carlisle, when the lieutenants of the First and Second Artillery now on duty there will proceed to join their respective regiments.

A [37].

[General Orders No. 46.—Extract.]

HEADQUARTERS OF THE ARMY, ADJUTANT-GENERAL'S OFFICE,
WASHINGTON, *August 19th*, 1841.

* * * * * * *

II. The following order has also been received from the Department of War:

"1. In the order of the Department of War, April 29th, 1840, adopting the '*Instruction for Field Artillery, Horse and Foot*,' it is said that so much thereof 'as relates to the manœuvres of horse artillery is for the present suspended, and will not be adopted in practice until otherwise ordered by the Department.'

"2. The President of the United States, through the Department of War, now directs that all parts of the said system be followed in future both by the horse and foot artillery, and to the exclusion of all other systems."

The foregoing addenda and order are announced to the army by the major-general commanding.

For the purpose of diffusing instruction, the lieutenants of the four artillery regiments will be passed through the school of horse artillery in their respective regiments, so that no lieutenant be in that school more than one year at any one tour. From this rule may be excepted lieutenants who are actually in command of companies, staff lieutenants, and such others who from accidental causes may be unable to ride; and the colonel will make all the other changes herein indicated.

A [38].

By Special Orders No. 96 of 1842 it was announced that, as the number of enlisted men allowed each company had been reduced by act of Congress, only four pieces would be manned by each company of light artillery; the other pieces would be stored for future use.

The detail of lieutenants for service with these companies was regulated by the following order:

APPENDIX.

[General Orders No. 33.—Extract.]
HEADQUARTERS OF THE ARMY, ADJUTANT-GENERAL'S OFFICE,
WASHINGTON, *July* 8*th*, 1844.

* * * * * * * * *

AFTER ORDER.

1. So much of General Orders No. 46 of 1841 having reference to the detail of subalterns for the four companies of light artillery as requires the first lieutenants to be annually relieved is hereby rescinded; and they will in future be attached to those companies in the same manner as the first lieutenants of the other artillery companies.

2. The respective colonels will accordingly select the first lieutenants who are to be permanently assigned to the light companies, so that the arrangement may take effect after the 30th of September next.

3. The brevet second lieutenants now attached to the light artillery companies will be transferred to other companies after the 1st of October, when they will be relieved by other brevet second lieutenants, so that the complement, including the graduates of this year, will be two for each light company.

A [39].

[General Orders No. 42.]
HEADQUARTERS ARMY, ADJUTANT-GENERAL'S OFFICE,
WASHINGTON, *October* 17*th*, 1844.

In order to extend the peculiar instructions now imparted to light companies of artillery by periodical changes in their regiments, and to have the number of officers and men necessary at each school to manœuvre with a full battery, instead of four pieces as at present, in the First regiment of artillery, company I will [be] exercised with K; in the Second, F with A; in the Third, F with C; in the Fourth, K with B.

Accordingly K company, Fourth artillery, will repair to Carlisle Barracks as soon as relieved by F company of the Third artillery, which will be put in motion for Fort McHenry the moment that transportation for it can be obtained.

Each of the additional four companies designated above for joint instruction in light artillery will remain as before, under the charge of its own officers, except in respect to the exercise and manœuvres, as field artillery, and in the care of batteries, horses, harness, and stables. In these particulars only the duties of the two companies will be blended and equalized under the orders of the senior officer on duty with the companies.

On the arrival of the additional company of the Fourth artillery at Carlisle Barracks the lieutenant-colonel of that regiment will become the commander of the post, and a field officer of the Third artillery will, as soon as practicable, be assigned to the command of the two companies of his regiment to be at Fort McHenry.

A [40].

ADJUTANT-GENERAL'S OFFICE,
WASHINGTON, *June* 18*th*, 1845.

Lieut.-Col. WM. GATES, or
  Com'd'g Officer Fort Moultrie, Charleston, S. C.

SIR: On the receipt of this you will immediately dispatch by sea company E, Third artillery, to New Orleans barracks to await further orders. I am, sir,

(Signed)   R. JONES, *Adj't-General.*

ADJUTANT-GENERAL'S OFFICE,
WASHINGTON, *June* 18*th*, 1845.

First Lieut. B. BRAGG, 3d Art'y, or
Comd'g Officer Co. E, Third Art'y, care U. S. Q'rm'r, New Orleans.

SIR: A battery of two pieces and two howitzers, fully equipped for service (with horses), and supplied with the necessary ammunition, has been ordered to New Orleans barracks for your company. You will take charge of it immediately on your arrival at the barracks, and then proceed as expeditiously as possible to join the brigade ordered to the Gulf of Mexico, near the mouth of the Sabine, under the command of Brig.-Gen'l Taylor, to whom you will report. I am, sir, &c.,

(Signed)   R. JONES, *Adj't-Gen'l.*

ADJUTANT-GENERAL'S OFFICE,
WASHINGTON, *June* 18*th*, 1845.

Brig.-General Z. TAYLOR,
Com'd'g First Dep't, Fort Jesup, La.

SIR: The colonel of ordnance has been this day instructed to send without delay to New Orleans barracks a field battery of two pieces and two howitzers, equipped for service with horses, with a full supply of ammunition. A company of the Third artillery has been ordered from Fort Moultrie to New Orleans, there to receive the battery, and will proceed thence to join you on the gulf. To avoid the delay attending the purchase and shipment of horses, it is deemed best to leave you the procuring of such number as may be required for the company, and you will therefore please give the necessary orders on the subject, &c. I am, sir, &c.,

(Signed)   R. JONES, *Adj't-Gen'l.*

A [41].

[Special Orders No. 74.]

HEADQUARTERS OF THE ARMY, ADJUTANT-GENERAL'S OFFICE,
WASHINGTON, *August* 15*th*, 1845.

Light companies A, Second artillery, and C, Third artillery, having been ordered to Texas, companies F of the Second and F of the Third artillery, united with them for the purpose of instruction, by General Orders No. 42, of 1844, will turn over to the ordnance department their sabres, &c., and resume their former equipments.

A [42].

[General Orders No. 218.]

HEADQUARTERS OF THE ARMY,
PUEBLA, *July* 16*th*, 1847

In compliance with General Orders No. 16, dated April 15th, 1847, from the War Department, the general-in-chief designates the following companies of the four regiments of artillery as those to be equipped as light artillery under the act of March 3d, 1847:

Captain J. B. Magruder's company I, First artillery.
Captain J. F. Roland's company M, Second artillery.
Captain T. W. Sherman's company E, Third artillery.
Captain S. H. Drum's company G, Fourth artillery.

By command of Major-General Scott:

(Signed)   H. L. SCOTT, *A. A. A. G.*

A [43].

[General Orders No. 14.]

HEADQUARTERS OF THE ARMY, ADJUTANT-GENERAL'S OFFICE,
WASHINGTON, D. C., *August* 24*th*, 1849.

For the purpose of diffusing instruction, the lieutenants of the four artillery regiments will be passed through the school of light artillery in their respective regiments, so that no lieutenant be in that school more than two years at any one tour.

From this rule may be excepted lieutenants in command of companies the captains of which are indefinitely absent, adjutants, regimental quartermasters, together with such others as from accidental causes may be unable to ride.

Two first lieutenants and a second lieutenant will be attached to each light company. No brevet second lieutenant will be allowed to a battery except where the captain is indefinitely absent.

To secure constantly with each battery at least one instructed subaltern, only a portion of the officers will be changed at the same time. Accordingly, one of the first lieutenants and the second lieutenant will be relieved the 1st of October next, the other first lieutenant October 1st, 1850, and so on in successive years.

Commanding officers of regiments will make the change herein indicated.

A [44].

[Special Orders No. 70.]

HEADQUARTERS TROOPS SERVING IN KANSAS,
FORT LEAVENWORTH, *September* 18*th*, 1857.

I. In obedience to instructions from the War Department, company M of the Second artillery will be furnished with the field battery of four guns (complete), now at this post. .

II. The quartermaster's department will procure without delay the necessary number of horses to equip this battery, including six horses to each piece and caisson.

III. The commanding officer of this battery will use every exertion to prepare it for the field as soon as practicable.

By order of General Harney:
    (Signed)   A. PLEASANTON,
    Captain Second Dragoons, Act'g Ass't Adj't-General.

A [45].

[Special Orders No. 52.]

HEADQUARTERS OF THE ARMY,
NEW YORK, *April* 10*th*, 1858.

I. Captain and Brevet Major John F. Reynolds' company C, Third artillery, is announced as one of the light companies of that regiment.

II. Light company C, Third artillery, now at Fort Monroe, will proceed without unnecessary delay to Fort Leavenworth, where its horses will be furnished. The company will thence join the Army of Utah with the reinforcements already designated for that command, and upon its arrival in Utah will be

equipped with the battery at present under the charge of Brevet Captain Jesse S. Reno, ordnance department.
By command of Bv't Lieutenant General Scott:
(Signed)   IRWIN MCDOWELL,
Ass't Adjutant-General.

A [46].

[Special Orders No. 141.—Extract.]

HEADQUARTERS OF THE ARMY, ADJUTANT-GENERAL'S OFFICE,
WASHINGTON, *June* 18*th*, 1870.

1. For the purpose of diffusing instruction, the lieutenants of the five artillery regiments are expected to serve in turn with the light battery of their respective regiments, not exceeding two years at any one tour, as directed in General Orders No. 14, Headquarters of the Army, August 24th, 1849. From this rule may be excepted lieutenants in command of companies the captains of which are indefinitely absent, regimental staff officers, and such officers as from accidental causes are unable to ride. Commanding officers of regiments will, in due season to carry out this arrangement, report to the adjutant-general of the army the names of officers who should be transferred under this order.

*   *   *   *   *   *   *

A [47].

[Special Orders No. 25.]

HEADQUARTERS OF THE ARMY, ADJUTANT-GENERAL'S OFFICE,
WASHINGTON, *February* 4*th*, 1878.

*   *   *   *   *   *   *

5. In conformity with section 1101, Revised Statutes, the President directs that company L, Second artillery, Captain John I. Rogers commanding, be temporarily equipped as a battery of light artillery. The commanding general, Department of Texas, will give the necessary instructions for the proper execution of this order.   *   *   *

A [48].

[Special Orders No. 208.]

HEADQUARTERS DEPARTMENT OF TEXAS,
SAN ANTONIO, TEXAS, *October* 13*th*, 1880.

*   *   *   *   *   *   *

III. To meet the requirements of General Orders No. 11, current series, and subsequent instructions from the headquarters military division of the Missouri, directing the movements of batteries E, G, and L, Second Artillery, the following will govern:

1. Batteries E (Fort Brown) and L (Fort Clark) will proceed to Little Rock Barracks, Arkansas; Battery G, to Jackson Barracks, Louisiana. Light battery L will move (mounted) to San Antonio, Texas, where the guns, horses, etc., will be duly transferred, under special instructions from these headquarters; thereafter the battery will proceed dismounted.   *   *   *

By command of Brigadier-General Ord.

                                              THOMAS M. VINCENT,
Assistant Adjutant-General.

A [49].

[Special Orders No. 246.]

HEADQUARTERS OF THE ARMY, ADJUTANT-GENERAL'S OFFICE,
WASHINGTON, *November 7th,* 1880.

1. In conformity with section 1101, Revised Statutes, the President directs that *Battery F, Second Artillery,* Captain E. B. Williston commanding, be temporarily equipped as a battery of light artillery. The commanding general, Department of Texas, will give the necessary instructions for the proper execution of this order.

* * * * * * * * *

A [50].

[General Orders No. 96.]

HEADQUARTERS OF THE ARMY, ADJUTANT-GENERAL'S OFFICE,
WASHINGTON, *August* 15*th,* 1882.

I. The following order has been received from the War Department:

WAR DEPARTMENT,
WASHINGTON CITY, *August* 14*th,* 1882.

The President, under the authority conferred by section 1101 of the Revised Statutes, providing that an additional battery in each regiment of artillery may be mounted and equipped as a battery of light artillery, designates the following as the additional light batteries:

1st Artillery, Battery E—Captain *Franck E. Taylor.*
2d Artillery, Battery F—Captain *E. B. Williston* (now temporarily equipped as a battery of light artillery).
3d Artillery, Battery F—Captain *James M. Lancaster.*
4th Artillery, Battery F—Captain *Frank G. Smith.*
5th Artillery, Battery D—Captain *Jacob D. Rawles.*

ROBERT T. LINCOLN,
Secretary of War.

II. The batteries named above will take station as follows:

Battery E, 1st Artillery, at Vancouver Barracks, Washington Territory.
Battery F, 3d Artillery, at San Antonio, Texas.
Battery F, 4th Artillery, at Fort Snelling, Minnesota.
Battery D, 5th Artillery, at Fort Omaha, Nebraska.
Battery F, 2d Artillery, will remain at Fort Leavenworth.

The batteries of the 1st, 3d, 4th, and 5th Artillery herein designated will proceed to the posts named, where they will be filled to a minimum strength of sixty-five enlisted men, and equipped as batteries of light artillery under the direction of the respective department commanders.

III. By direction of the Secretary of War, on the recommendation of the General of the Army, the tour of service of captains with light or mounted batteries of artillery shall hereafter be three years, commencing with January 1st, 1883, and of lieutenants as at present detailed—two years.

IV. Such of the captains as shall have commanded light batteries three or more years on the date named in the last preceding paragraph of this order will be relieved by others, to be designated in orders from this office.

V. Regimental commanders of artillery will, respectively, as occasion requires, nominate to the Adjutant-General, as is now done in the detail of lieutenants, the captains to replace those whose tours of duty with the light batteries are about to expire.

VI. To avoid complaints of injustice having been done in the selection, and that the instruction in regiments may be as uniform as practicable, the regimental roster for the detail of captains shall commence with the senior captain eligible for detail, and continue downwards, until all the captains shall have had instruction as such in the command of light batteries, when it will again commence with the senior captain.

Those captains relieved on the first operation of this order, or who have recently been in command of light batteries for three years or longer, will not be regarded as eligible for detail until all the other captains of the regiment have had a tour of duty in command of the light batteries.

VII. To insure that none but those possessing the more soldierly qualities and regimental *esprit* should be attached to so favorite and distinguished an arm of the service, an officer who has not served with his regiment continuously (including cumulative leaves) for at least the previous two years will not be considered eligible for detail to the light batteries. Exception will only be made by the special order of the Secretary of War, and where the circumstances attending the absence of an officer do not indicate a desire to avoid the performance of ordinary regimental and company duty.

A [51].

[Special Order No. 168.]

HEADQUARTERS ARMY OF THE POTOMAC,
CAMP NEAR NEW BRIDGE, VA., *June 2d*, 1862.

* * * * * * * * *

V. Commanders of army corps will, with the least practicable delay, organize from the field batteries attached to the divisions composing their respective corps an artillery reserve, to consist of about one-half the whole field artillery force attached to the corps, and to be placed under the command of a suitable light-artillery officer. This reserve will be subject only to the orders of the corps commander.

* * * * * * * * *

By command of Major-General McClellan.

S. WILLIAMS,
Ass't Adjutant-General.

A [52].

It will not be uninteresting to notice the organization of the artillery-brigades of the Union, the artillery-battalion of the Confederate, and the artillery-divisions of the German and Austrian armies.

1st.—UNION ARMY, ARTILLERY–BRIGADE. (Robertson's, in 1863, is taken for illustration.)

One commander, senior captain of brigade, *ex-officio* chief of artillery of the army corps. Staff—1 assistant adjutant-general, from lieutenants of brigade ; 1 acting inspector-general, from lieutenants of brigade ; 1 acting ordnance officer, from lieutenants of brigade; 1 quartermaster (assigned from that department of U. S. volunteers); 1 commissary officer (from that department of U. S. volunteers); 1 or 2 medical officers (from that department of U. S.

volunteers.) Non-commissioned staff—1 sergeant-major, from sergeants of the batteries; 1 ordnance-sergeant, from sergeants of the batteries; 1 commissary-sergeant, from sergeants of the batteries; 1 hospital steward, from regular medical department. Troops—6 batteries, four of them each with six 3-inch rifles, and two each with four 12-pounder Napoleons.

In addition to the ammunition wagons forming part of the regular war organization of the batteries, there were for its exclusive use attached to the brigade 75 wagons for transportation of ordnance and other stores; or the total number of supply wagons accompanying and forming part of the brigade was about 3⅓ per gun.

2d.—CONFEDERATE ARMY, ARTILLERY-BATTALION. (Alexander's, of Longstreet's corps, in fall of 1863.)

One colonel commanding, and 1 major. Staff—1 adjutant, 1 acting ordnance officer, (with sergeant and train of reserve ammunition-wagons, forges, and battery wagons); 1 quartermaster, from that department, with sergeant and wagons; 1 commissary, from that department, with sergeant and wagons; 1 or 2 medical officers. Troops—6 batteries, five of them each with four and one battery with six pieces.

Enlisted strength of batteries: to every 4 guns, 100 enlisted men; to 6 guns, 150 enlisted men, *i. e.*, these numbers were allowed by regulations. There was no regular non-commissioned staff.

3d.—ARTILLERY-DIVISION, GERMAN ARMY.

One major or lieutenant colonel. Staff—1 adjutant, 1 paymaster (from regimental staff), 1 medical officer (is part of regimental staff, but may be *attached* to the division staff). Non-commissioned staff—1 sergeant-clerk, 5 corporals and privates, to assist in various ways. Troops—4 batteries, each 6 guns and 8 caissons.

4th.—ARTILLERY-DIVISION, AUSTRIAN ARMY.

One field officer. Staff—1 lieutenant-adjutant, 1 lieutenant-paymaster, 1 quartermaster and commissary (from the supply department), 1 officer charged with money accounts (from the supply department), 1 medical officer. Non-commissioned staff, etc.— 1 veterinary (with horse artillery), 3 non-commissioned officers, 5 drivers and cannoneers, 5 orderlies. Troops—2, 3, or 4 batteries, each 8 guns; generally 3 or 4 batteries.

Superficial examination might lead to the conclusion that the administrative machinery of the Union artillery-brigade or the Confederate artillery-battalion was more complete than were those of the artillery-divisions of the German and Austrian armies. If we more fully consider the organizations of the latter, it will be evident that this is not the case.

1. The artillery-brigade of the Union army embraced all the batteries assigned to the army corps. Every principle of organization demanded that its staff should be perfect. There was in the corps no artillery authority above that of the artillery-brigade commander, who *by law* was chief of artillery and ordnance of the corps. Under these circumstances, it was absolutely necessary that the brigade should have within itself facilities for securing supplies and administering its affairs equal to the demands and exingencies of service. Had it been otherwise, the artillery would have been left helpless, dependent perhaps, at the supreme moment upon others who did not understand its wants.

The commander of artillery at army headquarters was often far removed from the batteries attached to troops. The supervision he exercised over them was general in character. It was not of that direct and energetic character which alone in an emergency could procure either sustenance for the personnel, matériel for necessary equipment, or munitions for the batteries in action. To attend to these indispensable matters, it was necessary that the staff of the artillery-brigade should be complete, embracing every branch both of administration and supply.

2. Few of the Confederate artillery-battalions were so completely organized as was Alexander's, previously mentioned. Some of them had neither ordnance, commissary, or quartermaster trains. The staff was limited to an adjutant detailed from the subalterns of the battalion, an ordnance officer (*i. e.*, artillery officer on ordnance duty) also a lieutenant, and a regular quartermaster and commissary. There was no non-commissioned staff. Each army corps had a reserve ammunition train of about twenty wagons, and the general ammunition train of the Army numbered about sixty wagons. This was the practice in the army of Northern Virginia, the most thoroughly organized army of the Confederacy. As this army was organized, August 31st, 1864, the first corps had eighteen batteries, arranged to five battalions; the second corps had nineteen batteries, in five battalions; so, likewise, had the third corps; two chiefs of corps-artillery were brigadiers; the other was a colonel; the chief of artillery of this army was a brigadier-general.

3. In the German army, although the arrangement is not uniform, the principle is the same throughout, *i. e.*, the artillery is distributed to army corps, each of which as a rule has an artillery brigade consisting of two regiments. One of these regiments, styled 'divisional artillery,' has eight batteries, grouped into two divisions of four batteries each; each division is part and parcel of one of the two infantry divisions which make up the army corps. The other regiment of the artillery brigade is styled 'corps artillery.' It has nine batteries, equally arranged to three divisions, which are held in a corps reserve.

The complete staffs of both the divisional and the corps-artillery regiments accompany the army corps. The artillery-brigade staff is also present with corps headquarters.

With each army corps there are six artillery ammunition columns. The personnel of each column is 1 captain, 1 medical officer, 1 paymaster, 1 veterinary (non-commissioned officer), and 169 men; the wagons of each are 19 caissons, 1 store wagon, 1 forge, 1 baggage wagon, and 4 park wagons.

These ammunition columns are under the orders of the chief of artillery of the corps; hence there is no danger of the artillery-divisions being left without a full supply of ammunition.

4. The same principles of organization govern in the Austrian service. One artillery regiment is permanently attached to each army corps. But this regiment on a war footing has fifteen batteries, while the German artillery brigade has but seventeen. The fifteen batteries are arranged to six divisions. Three of the divisions, embracing each three batteries, are attached to the infantry divisions of the corps. The six remaining batteries, grouped in divisions of two batteries each, form together the corps or reserve artillery.

The colonel of the regiment is chief of artillery of the corps. He has a staff sufficiently numerous to enable him, with the assistance of the small staffs of the artillery-divisions, to administer all the affairs of the regiment.

Four ammunition columns, embracing a total of ninety wagons, and all under the orders of the colonel, supply the six divisions with ammunition. The personnel of the four columns embraces 6 officers and 448 men.

From the foregoing, it is evident that, as the arm is at present organized, it is not necessary that the administrative arrangements of the German and Austrian artillery-divisions be so complete as was required with the brigades of the Union artillery, for this administrative machinery is supplied in their respective regimental and brigade staffs, which invariably accompany the army corps to which the regiments are permanently attached. As with these, so with the other armies of Continental Europe.

Questions of administration and organization have not, however, primarily determined that in all large armies of recent times artillery should be handled by grouping the batteries together. This has been decided from purely tactical considerations, which, in battle, should and do dominate all others. It is seen that, to use artillery effectively, massing to a greater or less degree is necessary. Correct tactical principles require that this arm must be used—not a gun or even a battery here and there, but that, when practicable, several batteries should come into action together, and, by weight of metal thrown, endeavor to beat down all opposition. And as tactics render it necessary that they must fight together, it is natural and proper that in the organization of the arm the batteries should be united in sufficiently large, yet not unwieldy masses, which, when necessary, may be moved from point to point with facility and effect. The question of administration in turn follows that of organization, and is only this: How shall the batteries thus brought together be commanded and supplied to insure the highest attainable degree of efficiency when they come on the field?

B [1].

PARIS, FRANCE, *September 16th*, 1776.—Articles of Agreement between S. Deane Agent for the United Colonies of North America, and Sieur Phillipus Charles John Baptist Trouson du Coudray, Adjutant General of Artillery, in the service of France.

I. Sieur du Coudray, under title of general of artillery and ordnance and rank of major general in the forces of the United Colonies, shall have direction of whatever relates to the artillery and corps of engineers, under orders and control only of Congress, their board of war, and the commander-in-chief, for the time being.

II. The corps of artillery and engineers, the officers and soldiers of the same, shall be under his immediate command, with all the privileges and authority annexed to such command respecting either rewards and punishments; and in case of vacancies in said corps by death, removal, or new creations it shall be for him to recommend to the Congress, or their committee of war, the persons proper for filling the same.

III. Whatever relates to the supplying the said corps with provision, to the construction of artillery and fortification, to any plan or scheme relative to these objects, will be consulted on with him, and the execution of whatever may be agreed on committed to him, as within his department.

* * * * * * * * *

V. Mons. du Coudray shall be furnished with an adjutant, two aids-de-camp, or one aide and a secretary, and designer, at the expense and in the pay of the United States.

* * * * * * * * *

X. Mons. du Coudray will exert himself in the dispatch of artillery and stores agreed on; also will embark himself as early in the season as is consistent with such dispatch.

His title and emoluments were to date from August 1st, 1776, and he was given the privilege of choosing for assistants 2 engineers, 4 captains, 4 lieutenants, and 1 adjutant-general. But his preparations were still more elaborate, as there arrived in the Amphitrite with him 1 doctor, 1 adjutant-general, 3 captains and 4 lieutenants of engineers, 1 captain and 2 lieutenants of mines, 2 captains, 3 captain-lieutenants and 6 lieutenants of artillery, 1 captain and 1 lieutenant of bombardiers, 1 lieutenant of workmen, and 12 sergeants of artillery. Among these captains of artillery was Louis de Tousard, who, in consequence of the loss of an arm while gallantly fighting his guns in an action against the enemy in Rhode Island, in 1778, was brevetted lieutenant-colonel, and given a pension of thirty dollars per month during life. This was the officer subsequently appointed major in the corps of artillerists and engineers, promoted lieutenant-colonel commandant, Second artillerists and engineers, and appointed inspector of artillery for the army of the United States. Being disbanded in the reorganization of 1802, he devoted himself to the completion of a task which he had undertaken at the special request of President Washington, and in 1809 published the Artillerist's Companion, the first elaborate and comprehensive work on the practical and scientific duties of the arm produced in this country. Considering the paucity of literary facilities at the time, the difficulty in procuring materials, the little interest in military affairs taken by a government still struggling to vindicate the principle that an army was not necessary to its existence, the publication of these volumes must ever be regarded as a remarkable achievement. They remain a noble, enduring monument to the patriotic zeal, high professional attainments, and indefatigable industry of the distinguished author. The artillery has reason to remember the advent of Du Coudray to American shores, if only for the felicitous circumstance that thereby the honorable list of its officers was embellished with the name of Louis de Tousard.

It may not be uninteresting to briefly note the fate of Du Coudray and his followers. It will be noticed that by the terms of his agreement he was to be chief of both engineers and artillery. But it transpired that provision for the former had already been made under authority of Congress, whose committee of secret correspondence had been instructed so early as December 2d, 1775, to procure four good European engineers. A contract was entered into February 13th, 1777, by Benjamin Franklin and others, at Paris, with certain officers, who received leaves of absence for the purpose.

On July 22d, 1777, Chevalier Du Portail, colonel of engineers, the officer highest in rank of these Frenchmen, was placed in command of all engineers in United States service—a position he retained until the end of the war. With Knox as chief of artillery and Du Portail as chief of engineers there was nothing left for Du Coudray except the ordnance feature of the Deane contract. He was accordingly, August 11th, 1777, chosen, with rank of major-general, to perform the duties of inspector-general of ordnance and military manufactories—an office created for him. He was not a man to be flattered with the shadow, while the substance of his agreement was being enjoyed by others. He declined the office, and informed the President that all he wanted was an opportunity to fight for America, with whatever rank Congress chose to give him. Upon this he was chosen captain, his officers lieutenants, and his non-commissioned officers ensigns, and commissions were ordered to be made out accordingly. Soon after, while hastening to join the army retreating from Brandywine, he was drowned in the Schuylkill river. Congress ordered his remains to be buried with the honors of war. The result of that battle was to bring foreigners once more into favor; the distrust and disappointment caused by the importunities, presumption, and incompetence of most of those already taken into the service of the States was again temporarily forgotten; and, October 11th, 1777, Du Coudray's friends, both commissioned and enlisted, were given the offices and pay stipulated for them by Mr. Deane. Had Du Coudray lived, he would probably, like De Kalb, have been appointed a major-general in the line.

B [2].

MARCH 23d, 1852.—Ordered to be printed.

Mr. Shields made the following report, to accompany Bill S. No. 304:

The Committee on Military Affairs respectfully reporteth—

That since the termination of the Mexican war, the artillery has been so much neglected that discontent and discouragement begin to prevail at the present time in that important branch of military service.

The exigencies of our extended frontier service, and the imperative necessity which compelled the department to make the whole military force as available as possible to act against the Indians and protect the frontier settlements, and the additional circumstance that the artillery consists nominally of four regiments, under four colonels, making four distinct and separate commands, subject to no common and recognized head, will sufficiently account for the present neglected and almost disorganized state of that important corps.

To avoid all misconception on this head, we wish to state distinctly that for the present condition of the artillery no blame or censure can justly attach to the department, to the general-in-chief who made every possible effort, under the circumstances, to preserve it in a state of efficiency, or to the officers of the corps who, as a body, are as intelligent and energetic as any other body of officers of equal number in any service; but to causes already alluded to, and to others, which it is unnecessary at this time to particularize.

There never was a time in the military history of the world when so much attention was bestowed upon the instruction and improvement of artillery as at present. The extraordinary progress of the present age in the arts and sciences is felt to the full extent in this branch of the military service.

The whole efforts of the nation should be directed, not to increase the quantity of this force, but to improve its quality, and to make it, both in its personnel and matériel, the most perfect of its kind in the world. It should be in every particular a model army—a nucleus around which the nation should rally in any great national emergency. Artillery is the work of time. Its efficiency depends upon a high order of intelligence and careful instruction, and its perfection can only be obtained by the zealous application to its service of time, intelligence, and practice.

Two companies of the forty-eight in service are equipped as light artillery; the remainder are, for the greater part, armed, equipped, and disciplined as infantry. They are thus deprived of any opportunity of acquiring that knowledge which is absolutely necessary for the defense of our coast in time of war—which includes the use of heavy artillery in all its forms. Great care and skill are now required in the preparation of the different species of munitions, in the arrangement of shell for efficient use, in the repair of carriages and the re-establishment of guns dismounted by accident or the enemy's fire, which can only be acquired by application and practice, and which are more necessary and essential now than ever, owing to the celerity with which steamers, or vessels towed by them, can pass, independent of wind and tide, to the object of their attack.

In addition to all this, there is the use of artillery in field and siege service, in which our troops will soon become lamentably deficient without competent instruction and practice. It is only within a few months that even a system of instruction in the manual exercise of the heavy artillery has been given to the army; for which the service is indebted to the general-in-chief, under whose orders it was compiled by a board of officers.

There are still other important duties belonging to the artillery, of which ours, under the present system of arrangement, can acquire no practical knowledge—such as the construction of their own batteries in field works, of siege works, including the parapets, embrasures, platforms, magazines, &c.

The condition and efficiency of the artillery as an arm of the military service may be taken as the best test at any time, and as a certain test at the present time, of the military efficiency of the nation to which that service belongs.

If the present condition of our artillery be taken as a test, ours might be considered as the most inefficient and worst managed military service in the world. But as this nation is anomalous in many respects, so it is in this. The personnel of our artillery, so far as it consists of the corps of artillery officers, is, in point of intelligence, scientific knowledge, and preparatory instruction, equal as a body to the officers of any other service; and with equal opportunities for practice and improvement, owing to the practical energy and inventive energy of our people, they would surpass in general efficiency any other equal number of artillery officers in any service. It must be gratifying to the American people to see the officers of the army, instead of concealing the defects of the service from the public, the first to point them out, and to call aloud for assistance and reform.

This is the spirit which should animate Americans in every branch of the public service, whether civil or military, and without which the public service is liable to become almost as much neglected and badly managed in a republic as under any other form of government.

The first essential to improve the condition of the artillery and render it efficient is *unity*. This is the first essential in every kind of military service, and is indispensable to the artillery. The committee propose, therefore, to give it a directing head, and to make the head, who ought to be one of the most efficient officers of the army, responsible for the condition and efficiency of this branch of the service. It is now a body without any head, or rather it has as many heads as it has regiments; but there is no one whose duty it is to superintend its management, supervise its instruction, and diffuse life and energy into the whole as a distinct corps of the army. The next measure is to authorize the chief of artillery, under the direction of the President, to eliminate from the present artillery force a sufficient number of officers and companies to constitute a competent corps for instruction, practice, and improvement in every species of artillery service, and employ the residue as cavalry or as infantry companies for the defense of the frontier. This new arrangement will not diminish the general efficiency of our little army for frontier service, and will not increase its expense; and yet, simple as it is, it will render our artillery disciplined and efficient, and keep it in a state of readiness, by which it can be expanded, in any emergency, to any extent commensurate with the wants and wishes of the nation.

B [3].

[General Orders No. 6.]

HEADQUARTERS OF THE ARMY, ADJUTANT-GENERAL'S OFFICE,
WASHINGTON, *January 30th*, 1866.

A permanent artillery board is hereby organized, to which questions pertaining to the artillery arm of service may be referred by the Secretary of War or the general-in-chief for discussion and recommendation.

The board shall also have the power to make original recommendations to the general-in-chief in reference to the interests and efficiency of the artillery arm.

The members shall sit on the board in accordance with their rank in the artillery, and the senior member shall be president. He shall have power to call meetings at such times and places as shall be approved by the general-in-chief, in addition to those called by the Secretary of War or general-in-chief.

A complete record of the proceedings of the board will be kept by the secretary, who, on being relieved, shall turn it over to his successor or the adjutant-general of the army.

*　*　*　*　*　*　*

By command of Lieutenant-General Grant.

E. S. TOWNSEND, *Assistant Adjutant-General.*

B [4].

Position and Functions of Brigadier-Generals and Lieutenant-Colonels, Royal Artillery, in the Field, British Regulations.*

The brigadier-generals and commanders of corps and divisional artillery in the field form an integral part of the army corps staff and divisional staff, respectively. They will encamp with the staff and receive orders from their respective generals.

The commanding officer of corps artillery will encamp with his artillery and receive his orders from the brigadier-general. When divisional artillery is withdrawn from its division for the purpose of being massed with the corps artillery, it will be under the immediate orders of the brigadier-general; but on other occasions the lieutenant-colonel in command of the divisional artillery will have the entire responsibility for the use of his batteries, under the orders of the divisional general.

In the field, brigadier-generals and lieutenant-colonels of artillery will be made acquainted with the general plan of operations and the part which the artillery under their command is expected to play. They will communicate as much of this information as may be necessary to the officers commanding batteries. The brigadier-general will, as a rule, accompany the general officer of the army corps, and only leave him when the artillery is massed. Similarly, the commanding officer of divisional artillery will accompany the generals of division, but will take personal command when the divisional artillery is massed.

---

* When the British army takes the field, there is, according to the published accounts of its organization, with each army corps a brigadier-general, chief of artillery. Each corps has three divisions; each division has three batteries (18 guns), commanded by a lieutenant-colonel. Each corps has an artillery *reserve*, called corps artillery, of three horse and two field batteries, commanded by a colonel.

APPENDIX. 379

Responsibility of Different Ranks of Officers.

In order that no question may arise as to the responsibility of officers of different ranks in action, the following general rules will be observed:

The brigadier-general will be responsible that the lieutenant-colonels or other officers in command of more than one battery in the field are acquainted with the position of the corps ammunition columns, the probable position of the corps staff, and every other necessary information which does not come strictly under the government of general officers commanding divisions. He will also be responsible, under the orders of the general officer in command of the corps, for the tactical use of the whole of the artillery not at the time under the command of general officers commanding divisions.

Whenever corps and divisional artillery are massed, he will take immediate command of the mass, assigning to each section the portion of the objective at which it is to fire, and the commanding officer of each section will divide the portion so assigned amongst the batteries under his command.

Any order given by him to the artillery is to be considered as coming from the general commanding the corps.

Lieutenant-colonels, or other officers of less rank, being in command of a section of artillery, will be responsible for the tactical handling of the batteries under their command, including the general choice of positions and the part of the objective to be fired at. When their batteries are massed, they will assign the position to be taken up by the wagons and spare horses, and direct the replacement of casualties.

Officers commanding batteries will be responsible for the range and nature of projectiles used, as well as for the actual movements of their batteries. In action, they should separate themselves from the smoke of the guns and watch carefully the result of the fire, correcting errors from time to time. They will note down the object, the apparent effect of the fire, and the changes made in projectiles, range and direction, the movements of their batteries, the hour at which movements and opening or ceasing fire occur, together with any useful remarks. The books in which these notes are made should be preserved for future reference. They will also be responsible, when acting singly, that the caisson-wagons are within reach, and that the guns in action are kept duly supplied with everything needful for their efficient working.

B [5].

The organization of the German artillery, for administrative purposes, in peace, is as follows:

1. A general or lieutenant-general as inspector of artillery.

2. Four artillery inspections, each supervised by a lieutenant-general or a major-general.

3. Fourteen or more artillery brigades, each commanded by a major-general or colonel, and each composed of two or three regiments.

4. Corps and divisional artillery; the former is in reality the *reserve* for the army corps, while the latter embraces the batteries attached to army divisions, two or three of which make up each army corps.

When the army takes the field in war, the inspector-general [1] joins the headquarters of the commander-in-chief; the sub-inspectors [2] join the headquarters of the operating armies, where they act as chiefs of artillery. The artillery brigade commanders accompany their corps headquarters, where they act as chiefs of artillery for their respective army corps.

The corps artillery (*i. e.*, corps reserve) is a regiment commanded by its colonel.

The divisional artillery embraces three or four batteries organized into an artillery division and commanded by a field officer.

Regarding the duties of the inspector-general, the following very general information has been secured through the American minister at Berlin:

"The inspector-general is both an executive and administrative officer. His duties consist in inspecting all the artillery in his district, in attending their shooting practice, &c. Questions of discipline, however, are settled by the army corps commander. On the declaration of war, his peace duties cease altogether, and he becomes the chief artillery officer at the headquarters of an army commander. In battle, it is his duty to secure good positions for the artillery of the different corps, but always in consultation with his commanding general.

"He is supposed to know the intentions of the general, and do all in his power to forward them in directing the artillery. He may form no independent plans, and consequently is not supposed 'to give any orders originating with himself,' except so far as, after knowing confidentially the general's plans, he believes they will be thus most successfully executed. There are no rules laid down to prevent conflict of authority between inspectors-general and commanding-generals of army corps. In time of peace the latter seldom interfere with the artillery of their district, but may, if they like, inspect it at any time. In time of war, the artillery-general of an army has to regulate the proper supply and disposition of ammunition as well as its reserves."

C [1].

Regulations United States Army of May 6th, 1813.

The artillery will be distributed for field service into divisions or half divisions. A division of artillery will consist of six pieces of ordnance, viz., four cannon of the same calibre and two howitzers or six cannon of not more than two calibres. A half division of artillery will consist of two pieces of cannon of the same calibre and of one howitzer, or of three pieces of cannon of the same calibre. To each pair of three-pounders will be allotted one ammunition-wagon or caisson; to each six-pounder the same; to each howitzer, double this allowance; to each gun of larger calibre than a six-pounder, two, or at most three, ammunition-wagons or caissons.

To each division of artillery will be allotted three wagons, provided with assorted and spare articles of equipment, ammunition, harness, entrenching and artificers' tools, &c.; to each half division, one wagon, with assorted spare articles and tools as above; to each division of flying artillery and every two divisions of foot artillery will be allotted one traveling forge. * * * Wagons will be provided with mining and laboratory tools and utensils, together with additional quantities of entrenching and artificers' tools, whenever necessary.

By the Regulations of 1820 each company of artillery, with six pieces of ordnance and their proper stores, constituted a division of artillery. The division was divided into subdivisions, each consisting of two pieces of ordnance of the same kind.

By the Regulations of 1835 the term *division* was changed to *battery*, and the artillery for field service was distributed into batteries, half-batteries, and sections, corresponding in composition to the former divisions, half-divisions, and subdivisions. We thus see that the Gribeauval system, not only as regards matériel, but as regards the organization of the personnel, disappeared in all its parts immediately after the introduction of the stock-trail system of carriages.

The inconvenience that results from having the legal designation of the artillery tactical unit—company—different from that prescribed by regulations—division or battery—is manifest. The incongruity remained, however, as part of the military system until the Fifth artillery was organized in 1861, when it was partially, and in the reorganization of 1866 it was wholly, abated by the introduction of the term *battery* to designate the smallest legal artillery unit.

As germane to the subject-matter of this note, the following extract from the fourth note of Napoleon's Dictations at St. Helena, made upon General Rogniat's "Considerations sue L'Art de la Guerre," published in 1861, will be interesting:

"The artillery division has been fixed by General Gribeauval at eight pieces—4, 8, and 12-pounders, or 6-inch howitzers—because it is necessary, first, that a division of artillery may be able to divide itself into two or four batteries; second, because eight pieces can be followed by a company of 120 men, having a reserve detachment in the park; third, because the wagons and carriages necessary for the service of these eight pieces can be harnessed by a company of the equipage of the train; fourth, because a good captain can look after that number of pieces; fifth, the number of carriages and wagons which composed a battery of eight pieces provide sufficient work for one forge and one ammunition-wagon, and because two spare gun-carriages are sufficient for the division.

"If the division were composed of a less number of pieces, so many more forges, ammunition-wagons, and spare gun-carriages would be needed.

"Napoleon suppressed the 4 and 8-pounders, and for them substituted the 6-pounder. Experience had shown him that the infantry generals made use indiscriminately of the 4 and 8-pounders, without regard to the effect they desired to produce. He suppressed the 6-inch howitzer, substituting for it the 5½-inch howitzer, because two cartridges of the first weigh as much as three of the second (5½-inch), and, besides, the 5½-inch howitzer is found to have the same calibre as the 24-pounder, used so much in siege-trains and forts. He formed his foot artillery divisions of two 5½-inch howitzers and six 6-pounders, or of two long-range 5½-inch howitzers and six 12-pounders; the horse artillery divisions, of four 6-pounders and two howitzers; but it would be preferable, if they [the horse artillery divisions] had the same compositions as the foot artillery, that is to say, two 5½-inch howitzers and six 6-pounders. ' The proportions of the various calibres were twelve-twentieths 6-pounders, three-twentieths 12-pounders, and five-twentieths howitzers.

"These changes modified M. de Gribeauval's system. They were made in his spirit, and he would not have disowned them. He reformed a great deal; he simplified a great deal. *The artillery is yet too heavy, too complicated; it must again be simplified, rendered uniform, and reduced to its simplest form.*

"The equipage of sixty pieces, formed on Napoleon's principles, was thirty-six 6-pounders, nine 12-pounders, fifteen howitzers, forming seven divisions and a half, and required thirty-two forges, ammunition-wagons, and spare gun-carriages for the divisions; eighty-one caissons for 6-pounders, forty and a half for 12-pounders, sixty-seven and a half for howitzers, twenty-nine wagons and carriages of the park, thirty wagons for infantry, twenty of bridge equipage—in all, three hundred and sixty carriages, or six carriages for each piece. By this means the supply was three hundred and six shot per piece, without counting what was in the small ammunition-chest.

"M. de Gribeauval, who had fought through the seven years' war in the Austrian army, and had a genius for artillery, made the rule that the extent of the equipage should be at the rate of four pieces to 1,000 men, or thirty-six pieces for a division of 9,000, or one hundred and sixty pieces for an army of 40,000 men. The imperial arrangement was 120 pieces for a corps d'armé of 40,000 men, composed of 4 infantry, 1 light cavalry, 1 dragoon, and 1 cuirassier division. Of the fifteen artillery divisions, two were attached to each infantry division, three were in reserve. Of the remainder—the horse artillery divisions—one was with the light cavalry, one with the dragoons, and two with the cuirassiers. The whole embraced seventy-two 6-pounders, eighteen 12-pounders, thirty howitzers, and nearly six hundred wagons, including the pieces, the double supply of stores, and the infantry ammunition-wagons.

"It is necessary that an army have infantry, cavalry, and artillery in just proportions. These different arms cannot supply each other's places. We have seen some occasions where the enemy had almost won the battle. He occupied a fine position with a battery of fifty or sixty pieces. It would have been in vain to attack him with 4,000 horse and 8,000 infantry. A battery of equal power was necessary, under the protection of which the colums of attack advanced and deployed.

"The proportions of the three arms have always been the object of the meditations of the great generals.

"They have agreed that it must be—first, four pieces for 1,000 men, giving one-eighth of the army for the artillery personnel; second, a cavalry equal to one-fourth of the infantry.

"A good infantry is without doubt the nerve of the army; but if it had to fight a long time against a very superior artillery, it would be demoralized and destroyed. In the first campaigns of the war of the Revolution, France had always the best artillery. I don't know a single instance in this war where twenty pieces of cannon advantageously posted have been taken by the bayonet."

C [2].

February 3d, 1840, the ordnance committee, when it had been in session nearly a year, addressed a letter to the Secretary of War on the subject of the proper metal for field ordnance, calling attention to the following facts: 1. The board of 1835 had recommended bronze. 2. The board of 1838, four to one, did the same, and also recommended that experiments be made to test the durability of cast-iron and malleable cast-iron. 3. The results showed that no dependence could be placed on iron guns of either description. 4. This was the opinion among artillerists abroad. 5. The committee therefore found no difficulty in unanimously recommending the adoption of bronze.

The Secretary replied in the following rather caustic letter, dated War Department, February 18th, 1840:

"The report of the board of ordnance in relation to the best material for field artillery has been carefully examined; and notwithstanding the concurrent opinions of so many boards of ordnance that have considered this matter, and that of the existing board, in favor of the exclusive use of bronze for field cannon, the Department of War does not deem it expedient to renounce altogether the use of iron for this purpose. Judging from the experiments quoted by the board, it appears certain that iron is abundantly strong, and that if guns sometimes fail, it is not because the gun is of iron, but because the founder is not perfect in his art. At present, he makes a good gun by accident, whereas it is by accident only he should make a bad one.

"The iron 6, 12, and 18-pounders in use during the last war prove that we formerly possessed the art of making strong, light, and serviceable guns. The uncertainty which attends the proof of the new iron guns arises from some irregularity in the selection, mixing, or the management of the metal; but the precise nature of the difference in this respect between a good and a bad gun is not fully known, and ought to be ascertained with all possible accuracy. This must be regarded as the first and most important thing to be learned, being more necessary even than to decide upon the pattern and other details. In fixing on the latter, however, it will be necessary to bear in mind that the uncertainty complained of is due in some measure to the frequent changes made by the ordnance office in the length and weight of the guns. No sacrifice of safety and solidity ought to be made to lighten the weight of the metal. * * * It would seem that it would be no less difficult to introduce the art of casting bronze than iron guns. We possess the best quality of iron; but copper is not found or not wrought in sufficient quantities, and tin not at all; and it is important that the armament of our navy, fortifications, and troops should be drawn from an independent source.

"The partial use of bronze field artillery is not objected to; but the board of ordnance must apply itself to acquire sufficient knowledge of the subject to cast the guns within our own arsenals, as this Department is not satisfied with those that have been hitherto made at private foundries. For this purpose an intelligent officer should be sent to visit the foundries of bronze cannon in Europe. A few pieces of field artillery may be purchased there, on condition of the privilege being granted of assisting at all the operations of mixing the metals and fusing and casting the guns. Two officers of industry and capacity ought to be immediately stationed at two of the principal foundries (in this country), in order to make themselves familiar with all the usual processes of iron work, so that when they enter the foreign establishments they may be able to discern what is new and peculiar, and lose no time in learning abroad things equally well understood and practiced at home.

"The Department will take measures to ascertain the method pursued by the Prussian Government in the reception of iron guns for its artillery, and pursue the same course in procuring a few light pieces from Sweden; and it is proposed that the officers spoken of above should, when sufficiently acquainted with the subject, proceed to that country, superintend the casting of our own guns, and acquire accurate information in relation to the selection of metals, their mixing, fusing, and casting, and the method of proving cannon, as practiced by the Swedish and foreign officers at those foundries. Connected with this subject is an inquiry into the effect produced by the increased strength of the powder now in use, both with regard to its application to common service and to prove guns." * * *

The rejoinder of the committee, dated February 20th, was as follows:

The board of ordnance officers has attentively examined the decision of the Secretary of War of February 18th, upon the proposition submitted to him of the best matériel for field artillery; and while it admits the correctness of his views and the propriety of the means to be adopted for accomplishing the objects to be attained, the subject is of so grave a nature, involving interests of such importance to the country as well as the reputation of the ordnance corps, that the board begs leave to submit the following remarks and propositions for his consideration:

1. The board is of opinion, as before stated, that iron field guns can be made. It also fully concurs with the Secretary that the means pointed out should be put in practice with as little delay as practicable, to insure castings of good quality; but it is evident some time must elapse before we can get the benefit of their results.

2. In addition to the field guns required for our own service, several of the States require iron field guns for arming their militia, and others require field guns of bronze. More than one hundred guns of this material have been issued to the States within the last two years; and in relation to this matter, the board is of opinion that the skill acquired in this branch of manufacture has been underrated. We have the principal French publications on the subject— Mouge and Dartein. They have been closely followed, except in moulding. We make use of a first-rate furnace, better moulding materials, and the same mode of mixing the materials as the French. We have succeeded in making castings perfectly sound and homogeneous, of the same specific gravity as foreign bronze, the actual weights of the guns corresponding with their computed weights. The durability of some of our bronze guns exceeds that of many foreign guns.

* * * * * * * * *

4. The board considers the ordnance department capable to furnish *immediately* bronze field guns fit for service, and they propose to make patterns of these guns the dimensions of which will be such that their carriages will be able to receive iron guns when prepared. Should the Secretary of War agree to this proposition, they will arrange all the details, so that our artillery could be supplied with field batteries complete immediately; and they could at the same time proceed to put in practice the measures proposed to perfect the manufacture of iron guns, which, when perfected, could be introduced without delay and without altering the system, as the same carriages, &c., would suit for both. The necessity of adopting a system at *once* is evident; and by pursuing the course here recommended, we would be able *now* to put our resources in operation to furnish what is absolutely necessary—*a system for the immediate use of our artillery.*

The subject of chambered guns will also receive the prompt attention of the board; but this, even supposing the principle established, would require some time and experiments to arrange the details.

FEBRUARY 29th, 1840.—The drawings of pattern field guns, brass and iron, were completed and sent to the Secretary of War, with the following statement for his consideration:

The board of ordnance officers, in conformity with the instructions of the Secretary of War, has the honor to submit drawings for bronze and iron field cannon, the latter of such dimensions as they confidently believe will impart to them sufficient strength, provided the material is of good quality, without which the board would have no faith in iron of any pattern. The patterns for the bronze guns are reduced somewhat in length from those established in 1835, so as to conform in length to the iron guns, for the purpose of allowing the latter to be mounted upon the carriages established for the brass guns, simply by a small increase in the width of the rondels and the length of the assembling bolts.

The 12-pounder bronze gun of 1835, being sixteen calibres long and weighing 1,800 pounds, is of too great weight for field service generally, though particularly adapted to field works and batteries of position. The pattern now proposed is for a light 12-pounder; and as it is not expedient to alter the diameters (which would affect the strength of the piece), they are obliged to reduce its length to thirteen calibres, which is nearly the same as the English light 12-pounder. This gun takes the place of the 9-pounder of 1835, which has been abolished.

The 6-pounders have been fixed at fourteen calibres length of bore, for the same reasons, viz., that the strength of the guns should be augmented without adding too much to their weight; and notwithstanding a majority of the board would prefer guns of an increased length, if made exclusively of bronze, they have yielded such preference to the necessity of preserving a uniformity between the length of the guns of the two metals and in the carriages for them, it being very important to avoid a multiplication of models for field carriages.

The board having considered the subject of chambered guns, is of opinion that a few field guns should be bored with chambers, and that their force and durability should be compared with the ordinary guns.

The reply of the Secretary of War to the above was dated War Department, March 5th, 1840:

The Secretary of War has attentively considered the remarks and proposals of the board of ordnance, made in reply to his communication of the 18th ultimo, on the subject of field artillery, and cannot concur in the one or the other. However important it may be that our artillery should be supplied at once with field batteries complete, it is more so that the guns which compose those batteries should be perfect, and the patterns to be adopted unobjectionable and permanent. The frequent attempts to adopt a system *at once* for the immediate use of our artillery, without an adequate acquaintance with the subject, have led to the protracted delay we have already experienced in this matter. The Secretary is therefore opposed to all temporary expedients. The patterns presented for approval, in conformity with the proposals, are confessedly defective, and have been devised because the material is supposed not to be good or the knowledge of the foundries imperfect. The weight is not considered material, but the length is very objectionable. It is not such as the board would have recommended if it had believed that the metal now in use would have borne such an increased number of calibres as would place our light artillery on an equality with that of Europe and suffice to fight the guns advantageously behind field-works. From a desire to use the same carriages, the bronze gun is likewise reduced, extending these serious objections to all the light artillery, whether iron or brass.

The board is satisfied "that such additions to the knowledge of founding bronze guns as could be made by visiting European establishments would undoubtedly enable them to perform the work at any one of the arsenals, in case a national foundry should not be authorized by Congress." The Secretary thinks this remark equally applicable to iron guns. And in the absence of authority to establish a foundry, the board ought to possess such additional knowledge of the subject as to enable its members to regulate the founding of bronze and iron guns by contract with the proprietors of private foundries, in such manner as to secure the strict application of scientific principles to the founding of cannon ; and *he is not satisfied that the corps, collectively or individually, possess that practical knowledge which the importance of the subject, both to the country and the reputation of the corps, would seem to require.* He repeats, therefore, his wish that this desirable knowledge should be acquired with as little delay as practicable, and for that purpose proposes that the three junior members of the board should proceed to Europe, accompanied by a practical founder.

Although the subject of light artillery alone is now under consideration, it may be well to advert to our defective system of heavy ordnance as a further motive for the course recommended. During the absence of the members of the board who are designated to proceed to Europe, it will be advisable to suspend the casting of light artillery, and to make no contracts for heavy ordnance.

386   APPENDIX.

C [3].

The following letter from Colonel Wadsworth to a prominent officer of the army, whose aid he solicited in the furtherance of the important work marked out in the letter itself, sufficiently indicates the prompt manner in which he proceeded to the task of introducing symmetry and simplicity into the artillery service. It is dated Washington, D. C., May 27th, 1813:

"Although it has been near a twelve-month since I came into this office, but little could be accomplished before General Armstrong became Secretary of War. At the commencement of hostilities we were destitute of seasoned timber for gun-carriages, as well as establishments and sufficient workmen for their construction. Heretofore they have been procured partly by contracts and partly constructed by the artificers of the artillery. Every superintendent selected whatever pattern and introduced whatever alteration his fancy suggested. The American artillery, including that belonging to the individual States, comprises, I believe, every calibre made use of either in the English or French service, by sea or land, with endless variations in the proportions of each calibre. The necessity of some regulation to secure *simplicity* and uniformity must be obvious to all; yet men of reflection and experience alone can duly estimate the importance of these two qualities. Every variation in the proportions of pieces of the same calibre exacts a corresponding change in the carriage, and for every distinct calibre will be required not only a suitable carriage but its appropriate equipments and ammunition. In a word, unless the number of our calibres and their variations be reasonably reduced, and the whole be settled by some permanent regulation, no possible exertion can give to our artillery that perfection its importance merits and which the public service requires.

"In France, by the Regulations of 1732, calibres for land service were reduced to five—24, 16, 12, 8 and 4-pounders. The military writers of that country date from that period the improvement of their artillery. Experience had taught the celebrated Vauban the necessity for such a reformation, which was solicited, however, in vain during his life.

"I feel anxious to get the following system established relative to the calibres of cannon in the United States:

"For field service, let there be:—light 3, 6, and 12-pounder guns on traveling carriages, and $5\frac{8}{10}$ inch howitzers, *i. e*, the diameter of the 24-pounder howitzer.

"For siege: heavy 18 and 24-pounders on traveling carriages, 8 and $5\frac{8}{10}$-inch howitzers on traveling carriages, and 8, 10, and 13-inch mortars.

"For fixed batteries on seaboard: heavy 18 and 24-pounders on fixed carriages, and 10-inch mortars.

"For movable batteries on seaboard: light 12-pounders and 8-inch howitzers on traveling carriages.

"Thus the whole reduced to five calibres of cannon, two of howitzers, and three of mortars.

"Were any alterations allowed, it might be in the entire suppression of the heavy 18-pounders, whose place should be supplied by the 24-pounders, on the supposition that a light 18-pounder might be annexed to the field train.

"The proportion of 3-pounders and 12-pounders in a field train should be small, letting* the division consist principally of 6-pounders and $5\frac{8}{10}$-inch howitzers.

"The difference between 3-pounder and 4-pounder shot or case is immaterial; but the former are preferable, used in conjunction with the 6-pounder, as they are not so nearly like each other—danger of mistakes avoided.

"The range of an 8-inch shell from howitzers exceeds that of random cannon shot, for this reason that piece is superior to all others for attacking a ship at anchor on our coast or in our bays and rivers. In attacking a ship with two or three 18-pounders or 24-pounders on traveling carriages commonly selected for the purpose, unless the ground should particularly favor the assailant, the chance is the fire of the ship, from the superior number of her guns, would compel him to give over the attack; whereas a single 8-inch howitzer placed out of the reach of a ship's guns would annoy her so as to compel a change of station, much more than which ought not to be expected.

"The light 12-pounder is perfectly adapted to impede and prevent the landing of boats.

"The 9-pounder is indeed a very good piece, yet need not be retained.

"If you require a gun heavier than the 6-pounder, let the 12-pounder be used; if lighter than a 12-pounder, use the 6-pounder.

"The 3-pounder will be particularly useful for the defense of distant posts on the frontier and interior, where the difficulties of transportation render economy of ammunition an important object.

"I give the preference to the 6-pounder rather than to either the 4-pounder or 8-pounder of the French, and, joined to the $5\frac{8}{10}$ inch or 24-pound howitzer, consider it capable almost of superseding all other kinds of field artillery.

"The influence of a single individual cannot reach far enough to attain *the object I have in view—of bringing our artillery to a system of simplicity and uniformity.* The public mind must be fully impressed with the idea of its necessity before a change can be wrought."

INDEX.

	PAGE.
ADMINISTRATION:	
General considerations affecting early artillery	108–112
Of artillery affairs from 1802 to 1812	164
Existing system of, in the United States artillery	178–188

AMMUNITION:
  Train, accompanying Army of Potomac 101
  Special, organized to accompany army 102
  Retained when army reserve (artillery) was broken up 102
ANDERSON, CAPTAIN ROBERT:
  Translates instruction for field artillery 305
        evolutions of field batteries 307
ARMISTEAD, CAPTAIN GEORGE, appointed major 3d artillery 39
ARMISTEAD, WALKER K., colonel 3d artillery 46
ARMY:
  Plans for peace establishment of the 17, 18, 19, 20, 21
  Detachment of, retained provisionally at the peace 22
  Measures adopted to secure small regular 22, 23, 24
  Of April 9th, 1787, composed of 1 infantry regiment and 1 artillery battalion 25
  Of confederation adopted under Constitution 25
  Reorganized into a legion 26
                upon Lieutenant-General Washington's plan 30
  Increase of, by 10 infantry, 2 artillery, and 1 dragoon regiment ... 38
  Of Potomac: Strength of Divisions and corps of 83
        Organization of artillery in (1864) 86
  Of Northern Virginia: Artillery organization of 93
ARTICLES OF WAR, provisions of, affecting the artillery 108, 109
ARTIFICERS:
  Recommended by Knox 4
  100 to be attached to artillery in the field 5
  Regiment of, formed of one of the proposed artillery battalions 7
  Regiment of, mustered out of service 14
  Large number provided for (act of March 16th, 1802) 114
ARTILLERISTS AND ENGINEERS:
  Corps of, organized 27
  Regiment of, organized 29
  Teachers authorized for cadets of 30
  Reorganization of corps and regiment of 30
  Failure of plan to make military school of 31
  Circumstances attending raising of corps of 191
ARTILLERY:
  Organization of, United States (Appendix A [1]) 1
  Volunteer companies of, before Revolution 1
  Colonial, associated with English Royal regiment 1
  One company Royal, accompanies Braddock's expedition 1
  Laws, customs, traditions of Royal regiment ingrafted into Colonial. 1
  Major John Crane's company of Rhode Island 2
  Gridley's regiment of, reorganized, Knox in command 3
  Standing of the arm in service secured by Knox 3, 4
  Two companies of Knox's regiment dispatched to Canada 4

(389)

INDEX.

ARTILLERY—*Continued.*

	PAGE.
Nine companies move to New York; one remains at Boston	4
Companies of Captains Beauman and Hamilton join Knox	4
Project for improvement of, submitted by Knox to Congressional Committee	4, 5, 6
Claim set up for superiority of British	5
Inadequacy of the, for needs of service	5
Proportion of, to other arms of service	5
The English taken as model for building up Colonial	6
Erroneous ideas regarding supposed influence of the French	6
General Washington authorizes raising three battalions	6, 7
Origin of the several regiments (or battalions) of *regulars*	7, 8
The regiments of *regular* Continental	8
Relative order of precedence established for regiments of	8
Colonel Ebenezer Stevens' corps of	9
Incorporation of companies of Stevens' corps into Crane's artillery	9
Companies and battalions of, belonging to Colonies, distinct from regular establishment	9
Colonial, status of, as compared to regular	10
Reorganization of regular	12, 14
Assignment, regular regiments of, to State quotas	14
At siege of Yorktown	14
First and Fourth regiments of, move South	14
Second and Third regiments of, remain North	15
Rule for promotion in	15, 16, 17
Views as to proper peace establishment for	17, 18, 19, 20, 21
Of peace establishment, organized into battalion	24
Position of, in the legion	26, 27
Reorganization of, as *corps* of artillerists and engineers	27
Organization of *regiment* of artillerists and engineers	29
Light, recommended; one regiment organized	33
Its equipment	34
Equipment first company as such	34, 35
Regiment of, concentrated at New Orleans	35
March of light company, Baltimore to Pittsburg	35
Company of light, dismounted	36
Condition of regiment of light, before war of 1812	38
Two additional regiments organized	38
Principal officers of, detached from their commands	40
Slight changes in personnel of	42
Corps of, formed by consolidation of First, Second, and Third regiments	42
Remarks on organization of *corps* of	42, 43
Reorganization of, act of March 3d, 1815	44
Designation of companies by letters of alphabet	45
Slight changes in organization of	45
Reorganization of	46
Light, one company of each regiment to be equipped as	46
(C), Third Artillery, equipped as	50
Four additional companies of, authorized	51
Career of, in Rio Grande valley	51
Report introduced by Senate Military Committee favoring chief of artillery	51
Bill introduced in Congress for reorganization of	51, 52
School of Practice for, at Fortress Monroe	52
Fifth regiment of regular, organized	53
Light, note regarding use of term	54, 55
Question of a proper mount for	56, 57
One company in each regiment of, equipped as field artillery	59

INDEX. 391

ARTILLERY—*Continued.* PAGE.
Light, letter of Adjutant-General concerning utility of..................... 61
    Excellence of captains, &c., commanding companies of........... 61
    Additional companies equipped as.................................. 62, 63
    Companies dismounted and remounted after Mexican war..... 63, 64
    Remarks of Secretary Conrad concerning............................ 65
    Money specifically appropriated for mounting....................... 66
    Companies re-equipped as... 66, 67
    Companies of, stationed on Indian frontier......................... 68
    Companies of, dispersed; condition at beginning of Civil war... 69
Fifth regiment of, organized with tactical units designated 'batteries'.. 69
Field, effort to organize powerful, in Army of the Potomac........... 69, 70
Horse batteries reorganized.. 70
    Formed into brigades.. 70, 71
Field, general dismounting of, after Civil war................................ 71
    Batteries retained as.. 71
    Effect of section 1101, Rev. Stats., regarding....................... 72, 73
    Companies equipped as (1884).. 73, 74
    Claims to recognition, of old light companies...................... 74, 75
Brigades of, formed after Chancellorsville................................... 83, 84
Advantages of assignment to large tactical units............................ 84
Erroneous ideas concerning proper organization of......................... 84
General reserve, Army of Potomac, broken up............................. 86, 87, 88
Results flowing from breaking up reserve.................................. 88, 89, 91
Siege before Petersburg, Va... 88
Recapitulation of changes in Army of Potomac........................... 89–92
Of Army of Northern Virginia... 93
Changes in.. 93–95
The organization of, into brigades an outgrowth of war................. 95
Reserves..96–107
Confederate Army of Northern Virginia organized on plan now universal in Europe... 94
Advantageous position of American, at beginning of Revolution.. 108–112
Better pay of officers of the... 110
Field batteries of, made schools of instruction.......................... 132–137
Posts of field batteries... 137–141
Target record of, in 1879, and results.. 145–147
Technical duties of, performed by artillery officers........................ 148
Commissaries for, appointed... 149
Attainments of the *personnel* from 1802 to 1812............................ 166
Recommendations made in 1811 for improvement of artillery arm...... 167
Views of Colonel Izard.. 167
United with the ordnance department... 168
Propositions looking to the securing a chief of......................... 186–188
Horse (or light), the organization of, advocated by the Secretary of War.. 192
Steps taken to fit the artillery for the field............................... 193, 194
The results flowing from efforts to organize artillery for active service in war of 1812.. 196–200
Character of the service rendered by, from 1815 to 1846................. 200
Companies of, equipped as light artillery in Mexican war................ 201
Functions of, usurped by ordnance.. 201–206
Chief of, question as to his proper function............................ 208–222
    Status of, during Revolution.. 208–210
        War of 1812.. 210
    As fixed by regulations of 1816....................................... 210
    By Scott's regulations.. 211, 212

ARTILLERY—*Continued.*
                                                                                    PAGE.
  Chief of, regulations of 1841 and of 1857.................................... 212
    McClellan's orders 213
    Hooker's position regarding.. 214, 215
    Meade's orders... 216, 217
    Confederate orders concerning.. 218, 219
    General remarks regarding position of............................ 220, 221, 222
    Matériel of.. 223, 298
  Personnel of the combatant always under command of the general-in-
    chief... 178, 179
  Authority of colonels of... 179
  Remarks on present condition of the combatant.......................... 180–182
  Proposed measures for improvement.. 187, 188
  Colonel Wadsworth's proposed system of matériel..................... 233–237
  English block-trail system of... 237–239
  Matériel of—Adoption of English system of, by France................... 239
      Americanized Krupp system............................... 272, 273
      Revolutionary system of................................. 275, 276
      System of, 1816... 278
          Proposed by ordnance board of 1818...... 279, 280
          1835.................................... 280
          Calibres of, proposed in 1835........... 281
          1839.................................... 282
          1850.................................... 283
          1861.................................... 286
          Contest between the smooth-bore and the rifle........ 289, 290
              Muzzle and breech-loader.......: 291–293
          Chamber introduced in construction of........................ 293
          Recent improvements in siege and field............... 294–295
          Report of board on light................................. 295, 296
          Systems of 1868 and 1880............................... 297, 298
          Mobility of the, at epoch of war of 1812..................... 315

BRIGADES OF UNION ARMY: Battalions of Confederate; divisions of German
    and Austrian Artillery... 370–374
BANKHEAD, MAJOR JAMES, assigned to corps of artillery......................... 44
    Retained in 1821 46
BARBOUR, SECRETARY OF WAR, remarks of, concerning school of practice.. 123
BARRY, GENERAL WILLIAM F.:
    Addresses General McClellan regarding field artillery..................... 69
    Principles formulated by, for organization of artillery................... 80
    Chief of artillery, Army of Potomac....................................... 82
    Relieved as chief of artillery, Army of Potomac........................... 82
    Appointed inspector of artillery.. 82
    Orders assigning to duty as inspector of artillery................... 186, 187
BEAUMAN, SEBASTIAN:
    Captain New York artillery.. 4
    Retained in service.. 350
BEAUMARCHAIS: contractor for artillery supplies............................. 224
BOARD—
    Of ordnance, recommended by Knox.. 5
    Of war and ordnance, remodeled... 10, 11
        Personnel of the, when remodeled..................... 11
        Attempts of, to supplant commander-in chief... 11
            Frustrated.................................. 12
    Of ordnance: Fenwick, Ewing, Talcott, Baker, and Mordecai.. 56
    Of officers, recommends measures affecting artillery..................... 167
        Appointed to improve condition of artillery...234, 243, 244, 245

INDEX. 393

BOMFORD, GEORGE:
    Lieutenant-colonel of artillery.. 46
    Labors of, as head of the ordnance department............................. 117
BRAGG, BRAXTON:
    Lieutenant, commanding company equipped as light artillery............ 62
    Captain, succeeds to command of horse artillery company............... 62
    Conduct at battle of Buena Vista.................................... 62, 63
BROOKS, MAJOR: regiment of artillerists and engineers......................... 29
BRASS:
    Foundry, recommended by Knox.. 4
    Ordnance, in which army stood in need 5
    The favorite metal for cannon during Revolution........................... 257
    Composition of early gun-metal... 257, 258
    Supplanted by cast-iron for field-guns...................................... 260
    Investigations begun looking to a return to brass................... 261, 262
    Manufacture of first ten bronze guns by Ames Manufacturing Co...... 263
    Definitely adopted for field ordnance.. 265
    Plan for converting field-guns into rifled ordnance........................ 266
BROWN: captain of artillery company attached to Harrison's regiment...... 12
BROWN, GENERAL:
    Gives reasons for establishment of artillery school of practice.......... 122
    Death of.. 124
BROWN, LIEUTENANT-COLONEL HARVEY, commandant school of practice.... 125
BUFFINGTON, LIEUTENANT-COLONEL, design of depressing gun-carriage........ 256
BURBECK, WILLIAM:
    Lieutenant-colonel Gridley's regiment... 2
    Knox's regiment... 3
    Note concerning his declining colonelcy..................................... 3
    Dismissed.. 4
BURBECK, HENRY:
    Captain of artillery.. 25
    Colonel commandant corps artillerists and engineers...................... 32
    Colonel of artillerists 32
    Retired from service... 33

CALHOUN, SECRETARY OF WAR:
    Plan to improve condition of the artillery............................. 115, 116
    for merging artillery and ordnance.. 169
    Not the originator of merging plan put in execution...................... 172
CALIBRES OF ARTILLERY:
    List of, during Revolution... 275–276
    At the epoch of the war of 1812.. 277
CAMP OF INSTRUCTION at Trenton, N. J.. 58
CARRIAGES, ARTILLERY:
    English patterns used by Americans during Revolution............ 223, 225
    Features of the Gribeauval introduced................................. 229, 230
    The Gribeauval system of... 231
    Purchases from France... 231, 232
    Wheels for, in British service, of same size................................ 227
    Colonel Wadsworth's pattern of... 233
    Efforts of board of 1831 to secure proper.................................. 247
    Recommendations of board of 1835 regarding........................... 248
    French stock-trail, adopted into United States service................... 248
    Metallic, advantages of early patterns...................................... 249
    Recent improvements in construction of.................................... 250
    Recommendations of light artillery board........................... 250, 251
    Difficulties in constructing proper..................................... 251, 252

CARRIAGES, ARTILLERY—*Continued.*   PAGE.
Systems of siege, garrison, and sea-coast.................................... 253
Introduction of cast-iron in construction of................................. 254
    wrought-iron 255
Depressing.. 256
CARRINGTON, EDWARD:
Lieutenant-colonel Virginia artillery regiment............................. 7
Claims colonelcy Fourth artillery.. 17
Quartermaster of Southern army... 190
CAPTAIN-LIEUTENANT, introduction of title into American service............ 331
CASS, SECRETARY OF WAR:
Reports on unsettled condition of the ordnance............................. 243
Appoints board for improvement of.. 243
Sanctions return to brass for field ordnance............................... 263
Introduces mountain howitzer into United States service.................... 282
CHANCELLORSVILLE, composition of Union Army at............................. 83
CHIEF OF ARTILLERY, the question of the status or functions of........ 208–222
COMMANDER OF ARTILLERY:
Recommendations of, favorably acted on by Congress...................... 5, 6
Authority curtailed by department of commissary-general of military
  stores.. 11, 12
New powers given by resolves of Congress............................ 154, 155
All artillery affairs placed practically under his control................ 155
COMMISSARY-GENERAL OF MILITARY STORES:
Department of.. 11
Resolutions of Congress concerning.................................. 150, 151
Its career short-lived... 152
Experiences of department.. 152–158
Field department of, or field ordnance department organized...... 153, 154
Readjustment of.. 158
COMMITTEE:
Of Congress, reports adversely to Gridley............................... 2, 3
    to investigate army affairs.. 4
    suggestions of Colonel Knox to..................................... 4, 5
    to consider subject of peace establishment......................... 17
Of ordnance officers, appointed by Secretary Poinsett..................... 264
    commission from, sent to Europe.................................... 264
Deliberation of, results in adoption of brass for field ordnance..... 264, 265
CONFEDERATE ARMY:
Organization of artillery in.. 84, 86, 93, 94, 95
The pioneer in present plan of artillery organization..................... 94
Rule for assignment of artillery officers in.............................. 86
Command and administration of artillery affairs in....... 218, 219, 370, 374
CONGREVE, CAPTAIN, improvements of, English artillery..................... 237
CONRAD, SECRETARY OF WAR, report of, regarding light artillery companies.. 65
CONWAY, GENERAL:
Made inspector-general... 11
Cabal, result of... 12
CRANE:
Major John's company Rhode Island artillery................................ 2
Major in Knox's artillery regiment... 3
Colonel of one of the artillery regiments raised by order of General
  Washington.. 7
The ranking colonel of artillery... 8
Regiment of Colonel, third in order of precedence.......................... 8
Chief of artillery, Department of the Highlands............................ 209
List of officers in regiment of, as first organized.................. 336, 337
    in 1780.. 341

INDEX. 395

	PAGE.
CRAIG, CAPTAIN ISAAC, promoted major Fourth artillery	17

CRAIG, COLONEL H. K., remarks of, relative to the performance of artillery duties by officers and men of the ordnance department............ 67, 68

DAVIS, SECRETARY OF WAR:
   Remounts three ot the field artillery companies............................ 66
   Proposes to re-establish artillery school of practice....................... 125
DEARBORN, HENRY:
   Secretary of War.. 34
   Authorizes equipment of light artillery company........................... 34
   Interest and labors in field of technical artillery.......................... 165
   Introduces many features of the Gribeauval carriage..................... 230
DEARBORN, GENERAL HENRY:
   Complains of scarcity of artillery officers.................................. 41
DE FATT, CAPTAIN, inspector of Georgia artillery................................. 10
DE LISLE, MAJOR ROMAN, commander Georgia artillery.......................... 10
DE SAGULIER, improvements of, English artillery................................ 238
DORSEY, CAPTAIN, artillery company of, attached to Harrison's artillery..... 12
DOUGHTY, BREVET MAJOR JOHN:
   Company of, provisionally retained at the peace (1783).................. 23
   Promoted to major artillery battalion... 24
   Declines appointment of lieutenant colonel commandant of infantry... 26
   Retires from the artillery.. 26
   Returns to it... 29
   Retires from service.. 32
DOUGLASS, CAPTAIN THOMAS:
   Commands artillery company on peace establishment 351
DU COUDRAY:
   Compact with American agent at Paris....................................... 111
   Results flowing therefrom... 375
DUCROT: Attack of, with cavalry at Sedan (note).................................. 105
DU PORTAIL, CHIEF OF ENGINEERS:
   Views of, regarding peace establishment.................................... 17

ELLIOTT, BARNARD: Major of South Carolina artillery battalion.............. 10
ENGLISH:
   Artillery of, taken as a model by Knox...................................... 6
      System of... 237
ENGINEERS:
   Two, distinct from corps of artillerists and engineers, authorized 31
EUSTIS, CAPTAIN BENJAMIN: Promoted to fourth artillery...................... 16
EUSTIS, DOCTOR WILLIAM, Secretary of War:
   Dismounts light artillery company... 36
   Remarks of, regarding use of horse artillery................................ 37
   Favorably inclined towards proposed plan of reorganization of artillery... 41
   Introduces Gribeauval carriage... 231
EUSTIS, ABRAHAM: Captain in light artillery, promoted to major............. 37
   Retained in 1811... 46
   Equips three companies of horse artillery.................................... 196

FENWICK, JOHN R.:
   Lieutenant-colonel of light artillery.. 40
   Commands artillery on Canadian border............................... 40, 196
   Colonel Fourth artillery.. 46
   President of board of ordnance.. 56
FIRE-WORKER, title of, introduced into American service....................... 332

INDEX.

	PAGE.
FLOWER:	
Colonel of so-called artillery-artificer regiment	7
Commissary-general of military stores	149, 151
Death of Colonel	156
List of officers in so-called regiment of Colonel	346
FORD, MAHLON, major of artillerists, discharged	32
FORNEY, DANIEL M., major Second artillery	39
FORREST, THOMAS:	
Major of Pennsylvania artillery regiment	7
Lieutenant-colonel Pennsylvania artillery regiment	16
FOUNDRY for casting *brass* ordnance recommended	4
FORT RILEY, KANSAS: School for light batteries there established	137
FRANCE:	
Army officers of that nation in service of colonies	6
Erroneous ideas concerning their influence	6
Embarrassments caused by officers of that nationality	166
FRANKLIN, BENJAMIN: correspondence of, with regard to artillery officers	111
FREDERICKSBURG: composition of the Union army at	83
FREEMAN, CONSTANT:	
Major of artillerists and engineers	28
Lieutenant-colonel of artillerists	32
Retired from service in 1821	33
GATES, GENERAL HORATIO:	
President board of war and ordnance	11
Is given a command	12
GERMAN ARTILLERY:	
Successful employment of, war 1870 and 1871	105
Organization of artillery in the field	371, 374
Function of artillery commanders in war	380
GIBSON, CAPTAIN:	
Marches company horse artillery to Albany, N. Y.	195
Letter of, to Secretary of War	197
GRIBEAUVAL:	
Artillery system of, unknown to Americans at time of Revolution	223, 224, 225
Features of carriage adopted by Secretary Dearborn	230
Carriage introduced into U. S. service	231
GRIDLEY, RICHARD:	
Colonel First regiment Continental artillery	1
Discontent in regiment of	2
Superseded in command of artillery	3
List of officers, regiment of	331
GRIDLEY, SCARBOROUGH:	
Second major artillery regiment	2
Dismissed the service for misconduct	2
HAMILTON, ALEXANDER:	
Captain New York artillery	4
Makes report on peace establishment	19
Inspector-general, work on system of discipline for the artillery	300
HAMPTON, MAJOR-GENERAL WADE:	
Complains of the inexperience of artillery officers with him	41
HANCOCK, MAJOR-GENERAL:	
Remarks of, relative to field-artillery schools, &c.	140
HARMAR: Lieutenant-colonel "First American regiment"	23

INDEX. 397

	PAGE.
HARRISON, CHARLES:	
Colonel of the Virginia artillery regiment	7
Third in order of rank regular artillery	8
Regiment of colonel, first in order of precedence	8
List of officers in regiment of	334–336

HINDMAN, CAPTAIN:
Appointed major Second artillery... 39
Retained in 1821... 46
HODGDON, SAMUEL:
Quartermaster-general... 26
Field commissary of military stores... 156
Retained in service after Revolutionary war................................. 158
HOLMAN, CHRISTIAN, major Virginia artillery regiment................... 7
HOOKER, MAJOR-GENERAL, policy of regarding functions of chief of artillery. 215
HOOPS, ADAM, major of artillerists and engineers........................... 29
HOUSE, CAPTAIN JAMES:
Appointed lieutenant-colonel... 39
Retained as lieutenant-colonel... 46
HUNT, GENERAL HENRY J.:
Commander of artillery reserve Army of the Potomac.................. 82
Succeeds to position chief of artillery Army of the Potomac....... 82, 83
Organizes special ammunition column...................................... 102
One of the committee on field artillery armament (note)............. 297

INSPECTOR OF ARTILLERY:
Appointed... 114
Duties of... 114
Colonel of artillerists performs the duties of............................... 115
Necessity for the office represented by Secretary of War............. 163
INSTRUCTION:
Artillery schools for, established.. 68
Consideration of general subject of, for the artillery.................. 112–147
Plan of Mr. Calhoun for artillery.. 115, 116
Plan of, inaugurated by G. O. A. G. O., 1859............................. 117, 118
Of artillery personnel, plan proposed by permanent artillery board.. 117, 118
Text-books for theoretical.. 118, 119
Importance of inspectors to supervise....................................... 120
Knox the first to recommend schools for artillery....................... 120
Inadequacy of scheme for, inaugurated in 1794......................... 121
Field batteries, made schools for... 132–137
General remarks upon the importance of field artillery posts...... 138–141
IRON, CAST:
Metal adopted for sea-coast carriages....................................... 254
Gradual introduction of, in constructing ordnance................... 258, 259
Supplants brass as a metal for field-guns.................................. 260
Dearborn's system of field-guns.. 260, 261, 262
Recommended to be superseded by bronze for field-guns......... 262
Circumstances attending readoption of bronze..................... 263–265
Pure and simple, for heavy ordnance................................... 267–269
Combined with other metals for heavy ordnance................. 269, 270
Malleable:
Experiments with, for field ordnance..................................... 263
IRON, WROUGHT:
Metal adopted for siege and sea-coast carriages......................... 255
Field-guns (note)... 259
Failure of guns for field ordnance.. 265

51

IRON, WROUGHT—*Continued.*
 General use of, for field artillery... 266
 Unsuitableness of, for heavy ordnance... 271
 Conversion of 3-inch field-guns into breech-loaders 274
IZARD, GEORGE:
 Colonel Second artillery.. 39
 Brigadier-general 39
 Plan for reorganization of artillery.. 41
 Organization of artillery for field service, 1814.................................... 77, 78
 Efforts to equip his regiment as field artillery....................................... 194
 Constructs some Wurst caissons... 232
 Correspondence of, concerning equipping light artillery...................... 198

JACKSON, DANIEL:
 Major of artillerists and engineers... 29
 Major of artillerists... 32

KING, MAJOR : design of depressing gun carriage.................................. 256
KNOX, HENRY:
 Volunteer in army under General-Washington.. 3
 Appointed colonel of artillery regiment, *vice* Gridley............................ 3
 On special duty at New York, Albany, and Ticonderoga 3
 Moves to New York city with nine companies 4
 Suggestions of, for improvement of artillery.. 4
 Recommends five battalions of artillery... 6
 Chosen brigadier-general of artillery... 7
 Secretary at War, reorganizes peace establishment into a legion 24
 Instructions of, to artillery officers on detachment........................ 76, 77
 Supervises department of technical artillery... 113
 Recommends schools for artillery officers.. 120
 Remarks of, concerning the ordnance department..................... 152, 153
 Proposes to unite the duties of Secretary at War and of master-general
  of ordnance 160
 Appointed Secretary at War.. 160
 Duties of, as such... 160, 161
 As Secretary at War, commands the army... 160
  surrenders command of the army to the first President
  under the Constitution.. 161
 Promoted to major-general, assigned to West Point........................... 190
 Receives manual of Gribeauval artillery from Lieutenant-colonel Nadal.. 224
 Views of, concerning qualifications of artillery officers...................... 110
 Submits list of artillery to be taken in campaign of 1779.................. 275
 Failure of plan for organization of militia... 300
 List of commissioned officers, the regiment of................................... 332
KOSCIUSKO : System of horse artillery manœuvres written by............. 300
KRUPP:
 Twelve-inch, gun, recommended to be purchased by board convened
  in 1872.. 272
 Attempt to graft breech mechanism of, on American conversions and
  new constructions 272, 273
 Failure of this attempt.. 272

LABORATORIES recommended by Knox.. 4
LALLEMAND, GENERAL HENRY: Treatise of, on artillery...................... 302
LAMB, JOHN:
 Major of Knox's regiment... 3
 Prisoner with the enemy... 4

INDEX. 399

LAMB, JOHN—*Continued*.
 Colonel of artillery regiment.. 8
 Colonel, second in order of rank.. 8
 Regiment of Colonel, second in order of precedence..................... 8
 Appointed surveyor of ordnance... 156
 List of officers in regiment of Colonel... 342, 344
LEE, GENERAL CHARLES, strictures of, regarding commander-in-chief......... 10
LINDSAY, WILLIAM :
 Major and lieutenant-colonel Second artillery................................ 39

MACOMB :
 Colonel of Third artillery... 39
 Appointed brigadier-general.. 39
 Chief of artillery for General Wilkinson... 40
 General-in-chief, views of, concerning school of practice................ 124
MACREA, WILLIAM :
 Major of artillerists.. 32
 Lieutenant-colonel corps of artillery... 44
 Retained... 46
MASON, DAVID :
 Major of Gridley's regiment.. 2
 Lieutenant-colonel of Knox's regiment.. 3
 Mustered out of service.. 157
MARCY, SECRETARY : Promulgates rule by which captains of field batteries
 are to be selected... 65
MATERIEL OF ARTILLERY :
 Gribeauval system.. 223
 Carriages.. 223, 256
 Sources whence America was supplied................................... 223, 224, 225
 Secretary McHenry moves against the Revolutionary system............ 227
 Modifications in, wrought by Secretary Dearborn...................... 228, 231
         Secretary McHenry................... 231, 232
         Colonel of the ordnance department...... 233
         And results.................................... 234–237
 Appointment of boards of 1831, 1835, 1837, 1838, and of the ordnance
 committee, to ameliorate condition of... 243, 246
 Result of their labors... 246, 249
 Recommendations of light artillery board concerning....................... 250
 The question of suitable metals for ordnance—brass, cast-iron,
 wrought-iron, steel... 257–274
 Calibres and natures of ordnance in the various systems of, that have
 been adopted... 275–298
MCDOUGALL, MAJOR-GENERAL : Court-martialed.................................. 209, 210
MCHENRY, SECRETARY :
 Advocates introduction of horse artillery... 192
 Remarks on necessity for educated officers....................................... 31
 Remarks concerning the failure of plan to educate cadets................ 121
 Observations on the unsatisfactory condition of the ordnance........ 163
MCINTOSH, CAPTAIN : Marches company light artillery *en route* to Canada.. 195
MCCLELLAN, GENERAL GEORGE B. :
 Assumes command of Army of Potomac... '80
 Remarks of, on organization of artillery.. 81
 Army commanded by, on Peninsula... 82
 Order of, defining position of the chief of artillery............................ 213
MEADE, MAJOR-GENERAL : Order of, defining status of chief of artillery...... 216
MIFFLIN :
 Quartermaster-General.. 11

400   INDEX.

                                                                    PAGE.
MIFFLIN—*Continued.*
  Member board of war and ordnance..................................... 11
  Resigns his commission.. 12
MILITARY ACADEMY:
  Influence of.. 78
  At West Point, placed on sound basis.................................. 121
  Character of education there acquired............................. 121–123
MITCHELL, GEORGE E.:
  Major and lieutenant-colonel Third artillery.......................... 39
  Retained at reorganization of 1821.................................... 46
MORTARS:
  Two thirteen-inch (13-in.), dragged through wilderness to Canada by
    companies of Knox's regiment.. 4
  Foundries for casting brass, recommended.............................. 4
  Rifle recommended... 273
MULLER'S TREATISE ON ARTILLERY the standard for constructions......... 224
MUSICIANS: Object of, in organization (1802).......................... 33

NICOLL, A. T., MAJOR: Adjutant and Inspector-General, resigned......... 44
NYE, SAMUEL: Major Third artillery.................................... 39

OFFICERS:
  Field; paucity of, in Royal artillery................................. 2
  Increased number of, in Gridley's regiment............................ 2
  Disputes among, concerning rank and precedence....................... 7
  Difficulty in obtaining, for Crane's and Lamb's regiments............ 8
  Number of, in reorganized artillery................................. 13
  Academy for instruction of, recommended.............................. 4
  Of American artillery equal to demands of service.................... 6
  Relative rank of colonels.. 8
  Of artillery battalion, Legion of United States.................. 24, 25
  Ranking, of artillerists and engineers........................... 27, 28
  Educated, efforts to secure from Europe........................... 30, 31
  Of light artillery, allowed forage for horses....................... 38
  Of artillery, habitually detached................................... 40
  Of old army, selected for vacancies in the increase given artillery.. 49
  Field, selected for Fifth regular artillery......................... 53
  Of artillery, unjustly discriminated against........................ 85
            Provisions made for technical instruction of.............. 112
  Protest of American, against Du Coudray's compact................... 111
  List of, retained in-service, when Revolutionary army was disbanded.. 350
            retained in service after June 2d, 1784................... 351
            in Pennsylvania detachment (1784)......................... 351
                                    (1785)............................ 352
            Artillery battalion, Legionary corps, in 1787............. 352
                                    under constitutional government... 353
ORGANIZATION:
  Of First Colonial regiment of artillery based on that of a battalion
    Royal artillery... 2
  Gridley's regiment... 331
  Battalion Royal artillery.. 332
  Major John Crane's Rhode Island company.............................. 2
  Knox's artillery regiment.. 333
  Five battalions recommended by Knox................................. 7
  The regular artillery and artificer regiments.................. 334–346
  Stephens' corps.. 338

INDEX. 401

ORGANIZATION—*Continued*.   PAGE.
  Of Colonial companies and battalions, other than those of regular
    establishment.. 9
  Regular artillery (1778)... 12, 14
  Corps of artillerists and engineers... 27
  Regiment of artillerists.. 29
  Second and Third artillery... 38
  Corps of artillery.. 42
  March 3d, 1815, corps retained.. 44
  Four artillery regiments.. 46
  Slight changes in personnel of artillery regiments...................... 48
  Artillery for field service in Revolution... 76
                in War of 1812... 77, 78
                under McClellan (1862).............. 78, 80, 81
  Artillery of army in Mexico... 78, 79
                in western armies during Civil war............................. 79
  Change in artillery, immediately after battle of Chancellorsville. 83, 84
  Elements of weakness in the artillery after 1821................... 170–173
  Propositions to modify that of the artillery............................... 186
  Measures proposed, looking to same end............................ 187, 188
  South Carolina artillery regiment... 347
  Artillery regiments, resolves of October 3d and 21st, 1780............ 347
  Troops retained when army disbanded in 1783........................ 349
  Proposed temporary force, in 1784.. 351
  Artillery, Legionary corps of 1787... 352
          under resolve of Congress October 3d, 1787.................... 352
  Legion of the United States under act of March 5th, 1792............ 353
  Corps of artillerists and engineers... 354
  Regiment.. 354
  Regiment of light artillery... 356
  Second and Third regiments of artillery................................ 356
  Plan of, proposed by Colonel Izard to Secretary of War................. 357
  Of military establishment under act March 3d, 1815..................... 358
  Reorganization of artillerists and engineers, 1799......................... 355
  Reorganization of artillerists pursuant to act March 16th, 1802............ 355
  Reorganization of artillery, March 2d, 1821.................................. 358
  Table showing reorganization of 1821.. 360, 361
ORDNANCE DEPARTMENT:
  Proposed reorganization of... 52
  Organized by act of May 14th, 1812.. 115
  Technical artillery duties confided to...................................... 115
  Assumes role of artillery staff... 143–147
  Of the Revolution.. 149
  Resolutions of Congress establishing................................. 150, 151
  Remarks of Knox concerning... 152, 153
  Merged in the artillery... 168......
  Result of the merging scheme... 168–172
  Of Confederate States (1861–'65)... 172
  Resuscitation of, in 1832... 173
  Career of the, United States, since 1832........................... 173–177
  Usurpation of artillery duties.. 201–205
  Ordnance Committee appointed by Secretary Poinsett................ 246
OSWALD, ELEAZER:
  Lieutenant-colonel Second regular artillery........................... 8
                Resigns September, 1778................................. 9
OVERTON, MAJOR W. H.:
  Assigned to corps artillery.. 44

INDEX.

	PAGE.
PARROTT: System of rifled guns	285, 286

PERKINS, WILLIAM:
  Major Third regular artillery... 8
  Commander of artillery at West Point................................... 209
PETERS, RICHARD: Member board of war and ordnance.................. 11
PETER, GEORGE:
  Captain light artillery... 34
  Company of, equipped as light artillery.................................. 34, 35
  Marches to New Orleans, Louisiana; resigns............................. 36
PICKERING:
  Adjutant-general.. 11
  Member board of war and ordnance.. 11
  Quartermaster-general 109
  Secretary of War... 259
PINCKNEY, MAJOR-GENERAL: Work on a system of discipline for the artillery. 300
PITTS, CAPTAIN THOMAS:
  Promoted major light artillery; resigns....................................... 42
POINSETT, JOEL R., SECRETARY OF WAR:
  Services of, for benefit of the artillery.................................. 50–54, 55
  Calls attention to our lack of light artillery................................. 58
  Sends ordnance commission to Europe... 174
  Results of its visit... 264, 265
  Introduces rocket service into United States............................ 282
  Controversy with ordnance committee as to construction of field guns.. 382–385
PORTER, MAJOR ANDREW: Lieutenant-colonel commandant Fourth artillery. 17
PORTER, MOSES:
  Major of artillerists... 32
  Colonel of light artillery; retained as colonel of First regiment......... 46
  Brevet brigadier-general commander of artillery, Northern Army....... 210
POPKINS, JOHN: Lieutenant-colonel Third regular artillery.................. 9
PRACTICE-FIRING, ARTILLERY:
  Plan for, instituted.. 116
  Successive changes wrought in plan....................................... 141–143
  Position of chief of ordnance in this feature of artillery instruction...... 143
PRINCE FREDERICK CHARLES at battle of Gravelotte (note)................. 106
PROCTOR, THOMAS:
  Colonel of Pennsylvania artillery... 7
  Fourth in rank in artillery service.. 8
  Regiment of, Colonel, fourth in order of precedence...................... 8
  Resigned his commission 17
PROCTOR, FRANCIS, JR.:
  Major Fourth artillery; retires.. 17
  List of officers in regiment of Colonel..................................... 344, 346
PROMOTION:
  Rule of, in regular artillery.. 15, 16, 17
    Variable in peace establishment.. 21
    Disregarded by President Adams.. 32
    Failure of this attempt.. 32
    For the three artillery regiments.. 39
    Executive attempts to set at defiance is defeated by Senate.... 42
    Followed in filling certain vacancies... 49
              created by act March 3d, 1847................. 51
PROPERTY, GOVERNMENT: No system of accountability therefor for many years after Revolution.. 162
PURVEYOR OF PUBLIC SUPPLIES: Office created; duties of.................. 162

INDEX. 403

	PAGE.
QUARTERMASTER:
   For artillery, recommended by Knox... 5
   Department remodeled... 11
   Failure of plan... 12

REED, GOVERNOR: Criticizes the construction of gun-carriages............... 157
RESERVE ARTILLERY:
   Organized during Revolution... 96
   Not used during War of 1812 or Mexican War.............................. 97
   Organization of, Army of Potomac.................................. 97, 98, 99, 100
   Of Army of Potomac broken up... 100
   Services rendered by, Army of Potomac................................ 100, 101
   Of Army of Potomac re-establishes itself...................................... 102
   Of Army of Northern Virginia.. 103
   General considerations affecting.. 104, 105
   Inexpediency of dispensing with.. 105–107
REYNOLDS, MAJOR J. F.: Proceeds to Utah with light battery (C) Third
   artillery... 67
RIFLED GUNS:
   Early experiments to test principle.. 284
   Give rise to so-called "punching system" of attack on iron-clads........ 287
   Development of heavy-rifle system retarded by Civil war............ 287, 288
   Experimental cast-iron.. 288
   Private foundries supply heavy during the Civil war..................... 288
RINGGOLD, SAMUEL, CAPTAIN AND BREVET MAJOR:
   Commanding company horse artillery... 55
   Secures modification of field-artillery instruction......................... 306
   Killed at battle of Palo Alto... 62
RIVARDI, J. J. U.:
   Major of artillerists and engineers... 27
   Disbanded at reorganization of the army..................................... 32
ROBERTS, OWEN:
   Lieutenant-colonel commandant South Carolina artillery battalion..... 10
   Mortally wounded at Stono River... 10
ROCHEFONTAINE, STEPHEN:
   Lieutenant-colonel commandant artillerists and engineers............ 27
   Dismissed the service... 29
RODMAN, LIEUTENANT:
   Develops system of cooling cast guns from the interior.......... 283, 284
   Develops a system of heavy ordnance.................................... 283, 284
   Member of committee to select field armament........................... 297

SANDERS, CAPTAIN JOHN:
   Appointed major of light artillery.. 34
   Note concerning successor to... 37
SCOTT, WINFIELD:
   Captain in regiment of light artillery (note)................................ 37
   Lieutenant-colonel and colonel Second artillery........................... 39
   Brigadier-general... 40
   Remarks concerning the equipment of light artillery.................... 66
   Regulations compiled by.. 211
   Makes proposition to War Department to go to Europe; proposition
   rejected.. 301
SCHOOL OF PRACTICE:
   Established... 122
   Broken up... 124
   Re-established.. 125

SCHOOL OF PRACTICE—*Continued.*
    PAGE.
  Career of.. 121–128
  Remarks upon course there pursued.................................. 128–132
  Light artillery... 137, 138
  European practices... 140
SCHOFIELD, MAJOR-GENERAL:
  As Secretary of War, establishes field artillery school........... 137
  Efforts to secure success of same... 138
SECRETARY AT WAR: Duties of.. 160
SECRETARY OF WAR:
  Fulfills functions of former Secretary at War....................... 161
  Has supervision of artillery technical affairs from Revolution to 1812.. 165
SERGEANTS, ORDNANCE: Grade established................................ 47
SHERMAN, CAPTAIN T. W.:
  Company commanded by, equipped as light artillery............ 62
  His company (E), Third artillery, re-equipped as field artillery........ 64, 65
SHIELDS, SENATOR: Introduces bill to create office of chief of artillery..... 186
SOUTH CAROLINA regiment of artillery................................... 9, 347
STEEL: Introduction of, in heavy ordnance construction.................. 271–273
STEVENS, EBENEZER:
  Lieutenant-colonel commandant of artillery in Northern Department.. 8
  Origin of corps commanded by... 9, 338–340
  Distinguished conduct of... 9
  Assignment of, to Second artillery, September, 1778............. 10
STEVENS, CAPTAIN WILLIAM:
  Remarks on personal armament of artillerymen.................... 190
  System of discipline for the artillery.................................... 299
ST. CLAIR:
  Appointed major-general... 26
  Defeated by Miami Indians.. 26
  Superseded by General Wayne.. 26
STODDARD, MAJOR AMOS, compiles system of artillery manœuvres............. 301
STROBAGH, JOHN MARTIN:
  Lieutenant-colonel Pennsylvania artillery regiment................ 7
  Death of.. 16
SUPERINTENDENT OF MILITARY STORES, duties of................. 161, 162
SURVEYOR OF ORDNANCE:
  Office of, created... 155
  Reports of, and results.. 157, 158

TACTICS:
  Instruction for field artillery... 59, 60
  Deficiency of artillery during Revolution............................. 77
  Stevens' System of Discipline the pioneer work in the United States.... 299
  Systems prepared by Hamilton, Pinckney, and Wilkinson.................. 300
  Proposition of Captain Winfield Scott to improve the......... 301
  Major Amos Stoddard's System of....................................... 301
  The Artillerists' Companion, to some extent a treatise on..... 302
  Works of H. Lallemand.. 302, 303
  Tyler's Translation of Manual for Artillery.......................... 303
              Gribeauval system of................................... 304, 305
  Anderson's instruction for field artillery.............................. 305
        modifications in, promulgated in 1845............................. 306
  Systems of, for siege, mountain, and heavy artillery............. 306
        field artillery of 1860... 307
  The assimilated, promulgated in 1873.................................. 308, 309
  Tidball's Manual for Heavy Artillery.................................... 309, 310

INDEX. 405

TACTICS—*Continued.*
Field artillery... 312–330
    Tactics of Revolution merely traditional................. 312
Tousard's mention of the Revolutionary............................ 312
The manual of the piece, by Revolutionary practices.............. 313
The main features of Kosciusko's system.......................... 313–315
    Stoddard's... 315, 316
    Lallemand's.. 316–318
    Anderson's Translation..................................... 319, 321
    The system of 1845... 321, 322
        1860.. 323–325
Early attempts at assimilating................................... 325, 326
Assimilation should not be indulged at a sacrifice of the natural tactical elements of the various arms of service........ 326
The assimilated system of 1872................................... 325–330
TIDBALL, CAPTAIN:
Company of, equipped as horse artillery.......................... 70
Major, manual of heavy artillery................................. 310
TOUSARD, BREVET LIEUTENANT-COLONEL LOUIS DE:
Major artillerists and engineers................................. 27
Appointed inspector of artillery................................. 29–114
Promoted lieutenant-colonel commandant Second regiment artillerists and engineers.. 32
Discharged from active service................................... 32
TOWSON, CAPTAIN NATHAN:
Assigned to light artillery...................................... 44
Nominated from paymaster-general to colonelcy Second artillery (note)... 46, 47, 48, 49
TROOPS provisionally retained in service when Revolutionary army disbanded... 349
TRUMBULL, JOSEPH: Member board of war and ordnance.............. 11
TYLER, LIEUTENANT DANIEL:
Services in the line of technical artillery...................... 239–242
Translations of tactics.. 303, 305

VALLEY FORGE:
Army encamped at... 10
reorganized at... 12

WADE, WILLIAM: Remarks of regarding artillery carriages......... 233
WADSWORTH, DECIUS:
Major of artillerists.. 32
Chief of ordnance.. 173
Devises a system of artillery matériel........................... 233
Strictures of, on report of an ordnance board.................... 235
Retirement of, from service...................................... 236
Recommends artillery system adopted in 1816...................... 278
Letter of, regarding this system................................. 386, 387
WALBACH, MAJOR JOHN B.: Retained at reorganization of 1821..... 46
WASHINGTON:
General, invested with extraordinary powers...................... 6
    authorizes raising three artillery battalions............... 6
    intrigues against... 11
    intrigues against result.................................... 12
Lieutenant-general, proposes plan for organization of army....... 30
General, apportions the field artillery to brigades.............. 76
    Order of, relating to artillery personnel................... 209
    recommends the procuring brass guns......................... 257

	PAGE.
WAYNE, MAJOR-GENERAL:	
Commanding the forces on frontier	26
Defeats Miami Indians	27
WILKINSON, JAMES:	
Letter of General, regarding light artillery company	36, 195
equipment of light artillery	198
Work of General, on a system of tactics	300
WILLIAMS, JONATHAN:	
Major Fourth battalion Second regiment artillerists and engineers	31
Appointed chief of corps of engineers	121
Translates Kosciusko's system of manœuvres	313
WOOLSTONECRAFT, CAPTAIN: Report concerning light artillery	195

www.ingramcontent.com/pod-product-compliance
Lightning Source LLC
Chambersburg PA
CBHW050844300426
44111CB00010B/1121